GRAND OLE OPRY

GRAND OLE OPRY

· CHET HAGAN ·

AN OWL BOOK

Henry Holt and Company · New York

Dedicated to the men and women—
and the music—of the storied Grand Ole Opry,
the long-lived radio program that
has now become the very soul
of country music

Published by Henry Holt and Company, Inc.,
115 West 18th Street, New York, New York 10011.
Published in Canada by Fitzhenry and Whiteside Limited,
195 Allstate Parkway, Markham, Ontario L3R 4T8.

Library of Congress Cataloging-in-Publication Data
Hagan, Chet.
Grand ole opry / Chet Hagan.—1st ed.
p.   cm.
"An Owl book."
Includes index.
ISBN 0-8050-0543-9 (pbk.)
1. Grand ole opry (Radio program)   2. Country music—History
and criticism.   I. Title.
ML3524.H22   1989
784.5'2'0097855—dc19   88-29231
                                                   CIP
                                                   MN

Henry Holt books are available at special discounts
for bulk purchases for sales promotions, premiums,
fund-raising, or educational use. Special editions
or book excerpts can also be created to specification.
For details, contact: Special Sales Director,
Henry Holt and Company, Inc., 115 West 18th Street,
New York, New York 10011.

First Edition

DESIGNED BY CLAIRE M. NAYLON
Printed in the United States of America
1   3   5   7   9   10   8   6   4   2

Special thanks to E. W. Wendell, Tom Griscom,
Grand Ole Opry management, Lisa Eubank, Bill Eiland,
Bill Ivey, Diane Johnson, John Rumble,
Charlie Seeman, and Chris Skinker.

The publishers are grateful for permission to use excerpts from the following works:
Johnny Bond, *The Tex Ritter Story*. New York: Chappell and Company, Inc., 1976.
Johnny Cash, *Man in Black*. Grand Rapids: Zondervan Publishing House, 1975.
Jack Hurst, *Nashville's Grand Ole Opry*. Introduction by Roy Acuff. New York:
   Harry N. Abrams, 1975.
Loretta Lynn with George Vecsey, *Loretta Lynn: Coal Miner's Daughter*. Chi-
   cago: Henry Regnery Company, 1976.
Jerry Rivers, *Hank Williams, from Life to Legend*. Denver: Heather Enterprises, 1967.
Elizabeth Schlappi, *Roy Acuff: The Smoky Mountain Boy*. Gretna, LA: Pelican
   Publishing Company, 1978.
"Paul Harvey News," ABC News, March 4, 1963.

GRAND OLE OPRY

Show me the way to go home,
I'm tired an' I wanna go to bed;
Had a little drink 'bout an hour ago
An' it's gone right to my head. . . .*

—Popular song, 1925

The year was 1925. The United States of America was in the midst of a post–World War prosperity. President Calvin Coolidge had declared from the White House that "the business of America is business." Yet the vaunted prosperity was a strangely urban phenomenon. Rural America was not sharing in it. Wheat growers in Kansas and cotton planters in Mississippi weren't sharing in it. Coal miners in Kentucky and textile workers in the Carolinas weren't sharing in it. Overall, farm income was plummeting. Mortgage foreclosures were increasing. A farm owned by a family one day was worked in tenancy the next.

In the Clinch Mountains of Virginia, and the Great Smokies of Tennessee, and the Appalachians of North Carolina, and the Ozarks of Arkansas, there were substantial pockets of stark poverty. There was virtually no money there. And no flappers and no stock market margins and no Jazz Age. There was only one kinship with the cities: illegal whiskey. Prohibition was as ridiculous in those mountains as it was in the canyons of Manhattan.

Much of rural America was made up of isolated enclaves. New York and Los

*"Show Me the Way to Go Home" by Irving King; copyright 1925 Piedmont Music Co., Inc.

Angeles, even middle-America Chicago, were as remote as the moon. What happened in the big cities was of little consequence to the farmers and mountaineers. They didn't *hear* what city folks heard; lyrics of the 1925 anthem from Tin Pan Alley—"I'm Sitting on Top of the World"—might as well have been written in a foreign tongue.

They made their own music, playing it on fiddles and guitars and mandolins and banjos and dulcimers. They sang the old songs of their ancestry; ballads with Scotch and Irish and Welsh roots, melodies that could be adapted and honed into something new by the untrained musicians as vehicles for tales of their own lives and times—of flood and fire, of train wrecks, of killings, of loves won and lost, of the hard times through which they had survived, of their rock-solid faith in God.

Indeed, they clung to the old values while the urban populations were casting them aside. What was happening in the little town of Dayton, Tennessee, in the summer of '25 was vastly important to them. For there, you see, one John Thomas Scopes, a young science teacher and high school athletic coach, was arrested for daring to teach the theory of evolution in clear violation of Tennessee's anti-evolution law.

The scientific suggestion that Man may have descended from the apes was abhorrent to anyone whose faith was bound up in the story of Creation as documented in the Bible's book of Genesis.

It might have remained a remote, little-reported trial, but for the two prominent lawyers it attracted: silver-tongued orator and erstwhile Presidential hopeful William Jennings Bryan, for the prosecution; able, quick-witted, liberal Clarence Darrow, of Chicago, for the defense.

Dayton was turned into a human circus by the "monkey trial," but it was all to come down to the battle of the judicial giants. Bryan's adherents had packed the Rhea County courthouse. When, during bitter cross-examination by Darrow, he seemed to make a telling point, there was favorable reaction from the audience. At one point there was loud clapping.

"Great applause from the bleachers," Darrow commented sarcastically.

Bryan: "From those you call yokels."

Darrow: "I never called them yokels."

Bryan: "Those are the people whom you insult."

Darrow: "You insult every man of science and learning in the world because he does not believe in your fool religion!"

Nothing in the twenties was as indicative of the wide gulf between the rural and urban Americas as was the Scopes anti-evolution trial. Big-city newspapers contended Darrow won because he had devastated Bryan in his cross-examination, making him out to be the pompous fool. Rural Americans simply pointed to the result of the trial: John Thomas Scopes was found guilty.

Kansas-born songwriter Carson Robison wrote a song about it—"The John T. Scopes Trial"—in which he closed with a moralizing stanza, warning the young schoolteacher of the dangers of doubting the "old religion." It was a regional hit.

However, there were two forces afoot in 1925 that would eventually be major factors in the *homogenization* of the diverse United States.

One was the phonograph record, the other was radio. Neither was really new.

An American, Thomas Alva Edison, invented the phonograph in 1877; it had become a popular home entertainment medium well before the days of the First World War. It wasn't until the twenties, though, that technical advances made it possible to take recording equipment out of the confines of studios and into the field. Recording entrepreneurs traveled far and wide, seeking new acts, new sounds. One of those pioneers was Ralph Peer, of Okeh Records.

He was to discover that there was a market for genuine rural music, having recorded Fiddlin' John Carson doing "The Little Old Log Cabin in the Lane" and "The Old Hen Cackled and the Rooster's Going to Crow" in a session in Atlanta in June 1923. That Peer thought Carson's singing was "pluperfect awful" was not important. The records sold!

Moving swiftly to capitalize on the newfound commerciality of rural music, Peer recorded others, among them Henry Whitter, of Fries, Virginia ("Lonesome Road Blues"/"The Wreck of the Southern Old 97"), and Ernest "Pop" Stoneman, of Galax, Virginia ("The Ship That Never Returned"/"The Titanic").

Other record companies recognized the trend. Victor permitted its most prolific star, Vernon Dalhart, to record two rural tunes: Whitter's "The Wreck of the Southern Old 97" and the weeper "The Prisoner's Song":

> *Oh, I wish I had the wings of an angel,*
> *Over these prison walls I would fly. . . .**

No one could have guessed how important that record would become. Years later it would be determined by researchers that it was the first "country music" record to sell more than a million copies.

At that time it was the practice of the record companies to designate that genre of music as "old time tunes." But it was in January 1925 that it received a new appellation, one that caught on, was highly "commercial," and persisted down through the years, even after the practitioners of the art denounced it.

It seems that a group of Pop Stoneman's Galax, Virginia, neighbors, encouraged by his recording success, banded together to journey to New York City to record for Ralph Peer. They were Al Hopkins, a hospital office manager, lead vocalist, and nominal leader of the group; his brother, Joe, a Railway Express agent and guitarist; storekeeper John Rector, a banjo player; and barber-fiddler Tony Alderman. They cut six sides for Okeh Records; included among the repertoire were such rural standards as "Silly Bill," "Old Time Cinda," "Cripple Creek," and "Sally Ann."

At the end of the session, Peer asked, "What do you call this group?"

Al Hopkins pondered for a moment: "We're nothing but a bunch of hillbillies from North Carolina and Virginia. Call us anything."

Laughing, Peer instructed his secretary to put "The Hill Billies" on the ledger sheets. In that moment native American rural music became "hillbilly music."

---

*"The Prisoner's Song" by Guy Massey and/or Vernon Dalhart; copyright 1924 Shapiro, Bernstein & Co.

Okeh Records moved quickly to exploit the phrase. In one of its 1925 catalogues it trumpeted:

Hear, folks, the music of the Hill Billies! These rollicking melodies will quicken the memory of the tunes of yesterday. The heart beats time to them while the feet move with the desire to cut a lively shine. These here mountaineers sure have a way of fetching music out of the banjo, fiddle, and guitar that surprises listeners, old and young, into feeling skittish. Theirs is a spirited entertainment and one you will warm to.

Hillbilly music was booming.

Just as precipitant was the growth of radio.

An Italian, Marchese Guglielmo Marconi, discovered the principles of radio signals in 1895, which he used initially to develop wireless telegraphy. In April 1912, when the White Star liner *Titanic* hit an iceberg in the North Atlantic, a young Marconi employee in New York, one David Sarnoff, gained fame by using the wireless telegraph to bring the news of the disaster to the world.

When voice transmission was married to the wireless signals, it was that same Sarnoff who recommended to Marconi officials (the year was 1916) that they manufacture a home receiver that would make radio "a household utility in the same sense as the piano or the phonograph."

Rarely has a man been so prescient.

A few years later radio mania would sweep across the nation like a fever, getting its first serious recognition as a public communications medium on November 2, 1920, when Pittsburgh station KDKA broadcast the Harding-Cox Presidential election returns.

Americans seemed intoxicated by the simple idea of *hearing* things through the air—an egg frying on a hot sidewalk, or a soprano singing "Silver Threads Among the Gold" from a makeshift studio in a garage. By 1924 the number of radio stations had jumped to nearly 1,400, most of them operated by hobbyists or as promotional sidelines to businesses. No community was immune.

Certainly not Nashville, Tennessee.

◄[ii]► Nashville of 1925 was a proud city. It was, of course, the capital of Tennessee. United States Presidents Andrew Jackson and James K. Polk had been part of the history of Nashville, and another President, Andrew Johnson, had been military governor of Tennessee there during the Civil War. It was the home of Vanderbilt University, and it boasted a replica of the Parthenon, erected as part of the Tennessee Centennial Exposition in 1897. The city liked to call itself the Athens of the South.

But there were other reasons for pride in 1925. The city had a symphony orchestra. Grantland Rice, a product of Nashville and Vanderbilt, was recognized as the nation's top sportswriter, his daily column, "The Sportlight," syndicated in newspapers from coast to coast. Nashville was getting daily airmail deliveries, small biplanes flying in from Chicago (in just three hours, twenty-nine minutes) to Blackwood Field, just beyond Donelson off the Lebanon Pike. And there was a substantial building boom under way.

On August 27 the Andrew Jackson Hotel opened in downtown Nashville, as one of the city's tallest buildings. On September 21 the War Memorial Building, a $2 million marble-and-granite tribute to the state's servicemen, was dedicated with Tennessee's Sergeant Alvin York, the nation's most decorated soldier, in attendance. Playing a role in the reconstruction of downtown Nashville was the National Life and Accident Insurance Company, owner of a brand-new five-story headquarters building at 7th and Union Streets.

National Life was just one of many burgeoning white-collar businesses in Nashville in those days. Founded before the turn of the century as the National Sick and Accident Association, it was bought in 1901 by a consortium of seven local businessmen who promptly changed the company name and put into being a growth plan that built the assets from $33,200 at the end of 1902 to $7 million by 1920. In the heady economic climate of the twenties those assets would nearly quadruple.

C. A. Craig, one of the original seven, was the president of National Life in 1925. His son, Edwin, not yet thirty, was a vice-president of the company. Edwin W. Craig was a radio "nut" with a plan to propose to his father and the other elders of the business. He wanted National Life to build a radio station.

Nashville already had two radio stations. One was WDAD, owned by a hardware company called "Dad's." The other was WCBQ, owned and operated by the First Baptist Church of Nashville. WCBQ had been built by a precocious teenager, John H. (Jack) DeWitt, Jr., who had had a ham radio license since 1921, when he was only fifteen. As a matter of fact, WCBQ was DeWitt's *third* radio station. At sixteen, he had put together WDAA for Ward-Belmont College, but it was allowed to lapse because it was thought to use too much electricity. Jack's second effort was a station in the living room of his home. An associate of that period, Luke Montgomery, said that station was closed down because DeWitt's mother got tired of "all those strangers [musicians and singers] traipsing through her house."

Then, about the time he started WCBQ, young DeWitt also made a battery-operated radio receiver for Edwin Craig. DeWitt remembered: "Mr. Craig became a long-distance radio enthusiast—or DX fan, as the hams call it. DX fans were people who would sit up all night listening to people around the country talk on the radio. It got Mr. Craig terribly excited."

Given that enthusiasm, and his position of influence as the son of the president of the company, Edwin Craig convinced the board of National Life to invest in a radio station. He pounded on the theme that a station could help promote the sale of life insurance policies and, once given the go-ahead, he wanted call letters that would prove it.

National Life's slogan was "We Shield Millions," and young Craig sought to get the call letters WSM for his station. Jack DeWitt again: "WSM were then the call letters of a Navy ship, a lifeboat of the *Leviathan*, I think. Mr. Craig got the Department of Commerce, which licensed radio stations then, to withdraw those call letters from the *Leviathan* lifeboat so somebody else—National Life—could get them. Herbert Hoover, the secretary of commerce, signed the license."

A special radio section in the *Nashville Banner* of Sunday, October 4, 1925, announced the plans for the initial broadcast of WSM the following evening. A big program was set—advertisements used the word "mammoth"—extending from 7:00 P.M. to 2:00 A.M. Jack DeWitt, now a student at Vanderbilt University, sat at the controls in the fifth-floor studio in his capacity as a part-time employee of the new station.

Edwin Craig was given the honor of inaugurating the broadcast. He did it simply: "This is WSM, 'We Shield Millions.' The National Life and Accident Insurance Company." After a prayer led by a Methodist pastor, and the playing of the national anthem by the Shrine Band, National Life president C. A. Craig dedicated the station to public service.

It was a high-class program that had been planned for that first evening. Tennessee governor Austin Peay spoke briefly; so did Nashville mayor Hilary Howse. And there were musical selections by concert baritone Joseph Tant McPherson, the Fisk University Jubilee Quintet, the Knights of Columbus Vocal Quartet, and any number of classical and semiclassical "concert" artists, both vocal and instrumental.

There was a nod to the popular music of the day with appearances by Beasley Smith's Andrew Jackson Hotel Orchestra and Francis Craig's Columbia Recording Orchestra.

But given the role WSM would shortly play in country music, it must be reported that there were no "hillbilly" entertainers on that first broadcast. The closest to that style, perhaps, was Miss Bonnie Barnhardt, billed as "The Lady o' the Radio," and introduced as a "singer of Southern melodies." But she was relegated to the post-midnight part of the broadcast, along with a saxophone soloist and a "syncopating pianist."

Not everyone who wanted to be party to the opening of WSM could be accommodated in the studio. Hundreds stood on the streets outside the National Life building and heard everything through loudspeakers. In its newspaper advertisements WSM had said: "The station regrets that it cannot invite the general public to be present at the studio . . . but in order that those who have no receiving sets who desire to hear the program can do so, the Western Electric Company will install large loud speakers in windows of the National building and as many as care to can assemble in front of the building and enjoy the broadcast."

Among the guests inside were three men who already had gained a reputation as radio personalities. One was Leo Fitzpatrick, of WDAF, Kansas City. Another was Lambdin Kay, of WSB, Atlanta, who nearly three years earlier had recognized the value of rural music when he put Fiddlin' John Carson on the air. And the third was George D. Hay, of the Sears, Roebuck station in Chicago, WLS ("World's Largest Store").

Hay might have been the best known of the three. He had just been named the most popular announcer in the United States in a poll conducted by *Radio Digest* magazine, getting more than 120,000 votes from radio set owners.

Before Hay left Nashville he would be offered the job as program director for WSM by Edwin Craig.

⸗⁅ iii ⁆⸗ George Dewey Hay, born in Attica, Indiana, began his career as a newspaperman. He was in his mid-twenties when the Memphis *Commercial Appeal* sent him to Mammoth Spring, Arkansas, in the foothills of the Ozarks, to cover the funeral of a Marine hero of the First World War. What he experienced was, in large measure, to change his life.

"The spring itself, from which the town got its name," Hay was to write later, "is really a small lake. It is said to be one of the largest open springs in the world. The water is almost icy cold. Near it there is a large country hotel, well appointed, where people of the old South come to spend the summers. . . . Mammoth Spring is one of the most typical small towns in America. . . .

"We rode behind a mule train thirty miles up in the mountains from Mammoth Spring, leaving very early in the morning. It was a beautiful day. The neighbors came from miles around in respect to the memory of this United States Marine who gave his life to preserve their way of life. The young man's father welcomed them as he stood on the crude platform in the country churchyard, but closed his brief remarks in this manner: 'Let all those who were against the government during the war pass on down the road.' We didn't see anyone leave. The minister conducted the services and the neighbors drove their mules and cars silently down the road. It was a very impressive scene at the end of a day when rural Americans took time out to check up on their lives.

"We lumbered back to Mammoth Spring and filed our story . . . [and then] spent a day in Mammoth Spring. It is a beautiful spot for rest and quiet. In the afternoon we sauntered around the town, at the edge of which hard by the Missouri line there lived a truck farmer in an old railroad car. He had seven or eight children and his wife seemed to be very tired with the tremendous job of caring for them. We chatted for a few minutes and the man went to his place of abode and brought forth a fiddle and a bow. He invited me to attend a 'hoedown' the neighbors were going to put on that night until 'the crack o' dawn' in a log cabin about a mile up a muddy road. He and two other old time musicians furnished the earthy rhythm. About twenty people came. There was a coal oil lamp in one corner of the cabin and another one in the 'kitty corner.' No one in the world has ever had more fun than those Ozark mountaineers did that night."

George Hay was never to forget that evening.

As it turned out, his days as a newspaper reporter were numbered. The *Commercial Appeal* owned Memphis radio station WMC, and Hay saw the potential of the new medium. He became an announcer on the station, a flamboyant one who identified his appearances by blowing an old wooden steamboat whistle he called Hushpuckena, the name of a very small town in northern Mississippi. Just why he singled out that name is not really clear, but it was all part of his show business flair. He also called himself "The Solemn Old Judge" on the air; this was the title of a newspaper column he had written. Years later there was a joke around the Grand Ole Opry in Nashville that Hay was neither solemn, nor old, nor a judge.

In 1924 Hay, having made a name for himself on Memphis radio, was offered a job as chief announcer on station WLS in Chicago. But he liked the South and didn't want to leave. Pressed to make a decision, Hay asked for $75 a week, a figure he thought was too high. WLS paid it and he was off to the Windy City.

One of his duties on WLS was to announce a new program put on the schedule by station manager Edgar L. Bill. It was called the "WLS Barn Dance," later to evolve into the "National Barn Dance" on network radio. The program was perfect for Hay, who remembered that night he had spent with the Ozark musicians in Mammoth Spring, Arkansas. On the WLS broadcast he dug into his bag of tricks: the steamboat whistle and the use of the handle "The Solemn Old Judge."

And all of that brought him to Monday evening, October 5, 1925, when he attended the opening of WSM in Nashville, was offered a job, and took it.

It's not recorded exactly when he began at WSM, but it isn't likely that it was before the first week in November. Ordinarily, that date wouldn't be important, except that Hay was to write, in 1945, a small history of a WSM show he had named the "Grand Ole Opry." By 1945, of course, the Opry was world famous. In his history, Hay was quite specific about when the "WSM Barn Dance," forerunner of the "Grand Ole Opry," began.

First, Hay's version: "Because the Grand Ole Opry is a very simple program it started in a very simple way. Your reporter, who was the first [program] director of WSM, had considerable experience in the field of folk music when the station opened in October, 1925. Realizing the wealth of folk music material and performers in the Tennessee Hills he welcomed the appearance of Uncle Jimmy Thompson and his blue ribbon fiddle who went on the air at eight o'clock, Saturday night, November 28, 1925. Uncle Jimmy told us that he had a thousand tunes. Past eighty years of age, he was given a comfortable chair in front of an old carbon microphone. While his niece, Mrs. Eva Thompson Jones, played his piano accompaniment your reporter presented Uncle Jimmy and announced that he would be glad to answer requests for old time tunes. Immediately telegrams started to pour into WSM.

"One hour later at nine o'clock we asked Uncle Jimmy if he hadn't done enough fiddling to which he replied, 'Why shucks, a man don't get warmed up in an hour. I just won an eight-day fiddling contest down in Dallas, Texas, and here's my blue ribbon to prove it.' Uncle Jimmy Thompson, Mrs. Jones and The Solemn Old Judge carried on for several weeks for an hour each Saturday night. . . .

"To the best of our recollection the first old time band we presented on the Saturday night show, which at that time we called the WSM Barn Dance, was headed by a very genial country physician from Sumner County, Tennessee, named Dr. Humphrey Bate."

And therein lies the controversy. Dr. Bate's daughter, Mrs. Alcyone Bate Beasley, challenged George Hay's claim that he inaugurated the first "barn dance" program on WSM on Saturday evening, November 28, 1925. If not Hay, then who? Her father did, Mrs. Beasley contended, and it should be her father who should get credit for originating what became the Grand Ole Opry.

Mrs. Beasley's story is that her father's group—with Alycone Bate, aged thirteen, playing the piano—did the first Saturday-night "barn dance" on WSM less than three weeks after the station went on the air, at the end of October 1925. She told a reporter: "I remember that night after it was over, we drove back home in the old Ford car and Daddy, who always called me 'Booger,' said, 'Booger, we might've started something down there tonight, you just don't know.'

"We played there for about four or five weeks before Mr. Hay came. We would drive into Nashville and perform on WDAD in the afternoon, then we would walk up the hill and play on WSM later in the evening. I remember we would give Jack Keefe, who was the WSM announcer then, a list of the numbers we were going to play during the hour we would be on the air. And within just two weeks or so, bands from everywhere began to come up to be put on the air. One of the first of them was Mr. Ed Poplin's band from Lewisburg, Tennessee.

"I never felt badly about it toward Mr. Hay, because he wasn't well, but the fact remains that nothing was ever said about Uncle Jimmy Thompson being the first one on the show until long after my Daddy died in 1936.

"How that came to be the story has been the puzzle of my life."

And a puzzle for researchers too. In the late 1960s, Norm Cohen, working under the aegis of the John Edwards Memorial Foundation, an archival and research center at UCLA devoted to the study of American folk music, dug through the files of the *Nashville Tennessean* to uncover mentions of country music broadcasts on Nashville stations for a three-month period—October 18, 1925, through January 17, 1926. What Cohen found lent credence to Mrs. Beasley's story.

In the Sunday, October 18, 1925, edition of the newspaper was an item under the heading "WSM ANNOUNCES WEEK'S PROGRAM": "Saturday . . . 10–11 (p.m.) Studio program featuring Dr. Humphrey Bates [*sic*] and his string quartet of old-time musicians, from Castalian Springs." That would have meant they appeared on Saturday, October 24, coinciding exactly with Mrs. Beasley's recollections.

Cohen's search revealed that Dr. Bate and his group, which had more frequent appearances on WDAD, played on WSM again on Saturday, November 14, on a program that also featured "Miss Sue McQuiddy, pianist, Miss Louise Harsh, mezzo-soprano." That would suggest that the time period (it was 10:00 to 11:00 P.M. again) had not formalized into a barn-dance format, but was merely an hour to present a variety of music.

Uncle Jimmy Thompson wasn't mentioned in the newspaper's radio listings until the December 20 issue: "Station WSM—Saturday (Dec. 26), 8:00 p.m.— Uncle Jimmy Thompson, the South's champion barn dance fiddler, and Eva Thompson Jones, contralto, will present program of old-fashioned tunes."

A week later, in the edition of Sunday, December 27, the *Tennessean* printed an article under the heading "WSM TO FEATURE OLD-TIME TUNES."

"Old tunes like old lovers are the best, at least judging from the applause which the new Saturday night feature at Station WSM receives from its listeners in all parts of the country; jazz has not completely turned the tables on such tunes as 'Pop Goes the Weasel' and 'Turkey In the Straw.'

"America may not be swinging its partners at a neighbor's barn dance but it seems to have the habit of clamping on its ear phones and patting its feet as gaily as it ever did when old-time fiddlers got to swing.

"Because of this recent revival in the popularity of the old familiar tunes, WSM has arranged to have an hour or two every Saturday night, starting Saturday, December 26. 'Uncle' Dave Macon, the oldest banjo picker in Dixie, and who comes from Readyville, Tenn., and 'Uncle' Jimmy Thompson of Martha, Tenn., will answer any requests for old-time melodies. . . .

"Uncle Jimmy made his first appearance a month ago and telegrams were received from all parts of the United States, encouraging him in his task of furnishing barn dance music for a million homes."

The article sounded suspiciously like the work of George D. Hay, plying his old newspaper skills. But whether Hay wrote it or not, two items stand out.

One—"WSM has arranged to have an hour or two every Saturday night, starting Saturday, December 26." This indicates that Hay did not solidify the barn-dance concept at WSM until the broadcast of December 26.

Two—"Uncle Jimmy made his first appearance a month ago." By simply counting back a month from the date of the article—Sunday, December 27—one comes to Saturday, November 28, exactly the date mentioned by George Hay in his memoirs of 1945.

What does it all mean? It means that Dr. Humphrey Bate and his aggregation *were* the first "hillbillies" to play on WSM, but not in a structured program like a barn dance. It means that Uncle Jimmy Thompson *did* perform on WSM on November 28, 1925. But was that the first "WSM Barn Dance"? Or was it on Saturday, December 26, as the newspaper article suggests?

More than a few years ago, the Grand Ole Opry decided to accept George Dewey Hay's 1945 recollections. Why not do so? No one kept any real records in those early days of radio; newspaper radio logs then were rudimentary, at best.

Thus, if George Hay contended that the "WSM Barn Dance" began on Saturday, November 28, 1925, with one hour of fiddling by an old man named Uncle Jimmy Thompson, so be it. The fiftieth anniversary of the Grand Ole Opry was celebrated on that basis; so was the sixtieth.

And, as time goes on, so will the seventieth.

You can talk about your evangelists,
You can talk about Mister Ford, too;
But Henry is a-shakin' more hell out of folks
Than all of the evangelists do.*

—Uncle Dave Macon song,
circa 1927

George Hay was having fun with his "WSM Barn Dance." It obviously delighted his promoter's heart when he discovered there was more to having Uncle Jimmy Thompson on his program than he had anticipated.

Just after Uncle Jimmy's debut, Hay read in the newspapers that Henry Ford, the auto manufacturing genius, had presented a prize for old-time American music to a New Englander named Mellie Dunham. That, of course, gave Mellie the title of America's Champion Old-Time Fiddler.

"WSM invited Mr. Dunham to fiddle a duel with Uncle Jimmy," Hay wrote, "but his advisors, realizing that he had nothing to win, refused to allow him to accept. Whereupon our Uncle Jimmy remarked, 'He's affeared of me.' The fact that Mr. Dunham was advised to refuse our invitation probably gave Uncle Jimmy more publicity than he would have received if the Hon. Mellie had come to Nashville. It added up to the fact that WSM had a good natured riot on its hands. After three or four weeks of this fiddle solo business we were besieged with other fiddlers, banjo pickers, guitar players, and a lady who played an old zither."

*Adapted from "Jordan Is a Hard Road to Travel" by Dan Emmett, 1853; new lyrics by David H. Macon, 1927. Public domain.

And what drew them? Certainly it wasn't money; there was no pay for anyone at the beginning.

Harmonica player Herman Crook, then the lone survivor of that first year, remembered: "When we first started out we played for two years for nothin'. But we didn't think much about that, because back there then, you see, radio was something new and we were just tickled to say that we got to play over the radio."

Those who came to "play over the radio" for Hay were from all walks of life. And The Solemn Old Judge, in keeping with his newspaper training, loved to write little biographical sketches of his artists.

He described Dr. Humphrey Bate as a "very genial country physician from Sumner County, Tennessee. Dr. Bate was a graduate of the Vanderbilt University School of Medicine and was very highly respected in his community as a physician and surgeon. He was in the Medical Department during the Spanish American War. Folk music was his hobby and he played a harmonica with considerable dexterity."

But Hay, while respectful of Dr. Bate's standing as a physician, was more concerned with the image of his barn-dance program. He quickly put a distinctive rural label on the doctor's band, calling it "The Possum Hunters."

Hay would write in 1945: "At the piano was seated Dr. Bate's little daughter [Alcyone], at that time thirteen years of age. . . . Other members of the original 'Possum Hunters' were Humphrey Bate Jr., known as Buster; Walter Liggett, with his banjo, who always insisted on crowing like a rooster every time he left the Opry stage . . ."

Liggett was a delight to George Hay, who had a warm spot in his heart for extroverts.

". . . Oscar Albright, whose brother was United States Minister to Finland after he had been editor of a Sumner County newspaper for many years; and Staley Walton, a good old country boy from the same neighborhood. A short time after the beginning of the Opry, Oscar Stone came on as a fiddler for the 'Possum Hunters' and since the death of Dr. Bate in 1936 has been the leader of the band. Oscar Stone is a carpenter by trade and has eleven children. He is a very kindly man. . . ."

There were three other such bands in the very earliest days of the "WSM Barn Dance." One was the "Crook Brothers" band, led by Herman Crook, a twist-maker for the American Tobacco Company, and his brother, Matthew, also a harmonica player. But Matthew would leave in 1930 to join the Nashville Police Department. He was replaced, in one of those oddities of show business, by a banjo player and singer named Lewis Crook, who was no blood relation to Herman whatsoever.

"I just let it ride as 'The Crook Brothers,' " Herman explained. "I never did change it. Same name, you know, and if the people didn't know, they'd think me and Lewis was brothers." (It should be noted that into the sixty-second year of the Grand Ole Opry, nonbrother Lewis Crook was still with the act.)

Yet another early band was "The Gully Jumpers" (more than likely the name was also invented by Hay), led by guitarist Paul Warmack, with Charlie Arrington on fiddle, Burt Hutcherson on guitar, and Roy Hardison on banjo.

Hay's sketch: "Paul Warmack is a skilled automobile mechanic who had his own shop for many years and now plies his trade for the State of Tennessee in one of its Nashville shops. Paul has been a great friend to all of the boys on the Opry. His heart seems to know no bounds. Even though he is a man of limited means his purse strings are always out [*sic*] for a friend in trouble. Charlie Arrington is a farmer who lives about twenty miles north of Nashville in a community known as Joelton. He is an Irishman with quick wit and is always ready with a funny story. Burt Hutcherson is a wood worker by trade who now has a job in the home office building of our parent company, the National Life and Accident Insurance Company. . . . Roy Hardison is another expert automobile mechanic who had his own shop in Nashville for many years."

The fourth such "hoedown band" on the early barn dance was "The Fruit Jar Drinkers," whose name alluded to the fact that moonshine whiskey was drunk from fruit jars serving as glasses. Hay, once more: "They are led by Grandpappy George Wilkerson, a red hot fiddler. The other members are Claude Lampley with guitar, Tommy Leffew, mandolin, and H. J. Ragsdale, bass fiddle which we call 'The Dog House.' The 'Fruit Jar Drinkers' have always been strictly country boys although they have lived in Nashville and have been mechanics with the exception of Tommy Leffew who is a barber by trade. They are very friendly fellows and all good citizens."

If George Hay seemed to suggest in his writings that everyone on the "WSM Barn Dance" was a standup individual without a flaw, it was understandable. The barn dance was a huge success right from the beginning; it was obvious that it was going to be important to the growth of radio station WSM and it was Hay's instinct to protect it.

Hay was a perceptive showman. He recognized what it meant when each week brought more and more people to the fifth floor of the National Life building to see the show. That phenomenon caused the first problems for WSM executives.

"Our first few broadcasts," Hay said, "originated in our Studio 'A.' . . . In the beginning it was a medium sized room, about twenty by fifteen feet, heavily draped by dark red curtains. The side next to the hall was glassed. In a few weeks that little hall was so filled with people that the station decided to build Studio 'B,' considerably larger than 'A.'

"Directly in front of the glassed-in side of 'B' was a large room, which held several hundred people. In addition to this hallway we admitted about fifty or sixty people to the studio, [in keeping with] the very informal nature of our show. They were all over the place. We scarcely had room to put on our show, but that was okay with us because we loved 'em and the applause helped put the show over.

"Each Saturday night brought more than its quota of people who wanted to watch our broadcast. They milled around for several hours and most of them stuck to the finish. They were hungry for the rhythm of the soil and the heart songs, plus the rural flavor and humor which spiced it.

"When Uncle Dave [Macon] came on we moved him back so that he would have plenty of room to kick as he played. He has always been an actor who thought the microphone was just a nuisance. It took a long time to 'hitch' him to it."

Hay realized, of course, that with banjo-playing Dave Macon his "WSM Barn Dance" had its first genuine star!

··◦[ii]◦·· He was born David Harrison Macon at Smartt Station, Tennessee, near McMinnville, in 1870, at a time when the South was struggling through the bitter Reconstruction period. Not far away, seven years earlier, blue-clad and gray-clad troops had clashed on the Stones River battlefield during the Civil War. His father, John Macon, had been a captain in the Confederate army; he tried now to scratch out a living as a farmer in hilly country that was perhaps best known for its sorghum molasses. It was not an easy time for the Macon family.

David was thirteen when his father decided to try a new venture. He moved the family to Nashville, where the captain became the manager of the old Broadway Hotel, a favorite stopping-over place for the traveling show people who came through the city. One of the shows to stop at the hotel, during a two-week engagement, was Sam McFlin's Circus with twenty-four men and four ladies in the troupe. Dave got free passes for the show.

Years later, he would write (in the third person, as he often spoke of himself): "Uncle Dave, being honest, always wanted to give 'honor to whom honor is due.' So, it was in the Fall of 1885 that he first met Mr. Joel Davidson, a native of Davidson County, Tenn., who was then a noted comedian and banjoist in the concert of Sam McFlin's Circus . . . then showing in Nashville on the corner of 8th Ave. and Broadway, at that time an open field. So it was Joel Davidson who proved to be the spirit that touched the mainspring of the talent that inspired Uncle Dave to make his wishes known to his dear old Mother, and she gave him the money to purchase his first banjo."

The young Macon was sixteen when his father died suddenly. His mother moved the family back to the farm. They settled near Readyville, on the Stones River in Cannon County. The banjo went with him and Dave played it whenever he had time off from his farm work.

In 1897 he married Mary Matilda Richardson; they were to become the parents of seven sons. At the age of thirty-one, in 1901, he started the Macon Midway Mule and Transportation Company, a freight-hauling business between Woodbury, the county seat of Cannon County, and Murfreesboro, the county seat of Rutherford County. The trip took two days; the first leg was eight and a quarter miles from Murfreesboro to Kittrell, the second leg was ten and three-quarter miles from Kittrell to Woodbury. Perhaps his most profitable cargo was Jack Daniel's No. 7 whiskey, carried at a fee of twenty-five cents a gallon.

Dave Macon became a familiar figure on those trips, sitting high on the wagon, four mules in front of him, playing the banjo and singing his songs. For nearly twenty years the mules-and-wagon transportation company prospered, until a rival motorized trucking company took his customers. Uncle Dave could never adapt to modern technology, especially the internal combustion engine. He never learned to drive a car. And in one of his songs he would declare: "I'd rather ride a wagon and go to heaven, than to hell in an automobile."

The freight business gone, Uncle Dave faced a turning point in his life. The year was 1920; he was fifty years old. He recalled in a letter to George Hay (writing again in the third person) what happened to him then:

"Early in the Summer of 1920, while in the Ozark Mountains of Ark for the benefit of his health . . . he gave himself up almost entirely to his favorite pasttime [*sic*], that of playing and singing on his banjo afternoons and evenings for the pleasure of the tourists stopping at his hotel. One gentleman came to Uncle Dave . . . and said, 'Uncle Dave, you saved my life.' The answer was 'How, my friend?' He replied, 'I was so blue and down and out I did not care for life any longer. But by seeing you at your age act out [*sic*] as well as playing and singing on your banjo . . . my spirits rose and refreshed my whole soul and body and has given me hope to go on with life's duties.' "

Thus encouraged, Dave Macon looked to a career as a professional entertainer. It was quick in coming.

"All of my life I had played and sung for fun," he said. "My neighbors always asked me to play at picnics and special occasions. Finally, one very self-important farmer approached me and asked me to play at a party he was planning. I was very busy and a bit tired, so I thought I would stop him. I told him I would play at his party for fifteen dollars. He said, 'Okay, it's a deal.' It was a large affair, and in the crowd was a talent scout for Loew's Theatres. My act seemed to go over very well. When I had finished, the theatre man offered to book me at a leading theatre in Birmingham, Alabama, at several hundred a week. They held me over for many weeks and booked me throughout the country. I was in the show business."

In 1923, after a chance meeting in a Nashville barbership, Uncle Dave teamed with a young Mount Juliet fiddler named Sid Harkreader for another Loew's vaudeville tour, starting with a three-week engagement in Nashville. Eventually they traveled as far west as Dallas, Texas.

In the following year, Macon and Harkreader went to New York City to record at the Aeolian Company, under the aegis of a furniture manufacturer who wanted his own special records to sell in association with the phonographs he was offering to customers. They were to receive expenses only, and they wound up cutting fourteen sides for Aeolian.

Harkreader told a story of Uncle Dave's reaction to the big city; it was his first visit to New York. Macon went into a Manhattan barbershop to "get the works." When he was presented with a bill for seven dollars and fifty cents, Dave tried to be nonchalant.

"I thought it would be ten dollars," he said.

George D. Hay, the "Solemn Ole Judge," holding his steamboat whistle, "Hushpuckena," with Uncle Jimmy Thompson, the "fiddler with a thousand tunes," on an early "WSM Barndance."

(C. 1925) GRAND OLE OPRY ARCHIVES

In spite of the coats and ties, the first hillbilly band to play on WSM: Dr. Humphrey Bate and his Possum Hunters. From the left, Dr. Bate, fiddler Oscar Stone, banjoist Walter Liggett, guitarists Staley Walton and Paris Pond, and bass violinist Oscar Albright.

(C. 1925) GRAND OLE OPRY ARCHIVES

Uncle Dave Macon, the "greatest banjo picker in Dixie."

(C. 1928) GRAND OLE OPRY ARCHIVES

In 1925, the National Life and Accident Insurance Company building was a prominent feature of Nashville's skyline. Radio station WSM had its initial broadcast from this building on October 5, 1925.

(1927) *LES LEVERETT COLLECTION*

The Crook Brothers in an early
publicity photograph staged at a
country store. On the top step are
Herman Crook with his harmonica
and Lewis Crook on banjo. Below
are, from the left, guitarist Blythe
Poteet, fiddler Kirk McGee, and
guitarist Bill Etters.

(C. 1930) LES LEVERETT COLLECTION

DeFord Bailey, the "wizard of
the harmonica," in WSM
Studio A. Discovered by Dr.
Humphrey Bate, Bailey thrilled
Judge Hay, who threw his
steamboat whistle in the
air the first time he heard
the black musician play.

(C. 1928) GRAND OLE OPRY ARCHIVES

With its increasing popularity, the Opry organized this troupe of performers to tour the RKO Theater circuit in 1931. Seated are Sam McGee and Uncle Dave Macon. Standing from left are Kirk McGee, Dr. Humphrey Bate, Dorris Macon, Humphrey Bate, Jr., Alcyone Bate, and Lou Hesson.

Later, though, he wrote on his expense sheet: "Robbed in barber shop . . . $7.50."

In 1925 the Macon-Harkreader duo was back in New York in April to record twenty-eight more songs in a four-day period. Then, on November 6 of that year, the two of them were in concert in Nashville's Ryman Auditorium. One contemporary report said: "A little fiddler by the name of Sidney Harkreader, introduced as the fiddling fiddler of Mount Juliet, [who was] teamed up with a banjo player by the name of Uncle Dave Macon of Readyville, Tennessee, introduced as the struttingest strutter that ever strutted a strut with a banjo or guitar, set the hundreds to stomping their feet with 'Turkey in the Straw,' 'Sugar Walks Down the Street,' 'Ain't Gonna Rain No More,' and 'Go Away Mule.'

"Six thousand people roared their approval."

The report was somewhat of an exaggeration—there was never a time when the Ryman could accommodate 6,000.

Yet when Uncle Dave Macon became a part of the "WSM Barn Dance" in December of 1925, George Hay could welcome a total professional (indeed, the *only* professional on the roster at that time), one with a vast repertoire of tunes, stage and recording experience, ample local popularity, and a keen knowledge of how to please an audience.

Also, Hay got a songwriter who recognized, as had Carson Robison, the impact on rural folks of the "monkey trial" in Dayton, Tennessee, earlier that year. Uncle Dave had his own song based on that event: "The Bible's True." It was a rollicking, hand-clapping, evangelistic tune:

> *Evolution teaches man came from a monkey,*
> *I don't believe no such thing in the days of a*
> *week of Sundays.*

> Chorus:
> *For the Bible's true, yes I believe it,*
> *I've seen enough and I can prove it,*
> *What you say, what you say, it's bound to be*
> *that way.*

> *God made the world and everything that's in it,*
> *He made man perfect and the monkey wasn't*
> *in it.*
> (repeat chorus)

> *I'm no evolutionist that wants the world to see,*
> *There can't no man from anywhere, boys, make a*
> *monkey out of me.*
> (repeat chorus)

God made the world, and then He made man,
Woman for his helpmate, beat that if you can.
(repeat chorus)*

As George Hay wrote, "The name of Uncle Dave Macon should always be remembered with gratitude by all of the members of the cast and by managers and officials of WSM. He has contributed so very much. . . . Our hats are off to this grand Tennessee farmer who has done . . . good wherever he goes with his three banjos, his plug hat, gates-ajar collar, gold teeth and his great, big Tennessee smile! God bless you, partner."

⌜iii⌝ With his *star* aboard, George Hay moved to make his show even bigger, with greater variety. Twenty-five acts were added to the "WSM Barn Dance" during the first two or three months of 1926.

"It was purely a labor of love," Hay said later. "Whoever showed up went on the air sometime, and usually several times, during the Saturday night show. By that we do not mean it was a free-for-all. We passed upon all of them in a crude sort of an audition."

Alcyone Bate Beasley recalled one early newcomer who even escaped the "crude sort of an audition"—black harmonica player DeFord Bailey. He had been discovered by Dr. Humphrey Bate on one of the programs on competing WDAD, and the doctor brought him to WSM on a Saturday evening.

According to Mrs. Beasley: "As they started in, Mr. Hay said, 'Doc, where you goin' with this boy?'

"Daddy said, 'Let this boy in here, Judge—let him play a tune.' And the Judge said, 'Why, Doc, I can't let this boy on the air without hearin' him.' And Daddy says, 'I'll stake my reputation on the ability of this boy, Judge.' So he went on the air and played, and Mr. Hay, he was just thrilled to death. He pitched his old steamboat whistle up in the air."

But DeFord Bailey was not the only find for the barn dance. There were, for instance, Sam and Kirk McGee, a brother act from the rural area around Franklin, Tennessee. They played all the stringed instruments, but Kirk was better known as a fiddler, and Sam was regarded as one of the finest finger-style guitar pickers of the early period.

Years later, Kirk would say: "I'll tell you, we got a lot of our pickin' from the colored people. My grandmother had a store by the railroad. At twelve o'clock the section hands would come over there to buy their lunch. An' after they were through eatin' they'd play an' we'd listen to them. They played some weird chords. They didn't know what they were an' we didn't either. Still don't.

"They'd get this fifth [of liquor] and break the neck off. They had a way of doin' this with water; they'd heat it, temper it with water, an' it would break off

*"The Bible's True," words and music by David H. Macon, 1926. Public domain.

clean. They used the bottle neck, you know, the way you use a steel on a guitar today."

Sam and Kirk McGee went to New York City in 1927 to record with Uncle Dave Macon. "I'da liked New York fine," Kirk said, laughing, "if I coulda seen it. Uncle Dave wouldn't let you go anyplace. He didn't care about anythin' but his show."

Of that recorded "show," musicologist Ralph Rinzler would write: "They provide us with some of the best examples of string-band ensemble playing ever recorded. Uncle Dave seems to revel in the sound of the reedy, yet elegant, fiddling of Mazy Todd (of Big Springs, Tennessee) and Kirk McGee. He crows and hollers with joy when Sam momentarily abandons his guitar bass line to beat out a clog rhythm on the top of his then-new Martin."

What George Hay would call "delineators of homespun music" were plentiful on the barn dance. Included were the Pickard Family, of Waverly, Tennessee, led by Obed (Dad) Pickard. And Theron Hale and his daughters, Elizabeth and Mamie Ruth. And two blind musicians, Uncle Joe Mangrum, a fiddler, and Fred Schriver, who played piano and accordion. "Each Saturday night," Hay noted, "Uncle Joe and Fred would hold a 'jam' session right on the air. It was one of the features of the show. All of the members of our company were delighted when the old man and the young man teamed up to give out their best."

Another early act of note was the Ed Poplin Band, consisting of the elder Poplin, a fiddling rural mail carrier; a friend, guitarist Jack Woods; and three Poplin children: Louise, also on guitar; Frances on mandolin, and teenager Ed Poplin, Jr., on piano.

"They played well," Hay remembered, "specializing in folk music, although once in a while, before we could or did stop it, Ed would slip into an old popular song, such as 'When You Wore a Tulip and I Wore a Red, Red Rose.' There is not much difference between that number and, for instance, 'Darling Nellie Gray,' except that we have always regarded the latter as strictly folk music. The line of demarcation between the old popular tunes and folk tunes is indeed slight. We have . . . much trouble . . . sorting them out."

That was a strange admission for George Hay, who was always a man with sure opinions. About almost everything. But since there *was* a difficult demarcation between what was acceptable "folk music" on one hand, and unacceptable "old popular tunes" on the other, Hay set himself up as the final arbiter. In that he had the full backing of Edwin Craig, who had played a mandolin in a string band in school and loved rural music. Indeed, Hay's fascination with the same kind of music was one of the reasons Craig hired him.

Thus, Hay took a hard-nosed approach about what went over the air during the "WSM Barn Dance." His most oft-repeated phrase was: "Keep it close to the ground, boys!" Hay decreed that *his* music would be played with stringed instruments. Other instruments bespeaking "pop" music—horns and drums, for example—were banned from the barn dance.

So determined was he in his quest to keep the program's music simple and earthy that his attitude persists among the old-timers on the show, even into the mid-eighties.

There was a revealing discussion in 1984 on a television interview show, "Yesteryear in Nashville," on The Nashville Network (TNN). Participants were Archie Campbell, the host; Jumpin' Bill Carlisle, who had been in the Opry for more than thirty years; and Herman Crook, who went back to the very beginning.

The subject was drums on the Grand Ole Opry.

"I remember," Campbell began it, "when Grandpa [Jones] came on and he saw some drums on the stage. And they asked him, 'Grandpa, you want drums on your number?' And he said, 'Very little, if any.' "

Crook was immediately vehement: "If I had my way about it, if I had the authority to do it, I'd take every one of them and carry them to the dump. And them tin things they bang on. Now, that's not music; there's not music to it. It's a lot of noise and racket!"

"Herman, I'm with you on the drums," Carlisle said lightly, trying for some levity, " 'cause they play everything in the same key. You ever notice that?"

Herman's peroration continued. "People argue with me. They say, 'Well, times have changed.' And I say, 'You don't change country music.' The music don't change. People change it. They just do it theirself, putting something that don't belong in there. Country music don't change, fellows, it don't change."

···⟡ iv ⟡··· Some change, though, was inevitable. In 1927 the power of WSM Radio was increased from its original 1,000 watts to 5,000 watts, vastly expanding the audience for its barn dance and other programs. That same year, WSM affiliated with the new National Broadcasting Company network.

Radio broadcasting had been going through some volatile times. Some of the early license holders, to which radio was little more than a lark, closed their enterprises. What had been 1,400 stations on the air in 1924 had dropped to only 600 by the end of 1926. Clearly, it was a time for professionals to sort it all out.

Once more the pioneering David Sarnoff came to the fore, proposing a "central broadcasting organization" to solve what had become the major problem—the lack of enough quality programming to assure the growth of radio. On November 15, 1926, the National Broadcasting Company—with twenty-five stations in twenty-one cities on the hookup—inaugurated its service in a broadcast from the old Waldorf-Astoria Hotel at 34th Street and Fifth Avenue in New York (now the site of the Empire State Building).

Presaging what wonders were ahead for radio, the broadcast presented the leading popular singer of the day, Mary Garden, performing "Annie Laurie" and "My Little Gray Home in the West" from Chicago, and humorist Will Rogers speaking from Independence, Kansas. There were five orchestras (including Vincent Lopez), a brass band, Metropolitan Opera soloists, a light-opera company, an oratorio society, and vaudeville comedians Weber and Fields.

Within two months, NBC was operating two networks, the Red and the Blue (later to become the American Broadcasting Company). WSM's affiliation in 1927 was with the Red network, an event important to the well-being of the station and to George Hay's show.

Part of the charm of the story of the barn dance, and what happened to it over the years, is that some anecdotes about it are wrapped in controversy. Controversy had cropped up again in another key anecdote, regarding the renaming of the "WSM Barn Dance."

Hay has said the incident, which was inextricably bound to Dr. Walter Damrosch's "Music Appreciation Hour" on the NBC network, took place on December 10, 1927. Yet subsequent research has shown the "Music Appreciation Hour" didn't premiere until the fall of 1928. Therefore, what happened on the "WSM Barn Dance" on that storied evening had to have been in 1928, most likely on Saturday, December 8. The correction does not make the event any less significant.

"It so happened that on Saturday nights," Hay reported, "from seven to eight o'clock, WSM carried the 'Music Appreciation Hour' under the direction of the eminent conductor and composer, Dr. Walter Damrosch.

"Dr. Damrosch always signed off his concert a minute or two before eight o'clock, just before we hit the air with our mountain minstrels and vocal trapeze performers."

Studio B's monitor was turned on, to listen for cues to the conclusion of the Damrosch program. George Hay heard the end of it, recalling what Dr. Damrosch said on that evening:

" 'While most artists realize that there is no place in the classics for realism, nevertheless I am going to break one of my rules and present a composition by a young composer from 'Ioway' who sent us his latest number, which depicts the on-rush of a locomotive. . . .'

"After that announcement the good doctor directed his symphony orchestra through the number which carried many 'shoooses' depicting an engine trying to come to a full stop. Then he closed his programme with his usual sign-off.

"Our control operator gave us the signal which indicated we were on the air. . . . We paid our respects to Dr. Damrosch and said on the air something like this: 'Friends, the programme which has just come to a close was devoted to the classics. Dr. Damrosch told us that it was generally agreed there is no place in the classics for realism. However, from here on out for the next three hours we will present nothing but realism. It will be down to earth for the "earthy." In respectful contrast to Dr. Damrosch's presentation of the number which depicts the on-rush of the locomotive we call on one of our performers, DeFord Bailey, with his harmonica, to give us the country version of his "Pan American Blues." ' "

"Whereupon, DeFord . . . a wizard with the harmonica, played the number."

Bailey's selection featured his imitation of a fast-moving freight train.

"At the close of it," Hay continued, "your reporter said: 'For the past hour we have been listening to music taken largely from Grand Opera, from now on we will present *The Grand Ole Opry.*' The name has stuck. . . . It seems to fit our shindig, hoedown, barn dance, or rookus."

The Grand Ole Opry.

It became the title for a radio show like none other in the history of broadcasting, a title of inestimable commercial value, and all because of a chance adlib remark by an enthusiastic announcer on WSM Radio in Nashville, Tennessee.

"Who's that knocking at my door?"
Cried the fair young maiden.
"It's only me from over the sea,"
Said Barnacle Bill the Sailor;
"I'm all dressed up like a Christmas tree,"
Said Barnacle Bill the Sailor.*

—Popular song,
circa 1930

It was 1930. The nation began a new decade sitting on an economic teeter-totter, unsure which end was up, which down. It was the start of a time of massive unemployment, uncounted business failures, bank closings, shantytowns, soup kitchens, bread lines, thirty-eight-cent wheat and six-and-a-half-cent cotton, farm foreclosures, and general despair.

In a peculiar way, the state of country music in 1930 was analogous to the economic situation. It was rife with uncertainty. On one hand, Jimmie Rodgers, the tubercular "Singing Brakeman," "The Blue Yodeler," was at the very peak of his popularity. It was reported that general-store customers would approach the counter and say: "Let me have a pound of butter, a dozen eggs, and the latest Jimmie Rodgers record." He was making an astounding $2,000 a week.

At the same time, however, there was a shuffling in the country music business that saw such songwriters as Carson Robison—composer of hillbilly compositions

*"Barnacle Bill the Sailor" by Carson Robison and Frank Luther; copyright 1929 Peer International Corporation.

"Way Out West in Kansas," "The John T. Scopes Trial," and "Goin' Back to Texas"—courting the "pop" market with the likes of novelty tunes like "Barnacle Bill the Sailor."

Change was in the air everywhere. The Grand Ole Opry included.

··◦[ii]◦·· By 1930 the performers on the Opry were being paid.

"They picked out the ones they wanted," Herman Crook remembered, "and put them on pay. We happened to be one of the lucky bands. They started us all at five dollars apiece on Saturday night. Each one got five dollars."

Kirk McGee found himself as a temporary member of the Fruit Jar Drinkers. "The way I joined them," he said, "Grandpappy George Wilkerson, he got disabled at work. He couldn't hardly breathe. The Solemn Old Judge asked me to do Grandpappy's number for him on the Opry. And I said, 'If you'll see that George gets the money.' And Hay says, 'We'll do that.' And they gave George the money. I played his show that way for about four years."

Thus, the family atmosphere of the Grand Ole Opry had already been established. As with any family it was growing. And changing.

In the early part of 1928 it got an important new member: Harry Stone, late of Jacksonville, Florida, who had been hired by Edwin Craig as an announcer and—more important—as associate program director to George Hay. Harry's brother, David, was also hired as an announcer about a year later.

It fell to Harry Stone to commercialize the Grand Ole Opry. Economic reality had changed the former "service" concept of radio to a commercial one—at WSM and across the industry. Stone was a good businessman, but he also genuinely liked the Opry program. And he made moves to improve it, first as Hay's assistant and then as Hay's superior.

In 1930 Hay was replaced by Stone as the program director. Brother David explained: "Judge Hay's health was not the best at the time, and he was in and out of work a lot. Another contemporary, Jack DeWitt, was more blunt about Hay: "He just wasn't a practical kind of man. He was up in the clouds all the time."

Just how much Harry Stone had taken over was revealed by Hay himself in his memoirs: "Along about 1930 or '31, *Harry Stone made a deal* with Asher Sizemore and his son, Jimmy, at that time about six years of age. The act was known as 'Asher and Little Jimmy Sizemore,' or more often as 'Asher and Little Jimmy.' Asher Sizemore came to us from Kentucky, where he learned the songs of the mountains and a number of sacred songs. Little Jimmy has unusual talent as a child singer. . . .

"Asher and Little Jimmy sang heart songs and closed their programmes with a prayer. They got out a song book, which sold by the thousands. The fact is, it was a phenomenal success. They broke records with their personal appearances on the road and people crowded into our studios to watch them work."

It must be obvious that the songbook sales by Asher and Little Jimmy were not undertaken without the approval of Harry Stone.

There were other personnel changes instituted by Stone. Robert Rainey Lunn, of Franklin, Tennessee, billed as "The Talking Blues Boy," came on the Opry in 1930. Hay would write: "There is never a dull moment when he is around. His infectious good humor, his practical jokes, and his ability to practice to a limited degree the ventriloquist's art keep the boys and girls in a mild uproar most of the time Robert is near."

Robert Lunn had a gimmick. His "Talking Blues" number had hundreds of verses, no one really knows how many, and he'd come forth with a few of them on every Opry broadcast. An example:

> *If you want to get to heaven let me tell you how*
> * to do it.*
> *Grease your feet in a little mutton suet.*
> *Fly right over in the promised land,*
> *Slip right over in the devil's hand,*
> *Go easy . . . make it easy . . . go greasy.*

Another "new" act on the Opry in 1930 involved the McGee brothers, Sam and Kirk, who teamed now with a superb country fiddler named Arthur Smith from Humphreys County, Tennessee. They called themselves the Dixieliners—old-timers considered it one of the best string trios ever to play the Opry.

"When the Dixieliners started," Kirk McGee said, "why, Arthur used to work on these here little railroads that ran through Dickson—the 'Dixie Line,' you know. Anyway, he was a lineman on the railroad. And we'd go get him at these work cars; they lived on the work car. And after he'd done his day's work, why we'd pick him up an' we'd go play a schoolhouse somewhere. And bring him back that night."

In 1931, Harry Stone took the Grand Ole Opry in an entirely new direction, hiring a vocal trio called the Vagabonds, a thoroughly professional group that had been on WLS in Chicago and KMOX in St. Louis.

George Hay called it "a new turn in the Opry road." It is not recorded whether he approved of the new turn; more than likely, given his preference for "down home folks," he objected. Certainly, he never would have hired them, so Harry Stone must have.

The Vagabonds were Herald Goodman, Dean Upson, and Curt Poulton. By the time he wrote his 1945 "history" of the Grand Ole Opry, Hay had found rationalization for their being on the Opry, although a perceptive reader can find tinges of The Solemn Old Judge's disapproval.

"Each son of a minister of the gospel," Hay wrote, "the boys were thoroughly familiar with sacred numbers and heart songs they introduced with great success on the show. Their backgrounds varied somewhat from the other members of the company, in that they had received more formal education. Born in the

Middle West, they had lived in small towns during their early years. They could hardly be called 'country boys,' but they loved folk music and handled it with a background of formal musical training, which smoothed it as against the usual renditions handled in a strictly rural fashion."

The early thirties brought a great many other changes to the format of the Grand Ole Opry. More and more Harry Stone was using other program time on WSM to develop acts that would later be put into key spots on the Opry.

One such act was a blackface comedian, Leroy "Lasses" White, described as "the dean of minstrelsy." White was hired to do a program on WSM titled "Lasses White's Minstrels," a radio adaptation of a theater act.

On the Opry itself, Lasses and partner "Honey" Wilds used material, according to Hay, "which fitted the Opry and [they] became stars of the big shindig almost immediately. The name of Lasses White was legendary throughout the South and Middle West. His high-pitched minstrel voice and delightful sure-fire comedy was a big attraction. Honey worked very well with him, with his deep voice trained to dialect so well that he lets it run over into his private life, and fed Lasses with perfect timing, so necessary to comedy routines. Their personal appearances made under the auspices of the newly-organized WSM Artists' Service were very successful. In fact, they 'had 'em hangin' on the rafters' in the schoolhouses throughout the territory served immediately by our station."

The WSM Artists' Bureau was another innovation of the early thirties, originally designed to book talent for church socials and schoolhouses. Hay ran it at first, but it soon became a major booking agency, given the pool of talent WSM had corralled. Acts were charged fifteen percent of their road "take" for the service.

Lasses White didn't stay at WSM very long, going to Hollywood to work in the movies. But Honey Wilds remained on the Opry with an act called Jamup and Honey. In our own time, when the blackface-minstrel concept is regarded as racially demeaning, it's difficult to understand the appeal of the genre. But Wilds claimed that his act was not offensive to blacks.

"We didn't think we were making fun of them," he said, "and evidently they didn't think we were making fun of them. Half of the people we drew [on the road] were Negro. They filled the balconies up at almost every show. And we didn't get along too well with some of the managers of theaters we played because of it, because they didn't care too much for the fact that Jamup and Honey were as popular with blacks and whites."

Indeed, in the context of the thirties, there was nothing strange about the Grand Ole Opry embracing blackface comedians. On the NBC radio network the most popular program of the day (starting in 1929) was "Amos and Andy," broadcasting five days a week, Monday through Friday.

Comedy had become more important for the Opry in the early thirties. There was the act of "Sarie and Sally," also begun in another time period and eventually moved to the Opry lineup. They were sisters from Chattanooga, Tennessee—Mrs. Edna Wilson (Sarie) and Mrs. Margaret Waters (Sally). They played rural women with hill country dialects; their act consisted of telling gossipy stories about their friends and relatives.

The Grand Ole Opry was diversifying, not only in front of the microphones, but also behind them.

⟨[iii]⟩ Harry Stone was promoted to the position of general manager of WSM in 1932. In that same year, Jack DeWitt returned to Nashville, after having worked for three years at Bell Laboratories in New York, and was named chief engineer of the radio station.

Of greater significance in '32, however, was the increase in power of WSM from 5,000 watts to 50,000 watts, and the assignment of a clear-channel frequency at 650 on the dial to the National Life and Accident Insurance Company.

That made it one of the "superstations" of radio, with enough uninterrupted power to spread its signal to fully two-thirds of the United States. Everything east of the Rockies could be considered WSM territory, enabling it to command greater commercial consideration and making its Grand Ole Opry virtually a "national" show.

As important as Stone and DeWitt would be to WSM and the Opry, and the other executives to follow, nothing would be quite as significant as being able to broadcast with 50,000 watts on a clear channel!

But the added coverage served only to exacerbate the live audience problems. Studio B had become hopelessly inadequate. By 1934 it was necessary for Edwin Craig to authorize the building of an entirely new studio on the fifth floor of the National Life building—an auditorium studio designed to seat 500 fans. It featured a portable stage and the latest acoustical treatment of walls and ceilings; a state-of-the-art studio for the day.

There was a plan devised for its use too. Three sets of varied-colored tickets were printed for each Saturday, one color to admit a holder to one hour of the Grand Ole Opry. Those 1,500 tickets—treasures to some—were placed in the hands of delighted National Life salesman in the field, perfect ice-breakers for an insurance sales pitch.

Studio C opened in February. It was an immediate victim of its own success.

George Hay's recollections: "The Opry audience promptly filled it. Things went along pretty well in that direction for some time. Finally the crowds stormed the wrought-iron doors of our Home Office Building to such an extent that our own officials could not get into their offices, when they felt it necessary to do so on Saturday nights. People in the crowds were apt to lose their heads and . . . the pay-off came one Saturday night when our two top officials were refused admittance to their own office building. They were forced to seek out the night engineer and be admitted through the back door. Our audience was very politely invited to leave the building.

"For some time we did not know whether or not the Grand Ole Opry would be taken off the air."

The initial temporary solution was to broadcast the Opry without an audience present. The summer of '34 passed with no audiences. "Something was lacking," Hay said. "It seemed that a visible audience was part of our shindig."

Thus, in the fall, the doors of Studio C were again opened to the fans. The same mob scenes prevailed. Talk started once more of simply canceling the Opry; it had become too big, too unmanageable.

"So we went into a huddle," Hay remembered, "and it was decided to rent the Hillsboro Theatre, a neighborhood house not too far from the center of Nashville. It was a great relief to the audience and to the performers."

WSM's publicity department trumpeted the change. In an October 21 release to *Broadcasting* magazine it was announced:

"The famous WSM Grand Ole Opry has again outdrawn [*sic*] its old clothes. Last February, when the new WSM auditorium studio was completed, WSM officials had felt that they had solved the problem of accommodating the crowds which assemble each Saturday night for the event; people who come from a dozen different states weekly and from as far distant points as a thousand miles. . . . The large auditorium studio of WSM proved inadequate.

"Saturday night [the date would be Saturday, October 27, 1934] WSM officials move to the Hillsboro Theatre in Nashville where many will be accommodated. Three different sets of colored tickets will be issued to admit a person to one hour of the Grand Ole Opry. Already the demand for the first night is taxing the capacity of 2,400 which may now see the WSM Opry. WSM has never charged for admittance to its Opry."

The theater offered amenities the Opry performers had never known: dressing rooms, a "control" of the audience, so to speak, with the ushers out front, and the feeling of being on a real stage. Hay had decreed that all of the acts were to wear costumes befitting a stage show.

Perhaps more important, the show had a stage manager for the first time—a gentleman named Vito Pellettieri.

Pellettieri was forty-five, the WSM music librarian. But before that he had been a musician, and a regional favorite.

He had grown up in a musical family: his father, Charles, was a prominent bandleader; his mother, Adelina, played the violin; an uncle, Emile, also led a band. Vito's future course was set by the father, who decreed his son was going to be a "great concert violinist."

He was a sickly child, unlike other children, always consumed by his violin lessons. He had talent. At seventeen, he formed a three-piece ensemble, playing at the Craggy Hope resort during the summer of 1906. Much in demand as a bandleader, Vito prospered and the father's dreams of a concert career for him faded.

By the 1920s, Charles Whited wrote in the *Nashville Tennessean* magazine, Pellettieri's group "played the colleges, the posh parties, the society blowouts. Everywhere the patrons demanded excitement, something new. Vito served it up with zest.

"In Jasper, Ala., he switched out all the lights in the ballroom and fired blanks from a .45 pistol 'just to wake 'em up.' Women shrieked and fainted. The lights came on and the sheriff rushed in shouting: 'Who got shot!'

"Then, one night in Chattanooga, Vito's arm went numb as he was playing the violin. He couldn't bend it, and he couldn't move his fingers. Doctors shook their heads: It was a breakdown caused by physical exhaustion."

His musical career was over, although he didn't fully realize it at first. He tried several times to come back with a band, only to be struck down by illness again. There was a period when he led a studio band at WSM Radio. And another time when he played a Gallatin Road ice cream parlor in Nashville—just to have the work. Finally, the Depression struck and the bottom fell out of the entertainment business.

He accepted a job as the music librarian at WSM. And on that October evening in 1934 he was assigned as stage manager on the Grand Ole Opry—seemingly an odd task for him: to shepherd a bunch of hillbilly musicians, many of them unable to read a note of music.

Vito himself thought it was ridiculous: "I went home, took me a big drink, and told my wife there wasn't enough devils in Hell to ever drag me back there."

But he did go back (frankly, he needed the money), and began to bring some order to what he felt was sheer chaos. First, he suggested the program be divided into manageable fifteen-minute segments. That was done. Then, he recommended that the segments be offered to sponsors. The first one was sold to Crazy Water Crystals.

Maybe the devils had dragged him back after that first night.

But he was to stay for forty years.

What a beautiful thought I am thinking
Concerning a great speckled bird,
Remember her name is recorded
*On the pages of God's holy word.**

—Roy Acuff hit,
circa 1930s

I f there was one thing that made life tolerable for the majority of Americans in 1935 it was *radio*. It had become the universal entertainment medium of the masses in those Depression-ridden years, bringing laughter and joyful music—even a bit of culture from time to time—into some very drab lives. Radio boomed. So did Nashville's Grand Ole Opry.

There were virtually no empty seats at the Hillsboro Theatre for the Saturday-night broadcasts of the Opry. The show was varied and, under Vito Pellettieri's firm hand, fast paced. Every taste within the country music genre was being catered to.

The old-timers were still intact—Macon, the Crooks, the Possum Hunters, the Gully Jumpers, the Fruit Jar Drinkers, DeFord Bailey, the Dixieliners, the Binkley Brothers (Gayle and Amos), and the Clodhoppers, et al.—but there were other acts in the Opry mix.

Zeke Clements and the Bronco Busters, for example, a group firmly in the cowboy mold. Clements would leave the Opry after a few years to test the en-

---

*"The Great Speckled Bird," traditional melody, original lyrics by the Reverend Guy Smith. Public domain.

tertainment climate of Hollywood. There he would gain a measure of lasting fame by being the voice of Bashful in Walt Disney's 1938 classic, *Snow White and the Seven Dwarfs*, the first animated full-length feature film.

And there was Jack Shook and His Missouri Mountaineers (Nap Bastien and Dee Simmons). They were all born in Illinois. And the Delmore Brothers, Rabon and Alton, who were to start an Opry tradition of duet-singing brothers. And the act of Curly Fox and Texas Ruby.

Fox was a fiddler out of Graysville, Tennessee. Hay said of him: "In addition to winning many blue ribbons with his fiddle he . . . [was] the only old-time fiddler ever to appear on the same program with the noted violinist, Dave Rubinoff. They gave contrasting versions of the art of playing the violin." (In those days, "Rubinoff and His Violin" was a popular feature on the Eddie Cantor network variety show; it was another example of radio's early flirtation with culture.)

Ruby Owens was from Fort Worth and billed herself as "Radio's Original Yodeling Cowgirl." "Miss Owens is proficient," Hay wrote, "as a blues singer and does very well with the heart songs which are used to a great extent on the Grand Ole Opry."

It could not be said that the Grand Ole Opry was the leading show of its type in 1935. That honor had to go to the "WLS Barn Dance" of Chicago, which had gone on the NBC Blue network in 1933 under the national sponsorship of Alka-Seltzer. That portion of it was renamed the "National Barn Dance." Its biggest star in '33 had been a cowboy singer named Gene Autry.

But if WSM's Grand Ole Opry lacked a network outlet, that seemed to be the only thing it lacked.

The Hillsboro Theatre couldn't contain it for very long and in 1936 it moved again, this time to the larger, if not more grand, Dixie Tabernacle on Fatherland Street in East Nashville. It wasn't much: The seats were benches without backs, the heating system was a series of pot-bellied stoves, there was sawdust on the floor. But a thousand or more could be jammed in for any one hour of the three-hour Opry; the same system of three sets of colored tickets was used.

Once more there was no charge for the tickets. National Life's insurance salesmen continued to be in control of the distribution.

There lived in East Nashville a young country music enthusiast named Vic McAlpin, who would later gain prominence as a songwriter and associate of Hank Williams. In '36, however, McAlpin was what might be called an "Opry groupie." He understood the ticket system thoroughly and he was aware that many of the Grand Ole Opry fans would drive hundreds of miles to Nashville without knowing that they had to have tickets.

McAlpin, being enterprising, would beg a couple of dozen tickets each week from several National Life agents, and then position himself at the door of the gospel tabernacle, scalping the tickets for the grand sum of a quarter each. Having concluded his business for the evening, he'd then talk his way past the attendant at the door.

One final anecdote, potent with poignancy, as reported by journalist Jack

Hurst in his entertaining fiftieth anniversary volume, *Nashville's Grand Ole Opry:*

"The evening before the first Opry performance at the Tabernacle, Dr. Humphrey Bate died of a heart attack at his home.

" 'Daddy knew he was going to die,' says Alcyone Beasley. 'He'd had angina for years. He was a doctor, and he knew when the attack came that it was a bad one. He looked down at his fingernails, because he could tell how bad it was from the way they looked, and he said, "Uh oh." Then he told my mother, "Ethel, this one's going to take me away from here."

" 'He was feeling his own pulse when it stopped.' "

⁓✦ ii ✦⁓ As the thirties marched on, there were developments destined to change the Grand Ole Opry for all time. In 1936, when it moved to the Dixie Tabernacle, Uncle Dave Macon was still the acknowledged star. The other acts were popular, of course, and had their loyal followings, but the old man continued to dominate the broadcast.

Maybe George Hay was responsible for that. He was a kindred spirit with Uncle Dave; the two of them fit together like bread and butter. Macon, for his part, admired Hay's "inquiring mind, friendliness, and command of the language." Hay's admiration for Uncle Dave was shown in his consistently lavish introductions of the veteran performer. He coined the phrase "Dixie Dewdrop" in those introductions and his characterizations of Macon in his writings were like no others.

Still, Macon was of an older school of performing and, to tell the truth, the developments in country music in the thirties indicated that "school was out." New kids were getting ready to matriculate at the Grand Ole Opry and go to the head of the class.

One was a young accordion player of Polish heritage named Julius Frank Anthony Kuczynski. In 1936 he had just married the daughter of his agent-manager and was playing on radio station WNOX, Knoxville, Tennessee, under the *nom de théâtre* of Pee Wee King.

Another was Roy Claxton Acuff, a tough-minded, fiddle-playing son of an east Tennessee preacher-lawyer. In 1936 he had begun his recording career, cutting twenty songs in Chicago for the American Record Company (later Columbia Records).

And the third was William Smith Monroe, a Kentucky-born direct descendant of the fifth President of the United States. In 1936 he was a member of the Monroe Brothers duo (with sibling Charlie), playing radio shows all over the country for Crazy Water Crystals and recording for Victor Records.

All had a single goal: the Grand Ole Opry in Nashville.

⁓✦ iii ✦⁓ Pee Wee King made it first.

Given his background he seemed an unlikely candidate for country music stardom.

"I was born in Milwaukee [February 18, 1914]," King said, "but when I was young my parents moved to a farm in Abrams, Wisconsin . . . about twenty-eight miles north of Green Bay. Dad had come from that area and so had my mother. And their parents had come from Poland.

"So I grew up in the Polish element, and was very fortunate to be associated with some Italians and Germans and Swedes. It gave me a broad knowledge of music of different countries. My dad played violin and concertina and he thought it would be an asset to him, as I grew up, to play sometime in his band—it was called the Midnight Four Plus One."

Young Frank (he was not called Julius) was the "Plus One." He started on the concertina, switching to the violin "when mother and dad decided that I ought to pursue violin. Not fiddle—violin." But his teacher was not enthusiastic about Frank's talents, declaring, according to King, "He won't ever be a good violinist because he's too energetic and he moves too fast."

An accordion came into his life at age fourteen, when he had saved enough money, by selling newspapers, to buy a secondhand instrument that came with a set of unused playing instructions. While still in high school, he had led his first dance band, a five-piece group that played on a Racine, Wisconsin, radio station. He called himself Frankie King, because he admired the music of Wayne King, "The Waltz King."

After graduating from high school he had a short-lived career as an apprentice mechanical draftsman in Milwaukee. But music drew him and he formed a group called the King's Jesters, playing engagements in Wisconsin, Michigan, and Illinois, and appearing frequently on Milwaukee radio stations.

"So as time went on," King said, "I was in an accordion shop in Milwaukee and there was a phone call from Mr. J. L. Frank. He was looking for an accordion player to work [on a tour] with Gene Autry at the time. And they had heard my radio show and I guess they said: 'Well, let's get this boy. He sounds like a nice, likable boy.' So I joined the Gene Autry group, thanks to Mr. Joe Frank."

At the time he called King—the year was 1934—Joe Frank was handling the career of Autry, whom he had placed on "WLS Barn Dance" in 1930. Autry was already recording and Frank was booking him in personal appearances around the Midwest. In 1935 Frank moved to Louisville, Kentucky, and placed Autry on WHAS as the leader of a group called the Log Cabin Boys.

Once more Frank called on King, and it was in Louisville that he got the nickname "Pee Wee." There were three musicians in the Log Cabin Boys whose first names were Frank. "Since you're the shortest one here, we're going to call you Pee Wee," Joe Frank told him. Pee Wee was actually five feet six. The name stuck; it was later legalized.

Autry didn't stay long in Louisville; the lures of Hollywood were too compelling. But Pee Wee King did stay, to start a new group called the Golden West Cowboys and to marry Joe Frank's stepdaughter, Lydia.

It must not be imagined that having a radio job in the depths of the Depression, or calling oneself the leader of a group (even one with the glowing name of Golden

West Cowboys) was a glamorous business. It was a coffee-and-doughnuts existence, at best.

In 1936 the newly married King was in Knoxville, at times wondering what he was doing in show business. "In those days," he recalled, "we got paid in scrip [discounted pseudo–paper currency redeemable at specific stores, often food markets]. . . . The Golden West Cowboys were having it kind of rough in the eastern Tennessee mountains. [The people there] weren't ready for western music . . . or western cowboy clothes. . . . [But] I took Mr. Frank's advice and became a standard-type musician. We didn't have day jobs or anything—we made our livings strictly from music. So, consequently, we took every chance we could playing radio jobs—even if they paid five or six dollars for the whole group."

Joe Frank recognized that King and the Golden West Cowboys needed to be in Nashville, broadcasting on a 50,000-watt, clear-channel station. He made a deal with Harry Stone to put them on the Grand Ole Opry.

Pee Wee's memory of their debut is vivid: "On the first Saturday in June of 1937 we did our first program on the Grand Ole Opry at the tabernacle on Fatherland Street, and we were invited to stay as regular members. It was a hard decision for me to make, because there was no pay at the Opry at that time. All we could do was play the broadcast and announce our dates, where in other cities they paid you for your staff programs, or commercial programs.

"Joe Frank drilled into my mind: 'You got to remember, kid, that one broadcast on the Grand Ole Opry means twenty weeks' work somewhere else.' And with that in mind, we stayed."

Pee Wee King was to contribute to some profound changes on the Opry. "I came in with a group—an organized group—and a group that belonged to the musicians' union. The Nashville local didn't want to accept our Louisville AFM cards right away, but they finally did. And others of the Opry members started becoming union members. . . . So I guess I had something to do with getting the Opry unionized.

"I remember when we came to the Grand Ole Opry," King went on, "it was free admission. . . . Now, the Opry was renting the tabernacle for their broadcasts, so Joe Frank went to Mr. [Edwin] Craig and said, 'Why don't you charge admission?' And Mr. Craig said, "No, we can't. It's just an advertising medium for our insurance company.' And Joe said, 'It's a known fact that you never give anything away if it's of any value, because that decreases its value and its importance.' "

(Perhaps that conversation would be remembered several years later.)

When Pee Wee King and the Golden West Cowboys were accepted on the Grand Ole Opry there was a performer in Knoxville who was wondering how King could get on the Opry and he couldn't. Roy Acuff had made several overtures to George Hay regarding the Opry and had been rebuffed; Hay told him the show had sufficient personnel.

But there was King. On the Opry! Acuff studied the situation carefully. And then he sought out J. L. Frank.

Lasses and Honey (Lasses White and Lee Davis Wilds) posing with their audience in the old National Life building studio.

(C. 1930) *GRAND OLE OPRY ARCHIVES*

Jamup and Honey (Bunny Biggs on right and Lee Davis Wilds on left) perform before an early WSM microphone.

(C. 1932) *GRAND OLE OPRY ARCHIVES*

The Vagabonds, Curt Poulton, Dean Upson, and Herald Goodman, were a professional vocal trio whose hiring in 1931 was for Judge Hay "a new turn in the Opry road."

(C. 1931) *GRAND OLE OPRY ARCHIVES*

O*pry stage manager, Vito Pellettieri,*
standing, when he was the leader of
an early WSM studio band.
(C. 1928) *GRAND OLE OPRY ARCHIVES*

The calendar in the upper right-hand corner of this photograph explains why Uncle Dave Macon is warming his feet.

(LATE 1930s) GRAND OLE OPRY ARCHIVES

The Delmore Brothers, Raybon and Alton (left to right), started an Opry tradition of brother duets.

(C. 1936) GRAND OLE OPRY ARCHIVES

Pee Wee King and one of the earliest
incarnations of his Golden West Cowboys
pose in the WSM studio for a publicity
photograph. Seated from the left are Pee
Wee King, Texas Daisey, and Milton Estes;
standing from the left are Curly Rhodes,
Jack Scaggs, and Abner Sims.

(1937) *LES LEVERETT COLLECTION*

Pee Wee King lassoes Lost John Miller
while Curly Rhodes and his sister Texas
Daisey help out the hapless Miller.

(C. 1938) *GRAND OLE OPRY ARCHIVES*

Zeke Clements was one of the first performers at the Opry to wear cowboy garb onstage.
(C. 1935) GRAND OLE OPRY ARCHIVES

Roy Acuff, with the fiddle, and his first touring band, the Crazy Tennesseans: Jess Easterday on guitar, Red Jones on bass, and Cousin Jody (James Clell Summey) on dobro. The black-face comedian is Jake Tindell and on the far right is Kentucky Slim ("Little Darlin' ").
(1936) GRAND OLE OPRY ARCHIVES/ROY ACUFF COLLECTION

Curly Fox and Texas Ruby spread the fame of the Opry on the road in the 1930s.

(C. 1937) GRAND OLE OPRY ARCHIVES

A popular band
from the early years
of the Opry in the
WSM studio: Jack Shook
and the Missouri
Mountaineers. From
the left, Jack Shook,
Dee Simmons, Bobby
Castleman, Fiddlin'
Arthur Smith, and
Nap Bastian.

(C. 1935) LES LEVERETT
COLLECTION

§[iv]§ In the summer of 1932, Roy Acuff, already twenty-eight years old and not settled on a career, went on the road with Doctor Hauer's Medicine Show, working mountain hamlets in east Tennessee and Virginia. There was no lightning-strike decision involved in Acuff's show business debut; he joined the show because it seemed to be something he ought to try for a season.

Young Acuff had dreamed other dreams; dreams that had turned to nightmares.

He had been a superb high school athlete, nicknamed "Rabbit" because of his quickness, and he had earned thirteen varsity letters at Central High School in Fountain City, Tennessee, the county area outside of Knoxville. He had four letters in football (he was a player in the first football game he ever saw), four in basketball, and five in baseball. He was only five feet seven and weighed a mere 130 pounds. But he was tough—very tough. And he never turned his back on a brawl, even when it might involve a police officer or two.

"There was nothing I loved as much as a physical fight," he has said, "an actual physical fight! It was a joy!"

Physical work, however, never had a high priority with him. As a teenager he loathed farm work. Some of his time in the fields was spent learning to balance a small hand-plow on his chin. He once went to Detroit for a production-line job at the Ford Motor Company and lasted two hours. His most permanent job, covering a period of nearly three years, was as a callboy on the Louisville and Nashville Railroad. But the tenure of that job might be attributed to the fact that he also played on the L&N semipro baseball team at the same time.

Baseball was his first love, and those youthful dreams were of major-league stardom. In the spring of 1929, New York Yankees scouts came through the Knoxville area, and it seemed that "Rabbit" Acuff was going to be given an opportunity to go to the Yankee training camp in 1930. It was not to be. Early in the summer of '29 he went on a fishing trip to Florida and suffered a blistering sunburn. Later, while playing for the L&N baseball team in Knoxville, he collapsed in the dugout, violently ill. Doctors diagnosed it as a sunstroke. Three more times that year, as he tried to resume normal activities, he collapsed. The warning came: Another attack might be fatal.

The next two years he spent at home; a good part of 1930 was spent in bed, recuperating and regaining his strength. During that time he picked up his father's fiddle and began to teach himself to play. Guidance came from his father, Neill Acuff, who was both a preacher and a lawyer, and from Victrola records of Fiddlin' John Carson and Gid Tanner and the Skillet Lickers.

He learned something, too, from his sister, Sue, who was a semiprofessional light-opera singer. Roy would mimic her and, as he did, he learned to sing from his diaphragm. Later he would say: "That's how I learned to rear back and sing, and come out with a lot of oomph. I used to knock some small stations off the air. They weren't used to my style. I was one of the first who ever put a real strong voice into country music."

By 1931 Acuff had recovered enough to make short trips to the corner drugstore, and there he discovered the yo-yo, a national fad at the time. His natural athletic ability made him expert with the yo-yo and he was never to put it down again.

Yet his fiddling and singing around the house and his mastery of the yo-yo did little to dispel the darkness of his life in those years. "When I found I was knocked out of a career of baseball," he recalled, "I just couldn't see any light at all—everything was dark." The fiddle, however, was to bring the light.

He sat one evening, early in 1932, on the porch of his home, idly playing a fiddle tune. It was heard by a neighbor, one Dr. Hauer, who ran a medicine show and who sold a homemade remedy called Mocoton Tonic, said to cure dyspepsia, sick headaches, constipation, indigestion, torpid liver, and countless other ills. Dr. Hauer offered him a job. Roy accepted.

"I didn't make much money at it, but I got a pretty good background in show business," he explained. "And when I found out I could fiddle, and I found out that I could sing a song, or sell a song, and I found out that people appreciated me, I began to see a new light, and that light has been brighter for me than the world of sports."

When the medicine show season ended in the fall of 1932, Roy Acuff was in show business to stay. But it was difficult. Money was scarce in those Depression days. Musicians often played engagements for fifty cents. Roy worked first with a group called the Three Rolling Stones. Then, in 1933 and 1934, they grew into the Tennessee Crackerjacks. In 1935, with some personnel changes, the band landed a regular daily show on radio station WROL, Knoxville, and became the Crazy Tennesseans. They began to tour in an old Reo sedan Acuff had purchased from Dr. Hauer.

"The height of my ambition," Roy said, "was to play a date where the box-office receipts would total as much as a hundred dollars."

It was during that period that Roy heard a song titled "The Great Speckled Bird," performed by a singer named Charlie Swain. The original six verses, based on the ninth verse, twelfth chapter, of Jeremiah, had been written by a Reverend Guy Smith; the melody was a traditional English tune. Acuff paid Charlie Swain fifty cents to copy down the lyrics for him. It became Roy's song.

By October 1936 the Crazy Tennesseans had achieved enough of a reputation to be asked to record for the American Record Company.

"They wanted 'The Bird,' " Roy said, "they didn't want me."

That modesty aside, the band went to Chicago for its first recording session. Twenty songs were cut, including, of course, "The Great Speckled Bird." Also recorded on that first session was "Wabash Cannonball," but Acuff didn't sing it at that time. The vocal fell to band member Red Jones. (Acuff's own vocal of "Cannonball"—which was to become his theme song—wasn't recorded until 1947.)

Now that he had recorded for a major label, only the Grand Ole Opry eluded Acuff. His biographer Elizabeth Schlappi has written: "Roy started making trips to Nashville as early as 1934, going at least once a year, sometimes as many as three times. He would drive, ride with others, take a bus, or hitchhike the almost 200 miles from Knoxville to Nashville. He usually talked with Judge Hay and was always told, 'Sorry, boy, but the show is filled and there are many applications in ahead of you.' "

He wrote letters, too. One of them was to Robert Lunn, "The Talking Blues Man." Lunn—as did many of the Opry regulars—got hundreds of letters like that every year. Lunn threw the Acuff plea into the wastebasket.

Then came the news that Pee Wee King had joined the Opry, another goad for Acuff. He made a telephone call to King's manager, J. L. Frank. As it turned out, Frank was meeting with David Stone, then head of the WSM Artists' Bureau, when Roy's call came through. There was a hurried consultation between Joe Frank and David Stone, and Frank asked Acuff what he was doing the following Saturday night. Roy answered, "Nothing." An audition appearance on the Grand Ole Opry was immediately arranged.

(The exact date of that first 1937 appearance on the Opry by Roy Acuff remains a matter of contention. But the best guess seems to be that it was on either October 9 or October 16.)

It was made clear to Acuff that he was being brought on for that one night as a fiddler, because the Dixieliners, who featured fiddler Arthur Smith, were out of Nashville that weekend. Roy and his band were to play the first fifteen minutes of the show, with fiddling predominating.

His own words tell it best: "I did an awful poor job of fiddlin'. I was scared to death. I played back of the bridge as much as I played in front of it, and it don't sound too good back of the bridge."

After struggling through versions of "Old Hen Cackle" and "Turkey Buzzard," Acuff tried to salvage the audition by launching into a vocal number he was sure of, "The Great Speckled Bird." But instead of belting it out, as was his normal style, he sort of crooned it, confusing the members of the Crazy Tennesseans, who also played badly.

In a phrase, the audition was a disaster.

When he got back to Knoxville he began to believe he had failed on his one great opportunity. The remainder of October went by without any word from the Opry managers. Then November. And December. Early in January, a letter arrived from David Stone (had J. L. Frank interceded again?) inviting Acuff and his band to make another audition appearance on February 5, 1938.

In the entire history of the Grand Ole Opry it was to be a landmark date. Once more the Crazy Tennesseans drove to Nashville from Knoxville: Roy Acuff, fiddle; Jess Easterday, guitar; Clell Summey, dobro; and Red Jones, bass.

It was a cold and rainy Saturday night. Acuff was a bundle of nerves. As David Stone was doing the introduction, Joe Frank stood in the wings with Roy. He tried to introduce a note of levity, trying to calm the young fiddler.

"Roy," Frank said, "is Mickey Mouse a dog or a cat?"

Acuff was annoyed: "Oh, Joe, I don't know nothin' about it. Please don't ask me stupid questions; I'm going on the air."

Biographer Schlappi picks up the story: "As he stepped out onto the stage, Roy tried to think of himself as singing before the medicine show audience, and in this rendition of 'The Bird' he put force and feeling into it. Clell played the kick-off on the dobro (it was the dobro's first appearance on the Opry) and Roy sang one verse. Then his knees began to shake. Clell had to play a chorus and another verse before Roy could resume singing. . . . [But] Roy felt that he had put the feeling over to the listeners."

The mail that began to pour into WSM by Monday afternoon—"by the bushel baskets"—proved that Acuff had been right. David Stone sent him a telegram offering him a tentative assignment on the Opry starting February 19; Roy wired immediate acceptance.

On Thursday, February 10, David Stone wrote this letter to Acuff's home in Knoxville:

I am in receipt of your telegram advising that you will be here for the programs starting the 19th. I will book you for a spot on the Grand Ole Opry and also a series of 7:00 A.M. programs starting Monday, February 21st. . . .

We have arranged for a commercial spot on the Grand Ole Opry for which there will be a small salary as long as the commercial runs. Of course we reserve the right to change the Opry schedule, but as long as you are on a commercial spot there will be something for you.

I am teaming you with the Delmore Brothers for several personal appearances. These boys have tremendous popularity in this territory, but they cannot build or manage their own unit so I think it would be a great combination for the two acts. I think I can get some good dates right away and start you out as soon as you can get here. This will save a great deal of time in getting your build up with the WSM audience.

We will talk it over when you get here and I feel sure that we can make satisfactory arrangements. If you have any photographs, cuts, or mats, please mail them to me at once so that we can get publicity started.

Thus, on February 19, Roy Acuff and the Crazy Tennesseans made their first regular appearance on the Grand Ole Opry. On Sunday, February 20, they appeared with the Delmore Brothers for a show at Dawson Springs, Kentucky. On Monday, February 21, they broadcast "live" on WSM from 7:00 to 7:15 A.M.

One thing remained to be done.

General manager Harry Stone didn't like the name of the band. "Crazy Tennesseans," he contended, was a slur on Tennessee. He recommended that since Roy came from the Smoky Mountains he adopt that name.

Acuff agreed.

From that day forward, starting with the Opry broadcast of February 26, 1938, it was Roy Acuff and the Smoky Mountain Boys.

A new era had begun for the Grand Ole Opry.

Late in the evenin' about sundown,
High in a hill above the town,
Uncle Pen played the fiddle,
Oh, how it would ring!
You can hear it talk, you can hear it sing.*

—Bill Monroe standard

Young country acts of the mid-eighties, traveling on wide interstate highways in lavishly decorated air-conditioned buses and hauling their sophisticated equipment in giant tractor-trailer rigs, can have no concept of what it was like for country music performers on the road in the late thirties.

Roy Acuff will stand as a textbook example.

Accustomed to jamming the entire act and its instruments into one car—five men and a girl (Imogene Sarrett, known as "Tiny," joined the band shortly after its Opry debut)—the Smoky Mountain Boys played every night somewhere within a 200-mile radius of Nashville. In schoolhouses and churches and fire company halls, able to charge only a dime for children and a quarter for adults. Never getting the guarantee of a fixed payment. Rarely did Acuff's percentage of the gate exceed $30; too often it was as meager as $10.

Roy had the band members on salaries—$22.50 a week. At the end of a week, after paying the musicians and the traveling expenses, if he had $20 left for himself

*"Uncle Pen" by Bill Monroe; copyright 1951 Bill Monroe Music, Inc.; Hill and Range Music, Inc.

he considered himself fortunate. Further, every engagement they accepted was tied to the necessity of being back on the air the following morning at WSM and, of course, performing on the Grand Ole Opry every Saturday night.

It was a constant grind, at times a bit mad. As Elizabeth Schlappi wrote in her biography of Acuff: "On Saturday they'd work all day and be back at the Opry for their 8:30 show, sometimes with not enough time to change clothes. On many occasions Mildred [Roy's wife] brought fresh clothing down to the Opry. Roy often went for days without removing his shoes." More than once he thought of quitting.

Years later Roy would stress how important it was that they get back for the Opry broadcast: "Only bad sickness or death was accepted as an excuse for not being there." And he talked of the terrors of driving over the bad rural roads of the thirties in all kinds of weather: "We'd drive all night with the snow or rain hitting against the windshield. Man, you'd think we'd be so sleepy from staying up that everybody but the driver would go to sleep. But we were all so scared we couldn't sleep."

There was no home life to speak of. The band members lived in the Clarkston Hotel in Nashville. Mrs. Acuff stayed in Knoxville and kept her drugstore job; her earnings were vital.

Yet it seemed that Acuff was on a mission. He was unrelenting in his drive to succeed, determined to develop a style of his own. "Every person who has been successful has created a style," he said later. "When I decided to be myself and create my own style, that's when the people listened to me and bought my records. That's when I became successful."

Maybe he didn't realize it, but he was filling a demand. The early Grand Ole Opry concentrated on string bands and, given the crude microphones and transmission equipment then available, the best that could be heard at home was a sense of the spirited performances. There were no nuances; nothing was clear-cut about the unrehearsed show. Acuff changed all that. Perhaps music chronicler Jack Hurst summed it up best: "In the din, Acuff's brief and impassioned solo spots stood out like gunshots at midnight."

Opry stage manager Vito Pellettieri would reminisce: "The string bands were the main thing. What little singing there was began with Uncle Dave, and the Delmores and Sam and Kirk. But there wasn't a lot of it. We hadn't got to the star business yet, not until the coming of a curly-headed fiddler."

If there was a turning-point year in the vivid sixty-three-year history of the Grand Ole Opry, it had to be 1939. For it was in that year it became clear that the Opry had "arrived." That its influence was being felt even beyond the reach of the powerful WSM signal.

The year began, however, with trouble in the camp of the show's newest star. First thing on New Year's Day three of Acuff's band members quit. Abruptly, Clell Summey, Red Jones, and Tiny Sarrett announced they were leaving, unable to agree with Acuff that their futures lay in the hillbilly music of the Opry. They meant to return to Knoxville to play "pop" music.

Roy had to act hurriedly. He meant to replace the defectors with performers who could be happy with his concept of what the Smoky Mountain Boys ought to be. He first reached out to an old medicine-show chum, Jake Tindell. Jake had worked for a time with the Crazy Tennesseans in Knoxville, and he knew a lot of tried-and-true comedy routines and could work in blackface.

Acuff also called on guitarist Lonnie Wilson, whom he had known during the days of the Tennessee Crackerjacks. And then there was a fellow named Beecher Kirby—everyone called him Pete—who played the dobro and had substituted for Clell Summey a time or two in Knoxville.

A telegram was sent to Wilson: "Get Pete Kirby at Kern's Bakery and see if you can play together." Kirby and Wilson had never met before, but they got together, played for a time, and Lonnie wired Roy that Kirby would do. The new band members arrived in Nashville on the morning of Saturday, January 7, and played the Opry with Acuff (and the loyal Jess Easterday) that night. The Smoky Mountain Boys never missed a beat.

Of note in all of this is that Roy selected the new members of the band with an eye to putting comedy in the act. He wanted a complete show unit—a package— to take on the road. Lonnie Wilson became "Pap," an old-man character; Jake played in blackface. But it wasn't until April that Roy met Rachel Veach and a brand-new comedy element was added. One that hadn't been planned.

Rachel was a shy little girl, an eighteen-year-old banjo player from Peytonville, Tennessee. She had never been away from her farm home before; things like showers and elevators and even locks on the door were foreign to her. But to Acuff she was so "country" that he believed she would be an invaluable addition to the act.

She was billed as "Rachel, Queen of the Hills," and Wilson and Kirby were introduced as "Pap and Oswald, Rachel's Two Country Comedian Boy Friends." Almost immediately though, Roy began getting mail chastising him for having a young girl traveling, unchaperoned, with all of the men in the act. He was sensitive to that kind of innuendo.

Later, in an interview with disc jockey Hugh Cherry, Roy explained what happened next: "Os would always sit in the car and give that big horse laugh, that 'Haaaaaaa' thing that he always did, and I'd get so tickled. We'd go through some little town, he'd see something funny and he'd laugh like that. It was a put-on laugh, of course, but it was funny to us. Well, it sounded like a backward, bashful laugh. So I said, 'Let me make you Rachel's brother and bring you two together as "Rachel and her Great Big Bashful Brother Oswald." ' So I teamed them together and it was a tremendous success right off, and my mail stopped immediately because they thought it was great to have a boy and his sister. So I fooled the public to protect the name of Rachel. I don't think that was wrong. I had to have a girl in my act."

Even after Rachel left in the mid-forties to raise a family, Kirby remained as

"Bashful Brother Oswald," his natural comedic talent highlighting the Smoky Mountain Boys' shows down through the years. And right into 1988.

Whenever personnel changes took place within the Smoky Mountain Boys, Acuff looked for someone who could do some comedy. Joe Zinkan, for example. At times he played a rube character called "Smilin' Joseph," because he never smiled. And then there was Oral ("Curly") Rhodes, who played bass and doubled on a rural alter ego known as "Odie." There were times with the billing as "Papa and Odie," or "Pap and His Son Odie."

But there was always comedy with the Acuff show. Kirby remembers: "It was our job to be crazy. In a lot of the shows all of us were out in the audience carryin' on and Roy was up there on the stage all by himself."

(A footnote regarding the early band: James Clell Summey would return to the Grand Ole Opry on a later date under the aegis of agent Joe Frank. He played with the Pee Wee King band for a short time and then developed a single act, "Cousin Jody," a rubber-faced, toothless rube. He remained on the Opry roster for many years.)

··◦❏ iii ❏◦·· The year 1939 was an important one behind the scenes as well. Jack Stapp, a Nashville native who had gone on to become a production executive at the CBS radio network, was on the WSM staff as second in command to Harry Stone.

Before leaving New York to return to Nashville, Stapp had visited NBC network headquarters and gotten the program people there to agree to accept "feeds" from its affiliate station in Nashville. It was Stapp's plan to produce those "feeds" himself.

But it wasn't the Grand Ole Opry he was going to offer to NBC. Instead, he put together an eighteen-piece staff orchestra and produced rather sophisticated pop music shows under the blanket title of "Sunday Down South." They were aired irregularly on NBC's Sunday-afternoon schedule, providing the initial national exposure for Nashville singers such as Dinah Shore and Snooky Lanson.

WSM had cracked the network barrier.

In July 1939 the Grand Ole Opry got yet another "home," the old Dixie Tabernacle having proved insufficient to the task of providing for the growth of the radio show. This time it moved to the imposing granite-and-marble War Memorial Auditorium in downtown Nashville, just across the street from the National Life headquarters from which it had been evicted just five years earlier.

The War Memorial could seat 2,000 plus for any one-hour portion of the show. It was hoped a twenty-five-cent admission charge would control the crowds somewhat. It didn't; the auditorium was soon overflowing each week.

It was during that period, just a few months after the move to the War Memorial Auditorium, that George Hay, in his capacity as the majordomo of the Opry, got a visit from "a big, good-looking fellow [who] had his own band with him. . . . He gave us a sample of folk music 'as she should be sung and played.' "

The visitor was William Smith Monroe, the youngest of eight children born in the Jerusalem Ridge section near Rosine, Kentucky. Few country music performers presented themselves to Judge Hay with a more intense musical heritage.

Monroe's father, a farmer and a sawmill operator, was forty-four years old when Bill was born in 1911; his mother was forty-one. His brother, Charlie, was the closest to him in age, and yet Charlie was eight years older. Bill had very poor vision as a youngster, and that caused him to be left out of a lot of activities with children his own age. He was a lonesome lad and painfully shy; he'd hide in the barn when visitors came to the farm.

What rescued him was the musical talent that he inherited from his mother's side of the family. Melissa Monroe sang the old-time ballads around the house; she also played the harmonica, accordion, and fiddle. And then there was Bill's uncle Pendleton Vandiver, the "Uncle Pen" about whom Bill would write an important song years later.

"When I first can remember him," Bill told an interviewer, "he'd bring his fiddle and he'd stay a night or so, and after supper, why, we'd get him to fiddle. We didn't have no guitar or anything, we'd just all gang up around him and listen to him fiddle—maybe an hour, hour and a half. My father would call bedtime then."

There was always singing around the Monroe household, but the shy youngster found it difficult to join in. His singing was done in the fields: "I used to go out in the field maybe a quarter of a mile from where any of 'em was at, so they couldn't hear me. I was seeing if I could sing numbers like 'Joe Clark' and that kind of stuff like some of the old ones in the family could do."

Bill's brothers were musicians. His first recollection of their music was from when he was about three years old. Charlie played the guitar; Birch the fiddle. As Bill got a little older, about ten, he started to play the mandolin and guitar. He selected the mandolin because no one else in the family played it. By the time he was eleven both of Bill's parents had died and he went to live with his Uncle Pen. That's when his real musical education began.

"Maybe if I hadn't heard him," Monroe would muse in later years, "I'd never have learned anything about music at all. Learning his numbers gave me something to start on. . . . When I was twelve, thirteen years old, we used to ride mules and go play square dances around the country. Any place that would want us, why, they'd send word to come and we'd make a little money out of it—never over five dollars a night and most of the time a couple dollars a night. [Uncle Pen] always gave me as much as he got."

Then, too, there was a second important element in young Monroe's musical education, an association with a black coal loader named Arnold Shultz, a guitarist and fiddler. Bill was given the opportunity to play guitar-backing to Shultz's fiddle at local dances, and something new was added to his musical education—the blues.

By the time he was eighteen Bill Monroe was an accomplished musician. It was then, in the summer of 1929, that he went to Whiting, Indiana, to join his brothers, Birch and Charlie, who had industrial jobs there. Young Bill got a job washing and loading barrels in an oil refinery. In their spare time, the Monroes played as a trio at square dances and house parties. They also did six shows a week on a Gary, Indiana, radio station. Take-home pay: eleven dollars a week.

In 1934, the "big break" came—an offer of a full-time performing job for Texas Crystals, a company that made a patent-medicine purgative. Birch elected not to continue, but Charlie and Bill began a duet act (guitar and mandolin) they called the Monroe Brothers. They went first to a ninety-day engagement on a radio station in Shenandoah, Iowa, then spent six months on the radio in Omaha, Nebraska. Next, Texas Crystals sent them to the Carolinas, where they played daily shows in Greenville, South Carolina, and Charlotte, North Carolina. From 1936 to 1938, they also did radio shows for the rival Crazy Water Crystals.

While they were in Charlotte, in February 1936, the Monroe Brothers first recorded for Victor Records. Their gospel tune "What Would You Give in Exchange?" became a best-seller, but they also had success with "My Long Journey Home," "Nine Pound Hammer Is Too Heavy," "On Some Foggy Mountain Top," and "New River Train."

In 1938 the brothers decided to go their separate ways. Bill went to Little Rock, Arkansas, for a job at KARK Radio, where he formed his first band, the Kentuckians. It didn't do too well, so he headed for Atlanta and some work there on a popular radio show, "Crossroad Follies." In Atlanta he formed his first Blue Grass Boys band. He couldn't have known then that the name of the band would become the designation for an entirely new subgenre of country music.

The act was polished and, in October of '38, Bill Monroe and the Blue Grass Boys auditioned for Judge Hay. The Judge, as already noted, was most enthusiastic, putting the group on the next Saturday-night Grand Ole Opry.

They debuted with "Muleskinner Blues," Bill's high Kentucky tenor knifing through the airwaves like a surgeon's scalpel.

"If you ever leave the Opry," Hay told Monroe that night, "it'll be because you fired yourself."

He never did.

❦[iv]❧ In the larger context of the entire history of the Grand Ole Opry, Monroe's introduction on the radio show must take a backseat to another development in October 1939. For it was also in that month the Opry—or a half-hour of it—went on the NBC Red network.

The deal was set through William Esty and Company, a major New York advertising agency acting in behalf of a client, the R. J. Reynolds Tobacco Company. The product to be sold was Prince Albert smoking tobacco and the thirty minutes of the Opry was to be called "The Prince Albert Show."

All of that was the brainchild of Dick Marvin, the radio director of Esty. Hay said: "His idea was considerably off the beaten track used by advertising agencies in the metropolitan areas of our country and he came in for much ribbing by many members of his profession."

The initial network show (the date was October 14, 1939) was carried on only a regional network of twenty-six stations. Hay remembered the opening night: "Representatives from NBC in New York and Mr. Marvin and his staff came to Nashville. The Opry House was crowded. Heretofore we had not made any attempt to produce the show, in the accepted sense of the word. We had to be snatched off the air at the end of our thirty minutes, but with that exception the half hour went over pretty well. Before the next week rolled around we had timed our opening and closing and had no further difficulty in the direction."

What was not mentioned by Hay in his writings on the first night of "The Prince Albert Show" was that Roy Acuff had been selected as the host—attesting to the heights Acuff had ascended to in the scheme of the Grand Ole Opry in less than two years.

"The Prince Albert Show" built slowly but steadily. By October 1943 it became a Saturday-night feature of the full NBC coast-to-coast network, initially with 125 stations, but adding stations as the network grew.

⚞ V ⚟ The Solemn Old Judge's concern for the network show seemed to be tied to what impact it would have on Hollywood moviemakers.

Sometime in 1938, you see, Republic Pictures had sent one of its associate producers—characterized by Hay as a "very intelligent young man"—to Nashville to get a look at the Grand Ole Opry. There was some thought that Republic would base a full-length feature film on it.

"We asked Uncle Dave [Macon] if he would mind entertaining our [Hollywood] friend at his farm in the Cannon County hills, knowing that the producer would get the right background and become acquainted with a true representative of the Opry. Uncle Dave was delighted. He asked his cook to prepare a real, sho' 'nuf Tennessee dinner with all of the trimmings and we drove down from Nashville on a beautiful day. . . .

"Uncle Dave asked the blessing and we were served a dinner which is not for sale anywhere in these United States, more is the pity. We were forced to be satisfied with rich country ham, fried chicken, six or seven vegetables, done to a Tennessee turn, jelly preserves, hot corn bread and white bread. Then came the cake. Oh, well, why carry this further?—

"After dining, Uncle Dave invited us to be seated under a large tree in his front yard, where we discussed the possibility of the Grand Ole Opry picture. . . .

"As the producer and your reporter drove back to Nashville, that experienced executive said, 'I have never met a more natural man in my life. He prays at the right time and he cusses at the right time and his jokes are as cute as the dickens.'"

But after the "very intelligent young man" got back to Hollywood nothing happened. "The project was pigeon-holed for more than a year," Hay admitted, "until the Opry 'went network' and was carried by one of the Los Angeles stations. Then it came to light. Republic turned it over to its ace producer, Armand Schaeffer. . . . Mr. Schaeffer meant business and after a short time he made a deal with

WSM to produce The Grand Ole Opry picture, with a picked cast from our show teamed with The Weaver Brothers and Elviry, nationally known rural comedians. Our show was represented by Uncle Dave Macon and his son, Dorris; Roy Acuff and his Smoky Mountain Boys, with Little Rachel; and your reporter, The Solemn Old Judge."

Which was reason enough for George Hay to be enthusiastic.

··✠[vi]✠·· But the more things changed with the Grand Ole Opry the more Hay struggled to keep what he was certain was the basic appeal of the show—the simplicity of the earthy music. His admonition was ever on his lips: "Keep it close to the ground, boys!"

There came a time as the thirties came to a close that Sam and Kirk McGee had bought an electric guitar and Sam had the temerity to play it on the Opry.

Judge Hay met him as he came off the stage: "Sam, that's purty but it's too modern. What we want to do is keep the show down to earth."

Years later Kirk McGee remembered, "We took the guitar home and never brought it back again."

That acquiescence by the McGees, however, would not end the controversy.

Just listen to the jingle
And the rumble and the roar,
As she glides along the woodland
To the hills and by the shore.
Hear the mighty rush of the engine,
Hear the lonesome hoboes call,
While she's trav'ling thru the jungle
On the Wabash Cannonball. *

—Roy Acuff "Theme"

Nashville, Tennessee, as the new decade began in 1940, was in the grip of a cold wave; old-timers said the city had never had one like it before. It was so cold in January that the Cumberland River froze solid, shore to shore, to the depths of several inches. Nashvillians of all walks of life delighted in slipping and sliding across the wide river. And one man set a record of sorts by driving his Ford across the Cumberland, from Inglewood to Donelson.

At the Grand Ole Opry things were a lot warmer, made so by the appearance of a bright, new star.

"In January of 1940," Eddy Arnold said, "I joined up with Pee Wee King and his Golden West Cowboys. I spent as much time selling songbooks and sweeping out auditoriums as I did on stage, but I learned a lot."

*"Wabash Cannonball" by A. P. Carter; copyright 1933 by Peer International Corporation.

Arnold, of course, was just one of King's sidemen in 1940—hired after he had sent a demonstration recording to Joe Frank. He was never much of a guitar player. As he said of his beginnings with the Golden West Cowboys: "I was singing and I was an instrumentalist also. I played the guitar, what we called his rhythm guitar. And I doubled on singing.

"It was tough. Very tough. I started off at twenty-five dollars a week."

But Arnold was to be something new in country music, although he and no one else at the Grand Ole Opry could have guessed it in 1940. He was to take country music into the pop field and, in essence, change the genre as it had never been changed since George Hay first introduced fiddling Uncle Jimmy Thompson fifteen years earlier.

Yet Eddy's beginnings were not unlike the beginnings of a host of other Opry performers. He was a country boy, born Richard Edward Arnold on a farm near Henderson, Tennessee, in 1918. He was poor, fatherless at an early age, and the family farm was lost in a foreclosure sale; he started in show business in a most modest manner.

"I was living on the farm," Arnold recalled, "and there was a little milling company in Jackson, Tennessee, that made flour and meal and that kind of thing. And they'd send out a man and his wife who had a little trailer they'd pull behind the car. It had a little stove on it, and they'd go out to these little country towns and she would cook biscuits. They'd want the people who came to town on Saturday afternoon to come up to the back of the trailer and sample the biscuits. So they hired me to go along to play a guitar to make a little noise to get the people over to the trailer. That was my first professional job; I got fifty cents."

His musical education began on a Sears, Roebuck Silvertone guitar borrowed from a female cousin. He taught himself to play, and one of the first tunes he could pick out was "Sweet Bunch of Daisies," a song his mother loved to sing. "I'd steal off by myself and start strummin' and singin'. I was beginning to discover what mattered deeply to me. I liked to sing. I *needed* to sing."

In 1929 his father died after a protracted illness. The date was May 15, Eddy's eleventh birthday. By the fall of that year everything had collapsed. He stood with his family and watched an auctioneer sell the farm, the livestock, the implements—everything—to satisfy the creditors. The Arnolds became sharecroppers on their own farm. Young Arnold made a promise to himself, vowing never to allow anything like that to happen to him again. By the time he was seventeen Eddy had decided to seek a better life away from the farm—as a singer.

The year was 1936. The place was Jackson, Tennessee. The act was Eddy Arnold and Speedy McNatt, a young fiddler Eddy had known for some time. They played on radio station WTJS in Jackson and at any little club or beer joint they could. Money was scarce, and Eddy took a job with a funeral director, driving an ambulance. He slept at the funeral home and was paid twenty-five cents every time he took the ambulance out to pick up a body. If he helped out at a funeral as a pallbearer he earned fifty cents more.

But Arnold and McNatt moved on, first to Memphis and then to St. Louis, where Arnold's married sister lived. She was good for an occasional free meal when show business simply didn't provide for them.

"Many nights during 1938 and 1939," Eddy remembered, "Speedy and I played clubs for fifty cents, or a dollar, or a dollar and a half a night, and sometimes just for tips."

Arnold decided he needed to be with a *real* country band. Having heard Pee Wee King and the Golden West Cowboys on the Grand Ole Opry—and having liked what he heard—he contacted agent Joe Frank, sent the audition recording, and was hired.

Eddy would never be the same again. Neither would the Grand Ole Opry.

❧[ii]❧ The big excitement at the Opry in 1940, however, was the Republic Pictures feature *Grand Ole Opry*.

It was scheduled to be shot—as were all B movies in those days—in a two-week period, extending from late April into May.

Uncle Dave Macon and Judge Hay were to go to Chicago and from there by train to Los Angeles. The Smoky Mountain Boys were going to make the trip west in Acuff's stretched-out Ford limousine. Six of them—Roy, Oswald, Lonnie, Jess, Rachel, and Dorris Macon. With all of their baggage and instruments.

Uncle Dave came to Acuff: "Roy Boy, we're gonna be out there a little while. Would you mind if I would take a country ham, so I'll have some good country ham to eat in California? If I boxed it up, would you mind hauling it out there for me?"

Acuff answered, "Why, I'll be glad to. I think we'll have room for it." Roy had no idea what problems his good nature would bring him.

"So he boxed the ham up and put it in the car," Acuff recalled. "And we got to the Arizona state line and they were searching for fruit flies, or whiskey, or something. Well, we had to take all the guitars out, and had to knock all the slats off Uncle Dave's ham, get it out, and show them what it was. They finally passed us and let us get into Arizona. We took off and got to the California state line and had to do the same thing all over again.

"We finally got the ham there to Hollywood and Uncle Dave was very grateful. He took it to his room, and he and his son, and I think some of my boys, ate it."

Roy had a sequel to the tale: "When we were finishing up the movie, Uncle Dave came back to me and said, 'Roy Boy, would you mind taking that box back with you that we brought the ham out in? I'd like awful well to have that to make a hen's nest out of.' "

Acuff would double with laughter over a retelling of that story. Something much less humorous to him, though, was the handing out of the wardrobe for the film.

The band members had gotten to the wardrobe department first and were given cowboy costumes. They were trying them on when Roy came in.

"What's this all about?" he demanded.

Bill Monroe, the
Father of Bluegrass
Music, on his farm
near Nashville.
*(C. 1940) GRAND OLE OPRY
ARCHIVES*

In October 1943, the
Opry's "Prince Albert
Show" went coast-to-
coast on the NBC
Network. The host of
the show was Roy
Acuff, far right. With
him are Velma
Williams (far left),
Jimmy Riddle (with
accordion), Rachel
Veach (at microphone),
Lonnie "Pap" Wilson
(under the
announcement),
Bashful Brother
Oswald (next to Acuff),
and Jess Easterday
(about to swat "Pap"
with his mandolin).
*(1943) GRAND OLE OPRY
ARCHIVES*

*O*pry stars plug one of their sponsors, RC Cola. At this time, Eddy Arnold was a recent addition to Pee Wee King's Golden West Cowboys. From the left: Pee Wee King, Ford Rush, Eddy Arnold, Redd Stewart, San Antonio Rose, Joe Zinkan, Judge George D. Hay, Dorris Macon, Louie Buck, and Uncle Dave Macon (seated).

(C. 1940) GRAND OLE OPRY ARCHIVES

Weaver Brothers and Elviry

GRAND OLE OPRY (A RE-RELEASE)

with ROY ACUFF

A REPUBLIC PICTURE

REPUBLIC PICTURES CORPORATION — HERBERT J. YATES, PRESIDENT

COUNTRY OF ORIGIN U. S. A.

R53-437

A publicity still from Republic Pictures' Grand Ole Opry, *which premiered in Nashville on June 28, 1940. The movie may be the only film record of Uncle Dave Macon (in passenger seat) and George D. Hay (with glasses, third from right). Others pictured in the cast are Frank Weaver (driver), and from the bottom left, Leon Weaver, Allan Lane (with cigar), June Weaver, Loretta Weaver (waving), Rachel Veach (behind Judge Hay), Lois Ranson, and Dorris Macon. In the rear of the car are (from the left) Roy Acuff, Jess Easterday, Pap Wilson, and Oswald Kirby.*

(1940) GRAND OLE OPRY ARCHIVES

While still pursuing an acting career, Sarah Colley had this publicity photo taken in New York City.

(C. 1947) *GRAND OLE OPRY ARCHIVES*

Sarah Ophelia Colley, a.k.a. Minnie Pearl, outside her wedding chapel, West End Methodist Church, in Nashville.

(C. 1947) *GRAND OLE OPRY ARCHIVES*

An early photo of Minnie Pearl, without the price tag on her hat, performing on the Grand Ole Opry.

(1940) *GRAND OLE OPRY ARCHIVES*

"The movie folks told us to get into this garb."

Roy exploded: "Take it off! We'll wear our regular Grand Ole Opry clothes, or go back home."

He sought out the producer of the film, Armand Schaeffer. "We just a bunch of country boys from Tennessee who've come out here to put on our little country show like we do back home. We're not cowboys! And we intend to wear our regular clothes." Then the punch line: "If you folks don't like my work, I can go back home. I can take my boys back. I've got enough to get back on."

The cowboy costumes were put back into wardrobe.

That problem out of the way, Roy was hit with another one. In her May 7 column, Hollywood's famous gossip columnist Louella Parsons reported: "Roy Acuff, young hill-billy brought here by Republic from Nashville, is suffering from appendicitis and will be operated on as soon as the picture is finished."

Meantime, Roy was packed in ice between scenes and was heavily taped around the abdomen when he was performing.

If Acuff wasn't having much fun in Hollywood, Uncle Dave Macon was. Hay wrote: "When Mr. Schaeffer let us see a few of the 'rushes' of our picture a day or two before we finished, Uncle Dave exclaimed with great glee and without a trace of self-consciousness—'Whee, that's me!' "

The final scene shot, Acuff and his band (with Uncle Dave's empty ham box jammed in the limo) made the long drive back to Nashville. There was no way that Acuff was going to be operated on in Hollywood. Immediately upon return to Nashville he was admitted to St. Thomas Hospital, the offending appendix was removed, and he missed one performance of the Grand Ole Opry because of the surgery. The next week he was on the stage at the War Memorial Auditorium, supporting himself by hanging onto a chair, and singing "The Great Speckled Bird."

In spite of the title, the motion picture was not really about the Grand Ole Opry. The screenplay dealt with politics in a small rural town. The stars were the Weaver Brothers and Elviry. Leon Weaver had the lead role, that of an honest mayor who seeks the governorship, defying the entrenched political establishment. Frank Weaver was a village constable, and Elviry, a veteran rural comedienne, played herself.

That's exactly what the Smoky Mountain Boys, Judge Hay, and Uncle Dave did—play themselves as country radio performers. Acuff and the band had three numbers in the picture: "Down in Union Country," "Wabash Cannonball," and the inevitable "Great Speckled Bird."

For his part, Uncle Dave, accompanied by his son, Dorris, played the banjo and gave out with a spirited version of "Take Me Back to My Old Carolina Home." It was vintage Dave Macon, featuring hollering, kicking up heels, and swinging the banjo wildly.

Judge Hay was a radio announcer, giving out with his lavish introductions of the act. (As far as is known, the movie provided the only film record of Uncle Dave Macon and George Hay.)

Grand Ole Opry was released quickly. On Friday evening, June 28, 1940, it had its world premiere at Nashville's Paramount Theatre, following a street parade with bands, square dances, and an appearance by special guest Sergeant Alvin York. WSM broadcast the festivities live.

The press wanted Acuff's views on his experience: "Of course, I was pleased to go to Hollywood, but I was glad to get back to Tennessee. They were all nice to us out there, but it just is no place for us kind of folks."

···❴ iii ❵··· Another invitation was added to the Grand Ole Opry superstructure in 1940—the tent show.

The idea was to put a major Opry tour on the road during the summer. This first one (for there were to be two others later) was headed by the blackface team of Jamup and Honey, with Honey Wilds as the nominal manager.

In a wide-ranging interview with writer Jack Hurst, Wilds detailed the trials and tribulations of the canvas caravan:

"The tent was eighty feet wide and two hundred twenty feet long, big enough to sit down sixteen hundred people under the canvas. It took twenty-five rough-necks to move it, and we moved it every cotton-picking day, feeding the roughnecks three hot meals a day in the process. With salaries, lot rent, advertising, and licenses, our daily operating expenses fluctuated between five hundred fifty and six hundred dollars a day. In other words, we had to make six hundred dollars a day before Jamup and I would make a nickel. Everybody said we were crazy."

Nevertheless, the tent shows drew big crowds—"monstrous," to use Honey's word. And the comedy routines of Jamup and Honey were augmented by appearances by Roy Acuff and the Smoky Mountain Boys and Uncle Dave Macon. WSM was clearly putting its biggest stars into the enterprise. Acuff and Macon had to be back at the Opry every Saturday night, but Harry Stone decreed that Jamup and Honey were to stay on the road, keeping the tent show operating.

It was rough. Wilds again: "We'd always have one or two trucks broke down that we'd have to overhaul. Lord, I've laid on the road many a time, with it anywhere from ninety-five to one hundred degrees, and put a transmission in a Chevrolet truck, laying flat on my back to get it in there.

"Not to mention the wrecks. We came off a mountain over in North Carolina one time, and the trucks were tailgating and five of them crashed. The front one went haywire, and then the first four behind him hit him. We had roughnecks, trucks, and seats thrown all over the place. We wound up with sixteen men in the hospital."

Honey Wilds became a scrounger of auto parts, especially tires, because the prewar mobilization program was in full swing. Priorities didn't go to traveling tent shows.

"A many a time," the comedian told writer Hurst, "I've gone down a little country road and seen a truck setting, and stopped and asked the farmer what he'd take for that truck. I'd buy the truck, jack it up, take the tires off of it, and leave the truck setting."

With all of those problems, the initial tent show made money. It was a good year for the Grand Ole Opry: there was the network radio show on NBC, a motion picture was promoting the Opry, the tent show worked out, a young singer named Eddy Arnold was on the scene, and, before the year was out, Sarah Ophelia Colley would be there.

··◦【 iv 】◦·· Sarah Colley was born in Centerville, Tennessee, in 1912, the fifth daughter in the family of a prominent lumberman. Centerville is some fifty miles southwest of Nashville, and very close to a "community" of two houses, an old barn, and a train switch—Grinder's Switch.

Tom Colley made a tomboy of his youngest daughter, teaching her how to whistle and how to recognize trees and birds. Her mother, known affectionately in Centerville as Aunt Fannie Tate Colley, was a cultured woman who organized book circles, played the organ at church, and had strong views about how proper young ladies should behave. She didn't want her daughters to walk around the town square, for example, because they would have to pass the smelly town stable.

As a child, Sarah showed interest in the stage; her mother gave her "expression" lessons. And on occasional trips to Nashville, while her mother went shopping, Sarah would sit in the Palace Theater watching vaudeville shows.

"I didn't realize at the time that this was going to be my life's work," she told interviewer Laura Eipper, "but I had this funny feeling about watching this one gal work. Her name was Elviry Weaver and she was a lot like Marjorie Main or Marie Dressler—a comic heavy. It was pure slapstick comedy and I ate it up. I'd sit through three or four shows. I'd sit there and see the lights. I didn't see that it was tawdry and I didn't see that half the canvas was off the backdrop and that it was in tatters. I didn't see that these were tired vaudevillians who had to get themselves back up for the four o'clock show. I thought it was delightful . . . that she could make people laugh."

When Sarah graduated from high school, she was enrolled in Ward-Belmont College in Nashville, an elite finishing school for young ladies. When she left there in 1932, after two years of majoring in speech and drama, she went back to Centerville to teach. It didn't really work. Two years later she took a job with the Wayne P. Sewell Producing Company in Atlanta, traveling the South to produce amateur musical comedies with people in remote rural areas.

"It gave me a chance," she recalled, "to really make a study of country girls. I became 'Minnie Pearl' in 1936 at Brenlea Mountain in Baileyton, Alabama, at a show. I was staying in a mountain cabin and met a fine old mountain woman who told so many tales and funny stories. After ten days with her, I began to quote her, and people would laugh. She was like Granny on "Beverly Hillbillies," a sprightly, brittle, hardy woman with a bun of hair on the top of her head. She told me once: 'I've had sixteen young 'uns. Never failed to make a crop.'"

With that background, Sarah kept working on the character and the hill dialect. By November 1940 (she was twenty-eight) she felt secure enough in "Minnie Pearl" to audition for a spot on the Grand Ole Opry.

"I auditioned in front of maybe eight or nine people," she remembers. "Harry Stone, Jack Stapp, Judge Hay, Ford Rush [then manager of the WSM Artists' Bureau]—all of those people standing in that old control room in Studio B on the fifth floor of the National Life building, and they just looked at me. They never cracked a smile. I didn't get through to them, I don't think."

It was Ford Rush who talked to her after the audition. He was low-key. And certainly not complimentary.

"He told me that they had done a little investigating about me," she said, "and he wasn't sure those people out there wouldn't think I was a phony. 'A phony!' I said. 'Why would they think that? I come from the country—you can go down there where I was raised and look at it yourself if you think I'm phony.'"

Rush admitted that the concern was based on the fact that Sarah had gone to the Ward-Belmont College. She pooh-poohed that concern and Rush told her it had been decided she was to have a tryout on the Opry the following Saturday evening. Then he told her that she was to report at 10:30 and be ready to go on the Crazy Water Crystals show at 11:05. He added that "normally there aren't many people listening to the Opry at that time, so if they don't like you it won't harm things very much."

Thus reassured, and wondering whether she wanted to show up at all, she did report at 10:30 that Saturday night.

"I went up to Judge Hay," she recollected, "and I said, 'I'm Minnie Pearl—' Well, I didn't say, 'I'm Minnie Pearl,' that was the funny part of it, I said, 'I'm Ophelia Colley,' which was the name then. And he said, 'Oh, yes, you're the young girl that's going to do the comedy.' And I said, 'Well, I'm going to try.' And he said, 'Now you just go back there in one of those dressing rooms and at eleven you come back here'—this was by the stage—'and we'll put you on at eleven-oh-five.'

"So I went back to the dressing rooms. And nobody knew me, nobody cared. At eleven o'clock I went back out and stood by Judge Hay. The house in the War Memorial was not full, because it was late and some of the people had come and gone. And the ones that were there were asleep because it was cold outside and a lot of people would come in to get warm. You could get warm for twenty-five cents." She laughed heartily.

"I was standing there shaking, scared out of my mind, and Judge Hay said, 'You're scared, aren't you?'

"I said, 'Yes, sir, I am.'

"And he said, 'Just love 'em, honey, and they'll love you back.'

"My mother was out front. And when I came out I said, 'How do you think it went?'

"And Mama said, 'Several people woke up.'

"I think that probably was the finest compliment that's ever been paid me!"

But Miss Colley knew the Minnie Pearl character needed work, and important help was to come from Roy Acuff. In December 1940, Acuff asked her to join his road show—at $50 a week.

"Well, that was just . . . my word, that was an enormous amount of money! I was making ten at the Opry."

She had never been on the road with a country music band and, as a matter of fact, was not too familiar with country music. There was something missing in her act; it didn't seem to meld with the Smoky Mountain Boys.

"There was one night," Minnie said, "that we stopped at an all-night truck stop and there was a jukebox, and I had a few beers, and I got up on the floor and started doing this dumb old dance.

"They all started laughing and Roy said, 'Minnie, why don't you do that on stage?'

"I stopped immediately and said, 'Oh, I couldn't do that. That's silly!'

"He said: 'That's what I've been tryin' to tell you, Minnie. Be silly. That's what they pay to see. Turn loose, Minnie.'

"Roy Acuff taught me that important lesson. Make a fool. Self-deprecation. He took a stiff, real frightened, plastic comic—a drama student who thought she had comedic talent—and made her into a crazy, carefree hillbilly comic."

Minnie Pearl, a.k.a. Sarah Ophelia Colley, was on the Grand Ole Opry to stay.

There's a star spangled banner waving somewhere,
In a distant land so many miles away;
Only Uncle Sam's great heroes get to go there,
Where I wish that I could also live someday. *

—World War II country hit, 1942

R oy Acuff's influence on what happened to and on the Grand Ole Opry was profound. He was always looking for ways to improve it, to bring in new acts. He assumed a leadership role at the same time he was maintaining a brutal personal schedule: touring, recording, broadcasting.

It was as if the old "Rabbit" Acuff were on the stage, driven by the fierce competitiveness that had marked his aborted athletic career. He was the hardest worker on the Opry; its keenest promoter. Very little escaped his attention, especially if it might benefit the Grand Ole Opry.

Take the case of the Wilburn Children. The story is pure Americana. A saga of the hard days of the Great Depression.

Benjamin Estes Wilburn was a disabled veteran of the World War (the first war didn't have a number then), and dirt poor. Timber on his small Arkansas farm had been "cut out" and what was left of the land couldn't support Wilburn's wife and their five children. His health was too fragile to allow him to hold a steady job.

*"There's a Star Spangled Banner Waving Somewhere" by Paul Roberts and Shelby Darnell; copyright 1942 MCA Music, a division of MCA, Inc.

But "Pop" Wilburn had seen one Slim Rhodes, teenage son of a local preacher, with two brothers and a sister, singing on a street in Hardy, Arkansas, in 1937.

"That gave me an idea," the elder Wilburn said, "that maybe our children could sing as a group. My wife and I had sung to them as babies, and I played the fiddle a bit. They learned to hum tunes before they could talk. So we ordered a mandolin, a guitar, and a fiddle from Sears, Roebuck. I built a platform of lumber in the backyard and the kids practiced. Neighbors came for square dances and songfests.

"Finally I thought they had enough practice to play on the street—so I traded some honey from our beehives for transportation by car eighteen miles to Thayer, Missouri. [The date was December 24, 1937.]

"We just went up there, got out on the street, and the kids started singing. Teddy was five, Doyle six, Geraldine ten, Leslie twelve, and Lester thirteen. We collected six dollars and forty cents that day.

"To wind up the day a neighbor took us to Hardy, and the merchants wanted the children to sing in their places of business."

It was a fitting conclusion to Christmas Eve.

Hardy merchants got behind the fledgling musical group, raising thirteen dollars and furnishing a car to send the youngsters to Jonesboro to compete in a radio station talent contest. They won first prize.

The Wilburn Children performed everywhere: at livestock auctions, farm sales, schools, churches, and radio stations, and on the streets. Pop Wilburn mortgaged his small farm for $100 to get a car to take them to Springfield, Missouri, for a talent contest at radio KWTO, where they won the first prize of ten dollars by singing "You Are My Sunshine."

In the winter of 1939 disaster struck. Their modest house burned to the ground; they took temporary refuge in a cleaned-out chicken house and then in a tent. But the Wilburn family persevered. It was a year later that their big break came.

The Wilburn Children were playing at radio station WAGF in Dothan, Alabama, when Pop heard about a Birmingham talent contest at which Roy Acuff, Bill Monroe, and several other Opry acts would be featured. The elder Wilburn piled the children into the car and headed for Birmingham. On the way a tire blew out and they arrived too late to enter the contest.

"My dad situated us at the side door of the auditorium," Teddy Wilburn remembered, "and when Roy came out Pop had us performing the song 'Farther Along.' Roy stood there watching us with tears in his eyes."

Although they weren't eligible for the Birmingham talent contest, Acuff presented them on the stage that night, having them sing again "Farther Along." Pop Wilburn recalled that "the folks almost tore the house down."

When Acuff got back to Nashville he spoke to David Stone, the WSM program manager, about the Wilburns. Stone sent a telegram to have them come to Nashville for an audition. (At the time Roy was on the way to Hollywood to make *Grand Ole Opry.*)

Pop Wilburn didn't need a second invitation. They rushed to Nashville, auditioned for Stone, and were hired for the Grand Ole Opry.

"Mail came in by the sacks," Teddy recollects. "Three sacksful a week. But the child labor laws were strong at that time. The authorities kept putting restrictions on WSM about what they could do and could not do with us, and it got to be a little too much for the Opry management. After six months we had to leave."

The Wilburn Children went back home after that, back to a more "normal" life.

In one of those marvelous stories of Grand Ole Opry continuity, Teddy and Doyle, billed as the Wilburn Brothers, became cast members of the Opry on November 10, 1956, on the basis of a whole string of hits for Decca Records. The audience was filled with disc jockeys that evening, attending the thirty-first–anniversary birthday broadcast of the Opry. Doyle told them: "Our hearts are here—we hope to help the Opry celebrate its sixty-second anniversary." Proud Pop Wilburn lived to see his youngsters reach real stardom.

As 1941 began, the draft was snatching up men from all walks of life. Opry musicians and WSM staffers were not immune. But perhaps the most important change U.S. mobilization was making was that southern boys, raised on the sounds of the Grand Ole Opry, were taking their "hillbilly" music with them into the armed forces. Radios in barracks were tuned to the Opry, record players on ships were giving out with the sounds of Roy Acuff and Bill Monroe. And city dwellers, side by side with their country cousins in uniform, were being exposed to those sounds for the first time.

At the Grand Ole Opry itself there was diminution of the size of the audiences at the War Memorial Auditorium; gasoline and tire restrictions caused that. But the Opry went on. And continued to change.

For one thing, a second Opry tent show was put on the road, this one headed by Roy Acuff. For another, Bill Monroe hired a new banjo player for his Blue Grass Boys—a tall, lanky fellow named David Akeman, who called himself "Stringbean, the Kentucky Wonder." In the years ahead the comedic Stringbean would become an integral part of the Opry roster.

And there was a third development early in 1941 that would bring embarrassment to the Opry. George Hay fired the black harmonica player, DeFord Bailey.

Even in the context of the attitudes of 1941, Hay's words of explanation must be characterized as racist. One writer has called the Judge's statement "savage."

"DeFord Bailey [was] a little crippled colored boy who was a bright feature on our show for about fifteen years. Like some members of his race and other races, DeFord was lazy. He knew about a dozen numbers, which he put on the air and recorded for a major company, but he refused to learn any more, even though his reward was great. . . . We gave him a whole year's notice to learn some more tunes, but he would not. When we were forced to give him his final notice, DeFord said, without malice: 'I knowed it wuz comin', Judge, I knowed it wuz comin'.' "

Subsequent developments suggested that Bailey did not accept the firing with the good grace that Hay suggested. He retreated to a shoeshine stand at Twelfth Avenue South and Edgehill, near his Nashville home and entered into forty years of virtual musical exile.

In 1978, when I was the line producer of the NBC television special "Fifty Years of Country Music," I went to see Bailey in an attempt to book him on the show to re-create that moment when he played "Pan American Blues" on the "WSM Barn Dance" and Judge Hay followed with his ad-lib comment that re-named the show "The Grand Ole Opry." "No," Bailey said firmly, "I don't wanna work with 'em again." Others had similar experiences: He turned down offers from the Newport Folk Festival, and a Burt Reynolds movie, *W.W. and the Dixie Dancekings*, and all recording contracts. I have no way of knowing why he made those decisions, but I do know that when I had finished my conversation with him in 1978 I came away with the distinct impression that he had been deeply hurt by his dismissal from the Opry.

···❧ iii ❧··· With more and more Opry fans going into the armed forces, Dick Marvin, the radio director of the William Esty and Company advertising agency, devised the idea of putting together an Opry touring show to visit military camps everywhere in the country. He called it "The Grand Ole Opry Camel Caravan."

"He had the bright idea," Pee Wee King said, "of taking Camel cigarettes and giving them away to all the men in the service—any branch of service in the United States. And he figured the easiest way to get a crowd together was by using the Grand Ole Opry acts.

"So Marvin and Harry Stone got together over lunch and invited Joe Frank, and they covered all the bases. Home base was the Grand Ole Opry, first base was the country people, second base was the pop acts, and third base would be novelty."

Before that luncheon was over the roster for the Camel Caravan was set. Perhaps because agent Joe Frank was involved, the starring act would be Pee Wee King and the Golden West Cowboys. Eddy Arnold, then with King, would get his first important exposure as a single act. Minnie Pearl was to provide comedy (the "novelty" of King's third base) and the pop acts would consist of a girls' trio and singer Kitty Carlisle. Ford Rush would go along to manage the unit and be master of ceremonies.

"It was put together," King went on, "and we rehearsed the show maybe two or three days here in Nashville before we took it on the road. We gave it away in Shelby Park. I'll never forget the audition for the Camel people—they liked what they saw and we stayed on that show for nineteen months, touring all over the United States and Panama and Guatemala.

"I've said this many times: That was the beginning of country music branching out, or leaking onto, the so-called 'pop' field. Everybody who saw the show learned to sing 'You Are My Sunshine.' And the girl trio sang modern pop songs like 'Don't Sit Under the Apple Tree.'

"We had six cigarette girls, and at the end of the show, just before the finale, we took just a small break and those girls would pass out free cigarettes.

"One of the biggest thrills during the whole nineteen months we were on the Caravan with Minnie Pearl, Eddy Arnold, the Golden West Cowboys, the cigarette girls, and all that, was a show we did in Buffalo in a football stadium— about thirty-five thousand people. Well, Ford Rush, who was with us as the emcee, conceived the idea that all the lights go out and everybody light a match. And I'll tell you, I was so choked up—that was one of the prettiest sights I've ever seen.

"And Kitty Carlisle sang 'When the Lights Go On Again All over the World.' "

·◄[iv]►· On December 7, 1941, the Japanese bombed Pearl Harbor. It would be a long time before the lights would go on again.

Nineteen forty-two, then, began at the Grand Ole Opry with the nation fully at war. And with entertainment being a vital part of the home-front morale effort.

A third big Opry tent show went into operation, with Bill Monroe and the Blue Grass Boys as the headline act. Uncle Dave Macon toured with that show. He was seventy-two at the time, but still spry and still sure of his appeal.

When the tent show audience was good, Macon would tell Monroe, "The old man can still draw 'em in." But if the audience was small, Uncle Dave would say, "You can't pull 'em like you used to, Mr. Bill."

Minnie Pearl remembered working one of those tent shows with Uncle Dave: "He used to carry a black satchel with him on those tours. In it was a pillow, a nightcap, his bottle of Jack Daniel's bourbon, and a checkered bib. He was quite a ladies' man, who proved to me that some men never cease to believe themselves irresistible, no matter how old they are. We would often sit in the back of the tent while others were performing, and Uncle Dave would talk of religion. He complained about preachers departing from the Bible. He could quote at great length from the Scripture and use it to solve all the problems of the world.

"Uncle Dave loved Jack Daniel's. He would usually take a toddy at night. Many people thought he'd be drinking all the time, but he didn't need it for that wonderful burst of energy. He was a born showman."

Other acts began to join the Opry. Among them in 1942 was an Arkansas mattress salesman named Paul Howard, soon to become Paul Howard and the Arkansas Cotton Pickers. It was the kind of a string-band aggregation close to the heart of Judge Hay.

Also arriving on the Opry stage in 1942 was an act George Hay did not select, Whitey Ford, the Duke of Paducah. He was brought in by the Esty agency and

NBC to beef up "The Prince Albert Show." He was a proven entity, a veteran comic who had starred on the rival "WLS National Barn Dance" in Chicago.

⹂[V]⹂ Benjamin Francis Ford was nothing if not self-assured. He was a complex man and a proud one, one who would still be honing his craft when he reached his eighties and who kept a carefully indexed and cross-indexed file of gags that exceeded half a million jokes in nearly 500 categories.

He was not the kind of a man to leave anything to chance; he wrote his own publicity releases: "The Duke [of Paducah] first saw the light of day in DeSoto, Missouri, on May 12, 1901. For a teething ring, they gave him a cob of corn. The cob wore out but the corn lingered on. . . . He attended Peabody Grammar School and received twelve years of book learning (nine years in the third grade). . . . The Duke says in later years he graduated from the University of Hard Knocks and he has the lumps on his head to prove it. . . . [He] ran away from home when he was seventeen years old and joined the Navy; stayed four years, five hours and twenty minutes."

Ford loved to appear on radio and television talk shows and reminisce about his show business days. One of his favorite stories was about his beginning in 1922 as an entertainer, playing banjo in a Dixieland band at a "barrelhouse" in Smackover, Arkansas. He told it one more time in a 1984 interview on Archie Campbell's "Yesterday in Nashville" program on The Nashville Network:

"It had the biggest oil boom in the world there at one time. [Then] Smackover was considered the largest city in the world of its kind. It was houses where you put down rocks or blocks, put a floor, come up about six feet with boarding, and two-by-four framing, and canvas over that. And that's the kind of town it was. . . .

"There was a big mud hole out in front of the barrelhouse where we were going to play. A barrelhouse was a dance hall, you know." A hearty laugh. "The job paid five dollars a night per person, and they gave you a room upstairs over the dance hall to sleep in. And what do you think the manager's name was? *Diamond-Tooth Blackie!* He had two gold teeth right here"—a gesture—"and he had two diamonds set in them, but he had picked the diamonds out and hocked 'em. And he was on parole from the Oklahoma State Penitentiary for bank robbery. This is not fiction. I'm telling you the God's truth! . . .

"Now, the barrelhouse charged twenty-five cents a dance a girl. The house got fifteen cents and the girl you danced with got a dime. . . . And a dance lasted a minute and a half. We didn't know that when we started and we were playing along and Blackie came by and said, 'Hey, what the devil do you think's goin' on here? A dance lasts a minute and a half and it's over!' Well, we learned real quick, you know.

"I wish you'da seen him. He didn't wear underwear. The hair on his chest looked like steel wool, and he wore women's pink chemises, and that hair comin' through there. And rough? Oh, he was rough! . . . One night a mule skinner— they hauled equipment back into the oil fields in huge wagons—was dancing with a girl and he was dancing a little bit out of line." Another hearty laugh. "And you had to go a long way to dance a little bit out of line at a barrelhouse. . . . And Blackie went over and grabbed him, and about that time the mule skinner came out with a switchblade. Blackie looked at him and laughed and grabbed some kind of wrestler's wrist lock on him. Got that knife and threw it and stuck it up in the wall, and took that mule skinner and threw him out in that mud hole in the middle of the street. . . .

"We lasted two weeks there. Well, I lasted longer than that 'cause I found a girlfriend. The others couldn't take it, but Benny Ford was still there with the banjo . . . and a girlfriend. While we were staying at a hotel there, I said one day, 'I'm gonna go back to Little Rock.' And I was lying across the bed and she flopped herself across the bed alongside of me. And the first thing I knew, something was on my neck—a switchblade knife. She said, 'You ain't goin' back to Little Rock.' And I said, 'I'll stay! I didn't wanna go anyway.' "

Ford managed to extricate himself from Smackover, leaving town on the next available train. But the experience in the rough oil-field town didn't dim his enthusiasm for show business. He did everything: medicine shows, tab shows, stage presentations, burlesque, dramatic tent shows, and vaudeville. He played the Keith vaudeville circuit with Otto Gray's original Oklahoma Cowboys, a trend-setting band in country-and-western music. He left Gray to work with Gene Autry's touring band, was a member of the original cast of the "WLS Barn Dance," had his own network radio show called "Plantation Party," and was in on the establishment of the "Renfro Valley Barn Dance" with John Lehr and Red Foley.

So when Whitey Ford came to the Grand Ole Opry with his Duke of Paducah character and his punch line, "I'm goin' back to the wagon, boys, these shoes are killin' me!" the WSM radio show got an experienced showman.

His routines were rapid-fire patter:

"I'll have you know one thing: I used to be a real outdoor boy. Oh, man! I had so many holes in my pants that most of me was outdoors most of the time. . . . I'll never forget how Mother used to keep me and my brother in a play pen. Many years have passed, but my brother still acts like a baby; he's still in the pen. . . .

"My Paw wanted me to go to college, but I wanted to go to a girls' school, and Paw said he couldn't understand it. I said, 'Well, Paw, a man can go to Harvard for four years and not learn nothing, and he can go to Yale for six years and not learn nothing. But you let him go to a girls' school for one week and, brother, he'll learn plenty!' . . .

"Talking about school, there was an old maid down home that took a correspondence course, and the first week she was supposed to get lessons on simple arithmetic. But us kids switched her mail with somebody else's and she got a package of love letters from a soldier to his girlfriend. She read about six of them and then she rushed out and sent a telegram saying, 'If this is simple arithmetic, rush course on higher mathematics immediately!' . . .

> "Well, *I'm goin' back to the wagon, boys, these shoes are killin' me!*"
> Vintage Whitey Ford on the stage of the Grand Ole Opry.

···{ vi }··· There was another development in Nashville in 1942 not directly involving the Opry, but having an impact on it anyway. Roy Acuff took what might have been the most important step of his career, a step of incalculable value to the entire country music industry. With only a handshake to seal the deal, and with $25,000 of "seed money" from Acuff, a music publishing partnership was struck with veteran songwriter and musician Fred Rose.

"People out of New York and California and all," Roy recalled, "were comin' in here tryin' to buy my songs, and I refused to sell 'em. But I realized that what I should do is get with some company to place my songs where they would be protected. When I first recorded they stole every song from me, and I was a young man and didn't know anything about it. I was green. But when I recorded the songs the record company just copyrighted them. They stole them."

At that time in the early forties, there was almost no protection for the less sophisticated country songwriter, and Acuff wanted to correct that. He wanted Rose to start a music publishing company. Fred, uncertain about becoming a businessman, hesitated. Acuff pressed him and Rose, after seeking the advice of Chicago music publisher Fred Forster, finally agreed.

Acuff remembered: "I said, 'Fred, I got twenty-five thousand dollars I'll place in the bank in your name. You use any amount of it you want to. I will never bother your publishing company.' He took my word, we went into a fifty-fifty agreement on it—a gentleman's agreement. This was our main point: that we were going to make sure that it be run as an honest company; that no man, or girl, that entered our door would be cheated out of a song, or one penny of anything that they've got coming. I said, 'Fred, if I ever find anything crooked about it, my name'll come off of it.'"

Roy's desire for integrity matched those of Rose and, on October 13, 1942, Acuff-Rose Publications was started. What most people didn't realize was that the formal partnership agreement was between Fred Rose and *Mildred* Acuff, Roy's wife. The "Acuff" in "Acuff-Rose" was not, in the legal sense, Roy himself. In spirit it was, of course.

Rose took two important steps to assure the future of the company. Almost immediately, he licensed the company's music catalogue with the comparatively new Broadcast Music, Inc. (BMI), receiving an advance of $2,500. That money was used to meet the early expenses of the then small company, and Rose never had to touch Acuff's initial investment of $25,000. Second, unwilling to tie himself down with business details that he feared would interfere with his songwriting, Rose persuaded his eldest son, Wesley, to join the company. Wesley wasn't sure he wanted to make the move from Chicago, where he was a well-paid accountant with the Standard Oil Company. But the elder Rose guaranteed his son that he would be in full charge of the business end, and Wesley, with the title of general manager, joined the fledgling company.

Acuff-Rose Publications was a huge success right from the beginning. At the end of the first year, Fred Rose also put together a publishing company to license some songs with the American Society of Composers, Authors and Publishers (ASCAP). It was called Milene Music, a name devised by using syllables from the first names of Mildred Acuff and Rose's wife, Lorene.

Acuff delighted in the songwriting ability of his new partner. "I remember one time Fred being backstage at the Opry," Roy said, "and he heard me sing 'Unloved and Unclaimed,' the one about the girl laying on a cold marble slab at the morgue, with thousands viewing her but none knew her name. They don't get no sadder than that. Well, Fred said, 'Lord, ain't nobody gonna want to hear that morbid thing.' And I said, 'I don't know, people love to cry, Fred.' Well, he went home and right away wrote 'The Day They Laid Mary Away.' "

With the Grand Ole Opry as the foundation, and with Acuff-Rose Publications as one of the cornerstones, a new "city" was being built in Nashville—*Music City, USA.*

It was not surprising that Roy Acuff was a key in both of them.

I'm walking the floor over you,
I can't sleep a wink, that is true;
I'm hoping and I'm praying
As my heart breaks right in two,
Walking the floor over you.*

—Ernest Tubb hit, circa 1941

It was in December 1942 that a lanky Texan named Ernest Tubb first walked onto the Grand Ole Opry stage and sang a song titled "Walking the Floor over You." He was called back for three encores.

A month later he moved to Nashville—permanently.

For more than forty years he was to exert an influence on the Opry second only to that of Roy Acuff. In some ways, perhaps, he was to have more impact.

Ernest Dale Tubb was born on February 9, 1914, near Crisp, Texas, in rural Ellis County, south of Dallas, the youngest of five children. That was cotton country and his father was overseer of a 300-acre cotton farm. His mother was one-fourth Cherokee Indian.

Music was in his life from the beginning; his mother played the piano and organ. When he was growing up in Crisp, and later in Benjamin, Texas, he was called "Wash" by his contemporaries. He had one ambition—he wanted to be a cowboy movie star. Then, at thirteen, he heard his first Jimmie Rodgers blue-yodeling record. That sound was to change, and dominate, his life. Having the latest Jimmie Rodgers record became almost an obsession with him. A brother, Calvin R. Tubb, Jr., recalled that "Ernest saved his nickels and dimes to buy them."

Tubb himself reminisced: "I just wanted to sing like Jimmie, and I didn't really have any idea of making a living with my singing when I first started out."

Starting out was not easy. His parents had separated when he was twelve, and his teen years were spent moving around Texas living with various family members. Schooling was virtually ignored; later he figured that he had had only seventeen months of formal schooling. "When I realized what I had missed," he said, "I began educating myself."

In 1933, when he was nineteen, he worked on a road construction crew near Benjamin and met a guitar player named Merwyn "Buff" Buffington, who was impressed with young Tubb's singing and urged him to learn to play the guitar. Ernest bought a secondhand instrument for $5.50, and Buff was his first teacher. Tubb was so intent on learning to play it that sometimes his fingers bled.

It was about that time, in May 1933, that Jimmie Rodgers died of tuberculosis. "I thought my world had come to an end," Tubb said. But it made him even more determined to emulate his hero.

Late in 1933 he was in San Antonio working on WPA construction projects at various military installations, a job he held only long enough to seek out employment at a San Antonio drugstore. His salary was $10 a week. Nevertheless, he was married in May 1934 to Lois Elaine Cook; a son, Justin, was born in August 1935. His drugstore salary was raised to $12.50 a week.

In San Antonio he again met Buff Buffington, who was playing on radio station KONO with the Castleman Brothers, Joe and Jim. Tubb sang with them several times and managed to wrangle his own fifteen-minute show, at 5:30 A.M., twice a week. While he was playing at KONO, he remembered that Jimmie Rodgers had resided in San Antonio at the time of his death and wondered if Mrs. Rodgers still lived there. He found a "Mrs. Jimmie Rodgers" listed in the phone book.

"I wanted a picture of Jimmie," he said. "I thought it might be possible she would help me get one somehow. I phoned and asked if she were *the* Mrs. Jimmie Rodgers. I was scared to death. I remembered the 'Thelma' in Rodgers's song and even wondered if maybe Mrs. Rodgers had treated Jimmie bad and was really the Thelma in the song! But I was determined to get that photo.

"She told me she was Jimmie's widow and I told her how much I admired Jimmie and how I played his songs and how much it would mean to me if I could have that picture."

Carrie Rodgers told Tubb she had several different photos of Jimmie and if he would like to come out to her home he could select his favorite. An excited young Tubb visited her the next Sunday afternoon:

"She was most gracious. She showed me Jimmie's guitar, boots, and souvenirs, and we spent the whole afternoon talking about Jimmie. I knew every note Jimmie ever sang. I told her if she would like to hear me sing Jimmie's songs she could tune in to station KONO some morning. Rodgers's songs were almost the only ones I knew then. When I left Mrs. Rodgers's home that afternoon, I felt like I was walking in the clouds. It was the greatest day of my life."

But three months would go by before he had any more contact with Mrs. Rodgers. Then she telephoned him: "She told me she had been getting up early to listen to me on the air and she liked the way I sang Jimmie's songs. She told me I had 'heart' in my singing and that she was impressed with my sincerity. She wanted to help me—to help *me*, even though she had turned down many others before."

She was not speaking idle words. Mrs. Rodgers contacted the executives of RCA Records and arranged for Tubb to have a recording session at the Texas Hotel in San Antonio in late October 1936. She lent the skinny young man Jimmie's guitar (she'd later make him a gift of it), and he cut four songs in that first session: "The Last Thoughts of Jimmie Rodgers," "The Passing of Jimmie Rodgers," "The TB Is Whipping Me," and "Since That Black Cat Crossed My Path." RCA released them, but with little enthusiasm. Four more songs recorded in a second session in 1937 were not released until Tubb had become nationally known in 1942.

Ernest continued to struggle. There were small radio jobs on a number of stations, dollar-a-night engagements in honky-tonks, two-dollar-a-night appearances at drive-in movies, and even a period when he sold mattresses, making free singing appearances to promote the product.

In 1940 he turned again to Mrs. Rodgers for help. This time she put him in touch with Dave Kapp of the newer Decca Records, and in early April he cut four sides for Kapp at the Rice Hotel in Houston: "Blue-Eyed Elaine," "I'll Get Along Somehow," "You Broke a Heart," and "I'll Never Cry over You." Tubb considers 1940 the beginning of his full-time professional career.

In quick succession he was the Gold Chain Troubadour for a flour company on KGKO in Fort Worth; his seventh Decca record (released in 1941), "I'm Walking the Floor over You," was a smash hit; he made cameo appearances in three Hollywood films; and he acquired a manager in the person of J. L. (Joe) Frank. And Joe, who had an "in" with the Opry management, got him the December 1942 audition on the Grand Ole Opry.

In January, then, he was on the roster of the Opry. He was home.

··◦⟧ ii ⟦◦·· Of all of the fascinating stories about the Grand Ole Opry, and the controversy attendant on some of them, none is more compelling, nor more confusing, than the story of the move of the Opry from the War Memorial Auditorium to its new home at the Ryman Auditorium in downtown Nashville.

When *exactly* did it take place?

In light of the importance of the Ryman to the history of the Opry, it would seem the question should have an easy answer. It doesn't. It's not carved in stone somewhere, it doesn't seem to be in anyone's files, it wasn't noted in contemporary newspapers, and personal memories seem vague on the specifics.

Minnie Pearl, though, strongly contends that the Ryman was housing the Opry in the winter of 1942, certainly in February 1942 when she made her debut on the Prince Albert network portion of the Opry. She remembers it vividly:

"It's imbedded in my memory irrevocably, because it meant so much to me to go network. The first night I went on the network ["The Prince Albert Show"] I got hit on the head with a sandbag. . . . You see, the stagehands changed those advertising flats back there and the rest of the people knew when it got time for the network *not* to come out on the stage until the scenery was changed. But I was so overeager, so avid, to get out there in position to go on, that I ran out there before they got it changed and one of those sand bags [counterweights for the scenery] came down and hit me."

"Did it knock you out?" she was asked.

Minnie laughed: "Well, it didn't help me any."

There are other contentions about the Ryman move, none of them exact as to the date. But Minnie Pearl's "irrevocable" memory to the contrary, the consensus of old Opry hands seems to be that the Ryman Auditorium became the home of the Grand Ole Opry "sometime in 1943."

In any event, the Ryman already had a colorful history before the advent of the Opry there, thanks to two strong personalities: a preacher from the hill country of north Georgia named Samuel Porter Jones, and a tough Cumberland River steamboat captain named Tom Ryman.

Sam Jones was going to be a lawyer, but he had become an alcoholic. In 1872 his life was turned around when he made a promise to his father, who was on his deathbed, that he would stop drinking. The promise made, and kept, Sam turned to the ministry. For eight years he was a Methodist circuit rider in the poorest counties of northern Georgia. He would write later that he began as a minister with "a wife and one child, a bobtail pony, and eight dollars of cash."

Reverend Jones had a gift. He could stir an audience unlike few other preachers. He began to build a reputation as a fiery evangelist, one with the common touch. "God projected this world on a 'root hog or die poor' principle," he would tell his audiences. "If the hog, or man either, don't root, let him die."

And he was a happy man: "Fun is the next best thing to religion. When I get up to preach, I just knock out the bung and let nature cut her capers."

In April 1885 a group of church leaders in Nashville called on Pastor Jones to conduct a three-week series of revival meetings in the city. He wanted a tent or auditorium that would seat 3,000; better yet, 5,000. What he got was a huge tent seating 8,000, erected on a lot on Broad Street. And when he began preaching on Sunday afternoon, May 2, 1885, the seats were filled and 2,000 more stood around outside of the canvas.

The evangelist began a series of four services a day: one at sunrise, another at 10:00 A.M., one in the afternoon, and then one again in the evening. He railed against worldliness, drunkenness, gambling, and any manner of sin he found around him.

One of the cigarette girls showers the GIs with Camels on the Caravan.

(C. 1941) GRAND OLE OPRY ARCHIVES

The Wilburn Children perform with the stars of the Grand Ole Opry. Doyle and Teddy Wilburn are in front. Behind, from the left, are Clyde Dillahay on guitar, Staley Walton on guitar, Goldie Stewart on bass, Herman Crook on harmonica, Zeke Clements on fiddle, Lewis Crook (obscured by Zeke Clements), unknown guitarist, Redd Stewart on bass, and Leslie and Geraldine Wilburn on guitars.

(1940) GRAND OLE OPRY ARCHIVES

The Grand Ole Opry Camel Caravan getting ready to depart from Nashville's Parthenon. From the left are a cigarette girl, San Antonio Rose, Ford Rush, Jr., another cigarette girl, Eddy Arnold, Kay Carlisle, Pee Wee King, Harry Stone, Joe Zinkan, Dolly Dearman, Ford Rush, Sr., Redd Stewart, Minnie Pearl, and the last cigarette girl.

(C. 1941) SPECIAL COLLECTIONS, VANDERBILT UNIVERSITY

B*enjamin Frances "Whitey" Ford,
the barefoot Duke of Paducah,
onstage for a special "Prince Albert
Show" performance. On the far right
is Pee Wee King with the accordion,
and behind him in the white
hat is Wally Fowler.*
(C. 1942) GRAND OLE OPRY ARCHIVES

P*aul Howard, behind the
microphone, and his Arkansas
Cotton Pickers, in a most
appropriate setting.*
(1942) GRAND OLE OPRY ARCHIVES

A *publicity photograph of Ernest Tubb with an early version of his Texas Troubadours: from left (standing), Leon Short, E. T., and Ray "Kemo" Head; from left (kneeling), Johnny Sapp, Jack Drake, and Jimmie Short.*

A rare, early photograph of the Union Gospel Tabernacle (the Ryman Auditorium). Note the roofline decoration, which, unfortunately, has been lost.
(C. 1904) COLLECTION OF THE NASHVILLE ROOM, NASHVILLE PUBLIC LIBRARY

The Ryman's Confederate Gallery packed for a performance of the Opry.
(LATE 1940S) GRAND OLE OPRY ARCHIVES

Crowds jam the entrance to the Ryman Auditorium for the Opry's Saturday night show.
(EARLY 1940S) GRAND OLE OPRY ARCHIVES

The Grand Ole Opry's tent show after one of the performances—the adult fare of 40 cents entitled the spectator to "The Best Show on Earth for the Money!"
(C. 1943) GRAND OLE OPRY ARCHIVES

Into this charged atmosphere came Captain Ryman, the wealthy owner of a fleet of "pleasure" boats plying the Cumberland—boats dedicated to dancing, gambling, and drinking. It's part of the legend that Tom and members of his rowdy crew went to the tent revival services determined to disrupt them. They meant to make sport of Pastor Sam Jones.

The Reverend Jones, however, was equal to the challenge. In the course of that evening's services, and during a stunning peroration on the subject of motherhood, the rough Tom Ryman was brought to his knees, converted to the ways of Christ. It is said Captain Ryman led his crewmen back to the boats to throw gaming tables and teakwood bars overboard.

Whatever the exact truth of that, Ryman *had* converted and he vowed to build Jones a tabernacle so "that Sam Jones will never have to preach in a tent again."

And he did. His initial effort was a temporary structure. On March 17, 1886, the proud Ryman sent a letter to Jones. If it reflected his lack of formal education it also clearly mirrored his zeal:

Dear Brother Sam Jones,

Myself & Capt Kendle [a riverboat partner in the venture] have just compleeted our gospell & Tempernce Hall, it is difernt to any thing in the country and truly is your production. It cost 3500.00$ and has six pictures on its walls some of them 20 feet long & 10 feet hy—life size. . . .

One of them was a portrait of Sam Jones himself. The other pictures dealt with the evils of alcohol. One, Ryman wrote, showed

a pile of whisky barells with snakes all around them, also bones skuls &cc, and the salvation army in the distance, women prevailing with the men, also an angel coming down with a drawn sword in the act of cuting [off] the heads of the snakes.

That much accomplished, Captain Ryman worked tirelessly to raise the money (and contributed large sums himself) for something more grand—a permanent edifice of brick and mortar, to be called the Union Gospel Tabernacle. It was begun in 1889; Sam Jones was soon to have his completed monument.

In 1897 a balcony was added—the Confederate Gallery—to accommodate a reunion of Confederate soldiers.

When Captain Ryman died in 1904, the Reverend Jones came from Atlanta to preach the funeral oration on Christmas Day. He praised Ryman's effort in building the tabernacle and urged that the name of the building be changed to the Ryman Auditorium. "All those in favor stand," Jones said. All 4,000 mourners came to their feet in approval.

Other evangelists were to follow Jones into the big brick tabernacle. One was the colorful Gipsy Smith, the son of a gypsy who had been an early member of the Salvation Army in England. Another was Billy Sunday, a former major-league baseball player with the Chicago White Stockings, who was perhaps the best known of the fire-and-brimstone preachers in the days before the First World War.

On one appearance at Captain Ryman's auditorium, Sunday took out after prostitution, calling Nashville's red-light district "the devil's backbone." One night two "ladies of the evening" attended Billy's revival meeting, sat for a time through his denunciations, and then got up to leave. As they walked up the aisle, the evangelist roared: "See, there goes two daughters of the devil!"

One of them turned back to Sunday, waved coyly, and shouted in reply: "Goodbye, Daddy."

From the beginning, though, the Ryman Auditorium was to be more than a gospel tabernacle. It was the largest such facility in middle Tennessee and it was recognized as an ideal vehicle to bring culture to the community. Very soon there would be Nashville audiences for Chicago, Boston, and New York orchestras, for the Metropolitan Opera Company's productions of *Carmen* and *The Barber of Seville*, for John Philip Sousa's noted U.S. Marine Corps Band, for Victor Herbert and his orchestra, for Ignace Paderewski, for Fritz Kreisler, for Helen Keller and her teacher, for Pavlova and Nijinsky, for Mischa Elman, for Mary Garden, for John McCormack, for Enrico Caruso, for lectures by Carrie Nation, William Jennings Bryan, and Booker T. Washington. In 1919 there was a concert by tenor Paul Ryman, a son of the builder of the auditorium.

Even after the National Life and Accident Insurance Company rented the building for its Grand Ole Opry in the early forties, Ryman Auditorium continued to be used for other purposes. Tyrone Power appeared there, and Faye Emerson, and Margaret Truman (in a piano concert), and Bob Hope, and Doris Day, and Les Brown and his Band of Renown. From time to time it was used as a recording studio for the likes of Red Foley, Rex Allen, the Four Aces, Woody Herman, and Ray Anthony. Trumpeter Anthony recorded the pop hits "Bunny Hop" and "Marshmallow World" at the Ryman.

With the coming of the Grand Ole Opry, one colorful era of the Ryman was to be replaced by another. And its new "hillbilly" ghosts would supercede the shades of the "Divine Sarah" Bernhardt playing the tragic role of Camille there.

❧[iii]❧ The Grand Ole Opry was ever changing, ever evolving. Its influence was growing. For one thing, its number-one star, Roy Acuff, had also become a full-fledged motion picture actor. In all, Acuff was to make eight movies between 1940 and 1948. Acuff's movie career served to bring more credit to the Grand Ole Opry, although Roy always rejected the idea that it was particularly important. But it did expose his songs to a wider audience. And while Acuff was spreading the name of the Grand Ole Opry far and wide, so were others.

Bill Monroe's tent show was prospering. It had great appeal, in those days before television, to a whole generation of rural people in Arkansas, Mississippi, Alabama, and Tennessee. The arrival of a Grand Ole Opry tent show was a major event in those small towns.

"The people would be watching for you," Bill Monroe remembered. "They knew you were coming because you'd been advertised for two or three weeks, and they'd be standing on the street corners and sidewalks, you know, watching the show come in. We had, I believe, seven trucks and a long stretched-out bus we traveled in.

"Around half past ten or eleven, we'd go out to where the tent would be put up. First you'd stretch the tent out, then drive the stakes down to where you could put the ropes up, just like the old carnival days. When the people got through with the work, they would shave and clean up and come on out to the show. Back in those days everybody wore a white shirt, it seemed like. They were just good, down-to-earth working people, you know.

"We started out charging twenty-five cents and seventy-five cents admission; after a while we went up to ninety cents tops. . . . We played in some places where there hadn't been a tent show in years."

Weather didn't seem to deter the public's enthusiasm for the Opry's tent shows. Sam and Kirk McGee traveled for a time with the Acuff show. "That was the joy of my life, right there," Kirk said later.

"You see, that ole tent," he went on, "there's something about it makes you want to get in there and see what's in there, you know. . . . And when it rained, well . . . we played one date in Mississippi with Roy, and the people sat there with their shoes in their laps, the water was coming through there that bad.

"They's paddlin' their feet in that water, keeping time with the music."

···❧ iv ❧··· Back at the Ryman Auditorium there was some stirring within the talent ranks in 1943. Eddy Arnold, for one, saw it as a time to make a move.

"Working with Pee Wee King was fun," Arnold said. "He was one of the funniest men I've ever known, and in those early days on the road a good belly laugh was about the only bonus you could get out of life. We used to hold our breath driving around in those dilapidated cars we traveled in. Pee Wee's was the worst of all and we were always afraid the bottom would drop right out of it. One day just before the war it did.

"He had picked me up and was driving me over to the radio station when we stopped for a light and the whole transmission fell right out of the car.

"Pee Wee didn't say a word. He just opened the door, got out, and looked around. We were at the top of a hill, and all of a sudden Pee Wee squinted at something off in the distance toward the bottom of the hill. Then he poked his head back in the car. 'I think I spotted somethin',' he said. 'Better get out and push.'

"The two of us got the car moving downhill and then he jumped in, letting ourselves coast and leaving the deceased transmission on the street behind us. As we rolled downhill we picked up speed, and by the time we got to the bottom we looked like any other car on the street—which is just what Pee Wee wanted. He glided along the curb and let the car come to a stop in front of a new-car dealer. Out we got, and in we went, and up came a salesman. I was holding my breath, but Pee Wee was as calm as could be. 'Just browsin',' he told the salesman.

"A few minutes later Pee Wee was letting the salesman talk him into a nice new shiny car.

" 'Well, I don't know,' he said, doing a good imitation of a final holdout. 'I really don't have the money for a down payment.'

" 'No need, no need,' the salesman said. 'If that's your car parked out at the curb, you've got your down payment.'

" 'Well, I don't know . . .' Pee Wee said, shaking his head.

" 'Tell you what,' said the salesman, 'suppose I take it for a little spin around the block and we'll see what she's worth to you.'

"Pee Wee held up his hand. 'Absolutely not! I never let anyone drive my car! Never have, never will!' And with that, he started to walk out, with me following right behind.

" 'Just a moment, sir!' the salesman shouted, and Pee Wee did a beautiful about-face, not too fast, not too slow. It was just right, and we ended up driving out of there with a brand-new car.

"The next day I was with Pee Wee when he got a call from the salesman, who had finally tried to take that little spin around the block. I could hear him screaming across the room. Pee Wee listened very patiently until the guy ran out of breath, and then he said, 'Well, you see what happens when I let somebody drive my car.' "

But by 1943 Eddy Arnold had to face other realities. "I began to realize that I wasn't progressing," Arnold said. "When the Camel Caravan road show ended, and my salary dropped back to what it was before, I had to do something. I was supporting my wife and my mother. I thought on it awhile and finally got my courage up and went to see Harry Stone, who ran WSM.

" 'Mr. Stone,' I said, 'I'm going to have to quit Pee Wee, and what I'd like to do is to go to work for you at this radio station.' And that's what happened. Harry Stone started throwing little spots to me, giving me appearances. And then he made a pitch to an old friend of mine—Fred Forster, the Chicago music publisher—regarding a record contract, and Fred got in touch with Frank Walker at RCA Victor in New York. On the strength of Forster's recommendation—and Harry Stone's—Mr. Walker sent me a recording contract although he'd never heard me sing!"

Stone also gave Arnold his own spot on the Grand Ole Opry and two live programs on WSM, one in the morning and one at noon. "Just me and my guitar," Arnold recalled. "And Harry did all this for me. He helped me greatly."

Thus, in 1943, Eddy Arnold's career started to blossom.

"There was a lot of fun on the Opry in those days," Eddy said. "Judge Hay, you know, was quite a dignified and fine old gentleman. And he had that steamboat whistle, which he would always leave in his desk at the radio station through the week. There were two boys there—Elmer Alley and Mickey Hopkins—who got that steamboat whistle one day and tore up little tiny pieces of newspaper and packed it full!"

A hearty laugh. "So Judge Hay on this particular Saturday picked up the steamboat whistle, put it under his arm, and went down to the Ryman. And that night he said, 'Hello, everybody, this is George D. Hay, The Solemn Old Judge, on the Grand Ole Opry!' And he blew into that whistle." More laughter. "It didn't make a sound! Nothing happened.

"I often wondered how he got all of that newspaper out of it."

··∘⟦ v ⟧∘·· There was another important network development at the Grand Ole Opry in 1943. Two, actually. In January the big Ralston Purina Company in St. Louis began to sponsor a second half-hour of the Opry on a regional network. And in October "The Prince Albert Show" went on the full NBC coast-to-coast network.

That was heady news for the Opry people. To celebrate, a party was planned on the Ryman stage, to which numerous dignitaries were invited, among them Tennessee governor Prentice Cooper. The governor, a crony of the powerful "Boss" Crump political machine in Memphis, declined the invitation, saying something about Roy Acuff and his friends and their bringing disgrace to Tennessee by making it the hillbilly capital of the world.

Acuff biographer Elizabeth Schlappi picks up the story at that point: "About 9:00 P.M. the following Sunday night some reporters were sitting around the *Nashville Tennessean* office with nothing to do. Since Cooper was going out of office, they were shooting the breeze about who could be elected. One of them, Elmer Hinton, said, 'I'll tell you one fellow who could be elected and that's Roy Acuff!' So they went around the office collecting names and within a few hours they had twenty-six, which they (not knowing whether Roy was a Republican or Democrat) filed with the State Democratic Party chairman to qualify Roy for the race."

In sum, Acuff declined to run as either a Democrat or a Republican in 1944, although he considered himself a Republican. Two years later the Democrats would try again to get him to run. He wouldn't.

But that wouldn't end the political efforts of the powerbrokers on behalf of the Smoky Mountain Boy.

Deep within my heart lies a melody,
A song of old San Antone;
Where in dreams I live with the memory
*Beneath the stars all alone. . . .**

—"San Antonio Rose," Bob Wills hit

T he Grand Ole Opry's move to the larger Ryman Auditorium, with its church-pew benches and stained-glass windows, seemed to breathe new life into the radio show and to give it new status. And the full-network coverage of "The Prince Albert Show" brought in special guest stars—flamboyant Bob Wills and his Texas Playboys, for example.

Wills was a major, nationally known star in the early forties. His "San Antonio Rose" was a runaway pop hit. His appearance at the Opry caused quite a stir. Minnie Pearl recalled: "You know, the Ryman is built in a semicircle and some of the seats in the balcony run clear back of the stage. And they were choice seats, because the 'groupies' could sit in those seats and holler down at the boys, and lean over and get autographs and all.

"When Bob Wills came on, there was this one woman in that section who just got carried away. *Oooh, Bob Wills and Tommy Duncan!* They were something special in their white western wardrobe and white hats. Anyway, she was leaning over and screaming, and in her excitement she fell forward onto the stage. She

*"San Antonio Rose" by Bob Wills; copyright 1940 The Bourne Company.

didn't hurt herself: I think she rather enjoyed the publicity. It didn't stop the show, but maybe it slowed it down a little, while they went and got her and picked her up."

But the Wills appearance caused another kind of consternation at the Opry. "That was the first time," Minnie said, "we ever put electrified fiddles on the Opry. Roy Acuff said it would ruin the Opry forever! I wish I had a nickel for every time I heard something like that."

However, it was a fact that George Hay's "prohibition" against electric instruments had already been breached by the time Bob Wills showed up with his wired fiddles. The Golden West Cowboys were using electric guitars, as were Ernest Tubb and the Texas Troubadours.

Tubb's reason was very practical. While Ernest was always careful to keep his act in the strictly country vein, he was not above innovation. When jukebox operators complained that the acoustic guitars of his early records could not be heard when business got a bit boisterous in the bars and honky-tonks, Tubb instructed his guitarist to attach an electrical pickup to his acoustic instrument. When the experiment met with the approval of the jukebox operators, Tubb acquired an electric guitar of his own. It came with him to the Grand Ole Opry.

There is one persistent fable that Bob Wills and the Texas Playboys brought the first drum on the stage when they made their guest appearance, with Opry officials decreeing that the offending instrument be hidden behind a stage curtain. However quaint and interesting that story may be, there is absolutely no documentation that it ever happened.

It may be—and this item is suspect, too—that Harold "Sticks" McDonald introduced drums to the Opry stage sometime in the early forties while playing with the Pee Wee King band. King himself told an interviewer that his group did use drums and he was told not to announce their use on the air. And after two or three such Opry performances, King was ordered, it is alleged, not to use them again.

Recalling that kind of thing brought an amused smile to the face of E. W. "Bud". Wendell, the chief executive of Opryland USA, Inc., in a 1985 interview: "That story about hiding the drums behind a curtain is just one of those old tales around here. As long as we remained at the Ryman, though, we never used anything other than just a standup snare drum. But that had as much to do with space restrictions as with the purity of country music. You just couldn't fit a whole set of drums on the stage at the Ryman; it just wasn't that big."

The entire issue of electrical instruments, and drums on the Opry stage, would not end with Bob Wills, Pee Wee King, or Ernest Tubb. It was not a controversy that would die easily.

❧[ii]❧ Sometimes show business history is made accidentally, and in an instant. With a chance remark not unlike the ad-lib of Judge Hay when he named the Grand Ole Opry. So it was in 1943 when Roy Acuff and the Smoky Mountain Boys were playing an engagement at the Dallas, Texas, Sportatorium. The show was sold out; in the streets around the auditorium several thousand people who couldn't get tickets were milling about angrily. Suddenly some of the mob began to tear down the side of the building in an effort to get inside. A frightened management appealed to Acuff to make a sidewalk appearance. He did, soothing the angry would-be patrons.

Once the show got under way, Roy introduced two distinguished guests who were seated in the audience. One was cowboy singing star Gene Autry, there in his military uniform. Autry came to the stage and sang a song. Then former St. Louis Cardinals pitching star Dizzy Dean was introduced.

Bounding to the stage, the grinning Dean embraced Acuff, telling the audience: "Friends, it's always a pleasure to appear on the stage with the King of the Hillbillies."

Diz had said magic words.

Within a very short time the media had amended the title to "The King of Country Music." Acuff was to spend his remaining years modestly denying it: "I'm one of the boys who's tried to work hard here at the Grand Ole Opry to make it in country music, and I don't deserve the title of being called 'king.' I don't deserve the title of being called anything but 'Roy Acuff.' "

Roy was enormously popular during the years of the Second World War. GIs from the southern states took his records all over the world. Even the Japanese-propaganda broadcaster Tokyo Rose played his recordings. And there is one story that a Japanese banzai attack on U.S. Marine positions began with the cry: "To hell with Roosevelt! To hell with Babe Ruth! To hell with Roy Acuff!"

⋯ᒍ iii Ւ⋯ New faces were appearing on the Grand Ole Opry in 1944.

One joined Bill Monroe's Blue Grass Boys. His name was Lester Flatt. He was born in 1914 near Sparta, Tennessee, in the Appalachian foothills, one of nine children of a sharecropper. Lester's parents played the banjo; his father was also a fiddler, and there were family "musicales" in which everyone sang and played. Flatt started with the banjo, but soon announced his preference for the guitar.

At seventeen, he went to work in a Sparta silk mill, met and married a young lady named Gladys Stacey, and a few years later moved to Covington, Virginia, to work for Burlington Mills. Gladys also played guitar and sang. It wasn't too long before Flatt was playing with a local radio group known as the Harmonizers, and later with the Happy-Go-Lucky Boys. In 1943, he and Gladys were hired by Charlie Monroe's Kentucky Pardners out of Louisville. But road work was tough, the money was short, and they quit after a year so that Lester could take a job with a trucking company.

His self-imposed divorcement from music didn't last. A telegram from another Monroe—this time Bill—took the Flatts to Nashville, where he joined the Blue Grass Boys on the Opry. He signed on as guitarist and lead singer. Neither Monroe nor Flatt understood then how significant that would be.

Also new to the Opry in '44 were the Poe Sisters, Nell and Ruth, described by George Hay as "two very charming country girls whose parents operate a farm near their home town" of Big Creek, Mississippi.

Somewhat more experienced were newcomers John and Walter, the Bailes Brothers, out of West Virginia. Judge Hay again: "Sons of a Baptist preacher, both of the boys started playing professionally at a very early age. Each one had his own group, but before long they joined hands and have been operating as the Bailes Brothers for several years. In addition to the two brothers the group is made up of Miss Evy Lou, a very charming young lady, who sings with the boys in trio numbers and does a solo every now and then. They carry two musicians who are strictly down to earth. . . . They have the 'feel' of folk music and their work rings true."

And Hay did verbal cartwheels over another new act arriving in 1944: "It is the opinion of your reporter that we have never had a funnier comedian than Rod Brasfield."

··◦⟦ iv ⟧◦·· "I was in the dressing room and I heard this loud laughter," Minnie Pearl recalled. "I was getting ready to go on the network [Prince Albert] portion and I was very conscious at that time of people who came on the Opry to do comedy. When I heard somebody getting a loud laugh, I'd run to the wings to find out what was going on. We were all competitive back in those days. I started for the stage and before I ever got to the wings I thought all of a sudden, 'That's Boob.' "

Her mind raced back a decade and a half, to when she was Miss Sarah Ophelia Colley in Centerville, Tennessee, and she went to see a Bisbee's Comedians tent show and was fascinated by a brother act of Boob and Rod Brasfield. Boob was the comic, Rod the straight man. She made her way backstage at that time and told the brothers she wanted to be in show business.

"No, you don't," they told the proper young lady.

"Yes, I do," Miss Colley said, "and I'm going to."

It was a jolt, then, when she thought she heard Boob Brasfield on the Ryman stage. But when she got to the wings she found that it was Rod Brasfield performing and not his older brother.

"He was wearing baggy pants and old, funny side-button shoes," Minnie went on. "He had on a suit that was five times too big for him, with galluses . . . and a tiny little hat. And he was just raking the audience over the coals, tossing them around any way he wanted to. When he came off the stage I grabbed him and hugged him and told him I was so glad he was there.

"Rod was the best comedian I ever saw, in country or any other kind of comedy, at getting an audience into his pocket. The women loved him, the men loved him, everybody loved him. He could get by with the rankest, bluest material and those old fat ladies would just laugh themselves to death. When he got into this old, clean-living, Bible Belt comedy on the Grand Ole Opry he never said anything bad—it was just that he couldn't help intimating things with the tone of his voice or with his face, which was like a piece of rubber."

Rod Brasfield was born in 1910 on a small farm at Smithville, near Tupelo, the son of a rural mail carrier. He saw little incentive to be a farmer. Or a mail carrier. At the age of sixteen he left Smithville to join an older brother, Lawrence "Boob" Brasfield, who was working with a traveling tent show. It was a small stock company road show touring the South, one of many such shows of those days. Rod played bit parts. He would say later that his "main job was running errands for the other actors."

Eventually, the brothers Brasfield graduated to the Bisbee's Comedians, a front-rank touring show fronted by one J. C. Bisbee, who had been a vaudeville magician for many years. Rod seemed content in his role of straight man.

There came a day, though, when Boob was late for a performance and Rod donned a red wig and filled the bill. He never went back to being a straight man, working with the Bisbee troupe until World War Two interceded and Rod found himself in the Army Air Corps. But he had a bad back, injured when he was a child, and was given a medical discharge in 1943, rejoining Bisbee.

It was in 1944 that Judge Hay auditioned him for the Grand Ole Opry and hired him. That first appearance on the Opry remembered so fondly by Minnie Pearl was on July 15, 1944.

The key comedy slot on the Opry then was "The Prince Albert Show," and Whitey "Duke of Paducah" Ford had that position nailed down. Along with Minnie Pearl. Rod was assigned to the other network portion of the Opry, sponsored by Ralston Purina.

❧[v]❧ Just about a month earlier another newcomer had arrived at WSM in the person of Grant Turner. He didn't sing, or play an instrument. He was to be just another member of the WSM announcing staff, but he was to have a substantial impact on the Grand Ole Opry.

Turner's road to the Grand Ole Opry began in Abilene, Texas, where he was born in 1912. What he remembers most distinctly about his youth is that he was fascinated by radio. "My grandmother had a radio and I wanted one of my own, so I built a crystal set. . . . When I was sixteen, they were going to move a station from Breckenridge, Texas, to Abilene, and I went and helped them move. We put up the transmitter and we used a windmill for a tower."

On that early Abilene station Turner got his first lesson about country music stardom when Jimmie Rodgers, the Singing Brakeman, came to town. He remembered: "Jimmie was in the neighborhood to take part in a jewelry auction. He got seven hundred fifty dollars for that. Of course, he was a big recording artist back then and he went around autographing his records.

"The Studebaker dealer found out that he was in town and paid him two hundred fifty dollars for an hour show on the station. That was a lot of money in those days.

"He was a chain-smoker. I remember the yellow stains on his fingers. And he didn't have a strap on his guitar. He stood up to perform and he just put one foot up on a chair and put his guitar across the leg.

For a time, young Turner thought he would be a newspaperman. He went to Hardin-Simmons to study journalism. And when he graduated he held newspaper jobs in Texas, eventually moving to *The Dallas Morning News.* But radio had not lost its appeal. There followed announcing jobs in Sherman and Longview, Texas, and in 1942 he moved to WBIR in Knoxville, Tennessee.

He was called "Tex" in Knoxville, where he worked with such country music acts as Carl Butler, Johnny and Jack, Kitty Wells, and Bill Carlisle.

And then came the offer from Nashville. Turner started his job there on D-Day—the day of the allied invasion of Europe—June 6, 1944. "The old WSM," he said, "was like a small Radio City. There would be writers, song pluggers, stars, and musicians around all the time. You felt you were in the center of a lot of activity."

It's clear that George Hay recognized Grant as a kindred soul, taking him under his wing and eventually having him assigned as the announcer on a half-hour portion of the Opry sponsored by Crazy Water Crystals. His tenure on the Opry was to take him all the way to the Country Music Hall of Fame.

··⟨ vi ⟩·· Those were fun days on the Grand Ole Opry. Turner, like Judge Hay, looked at the Opry performers through the eyes of a newsman. Uncle Dave Macon especially drew his attention.

"I remember we had a restaurant across the street from the Ryman," Grant said. "Across Fifth Avenue from the Opry; the name of it was the Victoria. And it was owned by a Greek family who just seemed to love the Opry people. Well, Uncle Dave would walk up to the side door there—they sold beer there and Uncle Dave would be wanting a drink—and he'd go in that door and he'd say, 'My name is Uncle Dave Macon and I wanna sing ya a little song.' So he'd crank down a little song, plunking the banjo and singing, and when he finished someone would say, 'Come on over, Uncle Dave, and lemme buy you a beer.' And that's the way he got his free beer.

"They tell a story about him when he went to Hollywood to make that *Grand Ole Opry* movie, and how he would hide a bottle in the shrubbery outside the studio. He knew how to get outside the studio door, but he didn't realize that the door had an automatic lock on it when they started filming and the red light went on. Anyway, they started shooting on this particular scene that Dave was supposed to be in. But when it came time for Uncle Dave to make an entrance, he was missing. He had gone to get a little nip and had been locked out.

"He was something special and he knew it. He put his name in big boxcar letters, maybe a foot high, all the way across the front of his house. It would read UNCLE . . . and there would be a window . . . DAVE, and there'd be a window . . . MACON. Everybody who traveled that road—it was a major one, 70 South—knew it was Uncle Dave's house. And they'd stop in and he'd entertain them."

Thus, even though the Opry was changing in the mid-forties, and new stars were coming on, the appeal of the old-timers, Uncle Dave particularly, was not lost.

Kirk McGee remembered when Roy Acuff and the Smoky Mountain Boys were to play a date in Baltimore on which the McGee Brothers and Macon were also booked. At that time Acuff had his own "airliner," named *The Great Speckled Bird.*

"I said to Uncle Dave," McGee recalled, " 'Uncle Dave, it'll take us two days to drive there, but if we fly you could leave here on Sunday morning, you'll be nice and clean, and you'll have that white shirt on, and you'll be ready to hit the stage no more'n you get off the plane.'

"He said, 'Before I do that, I'll quit and help my boy make a crop.'

"And I got Roy and we took him out to the plane and we drove up under the wing and he got to looking around it and I kind of figured he was weakening then. And I said, 'Let's get up in there, Uncle Dave.'

"He said, 'Reckon they would care?'

"I said, 'No.'

"We got up in that plane and he got that ole pipe out, you know, and he filled it and he says, 'Does everybody get killed when they have a wreck?'

"I said, 'No, a lot of them live sometime.' "

Apparently that logic convinced the old man. He agreed to take his first airplane ride to make the engagement in Baltimore.

McGee picked up the story: "So we was going over Roanoke and I asked the pilot, 'How high are we?'

"And he said, 'About ten thousand feet.'

"And I said, 'Uncle Dave, we're up ten thousand feet.'

"He said, 'By God, I'm gonna lay with it.' "

Uncle Dave Macon, a man who wouldn't even drive a car, had made his peace with modern travel.

All in the early month of May,
When the green buds they were swelling,
Sweet William on his death-bed lay
For the love of Barbara Allen.

—Traditional folk song

Most people would not remember the year 1945 because of what happened on Nashville's Grand Ole Opry in its twentieth year. For there were worldwide developments of far greater significance, overwhelming not only the Opry, but just about everything else in our lives as well.

World War Two ended.

What joy was occasioned by the Axis surrender—and there was a great deal of it—was tempered by what had happened in Warm Springs, Georgia, on Thursday, April 12. There, a massive cerebral hemorrhage took the life of President Franklin Delano Roosevelt in the thirteenth year of his unprecedented administration.

While it can be only a minor footnote in the history of 1945, Mr. Roosevelt's death contributed another "first" on the Grand Ole Opry.

Magazine writer Lena Ellis explained: "A barrier was broken [when] President Roosevelt died. When the Opry musicians tried to find a way to express their grief, Pee Wee King suggested a solo of 'Taps' played on the trumpet. The forbidden instrument was heard that night [Saturday, April 14] and the public reaction was favorable. The trumpet stayed."

Well . . . not really.

⋅⋅◦[ii]◦⋅⋅ Meanwhile, traditionalism was mightily served on the Opry in 1945 when Bradley Kincaid, "The Kentucky Mountain Boy," was signed to the roster. He was a folksinger, pure and simple; a vocalist with a notably unemotional style. His repertoire included such sad and beautiful ballads as "Fatal Wedding Day," "The Legend of the Robin Red Breast," and the seemingly ageless "Barbara Allen."

Music scholars have identified as many as thirty versions of "Barbara Allen," going back as far as 1666, when the noted British diarist Samuel Pepys mentioned it as a stage song. In any event, it was that type of material embraced by Kincaid.

Bill C. Malone, in his landmark book of 1968 written for the American Folklore Society, *Country Music U.S.A.*, wrote of Kincaid: "Although born in the foothills of the Kentucky Mountains and thoroughly knowledgeable about the folksongs of the region, Kincaid made no deliberate efforts to become a professional folksinger; he became one largely by accident. While attending George Williams College in Chicago, preparing for a career as a YMCA secretary, Kincaid began singing occasionally with the college quartet. A fellow classmate and member of the quartet informed Don Malin, the WLS Music Director, that Kincaid was a folksinger. Malin contacted Kincaid about doing a fifteen-minute show on WLS, and Kincaid, who had not sung folksongs for years, borrowed a guitar and began brushing up on the old songs from back home. His initial show evoked a tremendous audience response, and by the fall of 1926 he had become a regular on the WLS Barn Dance, where he remained for about four years."

From Chicago, Kincaid went on to WLW in Cincinnati, and then began touring extensively with a group that would eventually include the talents of another Kentuckian, Louis Marshall Jones, whom Kincaid was to nickname "Grandpa."

The folksinger hated the term "hillbilly." He bitterly resented it, as a matter of fact. He preferred to be labeled a "singer of mountain songs."

In that he found a kindred spirit on the Grand Ole Opry in the person of George Hay. "We never use the word 'hillbillies,' " Hay wrote, 'because it was coined in derision. Furthermore, there is no such animal. Country people have a definite dignity of their own and a native shrewdness which enables them to hold their own in any company. Intolerance has no place in our organization and is not allowed."

Ernest Tubb was another on the Opry who resented the term. Taking direct action, he pressured Decca Records on the subject, insisting that the word "country" be substituted for "hillbilly" in merchandising records. Decca, in turn, used its muscle with other companies and with the music trade publications. Eventually there was full capitulation.

Roy Acuff, though, who might have used his influence in the argument, didn't really care. As late as 1974, he was telling an interviewer: "I was raised back in the hills, back in the mountains. The word 'hillbilly' was a real good word. Back in Maynardville, Union County, where I'm from, we were considered hillbillies. We didn't resent it; we took it proudly, because there's nothing wrong with a hillbilly. I love people from the rural sections. I like people in the city too; it takes us all to make the world go. But we should never forget that the hillbilly, the guy that's out in the early morning on the farm milking the cow, followin' the plow through the day, and feeding the stock at night, is making the living for you and me."

To Acuff, the phrase "hillbilly fiddler" was a badge of honor.

⁘[iii]⁘ Lew Childre, from the marvelously named town of Opp, Alabama, also joined the Grand Ole Opry in 1945. He was a versatile performer, capable of cornball rural comedy and soul-stirring ballad singing. Having started his professional career at sixteen, he had been nurtured in small-town vaudeville and had played radio stations throughout the South for fifteen years before coming to the Opry.

While he might have gained a bit of sophistication with two years of schooling at the University of Alabama, Childre understood perfectly the country genre of the WSM radio show.

"My parents are just plain, everyday people," he said, "my dad being judge for many years and my mammy keeping the home together and flapjacks and syrup handy for three of us young 'uns."

Pee Wee King, meanwhile, had hired a singer-guitarist to replace Eddy Arnold in the Golden West Cowboys. His name was Lloyd "Cowboy" Copas and he hailed from Muskogee, Oklahoma. There could have been no greater contrast between two performers—Eddy had a smooth pop style, Copas was a gutsy honky-tonk singer. At the time, however, the honky-tonk style was not fully appreciated. Cowboy Copas would do his part to change all that.

Following in Copas's wake would come the ultimate honky-tonk singer. Minnie Pearl, on tour with the Golden West Cowboys, remembers the first brief glimpse she had of a fellow named Hank Williams:

"We were going to play Dothan, Alabama," she reminisced, "and after we checked into a hotel Pee Wee said we were going to do a radio show that afternoon to plug the show for that night. So we went down to the radio station, and sitting out in the lobby on a sofa was this long, tall man—put together like a stick man with his angular arms and legs. And next to him a beautiful blonde woman. He got up when we walked in, and Pee Wee spoke to him. He was peddling songs. He was down on his luck; his hat was dirty and his suit was wrinkled. Anyway, he sold Pee Wee a song called 'I'm Praying for the Day That Peace Will Come.' Little Becky Barfield was on the show with us and she used to sing it.

"Pee Wee told me he paid ten dollars for the song. Can you imagine—ten dollars for a *Hank Williams* song?!"

(For the record: The song was formally published in 1944 by Fred Rose Music, Inc., under the names Frankie "Pee Wee" King and Hank Williams.)

⁘{ iv }⁘ There were other developments in Nashville in 1945, all Opry related or WSM related, that pushed the city closer to ultimately becoming Music City, USA. Roy Acuff and Fred Rose had started it in 1942 with their Acuff-Rose Publications. Now a native Chicagoan named Paul Cohen entered the picture.

In those days the Decca Records empire of Jack and Dave Kapp was strong in country music, with such stars on the label as Ernest Tubb, Milton Brown and the Brownies, Bradley Kincaid, Jimmie Davis, Cliff Bruner, Johnnie Lee Wills, Rex Griffin, Bill Carlisle, and young Red Foley. Dave Kapp had turned the country division over to Paul Cohen in the early forties and Cohen immediately began to look to Nashville as a potential recording center, primarily because of the large pool of talent the Grand Ole Opry had attracted to the city.

It was in either March or April 1945 that Cohen rented WSM's Studio B, the second home of the Opry, for a recording session with Red Foley. No written records exist of that historic session; not the exact date, nor the titles of the songs recorded. Foley had told an interviewer years later (and somewhat hesitantly) that he thought three of the four songs cut then were "Tennessee Saturday Night," "Blues in the Heart," and "Tennessee Border." The last song, however, wasn't copyrighted until several years later, and there's no hard evidence about just what exactly was recorded then.

What was clear, though, was that the Foley/Cohen session in Studio B in the spring of 1945 was the first modern recording date in Nashville's musical history. Writer Robert Shelton, in his book *The Country Music Story,* suggested: "Whenever the first date of the first commercial session in Nashville is established, some sort of public celebration will be in order."

More precise is the information about Paul Cohen's second Decca recording date in the WSM studio. That was on September 11, 1945, when Ernest Tubb recorded "It Just Don't Matter Now" and "When Love Turns to Hate."

Cohen's pioneering example encouraged others. Three WSM engineers, Aaron Shelton, Carl Jenkins, and studio supervisor George Reynolds, banded together in a moonlighting operation that saw them establish the first commercial studio in the city: Castle Recording Studio, headquartered in the Tulane Hotel.

Shelton said the Castle studio came into being because the engineers believed that "with the pool of talent gathering here, it would be a natural. We knew that it would be easier and much less expensive to come here [to Nashville] to record the talent than it would be to take the talent to New York or Chicago."

Ernest Tubb was one of the earliest customers, recording "Blue Christmas" at the Castle studio.

The studio was used frequently by Cohen and his associate, Owen Bradley, a studio piano player at WSM and later the station's music director.

The big RCA Victor company quickly became aware of what was happening. Steve Sholes, the head of country music for RCA, came to Nashville in 1946 to record at a second commercial studio which had been established: the Brown Brothers studio at Fourth and Union Streets, on a site that had once housed the law offices of Andrew Jackson.

Sholes visited the Grand Ole Opry on his first visit to the city. "I had never seen it," he told an interviewer, "and when I got down there and saw the Opry . . . [and] saw everything that was going on I thought this is the place we ought to be recording. It seemed to be the center of everything. . . . I agitated

The two modes of transportation for Bob Wills and his Texas Playboys. Bob Wills brought electrified fiddles to the Opry's stage.

(C. 1941) COUNTRY MUSIC FOUNDATION LIBRARY AND MEDIA CENTER

The Dean of Opry announcers and Country Music Hall of Fame member, Grant Turner, motions for the crowd to applaud the next performer.

(1960) WSM PHOTO/LES LEVERETT

Curly Fox (left) plays straight man to Rod Brasfield
on the Ralston Purina segment of the Opry.

(1947) GRAND OLE OPRY ARCHIVES

West Virginia's Bailes Brothers, John (standing on the left) and Walter (standing on the right), were most famous for their song, "Dust on the Bible." Evy Lou, a vocalist who appeared with the Bailes Brothers, is seated in this photograph. Kneeling are (from the left) Dale Hecht and Ernest Ferguson.

(1944) GRAND OLE OPRY ARCHIVES

Bill Monroe and the Blue Grass Boys. What some people consider the finest bluegrass band ever assembled: (from the left) Chubby Wise on fiddle, Bill Monroe on mandolin, Lester Flatt on guitar, and Earl Scruggs on banjo. Cedric Rainwater is on bass, behind Bill Monroe. Ken Marvin ("Lonzo") is the comedian on the far left.

(1947) GRAND OLE OPRY ARCHIVES

for us to build a studio in Nashville, and we were the first company to establish a permanent office and permanent employees, including an engineer."

All that because of the influence of the Grand Ole Opry.

It should be noted that perhaps the first recordings of any kind in Nashville were made in 1928, when Victor Records brought in its portable field equipment and cut with several of the Opry string bands. Among them were Sam and Kirk McGee.

"We were outstanding in our field," Kirk quipped later. "And that's where they found us—out standing in the field."

··◦⟦ v ⟧◦·· As 1945 came to a close—it was sometime in December—there was another development at the Grand Ole Opry that would further enhance its colorful history. For in that month a sober-faced, somewhat shy, young Carolina banjo picker named Earl Scruggs joined Bill Monroe's Blue Grass Boys.

Earl was born in 1924 at Flint Hill, North Carolina, in the foothills just east of the Appalachians, some 250 miles from Nashville. His earliest days were filled with music. Two brothers and two sisters played banjo and guitar. So did his father, although he died when Earl was only four. His mother played the organ.

The area around Flint Hill was alive with banjo players who used a "three-finger" style of playing, picking the strings with the thumb and index and middle fingers. It gave a more fluid sound to the banjo and made it a solo instrument instead of using the banjo only for rhythm. Earl, in attempting to duplicate what his neighbors were doing, developed a distinct style all his own. It would later be known as "Scruggs pickin'."

Earl was a child prodigy on the banjo. By the age of six he was performing in public. As a teenager he played with the Carolina Wildcats on a Gastonia radio station, and then with the Morris Brothers on WSPA in Spartanburg, South Carolina. He worked briefly in a textile mill, but he continued to play: with Carl Story on WWNC, Asheville; with "Lost" John Miller in Knoxville.

Miller moved to a Saturday-morning show on WSM in Nashville, Scruggs going with him. But Miller decided to stop playing on the road, and Earl needed a job. He went to talk to Bill Monroe. He was hired.

He joined a Monroe group that consisted of Lester Flatt on guitar, Chubby Wise on fiddle, Cedric Rainwater on bass, Bill Monroe on mandolin. With the addition of Earl's driving banjo there was molded together what many consider to be the finest bluegrass band ever.

A dictionary definition of "bluegrass" says: "country music played at a rapid tempo on unamplified stringed instruments . . . characterized by free improvisation." But Bill Monroe's own definition is more emotional: "It's got a hard drive to it. It's Scotch bagpipes and ole-time fiddlin'. It's Methodist and Holiness and Baptist. It's plain music that tells a good story. It's played from my heart to your heart, and it will touch you. Bluegrass is a music that matters. It's not a music you play, get it over, and forget it."

Earl Scruggs understood that latter definition when he brought his skills to the Grand Ole Opry. Backstage there was much talk about him, and some of the wags went out of their way to report on the new banjo player within the hearing of Uncle Dave Macon, who billed himself as "The World's Greatest Banjo Player."

Macon, goaded by all the stories of Scruggs's three-finger technique, made certain he was in the wings on the night Earl debuted with the Blue Grass Boys. He stood watching the newcomer for a few moments. Then he turned and stalked away.

"He ain't one damned bit funny," Uncle Dave grumbled.

I was waltzing with my darlin'
To the Tennessee Waltz,
When an old friend I happened to see;
Introduced him to my loved one
And while they were waltzing
*My friend stole my sweetheart from me.**

　　—Pee Wee King–Redd Stewart hit,
　　　circa 1946

Eddy Arnold would call 1946 his "golden year."

It might have been the same for the Grand Ole Opry. The war over, business was booming at the Ryman Auditorium. The hottest ticket in town was for an Opry broadcast.

There was a churning of activity, a flux of creativity, a steady flow of new enthusiasm that seemed to overwhelm the old gospel tabernacle. But there was also some discontent. Together it would make 1946 a year not easily dismissed from memory.

First and foremost, without question, was the Opry's loss of its major star.

Roy Acuff quit.

Sponsor, a leading radio trade journal, summed it up in a long, prominently displayed article under the heading: "A STAR WALKS . . ."

"When Roy Acuff, star for seven years on the Grand Ole Opry," the article reported, "decided that he wanted more than folk-music men are usually paid

---

*"Tennessee Waltz" by Redd Stewart and Pee Wee King; copyright 1948 Acuff-Rose/Opryland Music, Inc.

(peanuts) and turned in his notice to the R. J. Reynolds Tobacco Company, the tobacco organization had more than usual star aches. Acuff was almost a religion in the mountain music territory. He had sold thousands of song books . . . a juke box didn't snag its share of nickels unless it had plenty of Acuff discs, and they still say he could have become governor of Tennessee, if he hadn't decided not to run.

"So when William Esty and Company, the advertising agency handling the Reynolds account, was told the sad news, it had trouble, real tall corn trouble. A reasonable facsimile of Acuff, even one better than the original, wouldn't work. The circuit-rider hold that the exiting star had on 'his people' wouldn't disappear just because he was playing one-night stands throughout the country to collect upon his national reputation. Something new had to be added to the Prince Albert section if the Opry was to hit a 13.1 Hooper rating [a very strong rating] in December, 1945, just as it had in December of the previous year."

The narrative of the *Sponsor* article is interrupted here to point out that Acuff didn't only quit "The Prince Albert Show" of the Opry; he severed *all* of his connections with WSM and the Grand Ole Opry.

Acuff never talked much about it, but there was hurt pride involved in it all. He had worked hard to make himself the heart and soul of "The Prince Albert Show" and he was, no one could deny, the Opry's most prominent star. On the road, where he was making good money, and through many lucrative movie offers he had learned what he was worth in dollars and cents. He wanted that recognized by both the Opry and the sponsor. When he was refused what he considered fair remuneration, he left.

Fair remuneration? It is not on the record what he asked for. But whatever it was, Acuff's actions were *not* taken because he needed money. He was the leading country music record seller of the day, he was commanding top dollar on the road, and the Acuff-Rose music publishing company was profitable. And then there were the songbooks.

Years later, in an interview on The Nashville Network, he rather gleefully recounted his experience with songbooks. "I went to Harry Stone," he said, "and asked him about my putting out songbooks. He told me: 'Roy, I don't believe I would if I were you, because Asher Sizemore and Little Jimmy have just about worked that territory out.' I said, 'Well, all my mail is asking for my songs—they really want my songs.' So I came up with the idea of a little folder and I put songs on one side and pictures on the other and sold it for a quarter.

"Mr. Stone didn't think it would go, but he said, 'I'll let you and your boys have ten o'clock [on the Opry broadcast], where you'll have fifteen minutes for eighty-five dollars to sell your song folder.' I went down to a printing company and had them print this thing. I went on the air on a Saturday night with it [the year was 1942]. By Wednesday there was ten thousand letters laying over there in the WSM mailroom! And WSM like to have went wild theirself.

"We didn't live in a house then; we had a house trailer. So WSM rented another trailer and sent six secretaries out there to take care of the mail. And we were carrying the quarters to the bank in big baskets.

"They caught one boy in the WSM mailroom who got to taking some of them quarters himself. And they found out he bought him a big, fine automobile."

It was the potential loss of loyal country music listeners that worried the R. J. Reynolds Tobacco Company when Acuff announced he was leaving in April.

The William Esty and Company advertising agency undertook a broadly based survey to determine how best to replace Acuff. Most listeners wanted the Opry to continue without changes. But it came clear after all of the questioning that a large percentage of Opry fans really wanted *more* music on the show—suggesting the need to replace Roy with an entertainer who was basically a singer.

But what singer? Esty checked all of the available data: record sales, jukebox plays, radio favorites, followed by interviews in the field. And it all came down to just one name: Red Foley.

§[ii]§ Clyde Julian Foley was born the son of a Berea, Kentucky, storekeeper in 1910. His birthplace was a little log cabin between Berea and Blue Lick in the east central part of the state. Before he was old enough to go to school, his father took in an old guitar in barter, and young Red learned to play it, using his thumb instead of a pick. When he went to school, it is said, he had a teacher who used a hickory stick on those who didn't sing loudly enough during the music period in class.

Although he was exposed to music from his earliest days (his father was a left-handed fiddler), it was sports that filled his dreams as he grew. Even then Kentucky schools were basketball oriented, and he used to practice by nailing a barrel hoop to the side of a corncrib and using an inflated hog bladder filled with buckshot as a basketball. In high school, Foley proved to be a good basketball player, and he excelled in track and field as well: 100- and 220-yard dashes, pole vault, shot put, and broad jump.

While he was in high school, his parents decided to give him formal singing lessons. A voice teacher was hired—for two short weeks. It's not clear whether young Foley rebelled against the voice training, or whether there was no more money to continue. The latter is probably true, because the teacher did urge him to enter the Atwater-Kent singing contests (Atwater-Kent manufactured radios), an important competition in those days to seek out talented youngsters for college scholarships.

Red won the local, district, and regional contests in which he sang, qualifying him for the state competition in Louisville. He was seventeen. What happened then was detailed by writer Paul Bryant in *The Mountain Broadcaster and Prairie Recorder*. Bryant said Foley, somewhat shy in those days, was overwhelmed by the big audience and forgot the words to the song he was to sing, "Hold Thou My Hand, Dear Lord."

The lad walked over to his accompanist-teacher and whispered: "What's the next word?" The teacher prompted him and he started over. On the second verse, he again forgot the words, and again started over. He finally finished the song and won third prize in the prestigious contest.

Bryant quoted the judge as having told Red: "Young man, that was one of the great examples of unconscious showmanship any of us have ever witnessed. . . . Your voice is good—yes, but you were awarded one of the prizes on the strength of your grit. Don't ever forget that when the going gets tough."

If his story *had* been a B-movie plot, Foley would have moved on from that experience directly to show business stardom. But it wasn't like that at all. He enrolled at Georgetown College in Kentucky. It was there that a talent scout for "WLS Barn Dance" in Chicago found him and convinced him to join the show.

There was no big money in those deals; opportunity was looked upon as more important than cash. His parents gave him the princely sum of $75 for the trip and, apparently, also gave him warnings about the ways of life in the big city.

"I limped around Chicago for several days," Foley recalled, "with my shoes full of five- and one-dollar bills. I was afraid to get it changed into bigger bills. Finally it got so painful that I took it out and pinned it inside my shirt pocket and kept my vest tightly buttoned. No one ever got to that money but me, but my feet still hurt when I think about that experience."

Bradley Kincaid was the star of the "WLS Barn Dance" when Foley came on the scene in 1930. Gene Autry also was there. One of Foley's initial stints on the show was to do short comedy bits with a girl singer named Lulu Belle, later to team with Skyland Scotty Wiseman in the famous Lulu Belle and Scotty duo.

Red's career developed slowly. A mid-thirties printed program for the "National Barn Dance" (it was now on the network) showed Foley was a member of John Lair's Cumberland Ridge Runners ("Old-Time Fiddling and Kentucky Mountain Songs"), along with Linda Park, "The Sunbonnet Girl," and Slim Miller, Karl Davis, Harty Taylor, and Clayton McMichen. Others on the program were the Prairie Ramblers; the Maple City Four; Grace Wilson, "The Bringing Home the Bacon Girl"; Georgie Gobel, "The Little Cowboy" (later to become a comedic star of radio and television); and Ralph Waldo Emerson, WLS staff organist, with his "Little Haywire Organ."

Tragedy struck Foley in those formative years. His wife, the former Pauline Cox, died during the birth of their only daughter, Betty. But Chicago was where Foley stayed. He made numerous personal appearances on WLS road shows, and he cut some records for the Sears, Roebuck Conqueror label. He also remarried in 1933; his new wife was Eva Overstake, a member of a sister trio on WLS, the Little Maids.

In 1939 Foley went back to Kentucky with John Lair to help organize the "Renfro Valley Barn Dance," another important pioneer country music radio show. It too developed a host of stars, including Homer and Jethro, Martha Carson, Old Joe Clark, and Whitey Ford, the Duke of Paducah. Red stayed for nearly three years at Renfro Valley and then returned to WLS as the star of the "National Barn Dance."

His return to Chicago led to a recording contract with Decca, and he got his own network show, "Avalon Time," with a former burlesque comic, Red Skelton, as the costar. In 1944 Foley had his first major hit on Decca, "Smoke on the

Water," a wartime song that promised victory in the end to the Allied forces. It went to the number-one position on the country music charts.

Thus, when the Grand Ole Opry beckoned in 1946, Red Foley was already an established star, as the substantial research by the Esty agency had clearly shown.

With him to Nashville came a twenty-two-year-old guitar player from Luttrell, Tennessee. His name was Chet Atkins.

···{ iii }··· "I ran into Red," Atkins remembered, "in his manager's office. Actually, I had gone to Chicago to try to meet Foley. Anyway, I played a tune for him and sure enough he said, 'How'd you like to go to Nashville with me, Ches?' Dreams do come true sometimes."

It was in late April 1946 that Foley took over on "The Prince Albert Show."

Minnie Pearl recalled: "Oh, he was the best-lookin' thing. He'd wear a white shirt and a white jacket, sort of zipped up in front—kind of an Eisenhower jacket, you know. And a white hat, black boots, black trousers, very tight; he had a good figure. He was a snappy dresser. Red Foley was snappy—that's the only word that describes him."

For Foley, though, the debut on the Grand Ole Opry was not without its trauma: "I guess I never was more scared than I was the night I replaced Roy Acuff. . . . The people thought I was a Chicago slicker who had come to pass himself off as a country boy and bump Roy out of his job."

Chet Atkins found that Nashville's burgeoning recording business offered much opportunity for a sideman to make extra money. Foley objected.

"Red, he wanted me to be his sideman," Atkins said. "He said, 'I don't want you recordin' for other people, Ches. I want you to play with me.' And I said, 'Hell, I wanna be a star like you, Red.' "

Indeed, Atkins was being given a solid opportunity to be a star in his own right. Each week he played a guitar solo on "The Prince Albert Show"; it was an important featured spot for him. Those were pleasant days and Chet enjoyed the unique ambiance of the Ryman Auditorium.

"I remember hanging out in the alley back of the Ryman," he said laconically, "and talking to the drunks. And watching Robert Lunn, 'The Talking Blues Man,' audition the hopefuls who always crowded around the stage door. He made a lot of them think he was the boss of the Opry. And he'd get 'em to sing and pick the guitar and he'd say, 'Now, can you dance while you're doin' that?' There's an old privy back there, and he'd get 'em up on top and get 'em to dancing and singing and picking on that tin roof."

But after six months the Esty agency's continual "tightening" of "The Prince Albert Show" caught Atkins.

He reminisced: "One day a telex came down from New York and said they didn't want my instrumental anymore. So I got mad and quit."

He would return.

·◦{ iv }◦· It must not be surmised that everything on the Grand Ole Opry floundered during this transitional period on the Prince Albert half hour.

Opry acts were on the road continually. The demand for them was unprecedented. One of the reasons was that a fellow named Jim Denny had taken over as the head of the WSM Artists' Service Bureau and was booking Opry performers everywhere.

Denny had risen through the ranks at the parent National Life and Accident Insurance Company. He had come to Nashville in 1922, at the age of eleven, from Buffalo Valley, Tennessee, a remote hill country village hard by the Cumberland Plateau. His family, the story is told, invested unwisely in mules during World War One and was financially destitute. Young Jim was sent to an aunt in Nashville, put on a bus with forty cents as his total capital.

The city frightened him at first: "I was alone and broke and scared. Heck, even the streetcars scared me. Four people standing together looked like a mob." But there was a toughness in him that allowed him to earn a living on Nashville's streets. He was at one and the same time a newspaper hawker in downtown Nashville and a $12-a-week telegram delivery boy for Western Union. His education was not a classroom thing; he learned about life in the seamier corners of the city.

At sixteen, he got a job in the mail room at National Life and became conscious of the vast amount of Grand Ole Opry mail pouring through his domain. And he saw an opportunity presenting itself. He began to work his way up in the insurance company—first from the mail room to the filing room. He took business courses at Watkins Institute in Nashville and moved up more—from filing to accounting to actuarial. He set up the mechanical accounting and record system for National Life and became a department head.

And to earn a few extra dollars, he was at the Grand Ole Opry every weekend. There he took telephone messages, ran errands, ushered, sold tickets, and even filled in as a bouncer when the occasion required it.

During World War Two he took over the operation of the Opry concessions. By 1946 he was running the artists' service bureau—the Opry booker. Because the Opry had the primary pool of country music talent, Denny ran a virtual booking monopoly. He knew every promoter in the nation and, when people wanted something in Nashville, it was Jim Denny they called.

Sunday through Friday, Opry acts were touring. And then they rushed back to Nashville for the Saturday broadcast. Someday someone will write a book on just that colorful phase of the country music business. When it is written, this next story will have to be included.

"It was a Friday night in 1946," Pee Wee King said in one of the retellings of the tale, "and we were coming back to Nashville from Texarkana. The luggage truck was the easiest place to concentrate. . . . Bill Monroe's 'Kentucky Waltz' was playing on the radio and Redd Stewart said, 'You know, it's odd—we're making a living in Tennessee, but nobody's ever written a Tennessee waltz song.'

"And so we took the old melody that we were using as our theme—the 'No

Name Waltz'—and Redd started writing lyrics on the back of a match box cover. Redd used to smoke cigars. This was one of the reasons he never rode in the limousine—the boys in the limo didn't want the smoke. We used to keep the dome light on in the luggage truck, and I'd make notes—what we'd have to do, what wardrobe to take, where we're going to stay. Anyway, on the back of this match box cover—a big nickel box of matches—Redd had written the lyrics. And we kept putting it together, putting it together."

When they got back to Nashville and turned the song in to Acuff-Rose Publications, Fred Rose did one bit of editing. Stewart's original phrase was "Oh, the Tennessee Waltz, oh, the Tennessee Waltz, / Only you know how much I have lost." That was changed to "I remember the night and the Tennessee Waltz, / Now I know just how much I have lost."

"Tennessee Waltz" was to become one of the most important copyrights in the world of country music. But not because of the recording by the Smoky Mountain Boys, nor because of an almost simultaneous recording by Cowboy Copas. Neither one of those sold a million copies. It wasn't until pop singer Patti Page recorded it in 1950 that it took off—and then it sold *multi*millions. In 1965 "Tennessee Waltz" became an official song of the State of Tennessee. In sum, there have been nearly 500 recordings of the song and sales in excess of $70 million. "I have never heard a bad rendition of it," Pee Wee King has said. "There's no way anyone can butcher it."

If 1946 was important to Pee Wee, it was just as special to his former employee—Eddy Arnold.

"My golden year was 1946," Eddy wrote in his autobiography, *It's a Long Way from Chester County.* "The song 'That's How Much I Love You' started it all.

"As I remember, I don't think I was crazy about the song the first time I heard it. It's a novelty song, and I like them slower than the public does. A ballad, a sentimental ballad, I know right away: I have a feeling for it. But after 'That's How Much I Love You' started hitting, I fell in love with it."

> *Now, if I had a nickel*
> *I know what I would do,*
> *I'd spend it all for candy*
> *And give it all to you . . .*
> *'Cause that's how much I love you, baby,*
> *That's how much I love you.**

"Steve Sholes at RCA Victor," Eddy continued, "had a favorite saying: 'They always sound so much better after they become hits.' How right he was! . . .

"When [manager] Tom Parker arranged for me to host a portion of the Grand

*"That's How Much I Love You" by Eddy Arnold and Wally Fowler; copyright 1943 Vogue Music.

Ole Opry . . . sponsored by the Ralston Purina Company, it was all almost too much for me—the record contract with RCA Victor, royalty checks from my records mounting rapidly, signing autographs, and being in demand. I was sure I'd tumble out of bed and the dream would be over."

Eddy also had a show on the Mutual radio network for Ralston, called "Checkerboard Square Jamboree." Longtime Opry performer Vic Willis, joined with his brothers, Skeeter and Guy, as the Oklahoma Wranglers, remembered it very well:

"It was June of 1946, and we had gotten out of the service about six or seven months before that in Kansas City and were working on a show on a CBS station there—'The Brush Street Follies.' We had sent out several audition discs to other stations, including WSM in Nashville. And Harry Stone called with a combination of things: The blackface team, Jamup and Honey, was looking for someone to go out on the tent show with them, and then there was the 'Checkerboard Square Jamboree' from the old Princess Theater on Church Street, from noon to one every Saturday. Eddy Arnold had one half hour and Ernest Tubb had the other half hour.

"So we said 'Sure' and Stone sent us train tickets and we came to Nashville and they let us do a song on each half hour of the Jamboree—one with Eddy and one with Ernest. Everybody seemed to like us a lot, and they said, 'Well, why don't you come down and sing on the eight-o'clock portion of the Opry,' which was also sponsored by Ralston. And Eddy was the host.

"The Bailes Brothers were on the Opry that night, I remember that. They did a song called 'Dust on the Bible,' and I was impressed with that. And I was *very* impressed with Eddy Arnold; I thought he was something extra."

Arnold, in turn, was impressed with the Oklahoma Wranglers. They became a regular part of his show.

Eddy's backup band in those days included his old, original partner, Speedy McNatt on fiddle, Little Roy Wiggins on steel guitar, Lloyd George (a.k.a. Ken Marvin) on bass, and Rollin Sullivan on rhythm guitar.

Sullivan hailed from Edmonton, Kentucky, where he was raised in a musical family of eight boys and two girls. In 1943 he came to the Grand Ole Opry to play with Paul Howard and the Arkansas Cotton Pickers; in less than two years he was with the Eddy Arnold band.

Teaming with Lloyd George, Sullivan began a comedy act known as "Cicero and Oscar." Sullivan was "Oscar."

"Eddy was a person who liked to be serious with his music," Sullivan recalled. "He said, 'I'm hiring you two guys to do my funnies, so I won't have to stand out there on the stage and pitch straight lines at you. So you just cut up and have yourself a good time. When I come out there it's all over.'

"Now, I had been called Oscar for some time—I was only nineteen years old, playing the mandolin on my first radio program, and the announcer couldn't think of 'Rollin.' He just could *not;* three or four times he had at it and he couldn't think of 'Rollin.' And he said, 'I'm gonna call you Oscar.' Eddy didn't like the name Cicero. He said, 'I want something plain, something everyday.'

"One night we were in Augusta, Georgia—the war was just over, prices were climbing, and hotels were hard to get. If you didn't have a reservation ahead of time you just absolutely wasn't gonna get into a first-rate hotel. So something had happened that we didn't get a reservation and we was downtown in Augusta looking for any place we could find to sleep.

"There was this little hotel, two stories, with no elevator, and we walked in at the desk and Eddy was checking in. And he heard a noise on the stairway; it had kind of a bending stairway. And all at once the desk clerk shouted out: 'Lonzo! Don't you ever bring those dirty linens down the front way no more!'

"Well, Eddy reared back and clapped them hands and he said, 'Ah! Lonzo! That's your name!' So there it was: Lonzo and Oscar."

The Lonzo and Oscar team was popular on Arnold's road show and on the Grand Ole Opry. "And then in 1947," Sullivan said, "Lonzo and Oscar made a record—'I'm My Own Grandpa'—and it sold 3,554,000 in six weeks. I mean, we zoomed right to the top!"

He laughed heartily. "Eddy fired us and the Grand Ole Opry hired us."

Whether it was really a "firing" is not clear. But Arnold himself was headed to greater things. He would write in his autobiography: "I always had the feeling in those days that maybe it wouldn't last; maybe I should save as much money as I could. I always had the horror of winding up a pauper. . . . I guess maybe [that feeling] goes back to seeing my daddy's farm sold out from under us. I don't know; I just know the fear was very real."

··⟩ vi ⟨·· And what of Acuff, the star who had left the Opry? First, it must be said that Roy contended he "had connection with the Opry at all times—through Harry Stone." Proof of that comes in the fact that he continued to bill his show as "Roy Acuff and His Grand Ole Opry Gang." That would not have been possible without Stone's approval.

Then there was the Roy Acuff Tent Theatre of 1946. He had put his own money into the equipment, a substantial investment, and it didn't go too well. The show started from Nashville, moved through the Virginias and Carolinas, then to Pennsylvania and Ohio. From there it snaked through the Deep South, into Texas, and by November it was in Florida. It had been a grueling, seven-day-a-week schedule and Acuff was exhausted. Even though the shows were making some money, Roy believed he could do better with a series of regular engagements. In Florida he called it quits, selling the equipment at a loss.

From California came an offer from Foreman Phillips and Marty Landau, prominent West Coast promoters, for a West Coast tour. Roy accepted and for the first three months of 1947 he covered the state, drawing big crowds everywhere he went. Biographer Schlappi wrote: "Roy had the satisfaction of earning *nightly* the amount the Opry had refused him."

When he returned to Nashville in April he was hospitalized for a minor ailment. Harry Stone and Ernest Tubb came to see him. The conversation at that hospital meeting is reported in Schlappi's biography.

"Harry said, 'Roy, the Opry is losing many of its people, and it looks like maybe we're going under if you don't come back and be with us. Please come and help us out.'

"Roy was surprised that he meant that much to the Grand Ole Opry.

" 'Roy, you mean everything,' Harry assured him. 'We wish that you would change your mind and come back.'

"Roy responded, saying, 'Harry, if I mean that much to WSM and the Grand Ole Opry, I will come back and I will do everything I can to help the Opry at all times.' "

While there doesn't seem to be any documentation that the Grand Ole Opry was in danger of "going under," it can be believed that Harry Stone—and Ernest Tubb—would want Acuff back on the Opry roster. Whatever was said in that hospital room, and whatever deal was struck, Acuff went back on the Opry on April 26, 1947, as host of the "Royal Crown Cola Show."

Smoke, smoke, smoke that cigarette,
Puff, puff, puff it, if you smoke yourself to death;
Tell Saint Peter at the golden gate
That you hates to make him wait,
*But you just gotta have another cigarette!**

—Pop hit, 1947

What was perceived as country music after the war was undergoing drastic changes. There was a new "pop" sound abroad totally unlike the folk tune–oriented "hillbilly" songs that had dominated the Grand Ole Opry.

Country music record charts in the trade magazines were being dominated with the likes of "Smoke, Smoke, Smoke That Cigarette," "So Round, So Firm, So Fully Packed," "New Jolie Blonde," "Divorce Me C.O.D.," and "Sugar Moon." Tin Pan Alley pop songwriters jumped on the rural bandwagon with such pseudo-country hits as "Sioux City Sue," "Doin' What Comes Natur'lly," "Gal in Calico," "Ole Buttermilk Sky," "Shoofly Pie and Apple Pan Dowdy," "Feudin' and Fightin' "—to mention just a few.

And if all that brought some consternation to the general country music community, the specific family behind the scenes at WSM Radio was also in turmoil. In reviewing such matters after the fact, a writer may be inclined to exaggerate

*"Smoke, Smoke, Smoke That Cigarette" by Tex Williams and Merle Travis; copyright 1947 Elvis Presley Music, Inc.; Unichappell Music, Inc.

their importance because of the strong contending personalities involved. But certainly there was trouble in the WSM hierarchy.

When the war ended, John H. (Jack) DeWitt, Jr., who had been the engineering genius behind WSM, returned from the service to be elevated to the presidency of the company. Edwin Craig, the founder, assumed the title of chairman of the board. Those moves put DeWitt in the position of being superior to Harry Stone, the longtime general manager of the station. The two men did not get along at all. One who was there at the time said: "Harry continued to run the property, and ignored DeWitt and refused to accept him."

Such a circumstance had to become intolerable. Before the forties ended, Stone was out, offering his resignation during a heated exchange with DeWitt and having it immediately accepted.

To a lot of people on the Grand Ole Opry the internecine warfare in the executive offices was of little consequence. But Eddy Arnold remembered Harry Stone's kindnesses to him when he was struggling to establish himself as a solo artist. "After Harry was out," Eddy said simply, "he had no income and I put him on salary for a time."

··◦[ii]◦·· At the Grand Ole Opry itself there were more additions to the roster. In spite of the pop influence invading the Ryman Auditorium one of the new acts was a *pure* country performer named Grandpa Jones.

Louis Marshall Jones came by his country music heritage naturally. Born in 1913, in Niagra, Kentucky, a small town near the Indiana border, he was the youngest of ten children. His father, a sharecropper, had been a fiddle player; his mother played the concertina. But it really wasn't music that dominated their home; it was work.

"Back then you raised tobacco," Jones recalled. "Thought you'd starve to death if you didn't raise tobacco, where we were from. You had to do everything by hand then—plant it, burn the plant beds, plow it with a walkin' plow, hoe it. I hated it. But I think it does you good to be poor when you start out. You enjoy a lot of other things better."

The Jones family moved around a lot while young Marshall (he was rarely called Louis) was growing up. "We moved about every two years. We moved so much that every time the wagon backed up to the door the chickens laid down and crossed their legs."

On one of the farms on which they lived, Grandpa remembered, "A sawmill was set up to take out some of the lumber that was plentiful there at the time. The workers lived in tents and one came to the house askin' to leave his git-tar so the moisture wouldn't hurt it.

"I got to sneakin' in and foolin' with that git-tar when I was about ten, and that was my first real introduction to a musical instrument."

When the worker left, so did the guitar, and the youngest Jones could only dream about having one of his own. His recollection was that a brother came home with a guitar one day for Marshall. "I like to went wild, seein' that git-tar, 'cause

I'd been wantin' one for so long. He got it at some old junkyard called Cheap John's. Paid seventy-five cents for it."

With that guitar, and with his friend Miff McKinley, also an amateur musician, Jones began playing local dances and parties.

In 1928 the family moved again, this time to Akron, Ohio, where the elder Jones hoped to get a job in a rubber plant. Marshall was enrolled in Akron's West High School, where he was painfully shy. But city life was to provide him with his first break. The year was 1930.

"There was a week-long amateur contest held in the Keith-Albee Theater," Grandpa said, "and it was sponsored by Wendell Hall, the old redheaded music maker who had that famous record 'It Ain't Gonna Rain No Mo'.' There were 450 contestants an' he'd go through an' weed 'em out every night. At the end of the week I won first place. The two songs I sang were 'Dear Old Sunny South by the Sea' and 'Goin' Back to Texas.'

"I won fifty dollars in ten-dollar gold pieces, so of course I went right out an' bought a better git-tar!"

The very next day he was given a radio show on WJW in Akron. It was an early-morning stint and he was billed as "The Young Singer of Old Songs." It wasn't long before he teamed up with the harmonica player Joe Troyan, and they made their way to Cleveland. In 1934 a Cleveland newspaper columnist wrote: "Word from WHK . . . reveals big things about Zeke and Harve, better known as Marshall Jones and Joe Troyan. . . . Jones has more than 500 songs of the hillbilly type in his library. Troyan hails from Cambridge, Ohio, and can do more tricks with his harmonica than a big-time magician. He carries 100 different harmonicas and can play two at a time."

That act drew the attention of Warren Caplinger and Andy Patterson, who had been recording artists in the twenties and then were talent scouts for the popular "Lum and Abner" radio show. Jones and Troyan became members of the house band for "Lum and Abner." When the show moved from Cleveland to Chicago, the young musicians elected to move to WBZ in Boston, where they joined the troupe of Bradley Kincaid. Marshall Jones's career was to change completely.

"We'd play the little theaters in New England," Jones reminisced, "performin' between pictures. Up on the East Coast as far as Maine, an' then drive back an' play an early-mornin' radio show. I never got enough sleep, an' Kincaid would say, 'Come on an' get up here to the microphone; you're just like an old grandpa.'

"Of course, I talked then like I do now, an' people got to writin' an' askin': 'How old is that old man? He sounds like he's eighty.' So we got the idea of makin' an old man out of me."

To enhance the "Grandpa" image, Kincaid gave him an old pair of mountain boots to wear; he told Jones they were already fifty years old. Lines were drawn on his face to suggest wrinkles, and a well-known blackface comedian of the era, one Bert Swor, helped Jones rig up his first mustache. From that time on—it was 1935 and Marshall Jones was only twenty-two—he was billed as "Grandpa Jones."

Eddy Arnold, at the microphone, began his solo career at the Opry as host of the Ralston Purina segment in 1946. With him are (from the left) Oscar Sullivan, Chubby Wise, Ken Marvin ("Lonzo"), Arnold, and Harold Bradley.

(1947) GRAND OLE OPRY ARCHIVES

Red Foley and Lulu Belle when they performed comedy bits for radio station WLS in Chicago.

(C. 1930) GRAND OLE OPRY ARCHIVES

Lonzo and Oscar did comedy sketches on the Ralston Purina portion of the Opry in the late 1940s. From the left are Vito Pellettieri (Opry stage manager), Harold Bradley, Oscar Sullivan, Chuck Wright, Ken Marvin ("Lonzo"), and Guy Willis.
(1947) *GRAND OLE OPRY ARCHIVES*

An early photograph of Grandpa Jones at his farm with one of his hunting dogs. The bushy mustache, the white eyebrows, and the numerous wrinkles were all a necessary part of his costume in the days when he was still a young man.
(C. 1947) *GRAND OLE OPRY ARCHIVES*

Red Foley, on the left, goes boating with Harry Stone on Old Hickory Lake near Nashville. Many of the Opry stars of this period bought boats with their earnings.
(1946) *GRAND OLE OPRY ARCHIVES*

The boots, resoled many times since then, are still used today. And the mustache of today is real. Obviously, the boots are dear to him. There's one story that when he was playing a park in Maryland some years back a drunken woman broke into his dressing room and made off with the boots. Jones was furious. When he found the woman, she had passed out on a hilltop above the park—with his boots on. "I tried to pull them off," he said, "and I guess I drug her halfway down the hill."

He worked a great deal, never making much money. There were stints on several West Virginia radio stations: WWVA in Wheeling, WCHS in Charleston, WMNN in Fairmont. Then, in 1942, Jones moved to WLW in Cincinnati to join the "Boone County Jamboree." There he met Alton and Rabon Delmore, Merle Travis, and Ramona Riggins, later to become his second wife. He also met a record store owner, Syd Nathan, who had an idea about starting his own record label. Grandpa Jones was one of the first to record for Nathan's King Records.

World War Two intruded on Grandpa's career; in the Army he tried to get assigned to Special Services, but he wound up instead as an MP in Germany. But he did organize a band called the Munich Mountaineers and broadcast daily over the Armed Forces Radio Network.

His Army stint ended, he went back to WLW. "You know at that time," he said, "when you come back from the Army who you was working for had to give you your job back—you remember that? When I got back to WLW the guy said, 'Well, I guess we'll *have* to give you your job back.' And it just sort of struck me bad, you know, and I said, 'No, you don't have to. I'll just leave.' And I just left. I came to Nashville an' started with Pee Wee King on a tent show. After I worked with him for a while they finally let me do a tune or two on the Opry."

The Grand Ole Opry got a thorough professional in Grandpa Jones. And although the money still wasn't great, he enjoyed working with the old-timers on the show.

"Uncle Dave was here," he said, "and I played some dates with him. I remember he rode home from Columbus with me. . . . He got to tellin' me a lot about his wagon train, you know, and a lot of things, and then he said, 'Well, I believe I'll take me a little nap.'

"An' he got back there and put on that hood—he had a hood—and he slept for a while. That night, we decided to stop at a motel, and he said, 'What time you get up?'

"I said, 'Oh, 'bout seven o'clock.'

"He said, 'Well, I'll be down in the restaurant.'

"So when I got down there the next mornin' he had on a bib, an' he had pancakes, an' he had a jar of homemade cherry preserves. An' he said, 'I'll tell you these cherry preserves beat that syrup all to pieces.'

"He got them preserves out of that little black bag he carried." Grandpa laughed. "There was no a-tellin' what he had in there."

❧[iii]❧ There were other Grand Ole Opry stirrings in 1947. Minnie Pearl got married in February to Henry Cannon, a commercial pilot who flew Minnie to many of her engagements. "I'm the luckiest girl in show business," she quipped. "I married my transportation."

Roy Acuff, conscious of all of the profitable country music parks that had sprung up around the country since the end of the war, got into that business himself. He bought a run-down old resort called Dunbar Cave at Clarksville, Tennessee, and began to refurbish it.

Ernest Tubb, who had already established a retail record shop on Nashville's Broadway, just around the corner from the Ryman Auditorium, bought an hour of time from WSM Radio and began a Saturday live show that would follow the Opry broadcast. He called it "Midnight Jamboree." In time it would become a starting point for many country music careers.

And Pee Wee King, ever conscious of the new developments in his business, wanted to get into television.

"In 1947, sorry to say," King remembered, "Nashville did not have television and from all indications was not interested in television. But we had an opportunity to open up on a new television station in Louisville and we thought that's where the future was going to be. So we decided to leave the Opry. And people said, 'You're crazy to leave the Opry and dig into something like television.' Mr. Craig actually told me, 'Pee Wee, it's a fad. It'll never make it.'

"So we went to Louisville with a one-year contract and stayed for twenty-one years."

···❧[iv]❧··· Although they were heard in the major metropolitan areas each week on the NBC radio network, the Grand Ole Opry acts had never really challenged the audiences of the biggest cities.

Then, in the fall of 1947, Ernest Tubb put together a country music package and took it into the bastion of classical music, New York's Carnegie Hall. Tubb and the Texas Troubadours headlined the show, which also offered Minnie Pearl, singer Rosalie Allen, the harmony team of Radio Dot and Smokey Swann, the Short Brothers, Jimmie and Leon, and George Hay, The Solemn Old Judge, as the master of ceremonies.

It drew well, and Tubb was quoted in at least one Manhattan newspaper as having said of Carnegie Hall: "This place'd hold a lot of hay."

"Whether he actually said it, I don't know," Minnie Pearl commented. "There wasn't much press coverage, as I remember. We were reviewed in *Variety* and panned, and I was pretty down about that."

There was no reason for Minnie to be "down," however, on the evening of Friday, October 31, 1947, when a Grand Ole Opry group played Constitution Hall in Washington, D.C. The promoter was a fellow who had come from Lizard Lick, North Carolina—Connie B. Gay.

Gay was a genuine entrepreneur who was absolutely convinced that country music was a salable commodity in the big cities of the nation. In the thirties he had supported himself as a street-corner pitchman. His product was a pocketknife sharpener, purchased for five cents apiece from a carnival supplier in Chicago, and "sold for a quarter in hick towns and for fifty cents in sucker towns like Washington."

A lesson had been learned: The so-called sophistication of the big city was a myth.

After the war, he set out to test his theories. In November 1946, with $1,000 as his total capital, he went to radio station WARL in Arlington, Virginia, which served the metropolitan Washington area. He told program manager Frank Blair (later on NBC's "Today" show) that he wanted one hour for a disc jockey show he meant to call "Town and Country Time."

"Blair thought I was crazy," Connie remembered. "But I told him I didn't want any salary; I'd just take a percentage from the sponsors. A *high* percentage, but then there weren't any sponsors in sight."

He broadcast from the basement of his home. "It took off like Blaylock's bull," he said. The program was soon expanded to three hours. "I couldn't beat the sponsors off with a stick. It was Katie-bar-the-door from then on. The show would sell anything. But I always kept half the commercial time for selling Connie B. Gay."

And that was selling something special: Connie B. Gay excursion trains to the Grand Ole Opry in Nashville; Connie B. Gay country music moonlight cruises on the Potomac River; Connie B. Gay country music concerts at Griffith Stadium; chartered country music square-dance trains from Washington and Baltimore to colorfully named Paw Paw, West Virginia; and the "Connie B. Gay Hillbilly Air Show" at Bailey's Crossroads in Virginia—stunt men in the air, country music on the ground, and 50,000 paid customers.

And then there was Constitution Hall. Owned by the Daughters of the American Revolution, Constitution Hall had housed an annual national folk festival prior to Pearl Harbor, and the DAR ladies were under the impression that that was the type of show Connie Gay had in mind when he approached them to rent the hall. He did nothing to dissuade them of that impression.

Thus, with a Grand Ole Opry package, Gay sold out Constitution Hall on the last evening of October, on an invitation-only basis. Invitations went out to cabinet members, senators, congressmen, lobbyists, diplomats, the "best society" of the nation's capital. For a six-dollar top.

"Oh, the other promoters laughed when I started to work on that," Connie said, "but I knew what the people I had booked were worth, and I wouldn't sell them for less. If you wanted to hear Eddy Arnold, Minnie Pearl, Rod Brasfield, T. Texas Tyler, Judge George D. Hay, Cowboy Copas, and Kitty Wells, you had to make it worth their trouble—and mine. I grossed twenty-two thousand dollars that night!"

The Solemn Old Judge opened the evening with a little talk about the Opry:
"We are not going to tell any jokes about Congress tonight," he told the

distinguished audience, "because Congress has a much better show than we have."

That was to be one of Hay's last appearances with an Opry troupe. A serious emotional breakdown followed shortly thereafter, virtually ending his career. On a limited basis he stayed around the Opry for the next decade, making brief appearances on the microphones. He also did, for a time, a series of short weekly radio talks about Opry stars.

A few of those talks have been preserved on audiotape. They are sad and spiritless. Each opens and closes with the blowing of Hushpuckena, the steamboat whistle. And then he ad-libs his stories, often failing to make a point before the time runs out. They show none of the enthusiasm George Dewey Hay, The Solemn Old Judge, once had for his beloved Grand Ole Opry.

Thus, as 1947 came to a close, Jim Denny, hard-driving head of the WSM Artists' Service Bureau, also became the manager of country music's premier radio show.

I'm sending you a big bouquet of roses,
One for ev'ry time you broke my heart;
And as the door of love between us closes,
*Tears will fall like petals when we part.**

—Eddy Arnold hit, circa 1948

On January 3, 1948, Grand Ole Opry star Eddy Arnold had the number-one record on the country music charts with "I'll Hold You in My Heart." It would stay number one for thirteen weeks. Before the year would end Arnold would have total domination of the country music charts, or nearly so. With the lone exception of "One Has My Name," by Jimmy Wakely, every other number-one record in '48 would be an Eddy Arnold record! No other country artist had ever done that; not Jimmie Rodgers, not Gene Autry, not Roy Acuff, not Ernest Tubb, not Red Foley. No one.

Even four decades later, as this narrative is being written, that mark is so impressive that it becomes necessary to detail the chart dominance:

January 3–April 2: "I'll Hold You in My Heart"
April 3–June 4: "Anytime"
June 5–June 18: "Texarkana Baby"
June 19–July 2: "Bouquet of Roses"

*"Bouquet of Roses" by Steve Nelson and Bob Hilliard; copyright 1948 Hill and Range Songs, Inc.

July 3–July 9: "Texarkana Baby"
July 10–October 8: "Bouquet of Roses"
October 9–October 15: "Just a Little Lovin' "
October 16–November 5: "Bouquet of Roses"
November 6–November 12: "Just a Little Lovin' "
November 13–December 3: "Bouquet of Roses"
December 4–December 24: "One Has My Name" (Jimmy Wakely)
December 25 into 1949: "Bouquet of Roses"

Arnold's manager, the mercurial and tough Colonel Tom Parker, moved quickly to capitalize on Eddy's amazing popularity. He had already placed him on a daily fifteen-minute show on the Mutual radio network for Ralston Purina. That show, broadcast from the Maxwell House in Nashville, opened each day with another Arnold standard, "Cattle Call."

Parker went to the WSM officials and made an audacious demand: He wanted a cut of the Grand Ole Opry gate receipts for his singer. With such a demand Eddy Arnold's days on the Grand Ole Opry were numbered.

When Parker was turned down—to no one's surprise—Eddy was faced with saying good-bye on the Opry. In his autobiography he wrote: "I had to give up my job hosting on the Grand Ole Opry, and all of my activities on WSM. It took Tom quite a while to convince me I had to do that, 'cause my ties were emotional there. It just didn't seem right to leave performers and friends like Minnie Pearl, Roy Acuff, Uncle Dave Macon, and that wonderful programmer for the Opry, Vito Pellettieri. I loved those people. I admired them. For years, my only ambition had been to work with them. . . .

"It was a real wrench to leave, but I knew if I were to keep goin' upward, I had to. It was 1948, nearly five years since Harry Stone had put his faith in me, and my world had changed. I didn't really know whether it was for better or for worse, the night I walked to the center of the stage on the Grand Ole Opry and told the audience I was resigning.

"I told them it was my last performance, and I felt inside as if it were my last performance anywhere. I thanked the people for being so kind to me, and I thanked Harry Stone and the station . . . then I hurried off stage and cried in the wings."

That final moment on the Opry was not a sudden thing, of course. A good many weeks had been taken in negotiations between Parker and the WSM executives. And during that time, when it came clear that a deal could not be struck to keep Arnold, Opry manager Jim Denny moved swiftly to replace him with another "sweet singer."

His selection was George Morgan, a native of Waverly, Tennessee, who at that time was a star of the WWVA "Wheeling Jamboree" after stints on WAKR, Akron, Ohio, and WWST, Wooster, Ohio.

Morgan was not familiar with Nashville and wasn't sure about the location of the Ryman Auditorium. He approached a man standing on the curb on Fifth Avenue: "Can you tell me where the Grand Ole Opryhouse is?"

The man laughed. "It's right behind you," he replied.

His informant was Eddy Arnold.

·⊰[ii]⊱· Morgan wasn't the only new member of the Opry that year. Little Jimmy Dickens also was added to the roster.

"I was working in Saginaw, Michigan, on a small station there with a five-piece band," he recollected, "and Mr. Acuff came to our city. I had made his acquaintance before that in Cincinnati in 1945. And then in '48, why, he asked me if I would come down to the Grand Ole Opry, and at that particular time Red Foley had the network show for the Prince Albert people on NBC. I came as a guest. . . .

"I had ten years of radio experience doing shows across the country . . . and I thought I was ready for that—you know, I was over the stage fright and all that. But when I walked on that stage of the Ryman I've never been no more scared and shook up in all my life. My knees were knockin' and I couldn't understand it, because I thought I was ready for that, but I wasn't.

"But I did very well, luckily—I mean as far as response was concerned—and then a month later they asked me to come down again, and when I came that time Mr. Acuff asked me if I would be interested in staying."

It had been a hard road to travel for Jimmy Dickens to get to the Opry from Bolt, West Virginia.

"My first performance on radio," he remembered, "was with my uncle and a couple of other guys called the Acorn Twins; a little fifteen-minute program. And where they went, I went. I didn't play guitar at that time—I was young, seventeen, still in junior high school—and I'd tag along with them. We were opening the station in the morning and they'd let me crow like a rooster. That would be my part."

Crowing like a rooster may have been demeaning to some, but not to Jimmy. He was a coal miner's son—youngest of thirteen children, five boys and eight girls, and he knew one thing for certain: He didn't want to mine coal.

"Boy, I was shootin' to be able to sing, you know," he said, "and I was doin' what they told me to do. I crowed like a rooster. But after that I worked with some professional groups like the Bailes Brothers and Molly O'Day. She was there on that radio station in Beckley, West Virginia.

"Johnny Bailes was the first person to have me sing on the radio. I sang one hymn a day on the [WJLS] show, and I performed at coal mining camps, small theaters, and in high school auditoriums with them. The Bailes Brothers taught me a lot about stage presence. They were good teachers. When I worked with them they treated me like a little boy. I think they just kept me as their mascot." Jimmy was eighteen at the time; four feet, eleven inches tall—which is his height today.

Within eighteen months he had moved on to WMNN in Fairmont, West Virginia, where he worked with Grandpa Jones and T. Texas Tyler. "Tyler took a likin' to me and when he left Fairmont to go to Indianapolis, he invited me to come along with him. And I went to Indianapolis and worked three years with T. Texas Tyler as a duet. We did harmony work—a good little duet. We had to train a long time for it, but we worked up a fine little country act and did basically all gospel. But we did real well there during World War Two."

There followed stints as a solo artist on the WLW, Cincinnati, "Midwestern Hayride," and on WIBW, Topeka, Kansas, and WKNX, Saginaw, Michigan. It was there that he crossed paths with Roy Acuff.

It's interesting to note that when Little Jimmy Dickens first came to the Grand Ole Opry he had no background at all as a recording artist. But being on the Opry brought him to the attention of Columbia Records, and his very first release, "Take a Cold Tater and Wait," was a smash hit.

❧[iii]❧ In the spring of 1948 there was a major development within one of the Opry's best bands—Bill Monroe's Blue Grass Boys. Banjoist Earl Scruggs left; Lester Flatt followed a few weeks later.

The three years they had been with Monroe—a long time considering the "revolving door" personnel changes in country music bands—had been vastly important ones for the Blue Grass Boys. *That* band had made history. Musicologists contend to this day that there never had been a better five-piece band in country music. Some of the songs they played are used by all bluegrass groups today: "Will You Be Loving Another Man," "Sweetheart You Done Me Wrong," "The Wicked Path of Sin," "I'm Going Back to Old Kentucky," "Toy Heart," "My Rose of Old Kentucky," and, of course, Monroe's classic, "Blue Moon of Kentucky."

With Flatt and Scruggs the Monroe band had recorded more than ever before—twenty-eight records in just two years. But anyone who worked for Bill Monroe toured a lot; he was on the road incessantly. That was one of the reasons Flatt and Scruggs left the Blue Grass Boys.

The departures, apparently, were *not* because they intended to start their own band. Yet within a month they started playing together and talking about looking for radio gigs. They recruited other sidemen: fiddler Jim Shumate, bassist Cedric Rainwater (his real name was Howard Watts), and guitarist Mac Wiseman. It was a "tight" group musically and they played on radio stations in Virginia and North Carolina. They also started recording for Mercury, taking the name of the Foggy Mountain Boys from the theme song they had chosen, A. P. Carter's standard, "Foggy Mountain Top."

There was no effort, however, to recruit them for the Grand Ole Opry. The Opry, after all, had the original: William Smith Monroe.

❧[iv]❧ A 1948 development that was to leave its mark on the Opry for a decade took place on "The Prince Albert Show."

Comedian Whitey Ford, the Duke of Paducah, had a disagreement with the R. J. Reynolds Tobacco Company and its advertising agency, and was replaced on the Prince Albert half hour by Rod Brasfield. Ford was used elsewhere on the Opry, but the honest truth is that when Brasfield went on the network portion of the show, and was teamed with Minnie Pearl, every comic on the Opry was eclipsed.

There was a rapport between Rod and Minnie, a chemistry, a magic, that was unique. Minnie Pearl said she was more funny when Brasfield worked with her, not because of any material especially, but because "I thought funny around him because I knew what the fool was thinking."

The basic scripts, including the comedy routines, were written in New York. "We had to come in off the road," Minnie recalled, "and go to Studio C on the fifth floor of the National Life building for rehearsal. And Rod and I would sit there and go over our material. We were allowed to edit it. They had given us free rein. If we didn't like any of it we could do our own stuff."

"Rod was so much smarter than me that he could just run rings around me, and he knew it. Sometimes on the network he would get me way off the routine we were supposed to be doing, just for the fun of gradually pulling me back into it again."

Putting the routines down on paper again—as we are about to do here—is sometimes unsatisfying. The jokes are somewhat dated now, some quarter of a century after the fact, and the printed word fails to transmit the nuances. But Brasfield, when he put on his oversized coat and his baggy pants and his undersized battered hat, and jammed his hands into his pockets and sauntered onto the stage in a kind of tentative and apologetic way, displayed a vulnerability about him that audiences loved instinctively.

He'd come on "The Prince Albert Show" to great applause and say, "Hi-dee, friends." And then he'd give the weather; those reports depended more on his mood than on the temperature. He'd say, "It's hot tonight, ain't it?" Or just as likely, "Ain't so hot tonight, is it?" and people would laugh. He made even those innocuous words funny.

Some examples of his routines have come down to us from the scripts of the shows. There was this item from November 20, 1948:

"By Ned, Buck, I don't know what restaurants are thinkin' about these days!"

"What's wrong *now*, Rod?" That from Louie Buck, an announcer on the show.

"I went in to have my supper tonight and I had a steak and I asked the waiter how it was cooked and he said it was smothered in onions. I took one bite and said, 'Boy, it sure died hard!' "

And another example:

Minnie: "Did I ever tell you what a lazy baby Brother was, Rod?"

Rod: "I don't believe you did, Minnie."

Minnie: "Well, Brother was so lazy he wouldn't shake his rattle like other babies do."

Rod: "Your brother was too lazy to shake his rattle?"

Minnie: "Yep. He'd jes' lay it on his stomach an' wait till he got the hiccups!"

Week after week it went on that way, to the delight of the millions listening to the NBC network broadcast of the Grand Ole Opry.

A lot of the jokes were about the frustrations of dealing with the opposite sex; "old maid" Minnie never getting asked to marry by her boyfriend, Hezzie, and Rodney, with a kind of worldly innocence, not really having much luck at all with women.

Example:

Rod: "Miss Minnie, I gotta be goin' now. I'm a-goin' over to my girlfriend Suzie's tonight."

Minnie: "Oh! Is Suzie entertaining?"

Rod: (after a meaningful pause) "Ohhh . . . not very, Miss Minnie."

Or:

Minnie: "Rod, do you know they're havin' just the grandest party down at Grinder's Switch tonight? How would you like to go to it with me?"

Rod: "Well, by Ned, Miss Minnie, you know I'd just love to go to the party with you. But I cain't tonight. I already promised Lem Puckett I'd help him get his pigs back in. They've rooted out of the fence, Miss Minnie."

Minnie: "Oh, Lem Puckett's pigs! Come on and go to the party. You'll have more fun there than you will chasing a bunch of hogs."

Rod: "But I already promised Lem, Miss Minnie."

Minnie: "Rodney, what do you care about Lem's pigs? Why, do you know there's talk they may even play a game of post office at the party?"

Rod: (mugging appreciatively at the thought; then sadly, almost as a confession) "Miss Minnie, I haven't sent a letter in years."

Laughter wells up from the audience. Just as the last of it dies away—

Rod: "Not even a postcard, Miss Minnie."

When they made personal appearances together on the road, free of the "continuity acceptance" people at the network, they had a routine that was a guaranteed laugh-getter, again largely on the basis of Brasfield's vulnerability. He was the perennial loser in his quest for a woman.

This particular "shtick" began with Brasfield coming onstage and rather boldly asking Minnie to sit down beside him.

She refused. "We don't have any chairs, Rodney."

With that, Rod would scurry offstage and return quickly with two chairs. They'd sit down and he would ask her for permission to put his arm around her. Protesting his "foolishness," she finally consented.

Then, acting the suave, sure-of-himself man-about-town, Brasfield would ask for a kiss.

Minnie feigned shock at first, but would finally tell him to close his eyes and promise not to look. He would, his mobile face mirroring a delirious joy at the thought of getting the kiss.

Then she would get up from her chair, move to the wings, and return in a second or two with a stocking-clad wooden leg, which she placed in the crook of his arm. Warning him again not to open his eyes, she quietly left the stage.

Rod just sat there alone, his eyes squeezed shut, a sad little man in a too-big coat. His hand touched the leg and the audience was convulsed in laughter as his face displayed a half-dozen kinds of delight. Rapture, even.

Then doubt. Maybe even a little shame. "Miss Minnie!" There was alarm in his voice now. "This ain't like you, Miss Minnie! What's got into you?!" But the hand continued to explore the forbidden leg until he touched the top. Only then did he realize he had been tricked.

"And I'd come to the edge of the stage," Minnie said, "and I'd be cackling up a storm at him. He would slowly open one eye and peek over at me. Then he would open both eyes wide and holler, '*Oh . . . Miss . . . Minnie!*' "

Embarrassed. But glad, too, that the leg hadn't really been that of Minnie Pearl.

Chase music would start, Rod would sweep up the chairs and the wooden leg and rush off the stage, the audience roaring its approval.

*There's a man that turned this country upside down
With his old-age pension rumor going 'round.
If you want in on the fun,
Send your dime to Washington,
And that old-age pension man will be around.**

—Satirical song, circa 1930s

I do not intend on keeping this matter flying around in the air," Roy Acuff said from the stage of the Grand Ole Opry. "I want to announce tonight that I am making the race for governor of Tennessee and making it to win.

"I have been nominated three times, friends; two times I refused to accept the nomination. I had my reasons and the reasons were good. This year I told them to leave my name on.

"I feel qualified for the job, for I started out as a business and have tried to build it as time passed. It isn't easy for a country boy like me to stand up here and try to make a political speech. I intend on staying up here with you, being one of you, and I promise not to bring politics again to the Grand Ole Opry."

Thus, in the summer of 1948, the King of Country Music was squarely into elective politics. He was a Republican (a "Yankee Republican," someone said) and proud of it. "My dad was a general sessions judge in Knox County," he explained, "and my granddad served in the Tennessee House of Representatives. I reckon it's in my blood."

If he was more moderate than most Tennessee Republicans of those days, he was still *staunchly* Republican. When songwriters Ralph Fulton and Sam "Dynamite" Hatcher turned out "Old Age Pension Check" in 1937, satirizing the Roosevelt New Deal and its cradle-to-the-grave welfare philosophy, Acuff bought all rights to the song, edited some of the lyrics, and eventually had it copyrighted by Acuff-Rose Publications.

Once again in 1948 his name had been placed on the primary ballot, with his acquiescence if not his announced approval. He was in Hollywood making a movie, *Smoky Mountain Melody*, when he learned he had been nominated without making a campaign of any kind. His primary opponent had been whipped by a margin of four to one.

This time, then, Acuff decided to run, even though his general election opponent would be a close friend, Democrat Gordon Browning. "If I have to criticize him," Roy said, "I'll withdraw." That may have been one of the reasons he decided to run in '48, believing that the gubernatorial campaign could be kept on a high level, without vitriol.

The other major contest in Tennessee that year was for a United States Senate seat, pitting longtime Republican congressman B. Carroll Reece against a young Democratic reformer, Estes Kefauver, who had beaten the entrenched and infamous "Boss" Crump machine of Memphis to get the nomination. On the national scene, President Harry Truman was seeking the office again on his own; few gave him much chance against the popular New York governor, Thomas E. Dewey.

Acuff campaigned as only he could, with the Smoky Mountain Boys at his side (Rachel Veach came out of retirement to join them). He worked hard, campaigning assiduously Monday through Friday. Saturday he had to be back in Nashville for the Grand Ole Opry; Sunday was a day off. And he discussed the issues with hill-country logic: TVA, more roads for Tennessee, tourism, labor, schools and education, taxes; he dodged nothing.

He drew massive crowds. One newspaper account said; "Boy! I've never seen anything like it. They're really coming out to hear Roy. The thing is, they're coming out clapping their hands and patting their feet to hear sweet mountain music. But they're going home with thoughtful brows and muttering in their beards over the seriousness, the earnestness and the homespun honesty of Roy Acuff. Oh, he still sings and fiddles, but they meet a new man, a plain, sincere man who impressed them as a fellow who wants to be governor to serve the average citizen, to do his best for the people regardless of party affiliation.

"It's evident that they are sold on Roy Acuff as an honest politician, just as much as they were sold on Roy Acuff the troubadour. How many of them will come back and vote for him, however, I don't know."

That was the key to it all: Could Acuff's popularity as an entertainer be translated into votes at the polls?

Senatorial candidate Reece appeared on the same platform with Acuff as often as possible; he wanted the exposure to Roy's big crowds. But there was one insider story that Reece, who controlled GOP patronage in the state after twenty-four years in the House of Representatives, didn't want a Republican governor to challenge his patronage hold. It was said that Reece supported Acuff only because he believed the Grand Ole Opry star could not win.

Democrats were worried by the masses Acuff was drawing in his campaign appearances. While opponent Gordon Browning kept on a high plain, other Democratic leaders were starting to poke fun at the "hillbilly fiddler" who wanted to be governor. And that finally was taken up by the newspapers who supported Democrat Browning. One Acuff rally at Sparta was reported by the *Nashville Tennessean* in this manner:

"Roy Acuff, hillbilly entertainer, found here last night that he could not hold his crowd for a full thirty-minute political address. The experience apparently rattled him. The crowd here began to empty the grandstand at Austin Athletic Field early in Acuff's speech. Acuff's anxiety apparently increased as the audience diminished and his irritation evidently resulted in his charge that the newspapers are 'making fun of me and my music.' "

As the "hillbilly fiddler" needling continued, Acuff finally struck back in a speech:

"Some of the people who have been active in this campaign, and especially some of the newspapers, have tried to make fun of me as a hillbilly fiddler; and have used various other forms of ridicule about me.

"Well, friends, I have no apologies for the kind of music I have been bringing to my people. . . . It is the folk music of the South, the songs and the hoedowns handed down from the sturdy pioneers who made Tennessee, and I am proud to do my part toward preserving it for the future. My people love it, because it is the music of their parents and grandparents. That's why three or four thousand of them come to the Ryman Auditorium every Saturday night and thousands of others listen on the radio; not just to hear me but to hear all those other fine boys and girls who play and sing this kind of music. I *am* a hillbilly fiddler and singer, and if that's a crime, I'll have to plead guilty to it. I'll even go farther than that and tell you I am *proud of it!*"

Acuff had taken no contributions to support his campaign. Not a dime. He paid for it all entirely out of his own pocket.

On the night before the election, 20,000 showed up in front of the War Memorial Building in Nashville to hear the music of Roy Acuff and the Smoky Mountain Boys, and to hear him say: "If you vote for me, I want to tell you now that I pledge you you'll never have cause to regret it. And for your support I thank you from the bottom of my heart."

The next day he learned that his great popularity could not be translated into enough votes to become governor. Gordon Browning beat him two to one. Carroll Reece lost too, and Estes Kefauver would go on to Washington to become a national figure. On the national scene, Harry Truman scored a stunning upset over Republican Tom Dewey.

Yet Acuff had received more than 167,000 votes—more than any other Republican candidate had ever received in a Tennessee state race.

Roy's wife, Mildred, breathed a sigh of relief; she had never wanted to see him as governor.

Acuff himself summed it up simply: "As governor, I would have been just another politician. As a singer, I can be Roy Acuff."

·◦⟨ ii ⟩◦· If there was disappointment at the Grand Ole Opry over Acuff's gubernatorial defeat, there was also concern in the executive offices of WSM because of a new challenge that seemed to strike at the very heart of the Opry's rock-solid hold on the Saturday night prime-time hours.

It came, although indirectly, from Tom Parker, Eddy Arnold's hard-nosed manager, who had already been instrumental in removing Eddy from the Opry roster. And it was a challenge to be met specifically by a man named Irving Waugh, WSM's commercial manager.

Waugh had come to WSM in 1941, under the aegis of program executive Jack Stapp, and he had started there as an announcer on the early-morning country music shows, just as all the newcomers did. Under no circumstances could Waugh be said to fit into the mold of a country boy. He was a native of Norfolk, Virginia, and Waugh's voice and demeanor reflected all that had gone into his make-up: education at the college of William and Mary, a stint at the Provincetown Playhouse, and air work on CBS's "March of Time" and at NBC.

He had been away from WSM during the latter part of World War Two as an NBC correspondent in the Pacific. When he returned to Nashville after his wartime service it was to go into the sales department—a traditional stepping-stone in a radio management career—and he soon became commercial manager.

Waugh was well aware of the significance of the challenge that faced him, and WSM, in 1948. "Tom Parker had sold Arnold—and Eddy was very hot at the time—to Ralston Purina for a daily Mutual show," Waugh said, "and he had also sold him to Ralston for a weekly half-hour transcribed show that was in about seventy-five markets.

"Gardner in St. Louis was the advertising agency for Ralston and they came to me wanting to place the half-hour transcribed show on WSM on Saturday nights."

What havoc that would have visited upon the Grand Ole Opry lineup was obvious.

"I said, 'We won't take it,' " Waugh continued. "And they said, 'Okay, then we'll go over to WLAC Radio and we'll put it on Friday nights.' After a lot of discussion, I went off to St. Louis to meet with the vice-president and advertising manager of Ralston Purina, as well as the agency people, and I very politely tried to say, 'WSM is the country station in Nashville and we can't permit you to put the Arnold show on a competitor. If you put it on WLAC'—and this took a lot of gall—'I'll put a half hour against you, a half hour in front of it, and a half hour behind it.'

"They got pretty incensed. But they finally said, 'Okay, we'll put the Arnold show on WSM Friday night, instead of Saturday night, but you'll have to do what you said you would do if we were against you. You'll have to build a show before and a show after the Eddy Arnold–Ralston show.'

"So that's how Friday night started with the Opry performers—to keep the Arnold show off the competition.

"Now, Edwin Craig called me upstairs and kept me there for three hours. He was the boss; all he had to say was, 'Don't do it.' But he wouldn't do that. He was trying to convince me that we were overdoing it, overexposing country music, and we would kill the Grand Ole Opry by starting a second night. And I kept arguing we were doing what he always asked us to do, that is, to appeal to the greatest number of people, make the greatest number of friends for the parent company, and make a buck—hopefully.

"Mr. Craig thought of himself as a great salesman, which he was, and he thought he could talk me out of it. But finally Mrs. Craig called him and told him to come home"—Waugh chuckled—"and I never heard another word out of it."

The new show, however, was not called the Grand Ole Opry. It was titled "Friday Night Frolics," and it originated from WSM's Studio C, the auditorium studio originally built for the burgeoning Opry, only to be found to be inadequate.

The year 1948 closed, then, with a new Opry show, regardless of the title. And it also closed with the good news from one of the first national radio surveys of local stations: WSM was reaching 10 million homes—an astounding figure in those days.

Waugh commented: "This, of course, was the Opry influence."

❧[iii]❧ Whatever else is written about the Grand Ole Opry—what has been put down before and what will be told at a later date—nothing will match the drama of what happened on the stage of the Ryman Auditorium on Saturday evening, June 11, 1949.

For it was then that a skinny, hollow-cheeked, sallow-skinned singer named Hank Williams made his Opry debut.

Hank Williams is an almost mythical figure now, some three decades and more after his death. A man who lived only twenty-nine years, who was nationally prominent only six of them. Yet no performer in the country music field has had more impact.

He wasn't a leader in the mold of Roy Acuff. Eddy Arnold sold more records. Dozens of other country music artists have made more money. So why was Hank Williams so special—to the Opry and to all of country music? No one can say for certain, but perhaps it was his universal commonality; the people simply identified with him.

Hank Williams was a man of brilliant light and dark shadows. But there is no *exact* truth about him; every anecdote concerning him has obverse and reverse sides; at times there are more sides than just two, with the truth buried there in the contradictions, perhaps never to be sorted out.

*E*ddy Arnold
*composes a song
while his wife, Sally,
looks on. In 1948,
Arnold dominated
the charts with
eleven number-one
records.*

(C. 1948) GRAND OLE
OPRY ARCHIVES

*J*immy Dickens, the Opry's
*"littlest" star, sings for the
Ryman crowd. Seated in the
rear are Gordon Stoker and
Mother Maybelle Carter.*

(1950) GRAND OLE OPRY ARCHIVES

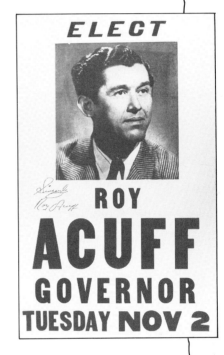

*R*ed Foley, Minnie Pearl, and Rod Brasfield swap tall tales backstage at the Opry.
(LATE 1940s) GRAND OLE OPRY ARCHIVES

A campaign poster from Roy Acuff's unsuccessful gubernatorial bid in 1948.
(1948) COUNTRY MUSIC FOUNDATION LIBRARY AND MEDIA CENTER

*F*red Rose (seated at the piano) was the song magician who edited and published the music of the great Hank Williams (seated with his guitar). Here, the two accompany the guests at a party singing "Happy Birthday" to Hank's eight-year-old stepdaughter, Lycrecia, standing next to him. At his knee is "Bocephus," Hank Williams, Jr., who was born on May 26, 1949.
(1951) COUNTRY MUSIC FOUNDATION LIBRARY AND MEDIA CENTER

There are some simple facts about which there are no doubts:

King Hiram Williams was born on September 17, 1923 (in a log cabin, actually), in the little community of Mount Olive, Alabama, some sixty miles south of Montgomery. His father was a sometime lumber-train engineer, sometime store owner, sometime berry picker. When young Williams—he was always called Hank—was seven, his father entered a Veterans Administration hospital, effectively removing him from the boy's life. It was his domineering mother, Lilly, a country version of the Hollywood or Broadway stage mother, who raised him. She was to be the posthumous source of much of the myth associated with her son. Nevertheless, Lilly *was* a church organist and little Hank sat on the bench beside her during many evangelistic services. In later years, although he was never a churchgoer, that upbringing manifested itself in the numerous country gospel songs that are included in his relatively small song catalogue, and in the moralistic recitations he recorded as "Luke the Drifter."

At about age five Hank was on the streets, selling peanuts and shining shoes. "The first day," his mother recalled, "he made thirty cents, and I remember how proud he was. He brought home some stew meat, tomatoes, and rice. 'Mama, fix us some gumbo stew—tonight we're gonna eat.' Hank always liked gumbo."

Lilly bought him his first guitar (others have claimed the same distinction), a secondhand $3.50 instrument. And he had one teacher on it—and only one. He was a black man named Rufe Payne, widely known as "Tee Tot." From him Williams learned chord progressions, bass runs, and the basic style of accompaniment. The techniques were nothing complex, but they were sprinkled with the blues idiom of the southern black, a musical background very similar to that of Jimmie Rodgers.

When Hank was twelve, the family moved to Montgomery. He sang his first original song, "The WPA Blues," in an amateur-night contest at Montgomery's Empire Theater, and he won the fifteen-dollar first prize. The die was cast. "He told me," his mother said, "he wanted to make a profession of singing and playing. He wanted to play the nightclubs and honky-tonks. He was only twelve but I let him do it. It was rough going."

Encouraged (or pushed?) by Lilly, Williams started his own band at thirteen— the first version of the later-famous Drifting Cowboys—and performed for a time on WSFA Radio in Montgomery. Lilly rationalized later: "He didn't learn much in school. It was too bad that Hank, worn out by playing and singing all night, often slept through his classes in school. But in a way it turned out to be lucky. Too much learning might have spoiled the natural flow of his songs."

By the time he was seventeen, Lilly claimed, her son knew "what makes a song." It was "love that makes the best songs," Hank was supposed to have told her. "Never in the history of country music," the mother said expansively, "has so much come out of a love of one boy for a girl, as in the case of Hank and Audrey. They loved each other like lovers in the old ballads."

Williams met Audrey Shepherd (already married and divorced at a young age and the mother of a daughter) at a medicine show in Banks, Alabama, and the romance was a stormy one from the beginning. Audrey was ambitious and given to prolonged nagging. Hank, who had started drinking at the age of twelve during those long nights in the tough honky-tonks, already had frequent bouts with booze. Nevertheless, they were married in December 1944 at a gas station near Andalusia, Alabama, during a brief respite from the rigors of a road tour. They were both twenty-one.

Two years later, Williams, apparently prodded by Audrey to make the effort, went to Nashville to see Fred and Wesley Rose.

It's an oft-told story. The Roses, father and son, were engaged in a table-tennis match at the WSM Radio studios (table tennis is still a way of life at Acuff-Rose Publications), and the game was interrupted by the arrival of Williams and his pretty blonde wife. Hank sang six songs for them, among them "Six More Miles to the Graveyard" and "When God Comes and Gathers His Jewels."

It has been written that Fred Rose, skeptical about the authorship of the songs just heard, gave the young visitor a test, propounding a hypothesis of a rich girl living in a fine mansion who rejects the love of a poor lad who lives in a mean cabin. Williams was sent alone into a room and a short time later—the length of time varies depending on which version of the story is heard—he emerged from his isolation with a new song, "Mansion on the Hill." The story is apocryphal; it didn't happen. It is used here only to illustrate how quickly the myths of Hank Williams developed.

It is fact, however, that his raw talent was obvious to the Roses. He was immediately signed to a contract with Acuff-Rose, the first *exclusive* songwriter's contract issued by the company.

To say that Hank Williams would not have become a star without Fred Rose would not be defensible; but to say that Hank's stardom would not have reached the magnitude it did without Rose is simply stating the truth. Williams was an unschooled musician; only semiliterate, really. The songs he heard in his head came out on scraps of paper, on the backs of envelopes, on matchbook covers. The Williams-Rose association was a perfect blending of two great talents—Hank's poignantly realistic songs, born of the experiences of his own life, and Fred's considerable trained skills as a song editor. What made it work so well was Rose's ability to change a note here, a lyric line there, and still retain the realism of Williams's original song.

Rose's first move with Williams—in addition to publishing his songs—was to get him on record. He turned to the Oklahoma Wranglers (brothers Vic, Skeeter, and Guy Willis), who were then playing with Eddy Arnold. Rose offered a flat-fee, no-royalty deal with Sterling Records of New York; Studio B of WSM was to be used as the recording studio.

"Sterling was looking for a western-sounding band, which we were," Vic Willis reminisced, "and a country singer. For the country singer Fred said he already had a fellow from Montgomery named Hank Williams. He said he wrote all of his own songs, but sang a little bit out of meter, meaning if he hit a note he liked he might hold it a little longer than he was supposed to.

"When I saw him at the studio, I remembered I had seen him once before. It had been at the Princess Theater two months before trying to pitch a song to Ernest Tubb. You couldn't forget him because of his appearance. He was a skinny, scrawny guy. Bobby Morris, who is a bass player here in Nashville, used to say Hank Williams was the only guy he ever saw who could sit back in a chair and cross his legs and still put both feet on the floor."

When the appointed time came for the Sterling Records sessions, the Oklahoma Wranglers recorded first. "While we did ours," Vic said, "he just hung around in the control room. He was nervous, the way you'd expect anybody to be before they made their first record."

There was a break for lunch. Williams and the Willis brothers walked to a nearby hotel to eat. Someone asked Hank whether he wanted a beer. "You don't know old Hank," he replied. "Old Hank don't just have one."

Back at the studio, the Willis brothers became the Drifting Cowboys to back Williams in cutting four sides—three were gospel songs and one was a country-blues tune. In one of the songs, "Wealth Won't Save Your Soul," there was the line, "My friend, it won't save your poor wicked soul." The Willises were supposed to sing along on that line.

"Hank couldn't say 'poor,' " Vic recalled. "Every time he sang it, it came out 'purr.' Fred, who had a low boiling point sometimes, finally said, 'Damn it, Wranglers, just sing it the same way he does.' And you can hear it on the record like that today. We sang 'purr.' "

The Willis brothers weren't impressed by the newcomer. He seemed an amateur; the songs crude, at best. Vic summed it up: "We hadn't been used to hearing a country singer who was as country as he was."

iv   It may be that Fred Rose had similar thoughts about Hank Williams. He arranged for him to appear regularly on the "Louisiana Hayride" radio show in Shreveport. "My father," Wesley Rose explained, "knew he'd get a straight reaction to Hank in Shreveport. The people there were real country fans."

From late 1946 through 1948, Acuff-Rose published at least twenty Hank Williams songs, among them: "Move It On Over," "(Last Night) I Heard You Crying in Your Sleep," "My Sweet Love Ain't Around," "I'm a Long Gone Daddy," "Honky Tonk Blues," "Honky Tonkin'," "I'll Be a Bachelor Till I Die," "I Don't Care (If Tomorrow Never Comes)."

He was touring extensively, building a reputation not only as a singer, but as a hell-raiser too. Stories of his drinking bouts began to filter back to Nashville and to Jim Denny at the Grand Ole Opry. But early in 1949, Williams—now on the MGM label—had a smash hit, a number-one record with "Lovesick Blues."

Ironically, that first major hit was not a song he had written. "Lovesick Blues" was an old country-blues standard, apparently first recorded as early as 1925 by yodeler Emmett Miller on the Okeh label, and then again in the thirties by Rex

Griffin on Decca. It's a difficult song to sing properly, its progressions are tricky, and the yodeling which is such an integral part of it has to be true. That Williams did it so well was indicative of how far he had come as a singer since that first recording session with the Willis brothers less than three years earlier.

"Lovesick Blues" was such a big hit, and Williams had become such a prominent fixture on the "Louisiana Hayride," that the Opry could ignore him no longer. He was booked for that June 11 debut.

And now the difficulty of separating myth from fact cropped up. Most accounts of that night place Williams on "The Prince Albert Show," and tell of a debut so successful that he was called back for six encores! These accounts have Red Foley quelling the uproar with a "little speech," promising that Williams would be heard again on the Opry.

Roy Acuff has always disputed that version of the Williams debut. Indeed, he had known Williams even before he showed up in Nashville in 1946 to audition for Fred Rose. Roy met him first in the early forties when the Smoky Mountain Boys played a concert in Montgomery and Hank had come backstage. In subsequent trips to Alabama, Hank became a regular in Acuff's dressing room. They'd sit there and "jam" and Roy remembered that Williams used to say: "Here's one of your songs, Roy, and I'll even play it on the fiddle to be sure it sounds like you."

Acuff liked the moody young man and, on one or two occasions, went to where he was playing and appeared onstage with him. "I would go out onstage and perform with him and Audrey," Roy said, "and he'd sing my songs and I sung his. We'd sing them together." Indeed, it may have been that Acuff recommended that Hank go to Nashville to see Fred Rose.

But once Acuff-Rose signed Williams as a songwriter, and he began to record, it would have made sense that Roy saw him as a potential Opry performer. In a March 1967 interview with Los Angeles disc jockey Hugh Cherry, Acuff told how he went to Vito Pellettieri with his thoughts about Hank Williams:

"I said, 'Vito, it would really be a feather in your cap if you could get this boy on the Opry.' . . . I was glad to take Hank under my wing. I introduced him to everyone backstage and then brought him out on the stage and introduced him to the crowd. You might hear it a lot of ways, but that's the way it happened."

In any event, Williams *did* stop the show on the night of June 11, 1949, and he *did* return for six encores. And it was seen from different perspectives.

Opry announcer Grant Turner witnessed it all from the wings: "I can remember about looking out into that audience. It was sort of smoky, although we had a no-smoking rule. It seemed as if the whole audience was just covered with a sort of blue haze, with him standing out there in the spotlight, and looking like he was suspended above the microphone. You got the impression that there was a coat hanger in his back attached to a rope strung to the ceiling, just . . . well, just suspending him there. And how he *worked* that audience! He focused his attention on the audience, drawing it close to him, becoming a part of it and the audience becoming a part of him."

Little Jimmy Dickens also recognized that about Williams: "You could hear a pin drop when Hank was working. He just seemed to hypnotize those people. It was simplicity, I guess. He brought his people with him. He put himself on their level."

And Minnie Pearl said: "He had real animal magnetism. He destroyed the women in the audience. And he was just as authentic as rain."

The Grand Ole Opry had a new, dominant star.

That big eight-wheeler rollin' down the track
Means your true lovin' Daddy ain't comin' back,
I'm movin' on. . . . *

—Hank Snow hit, 1950

In retrospect, it can be said that the decade of the fifties muddled through. So too did the Grand Ole Opry.

Nineteen fifty opened with the introduction of a new star to the stage of the Ryman Auditorium. He came from Canada and his name was Clarence Eugene Snow—Hank Snow, "The Yodeling Ranger." His entrée to the Opry was Ernest Tubb. They had something in common; both were unyielding devotees of the style of the late Jimmie Rodgers.

The date was Saturday, January 7, 1950.

"I guess my fondest memory of the Opry was the first night I came to it," Snow said. Then he laughed derisively. "I don't mind telling you that I bombed. The people just sat there while I sang. And sat. No applause, no nothing, almost. Just sat.

"I was scared, really scared. I sang a song that had been number one in Dallas, Texas, for sixteen weeks: 'Brand on My Heart.' But when I finished there was only moderate applause, probably sympathy more than anything." Another laugh.

"My wife had come to the Opry with me, and when we were driving home I said, 'I'll never go back there again. Never as long as I live. I can find something

*"I'm Movin' On" by Hank Snow; copyright 1950 Hill and Range Songs, Inc.

143

better to do than that.' I had been used to Canada, where I'd go out on the stage and tear the house down. But at the Opry it was a different story. And I tell you that hurt."

But Hank Snow was not a stranger to adversity. He had been born to it in 1914 in Liverpool, a small town in the Canadian province of Nova Scotia. His family, like those of so many Opry performers, was dirt poor. When he was eight, there was the added trauma of his parents' divorce and the complete breakup of the family. Two of Hank's sisters went to an orphans' home; a third sister—the eldest—was sent to work in a shoe factory. Young Hank was placed in the home of grandparents, where he wasn't really wanted and where he became a victim of physical abuse.

His mother was the only somewhat stable element in his unhappy life, and he ran away from his grandparents to return to her; at the time she was employed as a housekeeper in Liverpool. "My mother was completely organized all the time," he said. "Years ago, I guess even before I was born, my mother was a piano player. She used to play for the silent pictures, you see. She was very talented."

Hank's mother was also a Vernon Dalhart enthusiast and his records were part of Hank's early days. So too was a mail-order guitar, complete with a fifty-two-lesson "how to play the guitar" instruction book. "That was for her," he said, "but it came in handy for me too."

The boy's return to his mother was not idyllic, however. She remarried and they moved to Lunenberg, a fishing village seventy-five miles from Liverpool. What might have been a new beginning turned into a nightmare. His stepfather beat him—frequently, sadistically. It got so bad that the day came when his stepfather physically threw him out of the house. He was twelve years old.

"My escape from all the turmoil and poverty of that particular time," he recalled, "was going to sea. That was my escape. Which took care of about four years."

At sixteen, tougher and self-reliant (the year was 1930), Hank was back in his mother's home briefly. His reminiscences have it that he was practicing his guitar one day when his mother came home with a Victor record by Jimmie Rodgers: "Moonlight and Skies." The impact of that record, of hearing the distinctive Rodgers blue-yodeling style, convinced the teenager that his final escape would be as an entertainer.

Meanwhile, he worked in fish plants and as a delivery boy, lobsterman, Fuller Brush salesman, stevedore—anything to exist. And he persisted in his ambition to be a singer in the Jimmie Rodgers mold. That persistence got him a nonpaying radio show on CHNS in Halifax, which eventually led to a sponsor and a Canadian network show.

In 1936 he signed a recording contract with RCA's Canadian division, recording first two of his own songs: "Lonesome Blue Yodel" and "Prisoned Cowboy." The record wasn't really a hit; his first royalty check was $2.96.

Also in 1936 he married. His wife, Minnie, was a six-dollar-a-week chocolate dipper. And the reality of his position as an entertainer—even though he had a network radio show and a recording contract—was illustrated by the fact that their son, named Jimmie Rodgers Snow (later to be an evangelist preacher), was born in a charity ward of a Salvation Army hospital.

Hank played his first professional, in-person engagement at the Gaiety Theater in Halifax "for three dollars a day, three performances, which was a dollar each. My wife made me a little neckerchief in yellow and red, a little bandana. She took a pair of black dungarees and she sewed a white strip of cotton cloth up each side. And that's what I did my first performance in the theater with."

Snow readily admitted that, initially, his "road work wasn't that great." His recollection of those days formed a classic picture of the development of a country entertainer.

"My wife used to act as my advance man. She'd go ahead and put up the posters and arrange for the little halls that we'd play in and then join up with us and sell tickets at the door. You'd get those little old schoolhouses and halls for three or four dollars a night, charge fifteen cents admission—that was big money then. One of our top crowds would have been, oh, 500; we figured we were really setting the woods on fire then.

"I think I played every honky-tonk and beer joint . . . well, probably I'm stretching it a little bit when I say every one, but I've played with no dressing rooms, dirt floors, no stage, standing on the dance-hall floor, you name it."

Snow, who said his greatest honor in life was becoming a United States citizen, didn't play the U.S. until 1944, when a fan named Jack Howard arranged two weeks of personal appearances in the Philadelphia area. That led to other appearances in the States and in 1946 he had a radio program on WWVA, Wheeling, West Virginia.

He also acquired a horse named Shawnee somewhere along the way, and that "trick" animal became a part of his act. He learned to ride it through sheer determination; his dreams were that he might make it as a movie cowboy. He even went off to Hollywood at that period in his career. It was a sad mistake. It broke him. Since he had a few friends in Texas, he headed for Dallas. When he got there in the fall of 1948, his wife and his son with him, he had exactly eleven dollars, and no job.

In Texas he met Ernest Tubb, with whom he had corresponded for almost a decade. They were drawn together by their mutual admiration for Jimmie Rodgers. Tubb helped him, and so did a Texas fan, Bea Terry, who badgered a local disc jockey into giving air play to Hank's latest Canadian release, "Brand on My Heart."

The RCA contract didn't extend into the United States, but he arranged to cut a record for RCA in Chicago. One of the songs he recorded (he never really liked it) was "Marriage Vow," and it was a modestly good seller in December 1949—good enough to keep RCA interested in him.

That brought him to January 1950 and his disappointing Grand Ole Opry debut.

It was only his wife's encouragement that got him to go back to the Opry again after that first night. Opry officials wouldn't have cared, apparently, if he hadn't returned.

"They were getting ready to drop me. I heard that later from Jim Denny. But I managed to stay around long enough to record 'I'm Movin' On.' And when it was released in mid-April of '50 . . . well, that's the only thing that saved my neck. That did it. Everywhere. Internationally. That did it all."

"I'm Movin' On" was such a smash hit that it received the ultimate compliment—a parody. Rollin Sullivan, of the Opry's Lonzo and Oscar, told how that happened:

"Hank's song took off like a jet. It was gone! And Jethro Burns—of Homer and Jethro, you know—wrote the parody, 'Movin' On Number Two.' And he called me up and he said, 'Boy, I've never been so disgusted in all my life. I got a hit, a follow-up on "Movin' On," but they won't let me do it on RCA Victor. You wanna cut it?' So, he sang me a little bit of it, you know, and I said, 'Heck, yeah!' The next week we went down and cut it for Decca: 'The old hound dog was feelin' fine, till he fell in a barrel of turpentine. He's movin' on.' " Oscar laughed heartily. " 'Passed the gate like an eighty-eight. He's movin' on.' Sold a lot of records with that!"

··◦[ii]◦·· There was another Grand Ole Opry debut of consequence in January 1950. As a matter of fact it was on the same night as the Snow appearance—January 7—and may very well have overshadowed Snow's performance in the eyes of the Opry-goers.

For this singer came all the way from the West Coast to appear on the Opry and he was featured on Red Foley's Prince Albert network segment.

The billing was that of Tennessee Ernie Ford, and he was a native son of Bristol, Tennessee, where he had started in the business as a radio announcer just before the outbreak of World War Two.

"The first time I went to the Opry I was still working at radio station KXLA in Pasadena," Ford said, "making a solid eighty-five dollars a week as an announcer. But I had started to make records for Capitol and when the first country record sold a little bit [his "Shotgun Boogie" would place high on the country charts in 1950], why, they had me on the Opry.

"My wife, Betty, insisted that I go to Nashville even though she was very pregnant with our first son. But she knew it was a big thing for me to be on the Grand Ole Opry, and she said, 'I'm not going to have the baby until you get home anyway.' Famous last words! I think I was over Oklahoma City in an old DC-6B when the boy was born, on January 6. Of course, I was getting all kinds of phone calls when I got to my Nashville hotel.

"With that happening, and my first time on the Opry, I like to went nuts! I was excited in two different ways, because we were married for seven and a half years with no children and this was a very exciting thing for us.

"Well, the next night—Saturday—I bought a box of cigars and threw them off the stage at the Grand Ole Opry."

And what did he sing?

"I don't remember," Ford laughed. "I had other things on my mind. But everybody was great to me."

Minnie Pearl, who was an eyewitness to Ernie's Opry debut, said he sang "Anticipation Blues."

Ernie Ford didn't become a member of the Opry roster; his career developed in different channels. But he made frequent visits to Nashville, at least once to substitute for an ill Red Foley on "The Prince Albert Show."

"I was in the Opry House," Ernie recalled, "and Hank Williams walked up to me and said, 'While you're here, why don't you stay with me. I'm tryin' to get part of my life together and if I had somebody with me I wouldn't get drunk and get into trouble.' I did that for a couple of weeks while Red was recuperating. I'd roam around with Hank, and we'd sit down and try to write a song, and we'd go bowling, and we'd have meals together. The association was just buddy-buddy. He was a brilliant writer and it seemed he could control everything but his own life."

❧[iii]❧ Later that year Mother Maybelle Carter and her three daughters, Helen, June, and Anita, joined the Opry as "The Carter Family." Maybelle, of course, had been a member of the famed original Carter Family out of Maces Spring, Virginia, along with brother-in-law A. P. "Doc" Carter and sister-in-law Sara Carter Bayes. When that act broke up in 1942, she began to work with her daughters.

They did some work in San Antonio, and made transcriptions for one of the high-powered Mexican X stations in Del Rio. Beginning in mid-1943 they spent three years on radio station WRNL in Richmond, Virginia, and then moved on to the "Old Dominion Barn Dance" on WRBA, Richmond, to WNOX, Knoxville, and finally to radio station KWTO in Springfield, Missouri, where they headed a small regional network show.

Chet Atkins had joined them in Knoxville and had gone to Springfield with them—as a fiddler. He remembered how they moved to the Grand Ole Opry:

"George Morgan was comin' up there to Springfield and doin' some syndicated radio shows and he liked the girls a lot—he liked all pretty girls a lot—and through him we went to Nashville and auditioned for the Martha White portion of the Opry. They liked us and offered us a spot.

"Now, I was making fifty dollars a week at Springfield and they offered me seventy-five if I'd stay. I called Fred Rose—the greatest man that ever hit Nashville—and I said, 'Fred, what shall I do? Could you use me on some records as a sideman if I come down there?' He said, 'Yeah, come on down.' So I came down with the Carter Sisters and I worked the Opry, and right away I started working as a recording musician. Jim Denny didn't like that too much, but Jack Stapp kept me on."

Mother Maybelle and the Carter Sisters became a starring act on the Grand Ole Opry, but Atkins left them after a year to pursue his own career.

"I was a guest on a lot of the pop shows on WSM," Chet remembered. "They had a lot of network radio feeds in this days, with shows like 'Sunday Down South.' Then I was also featured as a soloist on 'The Prince Albert Show.' Stapp put me on there just as a filler, you know, if they needed a pad for time."

Just a few years earlier, Atkins had been fired from the very same show, and he got some satisfaction out of being back on it.

"Then I had my own show on the Opry—a fifteen-minute show—for a little while," Chet went on. "And I just worked with myself mostly, and worked spots with other people. But the Opry never really did hire me, not in any formal sense."

·· ₹ iv ₹ ·· With all of the changes, and all of the portents of changes, that the beginning of the fifties brought, one thing remained constant at the Grand Ole Opry: Roy Acuff. He was still the rock.

In the summer of 1950 Acuff and his troupe went out on what was to be called "the last of the great medicine shows"—the "Hadacol Caravan." It was promoted by a flamboyant sometime Louisiana state senator, Dudley LeBlanc. He manufactured a patent medicine called Hadacol, one of those good-for-man-or-beast remedies. With his free-spending promotions he had made Hadacol one of the best-selling patent medicines of all time.

The joke was: "They hadda call it something, so they called it Hadacol."

But the "Hadacol Caravan," starring Roy Acuff and the Smoky Mountain Boys, was no joke.

Roy remembered it enthusiastically: "The senator spent a tremendous amount of money. All expenses were paid. We couldn't hardly buy a toothpick. It was a real caravan. The lead car was filled with Old Forester whiskey and we had a party every night. We played all over the South.

"Every county or town had a queen, and if the queens wanted to stay with the tour they could. So we kept accumulating queens. As we entered a town we would sit on a flatbed truck and throw out chewing gum and candy to the kids. The admission to the shows was a Hadacol box top.

"When we played a city, Hollywood stars would join. During our stay with the tour Harpo Marx and Mickey Rooney came. . . . That was the doggonest tour I've ever been on! It was amazing the amount of money that man spent!"

And *made*, more than likely. Every box-top admission "ticket" meant a bottle of Hadacol sold.

·· ₹ v ₹ ·· Not all of the stories of the Opry came from those who were on it. As 1950 slid into 1951, two young men were seeing the Opry for the first time. One was a Nashvillian whose initial interest in the Opry had very little to do with country music. The other was a Carolinian, a teenager who was an admitted Grand Ole Opry nut.

The Nashvillian was Charles Eugene Pat Boone. Everyone called him Pat.

"Though I grew up literally in the shadow of the Grand Ole Opry," Boone said, "I had little acquaintance with the Opry itself until I met Shirley Foley. We were juniors in high school; she had been transferred from West High to become a dorm student because her mother was in the hospital, and I asked to be introduced. When I learned she was the daughter of the legendary Red Foley I became interested in country music immediately.

"I went with Shirley and her sisters several times to the Opry, in the old auditorium, and stood in the crowded wings to watch Red Foley perform on the Prince Albert portion. It was one of the most fascinating human experiences ever: the performers 'working up' their songs together just minutes before they were to perform them on the air, all kinds of folks walking on and off the stage during the performances, people from all over the country sitting for many hours to enjoy their favorites in live performance, eating (and drinking) from paper bags, mamas nursing their babies right in front of God and everybody, an incredible intermingling of great national celebrity with rural and grass-roots citizenry. There's never been anything like it!

"I married Shirley, my career headed toward New York and Hollywood, but I eventually made it back to the Opry. While in Nashville recording an album of my country favorites, I had an opportunity to appear with Hank Snow on his long-running portion of the Opry.

"I had just recorded his song 'Golden Rocket' and sang it live with him that Saturday night. It was a real 'knee-knocker' for me, because I was afraid Hank's loyal fans would not want me attempting to sing one of his classics—but Hank so obviously enjoyed it that his audience did, too."

The Carolina lad who was the acknowledged Grand Ole Opry enthusiast was named George Hamilton IV:

"I was one of those guys who grew up as a fan of the Opry. Although I was born in Winston-Salem, and was a 'suburban hillbilly,' my granddaddy Hamilton was a real mountain man out of Beaver Creek, Ashe County, North Carolina, who came to Winston-Salem to work on the railroad. My earliest memories of country music were sitting on my granddaddy's knee and listening to the Grand Ole Opry on Saturday night. It was a magical, wonderful fairyland in the sky to me, like the air castle of the South, you know.

"Well, when I was about twelve or thirteen years old my parents let me catch the Greyhound bus and go to Nashville; I had saved my money from my paper route. I stayed at the YMCA, across from the old National Life building, and I got me a room on the corner where I could look down and see Red Foley and Ernest Tubb and all my heroes going into the National Life building to rehearse 'The Prince Albert Show' on Saturday morning.

"When I saw them go in, I ran across the street and went up to the fifth floor, where I knew the rehearsal would be held; I was a real backstage spook. And when I got up there, there was Chet Atkins leaning against the wall. I was so thrilled. And I walked up and said, 'Mr. Atkins, my name is George Hamilton.

I'm from North Carolina and I just think you're great.' He just sort of yawned in my face and I thought, 'Man, this is the rudest guy I ever met.' I didn't realize how very shy he was, how unassuming. Anyway, I went away with my feelings hurt because I was disillusioned.

"A little later in the morning I was watching the rehearsal and I heard somebody say, 'Hey, kid.' And I turned around and it was Chet. And I said, 'Yes, sir?' And he said, 'I'm gonna get a haircut. You wanna go with me?' "

Hamilton laughed in remembering the incident.

"So we went down to the Hermitage Hotel barbershop and I went in and watched him get a haircut. He didn't say three words to me, but it was just such a nice gesture. He realized that I was a hopeless fan and although he wasn't a backslapper and a glad-hander and a loud-personality kind of guy, in his own quiet way he took me under his wing.

"After the haircut, we were walking back up to the National Life building and he said, 'George, would you like to come backstage at the Opry tonight?' and I said, 'Are you kidding? I'd love to.' He said, 'Well, meet me back in the alley there—' And Chet took me backstage and introduced me to Hank Snow—I still got Hank's guitar pick that he gave me that night—and to Ernest Tubb. All those people were so kind to me; I didn't have anything to offer them, but they were so good to me. And Chet stands out in my mind because my first impression was that he was a cold fish, and he turned out to be the warmest of them all."

❧[vi]❧ In the early fifties the pop trend in country music really began to dominate the trade charts. Red Foley had crossed over from country to pop with his "Chattanooga Shoe Shine Boy" in 1950. In 1951, Pee Wee King had a number-one hit with "Slowpoke," Hank Snow was big on the charts with something called "Rhumba Boogie," and one William Orville "Lefty" Frizzell had scored with "Always Late (with Your Kisses)."

But it was Hank Williams who was "owning" the charts with such hits as "Why Don't You Love Me?," "Long Gone Lonesome Blues," and "Cold, Cold Heart" (saloon singer Tony Bennett also had a major hit with "Cold, Cold Heart").

Williams and Frizzell were very much alike; both had reputations as two-fisted drinkers, both were honky-tonk singers, both were excellent songwriters. It was inevitable that they would become friends. And there came a point in 1951 when Lefty eclipsed Williams on the best-seller charts, however briefly.

Frizzell's "Always Late" was number one, "Mom and Dad Waltz" was number two (those two were back-to-back on a single release), "I Want to Be with You Always" was number seven, and "Travelin' Blues," a Jimmie Rodgers tune, was number eight. All at the same time.

Hank, being friendly, touted Frizzell on the Grand Ole Opry.

"I forget where we were at the time," Frizzell said, "but one day he says, 'You need to join the Opry.' I looked at him an' said, 'Look, I got the number-one song, the number-two song, the number-seven song, and the number-eight song on the charts. An' you tell me I *need* to join the Opry?' Hank thought about it awhile, then he laughed an' said, 'Darned if you ain't got a heck of an argument.' "

Williams was busy, of course, with his own runaway career and probably didn't give the Frizzell-Opry matter another thought. Again in 1951, Louisiana senator Dudley LeBlanc put his colorful "Hadacol Caravan" on the road, with Hank Williams and the Drifting Cowboys and Minnie Pearl as the country headliners on the star-studded extravaganza.

As the tour progressed, LeBlanc kept moving Hank on the program, getting him closer and closer to the top-billed closing spot. Finally, in Louisville Williams was next-to-closing in the order of performance, just before Bob Hope.

Jerry Rivers, fiddler with the Drifting Cowboys, recalled that "the packed stadium seemed to explode, the ovation was so great" when Hank finished. All efforts to quiet the crowd were unsuccessful and when Hope was introduced the cheering for Williams still continued.

"They just brought on Hope anyway," Rivers wrote, "and he stood there in front of the microphone for several minutes while the applauding gradually died down. When the roar was down to the point where his voice could be heard over the sound system, Bob pulled a big ragged cowboy hat down on his ears and said,'Hello, folks, this is Hank Hope. . . .' The roar went up again, and Bob Hope shared in some of Hank Williams's glory."

Unhappily, the glory was to be short-lived.

It wasn't God who made honky-tonk angels
As you said in the words of your song;
Too many times married men think they're still single:
*That has caused many a good girl to go wrong,**

—Kitty Wells hit, 1952

Almost any year of the sixty-odd that have made up the history of the Grand Ole Opry can be classified as significant, trend-setting, unprecedented. But 1952 was all of those things simultaneously—and more. This was the year in which country music was *urbanized*. That shouldn't be considered too strange, however, because the whole country was undergoing the same change.

Since the end of World War Two there had been a tremendous moving about of the American population; old home ties were being unraveled. Country boys who had seen the rest of the world during their years in military service were not content to return to the farms or the hills when the war ended. There was a song in the days of World War One with the lyrical question, "How ya gonna keep 'em down on the farm after they've seen Paree?" That was more true after World War Two.

Cities offered not only greater job opportunities but also greater excitement. Country music songs reflected that freedom. They had titles such as "Back Street Affair" and "The Wild Side of Life" and "Give Me More, More, More" and "Your

*"It Wasn't God Who Made Honky-Tonk Angels" by J. D. Miller; copyright 1952 Peer International Corporation.

Cheating Heart" and "You're Not Mine Anymore" and "We've Gone Too Far."

If there was a social revolution in the twenties when Grand Ole Opry was born, there was an even bigger one in the fifties when the Opry reached its twenty-fifth birthday. This time, though, women were having a say; it was no longer just a man's world. Then, too, there was television, expanding so rapidly as to defy description and just as rapidly acting to homogenize America and American tastes. In that kind of world, country music, once a regional phenomenon, was now acceptable in markets where only a few years earlier it had been almost unknown.

Former Opry star Eddy Arnold was selected as pop singer Perry Como's summer replacement on NBC-TV, Bing Crosby was singing country, Tony Bennett and Rosemary Clooney and Frankie Laine and Doris Day and Jo Stafford were singing Hank Williams's songs, and Williams and Roy Acuff were appearing as special guests on the highly popular Kate Smith television hour.

There was also an inevitable changing of the guard on the stage of the Ryman.

ii   On Saturday, March 1, 1952, Uncle Dave Macon made another appearance on the Grand Ole Opry. It turned out to be his last. He contracted a throat ailment shortly after that Opry appearance, entered a hospital in Murfreesboro, and died three weeks later.

Uncle Dave's Grand Ole Opry friends erected a monument to him on a hillside just outside Woodbury, Tennessee, overlooking U.S. 70, the road on which Macon used to drive his mule-drawn freight wagons. A banjo is carved on the stone, with a likeness of the old gentleman, and the title of one of his favorite hymns: "How Beautiful Heaven Must Be."

But David Harrison Macon was his own memorial. In a letter he had written to George D. Hay, he had said: "Uncle Dave, not satisfied with what he now does, is looking forward to television that he might add one more attraction to his radio programs."

That letter was dated May 23, 1933!

iii   The summer of 1952 in Nashville was hot. Very hot. There had been a protracted dry spell and there were many days in July with recorded temperatures in excess of 100 degrees. On July 27—that was a Sunday—the mercury soared to 107.3 degrees, the hottest temperature ever recorded in the city.

Gradually, a relieving front moved in and the rains came. Temperatures subsided, only to be replaced with torrential rains, storms, flooding. A few tornadoes touched down in the area. Attesting to the international reputation the Grand Ole Opry enjoyed by this time, WSM received numerous letters from country music fans in Japan who wanted to know whether any of the Opry stars had been victims of the tornadoes.

The Japanese could be told that the Opry folk were well. But it's not likely that the letters of reply mentioned the stifling heat inside the old Ryman Auditorium. Under normal circumstances, the Ryman was very nearly intolerable during the summer. In 1952, it was just plain terrible. Many Opry-goers were overcome. Onstage, picking an electric guitar with sweat running down arms and hands could be a dangerous challenge.

But the performers persisted. And the fans kept coming. New faces were bringing them in now. Among them was a young man, just twenty, from Shreveport, Louisiana. He was Faron Young.

"A disc jockey here in Nashville named Hugh Cherry had gotten a record of mine," Young explained, "and Hugh took it over to Jim Denny and Jack Stapp at WSM. And he said, 'This boy here's from Shreveport, he's on the "Louisiana Hayride," and he's gonna be a big star.' They listened to the record and they called me up here on a two-week trial. An' from that two-week trial I stayed at the Opry for fifteen years.

"You know, everybody listened to that darned Grand Ole Opry. I was on the Hayride and they heard it out through Texas and Oklahoma and New Mexico, but this Opry was a 50,000-watt clear thing. And back then the Opry could make a star out of you. They took me and literally made me into a big name, and it was just because of the exposure on the Opry itself."

But Faron wasn't making a lot of money when he first came to the Opry.

"Oh, hell, I think it was seventeen dollars for an Opry shot," he said. "And five days a week I had a morning show, and I got fifteen dollars a show for that. Chet Atkins was my guitar player; he got seven dollars. Owen Bradley [later head of Decca Records in Nashville] was the piano man, and he got seven dollars.

"But hell, I had been makin' three hundred dollars a week down there in Shreveport in those nightclubs. An' I couldn't see what the devil I was doin' in Nashville, gettin' up every mornin' an' workin' my butt off an' not makin' a hundred fifty a week. So after a few weeks here, I said one night at the Opry, 'I'm gonna go back to Shreveport an' get my clothes. I'll be back up.'

"Now, this is a weird thing. Roy Acuff was standin' there an' he said, 'Come on over here, I wanna talk to you. You come out to my house tomorrow and see me and Mildred.'

"Well, I went out there the next day and he said, 'You're fixin' to leave here an' not ever come back, ain't you?' That's *exactly* what I had planned! I wonder how Acuff knew that.

"An' he said, 'I'm gonna tell you what you better do, boy. You better stay here, because if you go back to them clubs that's where you'll be twenty years from now—still workin' them honky-tonks.' And then he said, 'You got what it takes to make it here on the Opry. Do yourself a favor. You can become a big name in this business if you stay here on the Opry.' An' I took his advice an' it worked.

"He was right, of course. 'Cause I'da been stuck in them honky-tonks. I worked places down there, when you'd come in they'd say, 'You got a gun?' You'd say, 'No.' And they'd say, 'Ya want one?!' "

Roy *Acuff and Minnie Pearl*
share a lighthearted moment at the Opry.

(1988) *DONNIE BEAUCHAMP*

Grandpa Jones and his wife, Ramona, still enjoy sharing the stage together.

(1978) *WSM PHOTO/LES LEVERETT*

Pickin' and grinnin', Grandpa Jones is familiar to many from his years as a regular on "Hee Haw."

(1984) *WSM PHOTO/LES LEVERETT*

Randy Travis follows in the footsteps of Marty Robbins as the darling of the Opry audiences.

(1988) *DONNIE BEAUCHAMP*

Always at home on the Opry stage, Ricky Skaggs introduces a guest on his segment of the Opry.

(1988) WSM PHOTO/LES LEVERETT

Ricky Skaggs, onstage with his band, delights Opry audiences with the traditional flavor of his brand of country music.

(1986) WSM PHOTO/LES LEVERETT

Bill Monroe, the solemn and stately creator of
bluegrass music, picks a mournful tune on his mandolin.

(1984) WSM PHOTO/LES LEVERETT

Loretta Lynn—from Butcher Holler
to the Country Music Hall of Fame in 1988.

(1988) *DONNIE BEAUCHAMP*

Hank Snow, a regular host on the Opry, jokes with the audience during his portion of the show.

(1978) WSM PHOTO/LES LEVERETT

Hank Snow's colorful costumes are a trademark of the versatile, veteran Opry star.

(1988) DONNIE BEAUCHAMP

Jimmy Dickens maintains an active touring schedule while still making frequent Opry appearances.

(1986) WSM PHOTO/LES LEVERETT

Jimmy Dickens, a friendly favorite of country fans, signs an autograph backstage at the Opry.

(1988) DONNIE BEAUCHAMP

❦ iv ❧ "Opry appeal" was beginning to spread to New York's Manhattan. Hank Williams and Roy Acuff were special guests on the highly rated NBC television show "The Kate Smith Hour." And the Astor Hotel, which had a posh nightclub on its roof, booked a Grand Ole Opry package show for an eight-week run in the summer of 1952. It was deemed such an important development that Tennessee governor Gordon Browning flew to New York City to sing "Tennessee Waltz" on the opening show.

But the Astor's experiment with country music was not a success. Business was bad; the hard-core country fans in the city simply couldn't afford the expensive tab to attend the nightclub. The Opry package was canceled after four weeks.

Yet one Opry act survived for the full eight weeks—an upbeat, gutsy gospel singer (in her own words, "a goer on stage") named Martha Carson. She liked Manhattan and, apparently, Manhattan liked her.

Martha had first come to the Opry in 1951 by way of Knoxville's "Midday Merry-Go-Round" on the strength of a Capitol hit titled "Satisfied," a hand-clapping gospel song that established her bouncy, spirited performance style. She was quickly a favorite of Opry fans, so much so that what happened to her is an incomprehensible part of Grand Ole Opry history.

She was on the Opry steadily until her first child was born in 1957 and then she took a sabbatical, which also included a year of working in New York. "I got a leave of absence from the Opry. I didn't quit and I wasn't fired. When I came back to Nashville, [Opry manager] Ott Devine said they had no openings." Then, sadly: "I never did go back. I never even got to be a guest."

Although hurt by the rejection, the memory of working the Opry is a bright one for her: "It was like a singer's or an entertainer's dream heaven. That was really what it was. Although the old Ryman was hot and uncomfortable it has such a friendliness to it. Everybody loved everybody. It seemed they had time for one another. It was just an experience like you'd never find anywhere else."

❦ v ❧ Of course, the Opry was different things to different people. Honky-tonk singer-songwriter Lefty Frizzell finally gave the Opry a whirl in 1952; it didn't work.

Writer Bob Oermann has described Frizzell as "a loveable, punch-drunk, boozy, puddin'-headed, bear-like kind of a guy who never really got along with Nashville or the Opry."

Frizzell himself said: "I just didn't like the Opry. It wasn't the dream I thought it would be." He left after a few months.

Another Texan, though, had a different view. Jimmy Dean has recalled his 1952 guest appearance: "I was twenty-four years old when I was asked to be on the NBC network show of the Grand Ole Opry—'The Prince Albert Show.' I had a pretty good record out called 'Bummin' Around.' Well, let me tell you, I've never been so scared before in all my life. And Rod Brasfield, that rascal, didn't make it any better. He told me just before I went on, 'Don't be nervous, there are only ten million people listening.'"

Dean would go on to become the host of a popular ABC television series in which he featured many Opry acts, giving some of them their first network TV exposure.

And then there was the 1952 Grand Ole Opry debut of Jumpin' Bill Carlisle.

Carlisle was born in the small community of Briar Ridge, Kentucky, but when he was age ten his family moved to the big city of Louisville, where his father was a music teacher. "Dad taught do-re-me-fa notes in church," Bill said, "but us kids listened to the Grand Ole Opry on those battery-set radios with earphones. I don't know, to me it was always a great, great thing and I just felt that if I ever got on the Opry that was as far as I could go."

It seemed inevitable that there would be a Carlisle family band, and it started on Louisville's WLAP Radio. For no pay. But by the time Bill was twenty-two he had made his first record, "Rattlesnake Daddy," and it was a hit on the Brunswick label. "You know, back when I started it was easier to get in the business," he said modestly, "because the record companies had scouts out looking for talent. And now you go looking for the A&R [artists and repertoire] man and, if he don't know you, why he's hiding back somewhere in the office, or he's busy in a conference, and you don't get to see him."

Bill and his brother, Cliff, a dobro player who had been featured on some of the Jimmie Rodgers records, recorded a great deal for Brunswick. "I got fifty dollars a song," Bill said. "I had a solo contract and I'd record twenty-five. My brother had a solo contract and he'd record twenty-five. And then we'd cut twenty-five together."

The Carlisle brothers began a radio odyssey that was typical of the early days of country music broadcasting—one station after another. Some good, some bad. A brief stay in Charleston, West Virginia, was on the minus side. "The hillbilly graveyard," said Bill.

Finally they got to WNOX in Knoxville, to start a long run on the "Midday Merry-Go-Round." It was there that the jumping started: "I did the comedy on our show, with a character called 'Hotshot Elmer.' We'd work as the Carlisle Brothers and then, while Cliff was handling the show, I'd go backstage and change into my rube clothes. That was Hotshot Elmer, and I'd be barefooted. During the act me and my brother had a mock fight and we'd get a chair between us and I could stand flat-footed and jump over the chair. And jump back. I just started doing that and people would laugh about it. So it comes natural to me when I'm singing sometimes just to jump, you know." He laughed. "Of course, I'm not getting as high as I used to"—a comedian's studied pause—"but I'm staying up there longer."

It was in 1952 that Carlisle recorded the comedy hit "Too Old to Cut the Mustard," which led directly to an offer to be a guest on the Opry's "Prince Albert Show." It also led to some . . . well, confusion.

"From there is where we started negotiating for me coming to the Opry full-time," Bill recalled. "They set a date for me to come down here and I turned in my notice at Knoxville. But then they decided at the Opry that they were going to wait for a while. In order to save face—I couldn't go back to WNOX—I just started to write letters; I wrote letters to, like, Wheeling and Shreveport, and most of them said they weren't looking for anybody.

"I told my wife, 'I'm going to write a song called "No Help Wanted." ' And sure enough I did, only I mixed up a little romance in it, and we recorded it. We went to the 'Louisiana Hayride' in Shreveport right after we recorded that song, and in six weeks it was way up in the charts. Then we had 'Is That You, Myrtle?' and 'Rough Stuff,' and finally the Grand Ole Opry brought us in.

"You know, you take milk and cream will form at the top. And that's the Opry—the cream on the top."

··◦[vi]◦·· The woman known as Kitty Wells was a paradox.
Almost a stereotype of the wife-mother, she broke the mold of that image with one spectacular recording—"It Wasn't God Who Made Honky-Tonk Angels." For the first time in the history of country music, it gave the woman's view on infidelity. Kitty Wells became the first female superstar in country music. And on the stage of the Grand Ole Opry.

Kitty was a rarity for another reason: She was a native-born Nashvillian. One of six children of a railroad brakeman, she was born Muriel Ellen Deason in 1919. One writer has called her childhood circumstances "average"; another used the word "unexceptional." What may have distinguished the Deason family from others in their south Nashville neighborhood was that there was always music around. Muriel sang in church as a youngster and began playing the guitar at age fourteen.

As a teenager, Muriel and her sisters, Mabel and Willie Mae, along with a cousin, formed a musical group called the Deason Sisters. They played numerous community functions, mostly for no pay, and also sang regularly on the "Old Country Store" program on radio station WSIX.

She began dating a young cabinetmaker/guitarist named Johnny Wright, who had moved to Nashville from Mount Juliet, Tennessee. They married in 1937 (Muriel was only eighteen) and their first professional experience together was as Johnny Wright and the Harmony Girls on WSIX. The third member of the trio was Louise, Johnny's sister.

It wasn't music that supported them, however, during those Depression days. Wright worked at a cabinet company for $15 a week, and Muriel was employed at a clothing factory, ironing shirts for $9 a week.

In 1939 Johnny teamed with his brother-in-law Jack Anglin, who had married Louise Wright, as the Dixie Early Birds on WSIX. By 1940 the decision was made to go into music full-time; they formed the Tennessee Hillbillies, later renamed the Tennessee Mountain Boys. They first went to radio station WBIG in Greensboro, North Carolina, but it didn't work out. Nearly broke, they wrangled a $30 advance from WCHS in Charleston, West Virginia, and went there to be regulars on what was called "The Old Farm Hour." Muriel was with the group, singing sometimes, but not featured. The Wrights' first child, Ruby, had been born, and Muriel was pregnant again when they traveled to West Virginia.

Though not a member of the Opry, Tennessee Ernie Ford made numerous guest appearances on the Ryman stage in the early 1950s.

(C. 1952) GRAND OLE OPRY ARCHIVES

In 1950, when the Carter Family joined the Opry, Chet Atkins was their guitarist. Here, he accompanies Mother Maybelle on guitar, with Anita on bass (obscured), and Becky Bowman on accordion, while June does a country can-can.

(1950) OPRYLAND USA ARCHIVES/JEANNE GORDON COLLECTION

Richard Norris, an Opry security guard (on left), and Hank Snow pose with a large, portable billboard thanking the disc jockeys for their support and promotion of Snow's concerts for Purina.

(C. 1953) OPRYLAND USA ARCHIVES/JEANNE GORDON COLLECTION

Jumping Bill Carlisle four feet in the air. Performing with him, but with their feet on the ground, are Dale Potter on fiddle, Dottie Sills on guitar, and Kenny Hill on bass.

(1953) OPRYLAND USA ARCHIVES/ JEANNE GORDON COLLECTION

*F*aron Young, at the microphone, credits Roy Acuff with keeping him in Nashville and on the Opry's stage. Pictured with him are (from the left) Gordon Terry, Tom Pritchard, Buford Gentry, Sleepy McDaniels, Young, Teddy Wilburn, Bubba Lunn, Dottie Sills, and Jud Collins.

(1955) *OPRYLAND USA ARCHIVES/JEANNE GORDON COLLECTION*

*T*he reigning "Queen of Country Music," Kitty Wells, pictured here with Leslie Wilburn.

(1953) *LES LEVERETT COLLECTION*

The entire troupe lived in two rooms in Charleston; Muriel and Johnny, with the baby, Ruby, plus Jack and Louise in one room; the other three members of the Tennessee Mountain Boys in the second. And while they were there the Wright's second child, Bobby, was born.

In June 1942 they moved to WNOX in Knoxville, Tennessee. But wartime gasoline rationing made it almost impossible to keep any kind of personal-appearance schedule, and they had to move back to Nashville. Johnny got a job at the Du Pont plant; Jack Anglin was inducted into the service.

A year later, the Wrights were back at WNOX to try again on the "Midday Merry-Go-Round." It was there that Muriel was renamed. Johnny reasoned that "Muriel Deason Wright" was too difficult for the fans to remember. He called her "Kitty Wells," a name taken from an old mountain folk song, "Sweet Kitty Wells."

It wasn't an easy life. With Knoxville as their base—and later Raleigh, North Carolina—they traveled in a car, dragging a trailer loaded with their instruments and luggage. When the war ended, Jack Anglin returned and the act of Johnny and Jack was begun, sometimes featuring Kitty Wells. In 1947 the Johnny and Jack act joined the Grand Ole Opry.

"We worked all that year at the Opry," Wright said, "and then we went to Shreveport to the 'Louisiana Hayride.' In '47 we were recording for Apollo Records and we didn't have any hits at all; so we got off of that label in the latter part of 1948 and got on RCA Victor, thanks to Chet Atkins."

The RCA connection opened the recording door—just a crack—for Kitty. "I started recording for RCA," she recalled, "singing gospel songs, but that was before a girl (any girl) had really got started in the recording field. And the fact is, they didn't really get the records out—at least in more than a trickle. I guess it was reasonable from their viewpoint. They were afraid the records wouldn't sell, and they'd be stuck with them."

Johnny and Jack, though, were to have some success at RCA Records, including a reasonably good seller titled "Poison Love." In 1952 they were welcomed back to the Grand Ole Opry.

"Kitty wasn't with us when we came back to the Opry," Johnny Wright said. "She had decided to retire and stay home."

Then came a chance meeting by Wright with Decca Records executive Paul Cohen at the Ernest Tubb Record Shop, where Johnny and Jack had gone to appear on the post-Opry "Midnight Jamboree." Cohen had an answer song to the Hank Thompson hit of the moment, "The Wild Side of Life," in which the story line was that men were led down the primrose path by ladies of easy virtue, characterized as "honky-tonk angels." Songwriter J. D. Miller's answer song—a *woman's* answer—put the blame on men. The title was "It Wasn't God Who Made Honky-Tonk Angels."

The melody was a familiar, oft-used public-domain tune readily familiar to those who knew "I'm Thinking Tonight of My Blue Eyes" or Acuff's "The Great Speckled Bird," as well as "The Wild Side of Life." From the melody standpoint, then, the answer song seemed solid.

"I think Kitty Wells could make a hit with this," Cohen told Wright. "Do you think she'd be interested in recording it?"

Wright took it home to his wife, who displayed something less than overwhelming enthusiasm. "Well, if you want me to record it we'll do it," she said. "At least we can make union pay scale out of the session."

Johnny remembered: "I played bass fiddle, Jack Anglin played guitar, Shot Jackson played the electric steel guitar, and Paul Warren played the fiddle. Those were the musicians on the session. That was on May third of '52, and by July it was number one. It took over Hank Thompson's spot of number one where he had 'The Wild Side of Life.' Kitty sold over a million copies of that record."

Later, Kitty herself commented: "I didn't think much about Hank Thompson's song—or that it needed an answer. I guess it just turned out to be the right song at the right time."

Kitty Wells's "retirement" had been ended.

"We were trying to get her on the Opry," her husband said, "but Vito Pellettieri, the guy that cleared all the songs on the show, says, 'You can't sing that song on the Opry because of the lyrics.' " Johnny laughed. "You know, that part about the trusting wife going wrong. Anyway, Roy Acuff went up and talked to Jim Denny and Jack Stapp and he told them: 'Kitty Wells is a female Roy Acuff. She sells songs with her sincerity.' And 'Honky-Tonk Angels' got to be such a hit, you know, that they had to let her sing it."

Acuff wasn't far wrong in his estimation of Kitty Wells. She followed up the million-seller with two more number-one songs in 1952—"I Heard the Juke Box Playing" and "A Wedding Ring Ago." The parade to the top of the charts was phenomenal: 1953—"I Don't Claim to Be an Angel," "I Gave My Wedding Dress Away," "I'm Paying for That Back Street Affair"; 1954—"One By One" (a duet with Red Foley), "Release Me"; 1955—"As Long As I Live" (with Foley again), "Making Believe," "Whose Shoulder Will You Cry on?"; 1956—"How Far Is Heaven?" (a duet with her daughter Carol Sue), "Searching," "You and Me" (with Foley once more); 1957—"Repenting"; 1958—"I Can't Stop Loving You," "She's No Angel"; 1959—"Amigo's Guitar," "Mommy for a Day"; 1960—"Left To Right"; 1961—"Heartbreak, U.S.A."; 1962—"We Missed You"; 1964—"Password," "This White Circle on My Finger"; 1965—"I'll Repossess My Heart," "You Don't Hear."

Not only had Kitty Wells broken a trail for other female singers in country music, she had built a four-lane highway.

She was voted the number-one female country artist for eleven consecutive years by *Billboard* magazine, for ten consecutive years by *Cash Box*, and the top female artist of the decade by *Record World*, and she was also the first female country singer to win an award from *Downbeat* magazine, which usually confined itself to jazz and pop artists.

In 1954 Tennessee governor Frank Clement created a Tennessee Womanhood Award for her.

And the Grand Ole Opry not only had the King of Country Music but was the home of the Queen of Country Music as well.

*Now you're lookin' at a man that's gettin' kind of mad,
I've had a lot of luck, but it's all been bad,
No matter how I struggle and strive,
I'll never get out of this world alive.**

—Hank Williams hit

It was fitting to the growing legend of Hank Williams that 1952 should begin with a New Year's Eve party at which Hank got roaring drunk, fired several shots at his wife, Audrey, and saw his troubled marriage end on that bit of boozy violence.

Williams was, by this time, the most dominant personality to hit country music since the days of Jimmie Rodgers. Everything he recorded turned to gold. A lot of gold. He had become wealthy beyond any dreams he might have had as a boy playing the honky-tonks of Alabama.

The only thing that was not gold was his personal life. He drank too much; he took too many pills, trying to stop the constantly excruciating pains in his back; and he led a generally profligate existence.

Yet the inner turmoil he must have felt spilled out into his songs. Many of them were autobiographical. And every one of them seemed destined to be a hit.

After he had scored his initial recording success with "Lovesick Blues" (not his composition), his other hit songs of 1949 had come from his own talents: "Mind

*"I'll Never Get out of This World Alive" by Hank Williams and Fred Rose; copyright 1952 Milene/Opryland Music, Inc.

Your Own Business," "You're Gonna Change," the humorous "My Bucket's Got a Hole in It," and "Wedding Bells."

In 1950 all four of his gold records were his own compositions: "Long Gone Lonesome Blues," "Moaning the Blues," "Why Don't You Love Me?," and "I Just Don't Like This Kind of Livin'."

Autobiographical? Well—

> *I just don't like this kind of livin',*
> *I'm tired of doin' all the givin';*
> *I give my all and sit and yearn*
> *And get no lovin' in return,*
> *And I just don't like this kind of livin'.**

His relationship with Audrey was a roller-coaster ride, alternate fighting and making up, all of which was reflected in his music. In 1951 he had seven top-ten songs: "Baby, We're Really in Love," "Crazy Heart," "Dear John," "Hey, Good Lookin'," "Howlin' at the Moon," "I Can't Help it," and "Cold, Cold Heart."

On the upside of the marriage was:

> *I run around in circles and turn in fire alarms,*
> *I'm nutty as a fruit cake when you're in my arms;*
> *If you're meant for me like I'm meant for you,*
> *Baby, we fit like a glove;*
> *If you're lovin' me like I'm lovin' you,*
> *Baby, we're really in love.†*

And on the downside:

> *Today I passed you on the street*
> *And my heart fell at your feet,*
> *I can't help it if I'm still in love with you.*
> *Somebody else stood by your side*
> *And he looked so satisfied.*
> *I can't help it if I'm still in love with you.‡*

Then, after the gunshot-punctured New Year's Eve party, everything fell apart. Hank and Audrey separated and then divorced. And his life turned into a personal hell. One associate has said: "I don't think he was so much a hateful guy inside. It was more like he . . . was burned out, as they call it. Blind crazy drunk and nothin' mattered."

---

*"I Just Don't Like This Kind of Livin' " by Hank Williams; copyright 1949 Fred Rose/Opryland Music, Inc.
†"Baby, We're Really in Love" by Hank Williams; copyright 1951 Fred Rose/Opryland Music, Inc.
‡"I Can't Help It" by Hank Williams; copyright 1951 Fred Rose/Opryland Music, Inc.

Jerry Rivers, the fiddler in Hank's band, remembered: "Hank brought some of his personal belongings to me to keep for him, and moved into an apartment with our new friend from Dallas, Texas, Ray Price. And we continued to record and work daily radio shows, but the pressure showed more on Hank each day."

But the hits continued: "Jambalaya," "Half as Much," "Honky Tonk Blues," "Settin' the World on Fire."

At the Grand Ole Opry the relationship with Williams was strained.

Faron Young remembered that "the Opry people gave him plenty of chances. You know, they run him off for a while and he'd come back and be drunk all over again. Jim Denny and Mr. DeWitt, they said, 'Look, we can't take any more of this crap. People drive all the way from Pennsylvania to see him and he walks out on the stage like that. We'd be better off without him.' "

As with all stories about Hank Williams, nothing can be considered to be simply black or white. The gray areas predominated in his life.

Former WSM executive Irving Waugh pointed out that, in an effort to help Williams, the Opry management persuaded him to check into Vanderbilt Hospital to dry out. "He had been on such a tear that it seemed necessary," Waugh said. "And his mother came up here and pleaded with us to have him released from the hospital. So I went out there and met with Hank, and now he had sobered up and he said if we'd let him go with his mother he'd be straight. Well, they got to about the second red light and he jumped out, leaving her there on the street with the car. And he disappeared for another three weeks.

"So he just wasn't booked on the Opry after that. Nobody fired him. I read that Edwin Craig fired him, or DeWitt fired him, or Denny fired him—but those stories are absurd! Everyone was just waiting for him to straighten himself out."

Williams left Nashville, surfacing at the "Louisiana Hayride" in Shreveport, returning to Nashville only to record. Faron Young recalled what may have been Hank's last visit to the city: "I was goin' with a girl named Billie Jones. I sent her back to Shreveport, but about three or four weeks later she came back up here. And Hank said, 'Hey, boy'—he never did call me Faron—'you get that girl you got an' I got one here from Pennsylvania, an' we'll go out on the town tonight.' I said, 'Oh, yes, sir.' It was like talkin' to God.

"Well, we got out to this little ole house he was rentin' an' he brought out a suitcase an' opened it up an' he musta had two hundred pistols in it. An' Billie said, 'Ooooh, what's this one, Hank?' 'That's a forty-five, gal.' An' it just went on like that. Finally, he called me into another room and he pulled a thirty-eight out of his pocket an' stuck it right in mah belly. He said, 'Now, I don't want no hard feelin's with ya, boy, but I'm in love with that girl, Billie.' And I said, 'Hey, she's yours! Put the gun up.' And we swapped dates that night. An' he wound up about two weeks later marrying Billie on the stage in New Orleans."

Williams did indeed marry nineteen-year-old Billie Jean Jones Eshlimar, a recent divorcee herself. It was a move apparently undertaken to strike back at

Audrey. The singer, encouraged by the no-holds-barred promoter Oscar ("The Baron") Davis, opted for a public ceremony during an engagement at the New Orleans Municipal Auditorium. Davis arranged to sell out the house for a matinee "rehearsal" of the wedding, and again in the evening for the "actual ceremony." Both were phony; the couple had been married by a justice of the peace the evening before.

No one seemed to care anymore; neither Hank, who had virtually disbanded the Drifting Cowboys because there was no work, nor those who attached themselves to his falling star. One of those was a paroled forger who had passed himself off as "Doctor" Toby Marshall and was supplying the singer with bogus prescriptions for the sedative chloral hydrate, a strong heart depressant that is sometimes used to treat alcoholics.

In late December 1952 (it apparently was Saturday, December 20) Williams was playing at the Skyline Club in Austin, Texas, as a single. One of those on the scene was a young man named Justin Tubb, a journalism student at the University of Texas, and the son of Opry star Ernest Tubb.

Tubb remembered: "I went out to the club and the old guy that was running it wasn't going to let me in. And I said, 'Will you please tell Hank that I'm here?' So he went back and Hank came storming out of the room in the back and said, 'Let that boy in here!' I stayed in his dressing room for the whole time—from like nine to one. When he wasn't on stage he was back there with me, and we talked. And he said, 'I just talked to Mr. Denny and they've agreed to take me back on the Opry. I got one date to play on New Year's Day and then I'm moving back to Nashville.' And we just had a long, long talk, and God, I never knew that would be the last time I'd ever see him.

"He looked a little thin—or, rather, a little *thinner*—and he had that screwy doctor with him that was giving him the shots for his slipped disc. And he had his hand bandaged up. He said, 'Billie hit me with a high-heeled shoe.' He was joking about it; he was in a good mood. He was happy about going back to Nashville."

⚬ iii ⚬ The engagement Hank had on New Year's Night was to be Canton, Ohio. The Opry's Little Jimmy Dickens was also booked on that show.

Hank sent word to the Drifting Cowboys to meet him in Dayton. Fiddler Jerry Rivers again: "The Drifting Cowboys had been working with Ray Price, working only occasionally with Hank when he would call from Shreveport. We got one such call about the show in Canton. Since Ray Price was also booked on another show nearby in Ohio the same night, I agreed to take a band and work the show with Ray, while Don Helms would take another band and work the show with Hank.

"On the morning of December 31, I drove out of Nashville in a spitting snow with our band. . . . We got as far as Louisville, Kentucky, where we encountered a blinding blizzard and the highway patrol informed us that the roads north were closed for at least twelve hours. So we turned the car around, arrived back in Nashville in the early morning and got into our warm beds. When I got up late in the morning, on January 1, 1953, I saw Hank's picture on the front page of the *Nashville Tennessean* and the headline which read, 'Country Singer Dies in Auto.' "

That snowstorm had been widespread, so Williams hired a young man named Charles Carr to drive him in his Cadillac from Montgomery to Canton. Hank sat in the back, dozing.

Did Carr carry out his informal driving contract? Apparently not. Williams arrived in West Virginia at the wheel of his car.

A different scenario emerges in a letter to the author from Hazel Wells Shultz, who had worked in a small all-night restaurant at Bluefield, West Virginia. Of that fateful night, she wrote: "He [Williams] walked into this restaurant without his [cowboy] hat, because he told us he didn't want people to bother him about songs, talk and the likes. He asked an employee if there might be someone around who would drive him to Canton, Ohio, that he had an appointment there the next day and that his driver had walked out on him. I believe his driver had left him somewhere in the area of either Knoxville or maybe Kingsport, Tn. Mr. Williams had managed to drive himself to Bluefield . . . and he informed us that he just couldn't drive any farther and had to be in Ohio the next day.

"We informed Mr. Williams that there was a cab driver present who had just checked off work who might drive him to Ohio. The cab driver I knew well, his name was Don Surface. He asked us if the cab driver would take a drink and we told him yes. Mr. Williams ordered two beers, took them to the booth where Don Surface was seated, they talk[ed], drank a beer each and left.

"Shortly after that a policeman came in the restaurant for coffee and informed us that Don had tried to wake Mr. Williams to get money for gas because they were running low, it was late, and not many stations [were] open at that time of night and he wanted to fill up so he could drive through without bothering about gas. The policeman told us that Don was being held in Oak Hill jail for a 72 hr. investigation.

"I talked about this with Don Surface many times before he died," Ms. Shultz wrote. "He told me that Mr. Williams asked him if he knew the way to Canton, and when he told him that he did, Mr. Williams said, 'Well, I'm going to sleep.' And that was the last word he ever spoke."

Thus, it was in Oak Hill, West Virginia, that Hank was found dead in the backseat of his car. The date was January 1, 1953; Hank Williams had not yet reached his thirtieth birthday.

Official cause of death was "alcoholic cardiomyopathy"; simply put, heart disease brought on by excessive drinking.

In Canton, Ohio, on that New Year's Night a spotlight was played on an empty theater stage while a recording of Williams's best-known gospel song, "I Saw the Light," blared from the loudspeakers.

Members of the audience wept.

Several days later, Hank's funeral in Montgomery, Alabama, was a massive outpouring of grief. Twenty-five thousand tried to get into a city auditorium that had seats for only 2,700. Women fainted; men cried openly.

One reporter wrote that the funeral was "the greatest emotional orgy in the city's history since the inauguration of Jefferson Davis."

And the Opry family gathered around. Ernest Tubb, standing beside the silver casket, sang "Beyond the Sunset." Roy Acuff performed "I Saw the Light," and Red Foley, choking back tears, sang "Peace in the Valley."

··◦[iv]◦·· There followed the inevitable exploitation of his fame. Both of Hank's wives went on tour, billing themselves as "Mrs. Hank Williams." Later, there was a biographical movie, *Your Cheatin' Heart*. Charitably, it was a travesty on Williams's fame.

What happened after Hank's death proved something. No matter how grossly the Williams story was handled, his music could not be subverted. All of the deep shadows of his life could not hide the light of his great talent. In a commercial sense, the Williams song catalogue (seemingly devoid of any really weak songs) is worth millions of dollars. In an aesthetic sense, the value of his songs is incalculable.

How do you sum him up? Many have tried.

Mitch Miller, onetime head of the popular music division of Columbia Records, said that Williams was in a class with Stephen Foster as an American songwriter. "He had a way of reaching your guts and your head at the same time."

Country music historian Bill C. Malone: "No one communicated as well as Hank Williams. . . . He sang with the quality that has characterized every great hillbilly singer: utter sincerity."

One final comment: Hank Williams, Jr.—"Little Bocephus"—was only four years old at the time of his father's death. Audrey's son knew the elder Williams only as a legend, as the man in the countless stories, many of them cruel, that survived him. It is the mark of Hank Jr. that he was able to overcome the pressure of the Hank Williams legend and carve out his own substantial career.

Wondering, wondering, who's kissing you,
Wond'ring, wondering if you're wondering, too,
Ev'ry hour of the day since you've been away,
*I keep wond'ring, just wondering if you're wondering, too.**

—Webb Pierce hit, 1952

If there could be a replacement for Hank Williams on the Grand Ole Opry it had to be Webb Pierce.

Indeed, that might have been in the minds of the Opry's executives when Pierce was invited to make a guest appearance on "The Prince Albert Show" in 1952 when the Williams "troubles" had grown to insolvable proportions. There is no doubt, though, that Webb would have been invited anyway. He was a major star of the competitive "Louisiana Hayride" and he had just scored impressively with his Decca release of "Wondering."

In one sense, Pierce, a native of Monroe, Louisiana, had the common touch attributed to Williams, and a unique style of singing in his wailing, whiskey-voiced tenor that grasped the listeners, holding them fast and wringing out of them every ounce of emotion.

There was a flamboyance about him, too, that excited the fans. He had once been one of them, having come from the modest circumstances of employment as a Sears, Roebuck clerk. But as soon as he started to become popular, there was no modest clerk in him; it seems impossible he had ever been anything but a star.

*"Wondering" by Joe Werner; copyright 1952 Aberbach, Inc.

He flaunted his success with lavish costumes and a custom-made automobile mounted with silver dollars, leather-encased steer horns as a radiator ornament, and seats designed to resemble saddles. Some in the music industry accused him of having a monumental ego, of bringing ridicule to country musicians, but Webb didn't care. And neither did the public.

In 1953, when he became a member of the Grand Ole Opry roster, he already had a number-one hit with "Back Street Affair," which was to become a country music standard about "cheating."

> *You didn't know I wasn't free*
> *When you fell in love with me,*
> *And with all your young heart you learned to care.*
> *It brought you shame and disgrace,*
> *The world has tumbled in your face,*
> *'Cause they call our love a back street affair.**

And he followed that with two more chart-toppers "It's Been So Long" and "There Stands the Glass." The latter became almost a national anthem for drinkers:

> *There stands the glass that will ease all my pain,*
> *That will settle my brain, it's my first today.*
> *There stands the glass that will hide all my tears,*
> *That will drown all my fears, Brother, I'm on my way†*

Pierce had an uncanny knack for picking commercial songs. And for making records that had a new, compelling sound to them, utilizing the wailing tones of the steel guitar. As Nick Tosches wrote in his book *Country: The Biggest Music in America*:

"There was steel in Pierce's music from the beginning, and with each record it pulsed stronger and louder. In 'Wondering' the steel is barely noticeable, but for a small flourish at the end; in 'That Heart Belongs to Me,' Pierce's second hit, there is a full solo; in 'Back Street Affair' and 'That's Me Without You' the steel flows through the whole of the music; in 'There Stands the Glass,' the steel is the dominant instrument; in 'Slowly,' the biggest country hit of 1954, the steel is the force of the song. Bud Isaacs, the man who played a Bigsby steel in 'Slowly,' birthed the Nashville steel sound that still prevails; those dark swoonings fluid as seaweed in a bay, and often as turgid."

If the intent was to have Webb Pierce replace Hank Williams on the Opry, he succeeded admirably. By the end of 1953 he was named the number-one country singer by America's jukebox operators, and he was well on the way toward becoming the biggest record-seller since Eddy Arnold.

*"Back Street Affair" by Billy Wallace; copyright 1952 Forrest Music Corporation.
†"There Stands the Glass" music by Russ Hill, words by Russ Hill, Mary Jean Shurtz, and A. Greisham; copyright 1953 Hill and Range Songs, Inc.; Jamie Music Publishing Co.

Webb enjoyed his time on the Opry, but the exigencies of taking advantage of his great popularity intruded. "You had to be there every Saturday night," Pierce said, "and that was too much, because, you see, most of our money, we made it on Saturday night. Of course, we'd be on a tour and then we'd have to turn around at the end of the week and be back at the Opry. I don't care if you was in Podunk, Canada!"

❧ ii ❧ It can be argued that the talent lineup on the Grand Ole Opry in the early fifties was one of the strongest ever to grace the Ryman Auditorium stage. Even after Williams's death there was real power in the roster: Roy Acuff, Red Foley, Minnie Pearl, Rod Brasfield, Ernest Tubb, Hank Snow, Jimmy Dickens, Bill Monroe, Kitty Wells, Webb Pierce, Faron Young, George Morgan, Carl Smith and his wife, June Carter (who worked as a single, as both a singer and a comedienne), and Ray Price.

And those were fun times, too. Faron Young remembered the comics: "Comedy was a great part of the show. Rod Brasfield was a funny sonofagun. You can take any of them other guys you wanna name and none of them was as funny as Rod. And him and Minnie Pearl together was a damned riot.

"Back then everybody traveled with a comic. I remember that Hank Snow had Sleepy McDaniels. After about three or four songs, Sleepy'd go back, put on his old bum clothes, and come around to the front of the theater. And he'd walk in and start hollerin': 'What's goin' on behind the stage?'

"An' Hank'd answer, 'Nothin'.'

"An' Sleepy'd say, 'Well, there ain't nothin' goin' on in front of it, either.' Then he'd say, 'Bureau, bureau.'

"Hank'd say, 'What are you talkin' about?'

" 'My girlfriend, Bureau.'

" 'No, no,' Hank'd say, 'a bureau is a great big thing standin' in the corner with drawers.'

"An' Sleepy'd holler, 'That's her!' "

Young continued: "One day Sleepy went out—up in Indianapolis—and by the time Snow did a couple of tunes he was supposed to make his entrance. Well, he didn't come in. The guard in the front thought he was really a bum and wouldn't let him come into the theater. Snow went on and sang three or four more numbers—and he was hot! Finally, somebody recognized Sleepy and he was let in. An' he started to holler: 'What's goin' on behind the stage?'

"An' Snow said, 'Not a damned thing, and besides that you're fired!' " And he was.

The conversation turned to George Morgan, a noted practical joker. "There was always somethin'," Faron said. "Limburger cheese in your guitar, or garlic rubbed on the microphone, or droppin' a stink bomb at the back of the stage—"

Vic Willis, often a fellow conspirator in Morgan's practical jokes, picked up the narration. "George had a fiddle player named Don Slayman, who was—and is—a very shy, quiet, kinda nervous-type person. And George got in a bathtub one time, and put some ketchup in it, and someone ran and got Don Slayman and said, 'George has finally done it—!' An' Don came in an' was shocked. 'Geez,' he said, 'somebody oughta call a priest.' An' then George rears up an' pounces on Slayman. He got him more than once on the death routine."

The name of Cedric Rainwater was brought up—a bass player with a number of bands. "We'd sit up there at WSM some mornings," Faron Young recalled. "Hank Williams would be there, and Ernest Tubb, and they'd be tellin' tales of things that happened to them on the road. Cedric always had to get in on the conversation somehow, regardless of what he had to say. Like somebody was talkin' about a shotgun he had, an' Cedric would say, 'I got a shotgun an' I gotta sell it.' An' Hank says, 'Why?' An' Cedric says, 'Well, I hit everythin' I aim at.' Hank says, 'That's the kind I'd want.' Cedric comes back with, 'Not me, hoss. I believe in givin' ev'rythin' a sportin' chance.'

"An' people'd get talkin' about drivin' a car an' Cedric would say: 'One year I drove a car 334,000 miles.' Somebody got a pen an' figured it up, an' said: 'Well, Cedric, you woulda had to average eighty-five miles an hour, twenty-four hours a day, for three hundred sixty-five days.' And he answers, 'Well, when I say a year, hoss, I sometimes mean eighteen months.' "

Rollin ("Oscar") Sullivan recalled the great influence that comedy had on the stage of the Ryman in those days. "Their concept of entertainment was different then," Sullivan said. "We had a guy here—Vito Pellettieri—an' they gave old Vito a challenge. They said. 'You keep that Opry *live*. While that commercial's on the air, we don't care what you do, but you keep after those comedians an' keep the audience entertained.' I'm tellin' you what—they had me in the R.C. cooler when we was on the R.C. Cola show, or if we was on for Stephens Work Clothes, somebody was tearin' my shirt off, or somethin', you know.

"We just did ev'rythin' to keep 'em laughin'. The people in that auditorium never heard a commercial."

···𝄞 iii 𝄢··· The early fifties also brought to the Opry a young man who was destined to become one of its most enduring stars. His name was Martin David Robinson, a.k.a. Marty Robbins.

Marty was a twin (his twin sister was Mamie), one of nine children of an oft-unemployed Arizona itinerant worker. To say that the Robinson family existed in desperate straits is to put a sugar coating on their poverty. There were times when the best home they had was a tent pitched in the desert near the small town of Glendale, Arizona.

Although he was always reluctant to talk about his personal life, Marty did tell one interviewer: "We were about as poor as you could get. I know what it's like to be laughed at because your shoes don't have soles on them."

Of his father, he added: "I never was one of his favorites. He had a bad temper and he'd whip me for nothin'. One time he got after me for somethin', chased

The legendary Hank
Williams at the Opry
with Chet Atkins as his
sideman on guitar and
Ernie Newton on bass.

(1951) *LES LEVERETT COLLECTION/
GERALD HOLLY PHOTOGRAPHER*

Over twenty-five thousand
people jammed Montgomery,
Alabama for Hank Williams's funeral
on January 4, 1953. His grave,
obscured here by thousands of
mourners, is in Montgomery's
Oakwood Cemetery Annex.

(1953) *COUNTRY MUSIC
FOUNDATION LIBRARY AND MEDIA
CENTER*

Webb Pierce serenades his wife, Audrey, at their home, perhaps with the biggest country hit of 1954, "Slowly."

(1954) OPRYLAND USA ARCHIVES/JEANNE GORDON COLLECTION

Marty Robbins uses a little musical persuasion to get Marion Worth to mark her ballot in his favor on the "Purina Grand Ole Opry Television Show."

(1955) OPRYLAND USA ARCHIVES/ JEANNE GORDON COLLECTION

The fifties decor in this photograph dates it to 1954, a big year for number-one country singer Webb Pierce.

(1954) OPRYLAND USA ARCHIVES/ JEANNE GORDON COLLECTION

Lester Flatt and Earl Scruggs and the Foggy Mountain Boys spread the fame of Martha White Flour from the stage of the Opry and also on tour in 1955. Pictured are (from the left) Jake Tullock on bass, Paul Warren on fiddle, Earl Scruggs, and Lester Flatt.

(1955) OPRYLAND USA ARCHIVES/JEANNE GORDON COLLECTION

me, and threw a hammer at me like a tomahawk. I stopped, picked it up, and threw it back just as hard. The hammer hit him in the chest. He never bothered me again."

His parents separated and his mother had to try to keep the family together by taking in washing. Marty was twelve at the time. The brutish father was written off: "I'm not sure whatever happened to him; never did check into it."

Those years at the end of the Depression had been a hell for the youngster. Teachers put him down as an incorrigible trouble-maker. He drifted, sometimes hopping freight trains, sometimes languishing in pool halls, sometimes picking cotton, sometimes herding sheep, sometimes digging ditches for ten cents a day, sometimes shoplifting, sometimes competing as an amateur boxer (he had more than seventy bouts), and sometimes just street-brawling.

"We were mean," he recalled, "and we fought dirty."

To writer Bob Allen, Robbins confessed some details of his teen years: "I had about fifteen or twenty phone booths [where] I wadded up napkins so they wouldn't return people's change, and I made the rounds of them for about ten months. They also had payoff pinball machines in a lot of stores back then. We would drill holes in their sides with an ice pick and rack up free games. Then we'd cover the holes back up with chewing gum. We had about a dozen machines fixed up like that, and we'd make about a dollar a night from each of them. They never did catch us."

What sunshine there was in Marty's youthful days came from two sources. One was Gene Autry movies. The boy would walk miles from his desert home to the movie theater on a Saturday morning to see Autry, sitting so close to the screen that he "could have gotten sand in [my] eyes from the horses and powder burns from the guns. I wanted to be a cowboy singer, simply because Autry was my favorite singer. No one else inspired me."

But someone else fascinated him almost as much as did Autry: his grandfather, who had spent some time as a traveling medicine show man. "They called him 'Texas Bob' Heckle," Marty said, "and he had been a Texas Ranger. Well, anyway, he said he was. He was a great storyteller. When I was a little kid, I'd sing him a song or two and he'd tell me a story."

In 1942, at the age of seventeen, Robbins went into the Navy. He spent three years in the South Pacific, and being an entertainer was far from his mind. He did buy himself a guitar in the service and taught himself to play it, but that was primarily to ward off boredom at sea. He returned to Arizona after his Navy stint, and moved aimlessly from one unfulfilling job to another.

"I was driving a truck hauling brick," he said, "and I heard some guy singing on a Phoenix radio station [KPHO]. The life of a singer sounded good to me because I liked to stay up late and never liked getting up early. Anyway, I went over to that radio station and told the manager I could sing better than the guy they had. I sang 'Strawberry Roan' for him and he fired his singer and hired me."

It would probably be more dramatic to report that Marty Robbins became an overnight sensation in Phoenix, but that didn't happen. He was happy with his radio job; he was making more money than he had ever dreamed of. And he was becoming popular in the tough Phoenix-area beer joints, where he first used the name Jack Robinson and then refined that to Marty Robbins, just because it sounded better to him. But he had no great motivation to go beyond that.

His old brawling days weren't ended either. "I got into fights almost every night," he recalled. "At some of those places I even had to fight the owner to get my pay. I only drank for two years out of my whole life, but during those two years I drank enough for the rest of my life."

Radio station KPHO also owned a television channel in Phoenix, which featured a live country music show. One day a scheduled guest star failed to appear and the station manager asked Marty to fill in. Marty declined. It was one thing to perform in front of a radio microphone, a place of comparative anonymity, but to "show" himself on television and to appear before a studio audience genuinely frightened him. He was told, however, that he *had* to take the TV spot: "If you want your job on radio, you'll do that television show."

He did, and continued it every week thereafter, although the singer who would later seem so at ease on the stage and in front of the cameras would frequently throw up before the telecast.

Robbins was doing that show in 1951 when Grand Ole Opry star Little Jimmy Dickens appeared on the station to promote a local concert appearance. Dickens was much impressed with the young singer and called him to the attention of Columbia Records. Columbia followed up on the Dickens recommendation, signing Marty to a recording contract.

His first record release was "Love Me or Leave Me Alone." It was his third release, though—"I'll Go On Alone"—that made the top ten on the charts in 1953, spreading his reputation to Nashville. Fred Rose, of Acuff-Rose Publications, flew to Phoenix to sign him as a songwriter.

"That was the highest compliment I've ever been paid in my life," Marty said later. "Fred Rose was one of the greatest songwriters that ever lived."

It was also in 1953 that Robbins was invited to make a guest appearance on the Grand Ole Opry, to be followed closely with an invitation to join the roster.

Perhaps no one could guess then that he'd stay for thirty years.

··◦❧[iv]❦◦·· There were other stirrings on the Opry scene.

A native Nashvillian, Adelaide Hazelwood, became a roster member in '53, after having turned down a two-week engagement with Bob Crosby the year before in order to accept an Opry guest spot. As Del Wood she was to bring a new sound to the Ryman stage: ragtime piano.

She had been playing since her parents gave her a piano for her fifth birthday. By the time she was a sophomore at Nashville's East High School she was an accomplished pianist. Her parents saw her as a concert pianist, but she always wanted to be on the Grand Ole Opry. Her rendition of "Down Yonder" got her there, and she was to become a fixture on the radio show.

The year 1953 also marked the beginning of Opry manager Jim Denny's career as a music publisher. He organized two BMI-affiliated companies: Driftwood, which was co-owned by Carl Smith and Troy Martin; and Cedarwood, a partnership with Webb Pierce (later Denny and Pierce were also partners in the ownership of three radio stations in Georgia). A third publishing company, Jim Denny Music, was set up as an ASCAP affiliate.

At the time it didn't seem to be a particularly significant move; Denny, after all, was simply moonlighting away from his Grand Ole Opry job. He was to learn that others would view his activities differently.

There was another development in that year that would have future repercussions on the Opry. It had to do with a longtime sponsor of the Opry, Martha White Flour.

Martha White was a small regional flour company begun in 1941 by a drawling Tennessee entrepreneur named Cohen Williams. He immediately saw the value of using country music to sell his Hot Rise flour and first advertised on the Grand Ole Opry in 1942.

"I think we had every fifteen-minute and every thirty-minute segment on the Opry," Williams said, "until we finally got the preferred eight-o'clock time spot." (In 1987, Martha White Flour was the longest continuous sponsor of the Opry— a period of forty-five years.)

It was in 1953, however, that Martha White's involvement with country music became all-consuming. At that time one of his salesmen came to Williams to suggest that Lester Flatt, Earl Scruggs, and the Foggy Mountain Boys "is who we need to sell flour." Williams had heard of them, of course, but he decided to follow up on his salesman's enthusiasm by going to see them himself—at WNOX, Knoxville, where the band was appearing on the "Midday Merry-Go-Round."

Satisfied with that initial look, he went on the road with them that night, to an engagement in Harlan, Kentucky. "That night they took in probably sixty-five dollars," Williams said. He offered to put them on the Martha White early-morning program on WSM and to get them on the Grand Ole Opry.

The latter part of that was easier said than done. Opry officials didn't want to offend Bill Monroe by bringing in a competitive act headed by two of Bill's former sidemen. As a matter of fact, there was even some doubt whether this new bluegrass band ought to be on the early morning show, but Cohen Williams went directly to WSM president Jack DeWitt to accomplish that.

But the Opry was off limits for Flatt and Scruggs.

Williams, however, recognized that there could be something very special in a substantial association of his flour company with Flatt and Scruggs, and he moved to put them on television, first with a weekly show on WSM Television, and then on similar shows throughout the South.

In those days before videotaped syndication of such programs the Foggy Mountain Boys became television circuit riders, driving 2,500 miles every week to meet their TV commitments. It spread the fame of Flatt and Scruggs, as well as Martha White Flour, and the Grand Ole Opry could not continue to ignore them.

By 1955 they were on the Opry roster. And not totally welcome at first. Lester Flatt remembered that other Opry acts were "steering around us as if we was a bunch of outlaws. But after we was there for a few weeks things changed, and they started coming around and patting us on the shoulder."

Not their former boss, however. Bill Monroe refused to speak to them.

As it turned out, that was only a minor distraction at the Grand Ole Opry. There was a larger tension building: the threat of rock 'n' roll.

It was on one moonlight night,
Stars shinin' bright,
Whisper on high
Love said good-bye;
Blue moon of Kentucky, keep on shining,
Shine on the one that's gone and left me blue. *

—Bill Monroe and Elvis Presley hit

It was in July 1954 that the small Sun Records company of Memphis released a single by a nineteen-year-old product of Tupelo, Mississippi, named Elvis Presley. On one side was Bill Monroe's "Blue Moon of Kentucky," sung with a physical intensity the Father of Bluegrass could never have imagined. On the other side was a Mississippi blues song, "That's All Right," which had been recorded by Arthur "Big Boy" Crudup in the mid-forties.

Sam Phillips, the perceptive and extroverted parent of Sun Records, knew he had a hit. But what was it? Country? Blues? It didn't fit easily into either category and a word would have to be coined to cover it: *rockabilly.*

Music historians would say later that the record marked the birth of rock 'n' roll. Maybe so. But it seems a Pennsylvania radio performer, a minor country singer with a spit-curl on his forehead and a broad grin on his open face, had been the father of that baby. Bill Haley's "Crazy, Man, Crazy" was already a genuine hit when Presley first recorded.

Nevertheless, Presley was something different; that much was very clear. On

*"Blue Moon of Kentucky" by Bill Monroe; copyright 1947 Peer International Corporation.

two different Memphis radio stations both sides of the record immediately scored with the listeners. And on WHIN in Gallatin, Tennessee, "Blue Moon of Kentucky" was the number-one record on the show of country disc jockey Justin Tubb, former Texas journalism student.

It was on Saturday, September 25, 1954, that Presley and his band (bassist Bill Black and guitarist Scotty Moore) came on the Grand Ole Opry to be introduced on the Hank Snow segment of the show.

Justin Tubb was there: "As best as I can remember, Elvis had on some red satin pants and a drugstore cowboy shirt. And he did 'That's All Right' on the Opry and it was just a little much. He just didn't go over that well. The audience was polite to him, no booing or anything like that, but I think he came expecting to set them on their ears and it didn't happen. I guess the country fans weren't quite ready for him."

Scotty Moore's recollection was that Elvis sang both sides of the record, "That's All Right" and "Blue Moon of Kentucky." But he agreed with young Tubb's evaluation of the reaction of the Grand Ole Opry audience: "It was really our first major appearance outside of Memphis, and it didn't go over so good. On a scale of one to ten I'd say it was something like a five—with an anchor.

"Anyway, that was Elvis's only appearance on the Opry. We'd come to Nashville for the disc jockey conventions in the early years. I remember that the first time we came to a convention Colonel [Tom] Parker had an elephant roaming around in front of the Andrew Jackson Hotel with an Elvis sign on it. A little bit of carnival."

It is part of the lore of the Grand Ole Opry that manager Jim Denny told Presley to go back to driving a truck (Elvis had a $42-a-week job then, driving a truck for the Crown Electric Company in Memphis), and that the young singer cried all the way back to Memphis.

Did Denny really say that? "He might have," Justin Tubb said. "Jim was capable of being very blunt."

Whatever the Opry manager may have said to him (if he made any comment at all), Presley was deeply disappointed by the lack of acceptance from the Grand Ole Opry audience.

Justin then took Elvis, Black, and Moore to the "Midnight Jamboree" at his father's record shop. "When he came to the record shop after the Opry [show] he was hurt, because his record was big all over the country. He said to my dad, 'Mr. Tubb, what should I sing? I love country music.' And Dad said, 'Well, son, on my show let's do "Blue Moon of Kentucky." But if you wanna make money, then you probably ought to sing your rock 'n' roll. If you get big enough, you can sing anything you want to.' That's exactly what he told him."

Grand Ole Opry star Billy Walker had another early remembrance of Presley: "Elvis worked his first public performance with me and Slim Whitman. Bob Neal had booked us at the Overton Band Shell in Memphis. Slim was hotter than a pistol back then, and I had this record, 'Thank You for Calling.' Charlie and Ira Louvin were on the show, too, and Neal put Presley on the show with us that night. We had about five thousand people at the band shell. Well, Slim went back to the 'Louisiana Hayride' and said, 'Hey, this kid up there named Elvis Presley is tearin' 'em up.' And the Hayride sent for him and he had to sign a year's contract. It was phenomenal! Presley changed the image of the 'Louisiana Hayride.' "

And the image, too, of all of popular music.

Rock 'n' roll's impact on country music was devastating. It appealed to the same basic audience, perhaps because its roots were initially in country blues and hillbilly; the Beatles were to recognize that later. Whatever the explanation, the impact was there. And the Grand Ole Opry was not immune.

◄[ii]► In 1953, the year that Bill Haley and the Comets had their first national hit with "Crazy, Man, Crazy," ticket sales at the Ryman Auditorium for the Grand Ole Opry had peaked at 243,721.

Then came Elvis Presley and Little Richard and Fats Domino and Chuck Berry and attendance started to drop. Slowly at first: 232,808 and 232,819 in 1954 and 1955, respectively. And then the dam burst.

Opry audiences declined to 209,695 in 1956, and to an alarming 172,144 the next year. There seemed no way to stop the slide: 144,464 in 1958; 140,710 in 1959; 136,520 in 1960. Thus, from 1953—when rock 'n' rock began—to 1960, Grand Ole Opry ticket buyers had fallen off by nearly forty-four percent.

Veteran Opry announcer Grant Turner recalled those days: "I can remember times when there were empty seats at the Opry. You remember back when Elvis Presley came along? Well, he and the other people in that rock 'n' roll era took away some of the audience.

"I remember especially one Saturday night. It was a Christmas Eve. I guess it was pretty cold that night. But there was hardly anybody there in the Ryman Auditorium. Some of the best shows were during the holidays when all the stars were home in Nashville. But that night nobody came to see them.

"Yes, I was worried about the Opry at that point—"

There was concern, also, in the corporate offices of WSM. "We began to say to ourselves," Irving Waugh recalled, "is this softening of attendance due to television? Or is it due to the world's becoming more accustomed to air-conditioning? That was another one of the big new things in those days. We wondered if we had a problem at the Ryman because of that."

WSM chairman of the board Edwin Craig was quick to put the blame on the "changes" that had been wrought at the Opry over the years. Waugh again: "Mr. Craig took the position that we had made a mistake by going to the star system rather than keeping the Opry the way it had been in the earlier years, but that we were going to have to keep it going, come hell or high water."

◄[iii]► In 1954, when the flood of audience decline was still a mere trickle, one of the stars to whom Edwin Craig objected so strongly left the Grand Ole Opry.

After eight years as the host of "The Prince Albert Show," Red Foley departed the Opry and Nashville to try his hand at television. He moved to Springfield, Missouri, to host what was called the "Ozark Jubilee," which had begun as a radio show on KWTO. It was a success.

Back at the Opry, the decision was made not to replace Foley with another permanent host. Some thought that Roy Acuff would go back to his old position; instead, rotating hosts were used, some drawn from the Opry roster, some from outside.

And in spite of the steady drop-off of audience at the Ryman it was clear that country music was still strongly supported in the hinterlands. The WSM Artists' Service Bureau released a year-end report in which it was revealed that it had booked 2,554 personal appearances of Opry acts in 1954, playing to some eight million customers. It remained huge.

·❦[iv]❦· No diminution of the Opry "live" audience was going to panic WSM officials into succumbing to the rock-'n'-roll fad. But they weren't ignoring new performers who would keep the Opry roster up to date. In the latter part of 1954, a Texas disc jockey named Charlie Walker came to the attention of the Grand Ole Opry brass. His story was almost too typical. Yet important to the Opry legend.

"When I was in the fifth grade in school—a little country school up north of Dallas," Charlie remembered, "they asked us to write down on a piece of paper what we wanted to do when we grew up. And at that age, most kids said they wanted to be a policeman, or a fireman, or a cowboy. But I wrote that I wanted to sing on the Grand Ole Opry. 'Cause that was our regular Saturday-night entertainment. I remember when Roy Acuff came on in '39—I was just a little boy— and we listened *every* Saturday night to hear him sing 'The Great Speckled Bird.' On Monday mornings kids in my school there would say, 'Hey, did you hear that joke that Minnie Pearl told Saturday night?' It was big-time radio.

"Anyway, in 1954 I lived in San Antonio, and I was with a CBS station down there for fifteen years as one of the top-ten disc jockeys in the country in those days. I had a hit record for Decca called 'Tell Her Lies and Feed Her Candy,' and they invited me to come up and sing it as a guest on 'The Prince Albert Show' of the Opry.

"My family and friends were excited. In fact, a friend of mine down there who was in the building business paid his own expenses to come to Nashville with me. And I remember that we stayed in the Andrew Jackson Hotel and I was sitting over there and listening to WSM on the radio in my room. And they came on with a tornado alert. The thought ran through my mind, 'Here's my big chance to appear on the Grand Ole Opry and it's gonna blow the damn place down before I get on it.' "

Walker laughed. "That first appearance I was scared to death. I'm not kidding. I guess I was in awe. Carl Smith was the host of 'The Prince Albert Show' that night. And just before I went on, Mr. Vito—the stage manager—came up to me and told me a little risqué joke that caused me to break out laughing. Just about that time the announcer said, 'And now here's that tall boy from Texas, Charlie Walker!' And I came out laughing and it broke the ice."

Walker was to make a series of guest appearances on the Opry in subsequent years. It was in 1967, after two hit records in a row—"Pick Me Up on Your Way Down" and "Don't Squeeze My Charmin"—that he moved to Nashville and became a member of the Grand Ole Opry roster.

South of the border, hey, I know a lad,
He's got more fun than anybody's had;
Don't got no worry, don't got no dough,
*Ev'rybody's wond'ring 'bout Mexican Joe.**

—Jim Reeves's first hit

Almost from the beginning of commercial television after World War Two there was talk around WSM about the TV potential of the Grand Ole Opry property. Talk, but not action.

But in 1955 a longtime sponsor of the radio Opry, Ralston Purina, cast its lot with TV, sponsoring a one-hour regional network show of the Opry. It aired every fourth week; the other three weeks Red Foley's "Ozark Jubilee" was in the time spot.

The shows weren't really called "The Grand Ole Opry," but they featured the Opry stars and were telecast from the stage of the Ryman Auditorium.

If the TV shows demonstrated anything, they proved once more that the comedy team of Rod Brasfield and Minnie Pearl could be translated to any medium. Television merely enhanced their comedy; both were inherently *visual* comics.

Here's a small sample of one of their routines:

Brasfield enters, dressed in an ill-fitting, long striped bathing suit, with swim fins on his feet, and carrying an inflated inner tube.

Rod: "I'm a-going' swimmin' with the purrtiest woman I ever seen."

*"Mexican Joe" by Mitchell Torok; copyright 1953 American Music, Inc.; Elvis Presley Music, Inc.; Noma Music, Inc.

Minnie enters behind him, wearing a gay nineties swimsuit that covers her from the neck to the ankles.

Minnie: "How-dee, Rodney!"

Rod: (turning to her in surprise) "Well, I declare, if it ain't Jane Russell!" (Double take) "An' it ain't! . . . Hey, Minnie, are you goin' swimmin' in that there swimsuit?"

Minnie: (coyly) "Yes. Do you think it's too daring?"

Rod: "Well, I don't know. Did anybody dare you to wear it?"

Minnie: "You're a big 'un to talk. Look at that what you got on."

Rod: (proudly) "Ain't it a fit?"

Minnie: "A fit? It looks more like a convulsion to me."

Rod: "This here's my divin' suit."

Minnie: "Well, you oughta know about the dive."

Rod: "How's that?"

Minnie: "You've been in plenty of 'em."

Rod: "Oh, Minnie, hush!"

Minnie: "Listen, Rodney, tell me how you feel about these girls that go out in these swimsuits like I've been lookin' at down yonder at the lake. Do you like bathin' beauties?"

Rod: (grinning lecherously) "I don't know, Minnie, I never bathed one."

Minnie: "Rodney, there are some girls down there that had on swim- suits . . . well, I ain't never saw nothin' like it. One of 'em had on what Uncle Nabob called a hobo bathin' suit."

Rod: "Hobo? What in the cat hat is a hobo suit?"

Minnie: "No visible means of support!"

⊰[ii]⊱ More and more the "Louisiana Hayride" in Shreveport was providing new acts for the Opry. Some eyes viewed it as a training ground: a minor-league farm club, so to speak, for the Grand Ole Opry. In 1955 the WSM radio show got one of its greatest stars from the Hayride.

His name was James Travis Reeves.

Reeves was a Texan, born in 1924 in Panola County, whence had come singing cowboy movie star Tex Ritter. He was a farm boy, raised on land along the Sabine River; his family produced cotton, rice, and watermelons. There's one story that he swapped a bushel basket of pears for his first six-string guitar, with three missing strings. As happened not infrequently to people in the thirties, young Jim was captivated by the recordings of Jimmie Rodgers.

His family encouraged his interest in music. At the age of ten, before his voice changed, he had his own fifteen-minute radio program on a station in Shreveport, Louisiana, just across the state line from his home.

As he grew up, however, his primary concern was baseball. He was a big, strong youngster, and a right-handed pitcher of sufficient ability to earn an athletic scholarship at the University of Texas. When he graduated from high school in Carthage, Texas, he was six feet two and weighed 185 pounds. The scholarship money and the side money he earned as a part-time performer sustained him during his college days.

Then came what he thought was his big break. He was signed to a professional baseball contract by the St. Louis Cardinals, at that time the operators of the best minor-league farm system in baseball. He was assigned to the Lynchburg, Virginia, club; in his second year he severely injured a leg while sliding into second base. Doctors told him his baseball career was ended.

Reeves returned to Texas, taking a job as a disc jockey at radio station KGRI in Henderson (later he'd buy the station). During his entire period in Henderson— five years—he sang on small dates whenever possible. Then, in 1953, another opportunity opened up for him. He went to radio station KWKH in Shreveport, Louisiana, where he became the master of ceremonies (singing occasionally) of the "Louisiana Hayride." In that same year his second record, on the rather obscure Abbott label, was released. It was "Mexican Joe," and it was a hit. "Bimbo," an even bigger it, followed shortly thereafter.

To test the show business waters, Jim secured a leave of absence from the "Louisiana Hayride" and undertook a nationwide tour. It too was a success. The venture quickly led to a recording contract with RCA Victor, a summer replacement stint for Red Foley on the televised "Ozark Jubilee," and an invitation, in the fall of 1955, to join the Grand Ole Opry.

He was to become, with his velvety pop style, the Opry's new Eddy Arnold.

···⚓ iii ⚓··· There were other personnel additions at the Grand Ole Opry. As already reported, Flatt and Scruggs joined the show, as did Charlie and Ira Louvin, Jean Shepard, the Ralph Sloan square dancers, and Justin Tubb, the son of Ernest.

The Louvin brothers, sons of a Sand Mountain, Alabama, farmer (the family name was Loudermilk), were raised on a remote family farm. Music was in their heritage. Their father was a fiddler and banjo picker and there were frequent weekends set aside for family musicales, with the father playing and Ira and Charlie joining their five sisters in singing harmony. Ira learned to play the mandolin, Charlie the guitar.

Eventually a brother act was begun and they competed in an amateur contest at radio station WAPB in Chattanooga, Tennessee, where they won three weeks in a row. They were offered a permanent job on the station. Ira, the older brother, took the radio position, but Charlie, then only seventeen, had to stay on the farm; his father thought he was too young to venture out into the world. But he finally relented and the Louvin brothers became a part of the Happy Valley Boys on WDOK.

It seemed that every time they began to make headway as an act, the U.S. Army interceded. Ira was drafted in 1943. He had no sooner returned from the service than Charlie was called up in 1946. It wasn't until late in 1947 that they were able to play together again; they caught on with a 4:30 A.M. show on WROL in Knoxville. It didn't pay much, though, and Ira's recollection was that they almost starved to death.

The King, Elvis Presley, visits backstage at the Opry House. Pictured with him are Hubert Long (on his left), Colonel Tom Parker (his manager), and Faron Young (on his right).

(C. 1956) COUNTRY MUSIC FOUNDATION LIBRARY AND MEDIA CENTER

Ronald Reagan has to settle for second billing to the King of Country Music at New York's Palace Theater in 1955.

(1955) ROY ACUFF COLLECTION

Justin Tubb, with the guitar, grew up at the Opry, where his father, Ernest, was one of the biggest stars. At 20, Justin became the Opry's youngest regular member, ever, in 1955. Pictured with him from left are Gabe Tucker, his manager at the time, and Paul Cohen, an A&R man for Decca Records.

(1955) OPRYLAND USA ARCHIVES/JEANNE GORDON COLLECTION

The Louvin Brothers joined the Opry in 1955. From the left are Ira Louvin, Chet Atkins, Grandpa Jones, and Charlie Louvin.

(1955) OPRYLAND USA ARCHIVES/JEANNE GORDON COLLECTION

A *publicity shot for one of the Opry's sponsors, Dr. LeGear's Animal Tonics. From the left are Grant Turner, Jimmy Riddle, Howdy Forrester, Roy Acuff (holding "Cow Prescription"), Brother Oswald Kirby (holding a wormer), Johnny Wright (holding "Hog Worm Powder"), Jack Anglin (holding "Pig Swig"), Kitty Wells, Joe Zinkan, and Pap Wilson.*

(1956) OPRYLAND USA ARCHIVES/JEANNE GORDON COLLECTION

M*innie Pearl in her checked apron and Rod Brasfield in his checked vest perform their comedy routine with guest star Buddy Ebsen, far left, and Carl Smith on the Ralston Purina television show in 1955.*

(1955) OPRYLAND USA ARCHIVES/ JEANNE GORDON COLLECTION

Enter Smilin' Eddie Hill, an announcer and promoter, who was driving through Knoxville and heard them on WROL. He contacted them.

"Charlie and I had just enough for a bowl of cornflakes for breakfast," Ira said, "but Eddie told us to eat ham and eggs and paid the check." He also financed their move to Memphis, where they joined Hill on a new radio program, remaining for two years before accepting a better deal back in Knoxville. Hill also interested Fred Rose, of Acuff-Rose Publications, in the Louvins' collection of more than two hundred original songs. And it was Rose who got them a recording contract with Decca, where their first releases were "Alabama" and "Seven Year Blues."

However, the act broke up again when Charlie was recalled to the Army during the Korean War. It wasn't until 1954 that they were able to be the Louvin Brothers once more. In the latter part of '54, Ira and Charlie were in Nashville for a recording session for Capitol and were invited to make a guest appearance on the Grand Ole Opry.

They sang one of their own songs, "Love Thy Neighbor," a song about family love at home in an isolated area where neighbors are friendly, and anxious to share their milk when the other fellow's cow goes dry. On February 29, 1955, they joined the Opry roster.

Before the year was out they had their first big recorded hit, "When I Stop Dreaming," and had won trade magazine recognition as the "most programmed group" of 1955.

Jean Shepard's road to the Grand Ole Opry was different, yet similar too. Born in a small town of Pauls Valley, Oklahoma, and raised on family music, she became a transplanted Californian when the family moved to Visalia, near Bakersfield, the western capital of country music. There, when she was only fifteen, she joined an all-girl country band called the Melody Ranch Girls as bassist and singer. While she was still in high school, Jean got a chance to record for Capitol Records; the release sank without a trace.

But she kept singing and came to the attention of Hank Thompson, who was touring that part of California. He was with Capitol Records at the time and once more brought her to Capitol's attention. Ken Nelson, an A&R man—an executive who hires talent and produces records—liked what he heard, and added her to the Capitol roster. Her first release was "Crying Steel Guitar Waltz."

Capitol then teamed her with one of its top male singers, Ferlin Husky. The result was a major hit in 1953, "Dear John Letter." The duo was in great demand and it seemed natural that they would be booked on a nationwide tour. Jean, however, was not yet twenty-one, and she couldn't legally leave the state on her own. To circumvent that problem, Husky was made her legal guardian for a few months. Later she told an interviewer: "Imagine having Ferlin Husky as your guardian!"

Her solo career was prospering too. In 1955 she had two top-ten hits: "Beautiful Lies" and "Satisfied Mind." She was asked to join the cast of Red Foley's "Ozark Jubilee" television show, and then, in 1956, came the call she had been wanting all along. Jean Shepard, blue-eyed, blonde, five feet one, only twenty-three years old, became a member of the Grand Ole Opry.

⋯∘ᗡ iv ᑕ∘⋯ Justin Tubb's initial introduction to the Opry was vastly different, of course. He grew up there.

"I made my first appearance on the Grand Ole Opry when I was about nine," he recalled. "In 1944, I believe. Dad had an early radio show on Saturday from the WSM studio for the Carter's Chick Company out of Illinois—they sold baby chicks. I was kind of a regular on that show in the summer until I would go back to school; I went to school in Lebanon [Tennessee] at a military academy. One night he took me down to the Ryman and put me on the Opry. Golly, I wish I could remember what I sang. It seems like he and I sung one together; 'Soldier's Last Letter' comes to mind."

Was that something he had wanted to do?

"Back then it didn't matter to me," Justin said. "I was just a kid. I was having fun. I was like a little stage rat at the Opry, because I hung around backstage. I knew everybody there and they knew me. And I used to travel with Dad on the road and he had costumes made up for me. And it was a big deal for me then. As I got older I sort of rebelled against it, because I got tired of hearing people say: 'He's gonna be just like his daddy.' I decided I wasn't going to be. And when I went to college at the University of Texas I had prepared myself for a journalism career and possibly a sportscasting career, because sports is my second love.

"Then, when Hank Williams died, and Dad recorded that tribute song I wrote, well—" Justin paused. "It all changed for me. I got into country music first as a disc jockey and writing songs. And then Paul Cohen said, 'Well, he writes pretty good songs, so let's cut them with him.' That's how I got on Decca, and after my fourth release I joined the Opry in 1955. I was the youngest regular member ever on the Grand Ole Opry. It was just three weeks past my twentieth birthday when I joined."

Was it difficult being the son of Ernest Tubb?

"It really was," he answered without hesitation. "I don't care what anybody says, it's hard. For a son to follow his dad, especially somebody who's in the Hall of Fame and a legend. For a long time my daddy and I were competing with each other. We sat down and talked this out before I ever got into it full-time. And I told him, 'I don't want to be part of your show. I just feel funny about you bringing me out onstage and everybody saying, 'Yeah, well, he wants us to hear his kid now.' So I went my separate way and I don't think I would have done it any other way.

"I'm completely happy with what I've done. I haven't been no superstar. I've had chart records, I've had number-one records, I've written songs that had been recorded about two hundred different times. It's been enough to satisfy me. Once you settle in your place in the scheme of things, it's pretty comfortable.

"Now, when I look back, I kinda miss some of the good times he and I might have had if we had traveled together. I went on a couple of trips when I wasn't supposed to be there. I just went along for the ride; just to be with him.

"He just loved that road. And he told his fellows, 'If anything ever happens to me while we're on the road, you put me in the back of this bus and bring me home.' That bus was more of a home to him than the home he had, you know."

[v] The major Opry acts were plowing new ground in 1955. Roy Acuff and Kitty Wells (along with Johnny Wright and Jack Anglin, of course) banded together to form a touring unit that was to stay together for two years.

They played everywhere in the United States and Canada. And when they were back on the Opry on Saturday nights, they worked in the same Opry segment.

Of special note was the November 1955 appearance in the Palace Theater on New York's Times Square, once looked upon as the pinnacle of success for any vaudeville act. "Playing the Palace" was the best you could achieve.

By 1955 the old vaudeville houses had turned to motion pictures. Only a few—like the Palace—still offered live stage shows, but now in concert with a feature film. That show business reality led to a marquee on the Palace that would, in later years, bring a lot of joy to Acuff.

A photograph taken at that time shows the billing on the RKO Palace marquee reading:

GRAND OLE OPRY
ROY ACUFF
RONALD REAGAN

Obviously, the Reagan billing referred to the motion picture being offered.

(Years later, when *that* Ronald Reagan became President of the United States, Acuff had a special print made of the photo and sent it to the White House. The President recognized the humor in once having received second billing to the King of Country Music.)

[vi] Even with the diminished audience at the Ryman Auditorium during that era, the enthusiasm of those country music fans who did buy tickets remained high.

Oswald Kirby, of Acuff's Smoky Mountain Boys, recalled: "A bunch of us were dancing out there on the stage in the middle of the show one night, just having fun and acting the fool, when this short, stocky fellow from Kentucky jumped onto the stage with us out of the audience.

"This fellow started dancing right along with us. I guess he thought it was open to anybody, and I suppose he had a little something to drink. Anyway, Roy could have stopped it by just going over to the boy and putting a hand on his shoulder and telling him quietly that members of the audience weren't supposed to be on the stage.

"But before Roy could do anything, Jim Denny went over to the boy and popped him on the chin!

"It started the awfullest fight you ever saw. That boy whipped Jim Denny all over the stage, then he whipped six policemen and half the musicians, before they could get him hauled off to jail."

Perhaps that was indicative of how much Denny would be beleaguered in the months ahead.

I keep a close watch on this heart of mine.
I keep my eyes wide open all the time.
I keep the ends out for the tie that binds.
Because you're mine,
I walk the line.*

—Johnny Cash hit,
1956

Carl Smith introduced him on the Prince Albert network portion of the Grand Ole Opry, saying that he was "the brightest rising star in country music."

The *Nashville Banner*'s Ben A. Green was there on that summer evening of 1956: "He had a quiver in his voice, but it wasn't stage fright. The haunting words of 'I Walk the Line' began to swell through the building. And a veritable tornado of applause rolled back. The boy had struck home, where the heart is. . . .

"As his last words filtered into the farthermost corners, many in the crowd were on their feet, cheering, waving and clapping. They, too, had taken a new member into the family."

That was the debut of Johnny Cash at the Grand Ole Opry.

What was so astonishing about Cash coming to the Opry was that he had been a performer for just a little more than a year.

**"I Walk the Line" by John R. Cash; copyright 1956 Hi Lo Music, Inc.; Hill and Range Songs, Inc.

Johnny was a child of the Depression in the South, which was something vastly different from the Depression in northern industrial cities. From age three to age eighteen, Cash lived in Dyess, Arkansas, a tiny community brought into being by the federal government to resettle poor families who needed the promised twenty acres of delta land, the mule, and the small frame house just to survive. It was in Dyess that he picked cotton. And it was there that he learned to sing, but with little thought that he would ever be an entertainer.

After graduation from high school, Cash joined the Air Force in 1950, serving most of his hitch in Germany. There he bought his first guitar, learned to play it, and did a lot of playing and singing in the barracks—mostly country and gospel tunes. On July 4, 1954, he was honorably discharged.

"I had a crooked nose from a fight with a paratrooper in a honky-tonk," Cash would write later in his autobiography, *Man in Black*, "a scar on my cheek left by a drunken German doctor who couldn't find a cyst he was trying to remove, and a left ear with the hearing temporarily impaired because a German girl stuck a pencil in it. Otherwise, I was in good shape to come back to my people and to a San Antonio girl named Vivian Liberto, whom I married a month later."

John set up housekeeping in Memphis, at first trying to make a living as a door-to-door appliance salesman. By his own admission he was a dismal failure at that. He tried to get a disc jockey job, then spent a few months in a radio announcer's school. A turn in the road came when Roy, his brother, introduced him to two auto mechanic friends—electric guitarist Luther Perkins and bass player Marshall Grant.

"We three became friends," Cash reminisced, "and 'made music' together practically every night at Roy's house or at mine. Friends and neighbors started coming in and listening, and we'd sing and play until the early hours of the morning, night after night, just for the love of it."

Memphis was a place to be in those days for anyone with musical ambitions. Sam Phillips, owner of Sun Records, was beginning to stir things up, especially with a young singer named Elvis Presley. Through persistence, Cash wrangled an audition with Phillips and eventually cut a record with two original Cash songs: "Hey, Porter" on the A side and "Cry, Cry, Cry" on the B side. It was released in mid-May 1955, and the Johnny Cash career was launched. John and the Tennessee Two began to play personal appearances around Memphis and in Arkansas, Louisiana, and Texas.

National recognition came with the release of "I Walk the Line." An earlier hit, "Folsom Prison Blues," had earned him a regular spot on the "Louisiana Hayride" in Shreveport. When "I Walk the Line" crashed onto the charts, the Grand Ole Opry beckoned.

Cash told the Ryman audience on the night of his debut there: "I am grateful, happy and humble. It's the ambition of every hillbilly singer to reach the Opry in his lifetime. It's the tops for us. I feel mighty lucky to be here tonight . . . and I thank everyone."

John R. Cash was on the road to superstardom. He didn't know then how many potholes there would be in that road.

··◦⟦ ii ⟧◦·· Louisiana, historians will tell you, was America's first melting pot. Beginning early in the eighteenth century there was a mixing of races and nationalities from all corners of the globe: Choctaw Indians, Frenchmen, Acadian refugees from Nova Scotia, Spanish planters, Dalmatian oystermen, Filipino shrimpers, Germans, tough "Kaintucks," and a generous sprinkling of fugitives from justice, *filles de joie*, and genuine pirates.

Northern Louisiana was very much like other areas of the Deep South. But southern Louisiana . . . well—that was, and is, a bewildering conglomeration of what one writer has called "an ethnic and cultural heterogeneity." Southern Louisiana conjures up visions of the serenity of Spanish moss and cypress trees on the banks of a misty bayou, the violence of a Gulf storm lashing at ancient live oaks, the languid pace of a steamy-hot summer day, the lightning speed of an alligator slipping into the river, and the intensity of energy-charged Cajun music.

Cajuns? Basically, they were French, which is a sadly inadequate explanation. There saga began in September 1755 during the French and Indian Wars, when the British ordered the deportation of virtually the entire French population of Nova Scotia. Eight thousand were driven from their homes, herded aboard overcrowded ships, and banished into exile. Nearly half of them died at sea of smallpox. They scattered along the Atlantic coast, slowly drifting southward looking for a hospitable area in which to resettle. Henry Wadsworth Longfellow told the heartbreaking story of their wanderings in his classic poem *Evangeline*.

It was Louisiana that welcomed them finally, and because most of the survivors of the exodus were farmers and trappers and fishermen, they settled in the bayous of southern Louisiana, which offered them succor. They were called Acadians, a name the American tongue soon corrupted to "Cajuns." And their French was corrupted, too, into a regional dialect also known as Cajun.

It was that colorful area that produced a star for the Grand Ole Opry in August 1956 in the person of Jimmy C. Newman, a one-hundred-percent Cajun who was a native son of Big Mamou, Louisiana. But he wasn't a Cajun performer. Not then. True, he had the unmistakable Cajun accent in his tenor voice, but he had to be a country performer if he wanted to progress. It's a fact that Hank Williams had a hit with the Cajun-like "Jambalaya," but Cajun music wasn't yet considered commercial in the mid-fifties.

Newman had been playing and singing with bands in his teens, and he made his first recording as a vocalist in 1946. In French. "For a long time," he said, "I couldn't get a record contract because of my French accent."

In the early fifties, however, Dot Records took a chance with him, and he began to perform on the "Louisiana Hayride." In 1954 he had a hit with his own country composition, "Cry, Cry, Darling," and in 1956 the Grand Ole Opry once more dipped into the Hayride talent pool for another Opry roster member.

"When I got to the Ryman," Jimmy recalled, "Webb Pierce was on the Opry, and George Morgan, Jimmy Dickens, Hank Snow, Carl Smith, Faron Young— it was probably the end of that certain era when the Nudie look was so big. [Nudie was a self-promoting Hollywood manufacturer of loud costumes, featuring multi-colored embroidery and acres of rhinestones.] The Nudie suits and the Cadillacs were the big things when I came to the Opry. I wore western suits then—I couldn't afford a costume by Nudie himself—but in '57 I had a crossover hit with 'A Fallen Star' and I went to the Ivy League look."

After he had been on the Grand Ole Opry only a few weeks, Newman went on tour with the Roy Acuff–Kitty Wells troupe. "We were playing in Canada," he remembers, "and someone called back to Nashville, and we learned that Jim Denny had been ousted as manager of the Opry, and Dee Kilpatrick was in."

꞉[iii]꞉ Newman, of course, knew nothing about the background of the inter-necine warfare being fought within the WSM hierarchy. Nor did a lot of other Opry artists; they didn't know, or they didn't care.

There was, if the truth be told, a kind of "armed camp" atmosphere in the corporate offices. Rancor had sprung up between WSM president Jack DeWitt and several of his executives. Perhaps the full story will never be written, and maybe it really doesn't matter in this case, except for the fact that it did affect the Grand Ole Opry in one of its manifestations.

The board of directors of WSM, concerned by the increased moonlighting of their employees, decreed that outside business activities would not be allowed, especially in those instances deemed to be in conflict with their WSM employment. "Make a choice," the directors said, "WSM or your outside jobs." Thus, engineers Aaron Shelton, George Reynolds, and Carl Perkins, who had founded the successful Castle Recording Studio, quickly got out of that and elected to stay with WSM.

Not so clear-cut was the issue of whether a music publishing company was a conflicting business. Jim Denny's Cedarwood had become a force in Nashville. WSM program director Jack Stapp had Tree Publishing, but it was a small company not yet of the importance of Cedarwood.

"The board of directors," executive Irving Waugh said, "had indicated that Denny and Stapp should be given the option of resigning or giving up their publishing interests. DeWitt didn't do that. He just fired Denny in September of '56 and brought in a new manager for the Grand Ole Opry."

It was on Tuesday, September 25, that DeWitt announced to the Nashville newspapers that Walter D. Kilpatrick, a thirty-seven-year-old ex-Marine and a former record company executive, had been hired to be what was described as the Grand Ole Opry's "general director." Kilpatrick would succeed Denny not only as Opry manager, but also as manager of the radio station's Artists' Service Bureau.

Effectively sidetracked had been program director Stapp, whose areas of responsibility had included overall management of the Opry. Kilpatrick's appointment removed Stapp entirely from the Opry picture. (Several months later he would resign.)

Denny's first act after leaving the radio station was the organization of the Jim Denny Artists Bureau, Inc. Grand Ole Opry talent, aware of Jim's widespread booking contacts, flocked to his agency, as did others not on the Opry roster.

An early brochure of the Denny booking agency listed representation of Webb Pierce, Minnie Pearl, Ray Price, Carl Smith, Kitty Wells, Johnny and Jack, Hank Snow, Jimmy Dean, Little Jimmy Dickens, Hawkshaw Hawkins, Jean Shepard, George Morgan, Jimmy C. Newman, Stonewall Jackson, Grandpa Jones, Lefty Frizzell, Marvin Rainwater, Carl Perkins, Porter Wagoner, Roger Miller, the Willis Brothers, Red Sovine, Archie Campbell, Norma Jean, Bill Monroe, Justin Tubb, Claude Gray, Bill Phillips, Carl Butler, Del Wood, Whitey Ford ("The Duke of Paducah"), Cousin Jody, Dottie West, and others.

Years later he would say that his dismissal by WSM was the biggest break in his life.

And he could point to a note he had received on the day he left: "You did a big job for WSM, and only a few know the problems you solved." It had been written by George D. Hay, The Solemn Old Judge, whose days at the Grand Ole Opry were also numbered.

…⟨ iv ⟩… Dee Kilpatrick did face a strong challenge at the Ryman Auditorium, and he thought he knew how to score in his new job.

"They asked me what I thought was wrong," he told journalist Jack Hurst. "Well, back when I was working with Mercury Records I was at the Opry every Saturday night I was in town, and I could look at the audience and see what was wrong. The Opry didn't have the appeal to the younger audience that you have to have if you're going to keep growing. All I could see there were older people and little teeny kids. There weren't any teenagers."

In the year immediately following his appointment, Kilpatrick moved to try to solve that problem. True, he hired some acts more or less in the "old" vein of the traditional country artists already on the Opry: the Wilburn Brothers (in a return), Stonewall Jackson, Wilma Lee and Stoney Cooper, and Porter Wagoner. But he also brought in Ferlin Husky, and Rusty and Doug Kershaw, and a very hot young act in the Everly Brothers.

On one hand he had to try to attract younger people to the audience; on the other hand he was smack up against the long traditions of the Opry, some agreeable to him, some not so agreeable.

That old bugaboo about drums on the Opry stage was revived again. Kilpatrick sided with tradition, not so much for tradition's sake, but because in his mind the drum was a symbol of rock 'n' roll.

"Why take the thing that's killing you and start giving in to it?" he said to Hurst. "I figured if we allowed drums then, with all the antagonism that there was between country music and rock 'n' roll, we would lose the traditional audience we had always had."

Yet tradition could be in the way sometimes. He had inherited four old-timey string bands from the earliest days of the Opry: the Possum Hunters, the Crook Brothers, the Fruit Jar Drinkers, and the Gully Jumpers. With each band getting its own spot on the show, time was being used that might more profitably go to newer acts—acts to attract audience and sponsors.

He proposed a consolidation of the older musicians, from four to two bands, on the theory that the groups weren't really the old-time groups anyway, many of the original members having died.

Herman Crook was incensed, taking his anger to WSM president DeWitt, arguing vehemently for status quo with the old string bands. He lost the argument. The old-timers were consolidated into the Crook Brothers and the Fruit Jar Drinkers.

Years later, Herman was still fuming: "It shouldn't have changed. . . . We had a lot of stuff [on the Opry] that didn't really belong. You need fiddles, guitars, banjos, and things like that. And play the old-time tunes and songs. That's what it's supposed to be. It made National Life, I'm telling you. It really made them money."

⋯⊰⟦ v ⟧⊱⋯ Of all the stories of the Grand Ole Opry, none has the rags-to-riches appeal of the tale of Stonewall Jackson, a young man from Moultrie, Georgia, who joined the Opry in 1956. And no one tells it better than Stonewall Jackson (yes, that's really his name) himself:

"Ah came into Nashville, in just mah pickup truck, an' Ah stopped out there at Acuff-Rose an' went in with some songs Ah had—a li'l ole song called 'Don't Be Angry,' which is still one of mah most requested songs. What Ah aimed to do was try to get some of mah songs out by other artists. Ah was gonna go the next day an' get me a job at a service station, or somethin', an' wait for somebody to pick up one of mah songs.

"That was mah intention; that's all Ah had in mind—not get into it mahself as an artist.

"Ah went into Acuff-Rose an' sang for Mr. Wes Rose's man; Ah didn't see Mr. Rose at all. Ah went to mah motel, lay down across the bed, an' the phone rang. Ah said, 'Well, who could be callin' up? Must be a wrong number.' Ah picked up the phone an' it was Mr. Rose. An' he said, 'Ah've been listenin' to that tape you cut an' I can hear somethin' in it. Ah cain't quite put mah finger on it, but Ah got some folks down at the Grand Ole Opry, they might can do a better job than Ah can.' An' laughed, you know. He said, 'Would you be interested in auditionin' for a spot on the Grand Ole Opry?'

"Well, he told me later he meant a guest spot. He hoped that if we could get me just to guest on the Opry that it would get mah name around town a little bit an' help me to place mah songs. That's all.

"Ah went down the next day an' auditioned for Judge George D. Hay. Ah'd never done any performin' professionally, you know, where you got paid for playin'. Just li'l ole parties an' things like that. Folks 'round home that Ah would sing mah songs to said, 'Those songs are as good as a lot of things we hear on the Opry. You should try to go to Nashville, you know, and do somethin' with that.' They just kept tellin' me that. When Ah was in the service Ah'd played a li'l show in front of the fellas, before the movie, an' that type thing.

"An' when Ah auditioned for Judge Hay Ah was pretty bashful an' Ah stood in the corner—facin' the corner—an' Ah said, 'You know, Ah'm a li'l bashful, 'cause Ah never did anythin' this important before. So Ah'm a li'l nervous.' Ah looked down an' seen mah kneecaps jumpin' up an' down, you know. Because Ah thought of the Grand Ole Opry as somethin' really special, an' Ah still do. So they carried me down the hall an' Ah did the same songs for Mr. W. D. Kilpatrick; he was the manager at that time.

"Well, they give me a contract. Ah had a five-year contract—never signed another with 'em since. Ah found out later it's the only time anybody's ever come an' just was hired right off the street.

"Ah didn't have decent clothes to wear an' when they put me on Friday night Ah had some patches on mah khaki. An' they thought it was a gag—Ray Price, an' the Wilburn Brothers, an' a bunch of 'em was there—so they went to laughin' at me while Ah was singin': 'Don't be angry with me, darlin', Ah fail to understand. . . .' It's really a serious ballad song. An' the audience was kinda laughin' at me too, see.

"But Ah got about halfway through that song, an' Ah was bearin' down on it. Ah was right in that mike, just whippin' it on, just the best Ah could do it, with all mah heart, an' that audience seen how serious Ah was, an' they just got quiet. An' Ah encored four times." He laughed. "Ah guess an older man mighta had a heart attack. . . .

"If Ah hadn't got that break, an' mebbe not got a song out in a few months, an' mebbe got tired of workin' at a service station—the way it happened Ah never had to get the job at a service station."

Bye, bye love,
Bye, bye happiness,
Hello loneliness,
*I think I'm gonna cry.**

— Everly Brothers hit,
　　1957

e was working on a show at the Richmond Mosque," Wilma Lee Cooper said, "and Johnny Cash was on it, Lester Flatt and Earl Scruggs—a big package. Dee Kilpatrick was there and he come to us after the matinee show and asked us to come and join the Opry."

Thus, in January 1957, the veteran duo of Wilma Lee and Stoney Cooper left the WWVA "Wheeling Jamboree" to become roster members of the Grand Ole Opry. They were a hard-core country act, with such songs as "Cheated, Too," and "Willie Roy, the Crippled Boy," and "There's a Big Wheel," and "Walking My Lord up Calvary Hill."

The Coopers were pleased to have been asked to be on the Opry; Wilma summed it up: "Back then, you know, the Grand Ole Opry was the top of the ladder for you in country music. If you could make that you had really reached the apex of the whole thing." But after several weeks in Nashville doubts began to set in. It had to do with economics.

*"Bye, Bye Love" by Felice and Boudleaux Bryant; copyright 1957 The House of Bryant, Inc.; Acuff-Rose/ Opryland Music, Inc.

In Wheeling, Wilma Lee and Stoney had been *the* stars on WWVA, and the unchallenged leaders in selling products through P.I. (per inquiry) accounts. "On a P.I., if you had a dollar item," Wilma explained, "you'd get five cents for every order."

What did they sell?

"Oh . . . carving knives, and little Bibles that they could carry in their pockets," she recalled, "and tablecloths with the Lord's Supper on it, baby chicks, so much a hundred, eyeglasses, getting people to order the Rock Dale Monument catalogue and if anybody bought a tombstone we'd get a commission. I just don't remember what all . . .

"So you knew how many orders you were getting, they had long tables and we had to go in every morning and take our mail—just boxes of it!—and dump it on one of those tables and slice those letters open and see how many orders were in an envelope and mark it. That's all we did; we didn't ship no orders or nothing. Just mark the envelopes: four orders, two orders, one order. And then they'd take the mail and send the products out.

"Well, our check most of the time—on five cents an order—ran anywhere from like $875 to a $1,000 a week. A week!

"When we came to the Opry they didn't have P.I. accounts. We made thirteen dollars a show, as I remember it. I mean, Stoney got thirteen dollars as the leader, and I always had to work as a sideman, and I think I got twelve dollars as sideman for the first show and eight dollars for the second. We had done so good at Wheeling that Stoney, after we was here for a short while at the Opry, said he believed we had made a mistake.

"And then in '57 the work was hard in the country business. Remember the rock 'n roll? But we worked for a whole year off the bookings we had made out of Wheeling—dates that had already been booked. So, we kept a-workin', where others were having trouble getting bookings."

The Coopers persisted, becoming one of the most popular acts on the Grand Ole Opry. When Stoney died in March 1977, Wilma went on alone. Carol Lee, their daughter, became the leader of the Opry's talented corps of background singers.

"The Opry is like home," Wilma Lee said. "I don't know, it's something there that you do. Like, if you're home, you gotta cook a meal, or clean house, you know. To come in an' do the Opry is just a part of your life. It's just home to me."

❦[ii]❦ Another performer to find his way home to the Grand Ole Opry in 1957 was Porter Wagoner, out of West Plains, Missouri. He had started as a performer at the age of fourteen, when he was a clerk in a grocery store. During slack business in the store, Porter would take his guitar and entertain the customers and the owner. The store owner liked him so much that he sponsored a local fifteen-minute radio show for his clerk.

Wagoner's first serious move in show business came when he was signed to

Red Foley's "Ozark Jubilee" television show in Springfield, Missouri. About the same time he also was given a recording contract by RCA Victor, even though he was hardly a "big name."

In 1956 he had a major hit with "Satisfied Mind," and that brought him to the attention of Dee Kilpatrick. He was invited to be a guest on "The Prince Albert Show."

"I was scared, of course," Porter said. "I was real nervous because of it being such a big show. And it was such a big thing for me because I had listened to the Grand Ole Opry since I was a kid. The thing I think that surprised me most was how right it felt once I was on the stage. Because once I got onstage and started doing my song it was kinda like I belonged there. The people had a way of making you feel you belonged. So all the nervousness really went away and that surprised me. The people were just so friendly with me and there was so much applause and so many smiling faces around me—it was really a neat feeling.

"Carl Smith introduced me. I had written a song for Carl back in 1955 called 'Trademark,' which was a number-one song for [him], and that's why I was on his show.

"That first night I appeared on the Opry, I came off the stage and went back to the little dressing room area, and I met Roy Acuff in the hallway there. And he came up to me and he said, 'Porter, I'm awful glad that you're becoming a part of the Grand Ole Opry. We need more of your kind of people here.' And he handed me a phone number. He said, 'This is my home number. If I can help you with your stay here at the Opry please call me.'

"Well, I just didn't know what to say. He had nothing to gain by offering his help to me. But me being new to Nashville, you can imagine the security that gave me. But it was one of the big thrills, becoming friends with people like that. Although I never had to call him to help me, I always knew that I could."

♪ iii ♪ The 1957 "youth movement" instituted by Opry manager Kilpatrick brought Kentuckians Don and Phil Everly to the Ryman stage. Don was twenty; Phil was only eighteen.

They had come from an impeccable country music background. Their parents, Ike and Margaret Everly, were country-gospel artists known throughout the South and Midwest since 1930. The boys had learned to sing country standards at a very young age; Ike taught them the rudiments of the guitar when they were first old enough to hold the instrument.

Don was eight and Phil was six when they made their public debut on radio station KMA in Shenandoah, Iowa. They toured with their parents every summer, and when they were both graduated from high school Ike and Margaret retired. The young men came to Nashville to further their careers.

In Nashville, as they sought new material, publisher Wesley Rose put them in touch with songwriters Felice and Boudleaux Bryant, who had just written

J ohnny Cash, the "brightest rising star in country music,"
shown here with Carl Smith on the right.

(1956) OPRYLAND USA ARCHIVES/JEANNE GORDON COLLECTION

Jimmy C. Newman, with his name emblazoned on his guitar, entertains at the 35th Grand Ole Opry Birthday Celebration.

(1960) WSM PHOTO/LES LEVERETT

Stonewall Jackson, often described as an overnight success, joined the Grand Ole Opry after auditioning for Opry manager, Dee Kilpatrick.

(1957) GRAND OLE OPRY ARCHIVES

Jim Denny began his Grand Ole Opry career in 1936 working in a variety of capacities, including manager, until his departure in 1956. Here he is shown outside the Ryman, standing next to the Purina Chow wagon used to promote Purina's television program.

(C. 1956) OPRYLAND USA ARCHIVES/JEANNE GORDON COLLECTION

D*on and Phil Everly perform for the Country Music Disc Jockeys' Convention in 1957.*

(1957) OPRYLAND USA ARCHIVES/JEANNE GORDON COLLECTION

T*he Cooper Family specialized in the traditional Appalachian mountain music they did so much to promote. From the left, Jimmy Elrod on banjo, Carol Lee Cooper, Stoney Cooper, Wilma Lee Cooper, Hank Snow (looking at his script), and the announcer, T. Tommy Cutrer.*

(1957) OPRYLAND USA ARCHIVES/ JEANNE GORDON COLLECTION

Hawkshaw Hawkins and Dee Kilpatrick backstage at the Ryman. As the Opry's General Manager, Kilpatrick brought the Everly Brothers and Ferlin Husky to its stage in 1957.

(C. 1957) GRAND OLE OPRY ARCHIVES

For twenty years, Porter Wagoner's syndicated TV show was a favorite of country music fans. On a set for an early 1960s show are (from left) Jack Little on fiddle, Don Warden on steel guitar, Speck Rhodes, Norma Jean, Porter Wagoner, and Buck Trent on guitar.

(C. 1964) COUNTRY MUSIC FOUNDATION LIBRARY AND MEDIA CENTER

"Bye, Bye Love." The Everly Brothers recorded it for Cadence Records. It was a smash hit. A gold-record hit.

And it catapulted them to the Grand Ole Opry.

Before the year was out they earned another gold record with "Wake Up Little Susie," also from the fertile talents of the Bryants. Don and Phil were national crossover stars, appearing on Ed Sullivan's "Toast of the Town" and Dick Clark's "American Bandstand."

In 1958 there were three more hits from the Bryant songwriter team: "All I Have to Do Is Dream," "Bird Dog," and "Devoted to You," plus another hit with their own composition "Cathy's Clown."

The Everlys were exactly the kind of act Dee Kilpatrick needed to bring teenagers into the Grand Ole Opry audience. But the Opry couldn't contain them; the lure of the good life of Hollywood was much more exciting.

But there was another young brother act corralled by Kilpatrick—Doug and Rusty Kershaw, out of the Cajun country of Louisiana. They were raised on Cajun music, and they didn't speak English until they went to school.

As a duo they were good enough by the mid-fifties to become cast members of the "Louisiana Hayride." Yet again the long arm of the Grand Ole Opry reached into the Hayride and snatched them away. Doug was twenty, Rusty seventeen.

Years later, Doug told an interviewer that the move to the Opry in 1957 was significant because there was a seven in the year. "It's really amazing," he said, "how the number seven is constantly popping up in my life. I was on the Johnny Cash premiere TV show, which was shown on June 7. I taped a guest appearance on a television show with Hank Williams, Jr., and on the seventh take it was right. The first money I ever made was seven dollars."

And he ticked off other "sevens," both lucky and unlucky, in his life. Doug was the seventh child in the family, his father committed suicide when he was seven, he signed a writers' contract with BMI in 1967, his solo recording contract was with Warner Bros.–Seven Arts, and his most important song, "Louisiana Man," was the seventh song he wrote.

None of that, however, had anything to do with the Kershaws' stay at the Grand Ole Opry. They left in 1958 to join the Army, reasoning that they were going to be drafted anyway, and that if they enlisted together they'd be discharged together.

Kilpatrick had a bit more luck, however, with another young singer he brought to the Opry in 1957—Ferlin Husky, a mercurial thirty-year-old who was born in Flat River, or Hickory Grove, or Cantrell, Missouri. A biographer could take his choice, because Husky was born on a farm located at equal distances from any of those three small towns.

There was also a choice of names. Early in his career he called himself Terry Preston, because he felt that Husky had the wrong sound for a performer's name. And then there's Simon Crum, Ferlin's alter-ego hayseed character he had made so "real" that many believed Ferlin Husky and Simon Crum were two distinctly different people.

With the acquisition of Ferlin Husky, the Opry had a guaranteed young recording star. He had already had major hits with his duets with Jean Shepard on "Dear John Letter" and "Forgive Me John," a follow-up song. And in '57 he had a number-one seller with "(Since You've) Gone," which was a remake of a song he had recorded in 1952 as Terry Preston.

Then, after Ferlin joined the Opry, he had a major hit as the comedic Simon Crum doing "Country Music Is Here to Stay," followed, as the decade ended, with the classic country-gospel tune "On the Wings of a Dove."

Husky would become one of the top stars on the Opry roster, and he would be there until he was caught in what can be called the "Purge of '64." But more on that later.

Whatever was thought of Dee Kilpatrick's job as manager of the Grand Ole Opry within the WSM executive offices, in public it was being applauded. In a story in the *Nashville Banner* in late March 1957, no less of an authority than Roy Acuff was quoted as saying that the Opry cast now represented "the highest quality of entertainment since I have been with the show."

Statistically, though, attendance in 1957 continued to slide, dropping under 200,000 for the first time.

··◦[iv]◦·· There were certainly tensions in the background.

Little Jimmy Dickens left the Opry after nine years. He had accepted an offer to head up a major road show for the Philip Morris tobacco company. But at that time the Opry's sponsorship by the R. J. Reynolds Tobacco Company prohibited any Grand Ole Opry member from traveling with a tour sponsored by a competitor. Thus, Jimmy departed Nashville. "There were no hard feelings ever," he insisted later.

The year also marked the departure of George Dewey Hay, The Solemn Old Judge, the man who had started it all in November 1925. Hay, at sixty-two, was retired by WSM and left Nashville to spend his last years with his family in Virginia.

Was it a bitter separation?

Well, in 1965 he would write a letter to Robert Shelton of *The New York Times*, who was preparing a book (with Burt Goldblatt) to be titled *The Country Music Story*. There were several strange phrases in the letter, indicating some discontent with the way his role in the Opry had been handled.

He wrote: "The following statement by George D. Hay may *correct much false opinion* [author's emphasis] regarding the WSM Grand Ole Opry, which was named by George D. Hay a short time after the WSM Barn Dance was started on November 28th, 1925. Mr. Hay was director of WSM at that time and arranged the programme and served as Master of Ceremonies thereon. From that time until he retired from WSM in the spring of 1957, Mr. Hay, as an employee of WSM, appeared on the Opry each performance, with the exceptions of times when he was out of the city or sick; more than thirty years over all time. He was in charge of the Opry much of that time.

"I do not now nor did I ever own any part of the Opry of the WSM. I was an employee of WSM. I do, however, have a great love for the Opry, which is in my heart protected from all *illusions and false opinions of certain members of the so-called human race* [author's emphasis]."

The tensions of 1957 were perhaps all encompassed in an incident early on a Monday morning in the spring. WSM president Jack DeWitt, who detailed the story for writer Jack Hurst in the fiftieth-anniversary book on the Opry, was awakened by a phone call from Bill Williams, then an announcer at WSM and later the Nashville editor for *Billboard* magazine:

"Bill said, 'Jack, we've got a very serious situation down here.'

"I said, 'What is it?'

"He said, 'Ernest Tubb has just shot up the lobby.'

"I said, 'Oh, for God's sake!' He asked me what to do, and I said, 'Well, you've got to get Ernest home.' He said, 'Oh, it's too late for that—the police are already here.' "

Hurst went on with the story: "Williams recalls that he had just walked into the lobby of the National Life building to go to work when a shot from a .357 Magnum pistol was fired over his head. Badly frightened, he turned and saw Tubb and shouted, 'Ernest, what are you doing?' All he can remember Tubb answering is, 'My God, I've shot the wrong man.' " Fortunately, Ernest hadn't shot anyone, but he had shot *at* the wrong man.

Hurst continued: "An engineer already on duty upstairs in the WSM studios called the police as soon as he heard the shot, Williams says, and they arrived almost immediately. Tubb told them he had talked on the telephone with a man he refused to identify, and that the man had threatened to kill him and said he would meet him [in the National Life lobby] for a shootout."

Police took Tubb to the city jail, held him for a mandatory three hours on a charge of public drunkenness, and then released him. Nashville newspapers carried the story for a few more days and then it petered out.

From the perspective of the passage of thirty years, it can be said only that the incident was something—the use of the gun—out of character for Ernest Tubb.

❧[v]❧ Considerably less dramatic were some 1957 executive shifts within WSM. Irving Waugh was named vice-president and general manager of the television station, and Robert Evans Cooper, a former sales manager, was given the comparable post as head of the radio station.

Thus, Cooper found himself directly responsible for the Grand Ole Opry; Opry manager Dee Kilpatrick reported to him. One of Cooper's first moves was to take "Friday Night Frolics" out of the WSM studios and shift it to the Ryman Auditorium. It was redubbed the "Friday Night Opry." No one objected.

Before the move was made, however, there developed one of those little, seemingly insignificant stories that would, with the passage of years, become part of the legend of the Grand Ole Opry.

It involved a twelve-year-old girl from Sevier County, Tennessee, in the Smoky Mountains foothills. Her name was Dolly Parton.

"Carl and Pearl Butler, who used to perform on the Opry," Dolly recalled, "They were friends of mine and we had worked on the same show in east Tennessee—the 'Cas Walker Show.' So they brought me down to Nashville. They had been working real hard at pushing me along. Along with my uncle Bill Owens, who had an old car with a caved-in side, we'd keep coming back and forth to Nashville, trying to get something going. He believed I was going to be a star, and I was fool enough to believe him.

"And we'd hang around the Opry; I wanted to be on it. They told me I was too young, and then they said, 'You can't be on the Opry, you're not in the union.' And I said, 'What's a union?'

"Well, anyway, they used to have this 'Friday Night Frolics,' and I went up there one night with the intention of being on it. I kept telling everybody, 'I'll just sing one song.' Most of the Opry artists had two spots on the show and I walked up to Jimmy C. Newman, who was going to sing his second song next, and I told him I wanted to be on. I didn't know why he did it, but Jimmy gave me his spot and I sang a George Jones song.

"I thought I was a star! I was kind of scared; I was excited because I knew that Daddy and Momma were listening on the radio. I didn't grasp all that it meant, but it was almost like being on the Saturday-night Opry."

Ev'rybody's goin' out and havin' fun,
I'm just a fool for stayin' home and havin' none,
I can't get over how she set me free,
*Oh, lonesome me.**

—Don Gibson hit, 1958

O ver the years, since the advent of Roy Acuff and "The Great Speckled Bird," there was one sure way to make it onto the Grand Ole Opry—on the strength of a great song.

That was the path followed by Don Gibson in 1958.

Gibson was, and is, an enigma, in the full dictionary sense of the word: something hard to understand or explain, an inscrutable or mysterious person. Although he was, and is, a fair enough singer and player, there is none of the charismatic appeal in him of a Hank Williams or a Johnny Cash. One gets the feeling, watching him perform, that he is almost too shy to be an entertainer.

What he was, and is, is a *great* songwriter. Certainly, on that score he must rank with Hank Williams, with Willie Nelson, with Lefty Frizzell, with Merle Haggard, with Kris Kristofferson—name them and Don Gibson must be placed near the top of any such list.

Gibson has been the kind of songwriter whose effect on other songwriters who study his catalogue is to bring them to take the gas pipe or, at the very least, go

*"Oh, Lonesome Me" by Don Gibson; copyright 1958 Acuff-Rose/Opryland Music, Inc.

home and want to smash their typewriter with a sledgehammer. The author is an admitted admirer of Don's talents. And with good reason. Over the years his songs, with intelligent lyrics and solid melodies, have made more than one routine singer sound good. And have made good singers sound great.

But to return to the narrative: Don came out of his native North Carolina as a youngster to begin his career as a performer on Knoxville's WNOX, where he was heard on the "Tennessee Barn Dance" and the storied "Midday Merry-Go-Round." He organized his own band and there was the obligatory series of one-nighters and club dates. And then he met Wesley Rose. Rather, Rose had heard some of his songs and sought him out.

There followed a songwriter contract with Acuff-Rose and a recording contract with RCA Victor. His first single, "Too Soon to Know," was adequate. But his second, "Oh, Lonesome Me," was a smash hit. The Grand Ole Opry wanted him.

It is part of the Don Gibson lore that on one afternoon in '58—hidden away in a Nashville motel room—he wrote both "Oh, Lonesome Me" and "I Can't Stop Loving You."

> *I can't stop loving you, so I've made up my mind*
> *To live in memory of old lonesome times;*
> *I can't stop wanting you, it's useless to say,*
> *So I'll just live my life in dreams of yesterday.**

In the year he joined the Grand Ole Opry, Gibson had no less than sixteen songs published. He was just as prolific in 1959, and in 1960 he wrote a song that can serve as a primer on how to write a sophisticated country composition:

> *If heartaches brought fame*
> *In love's crazy game,*
> *I'd be a legend in my time.*
> *If they gave gold statuettes*
> *For tears and regrets,*
> *I'd be a legend in my time.*
>
> *But they don't give awards*
> *And there's no praise or fame,*
> *For a heart that's been broken*
> *Over love that's in vain.*
>
> *If loneliness meant world acclaim*
> *Then ev'ryone would know my name,*
> *I'd be a legend in my time.†*

*"I Can't Stop Loving You" by Don Gibson; copyright 1958 Acuff-Rose/Opryland Music, Inc.
†"(I'd Be) A Legend in My Time" By Don Gibson; copyright 1960 Acuff-Rose/Opryland Music, Inc.

ii Yet another graduate of Knoxville's "Midday Merry-Go-Round" came to the Opry in 1958—Archie Campbell, a singer and comedian who had been doing a grandpappy character for some twenty-five years. But the Opry already had Grandpa Jones and Campbell wisely sought another persona.

"One particular night at the Opry," he recalled, "I took a look at Ferlin Husky. He was one of those well-dressed cats; he'd come out in them mohair suits. And I thought, 'My God, that's it!'

"So I bought a new mohair suit, white shirt, and a white tie. When I came out that night, they said, 'Where's your costume?' And I said, 'This is it.' And they said, 'Hell, you can't go out in stuff like that. That's no outfit for a comedian.'

"I was always of the opinion that your delivery, whatever you did, was the important thing. So I walked out—I saved my best stuff for that night anyway—and I really laid 'em in the aisles. I proved my point. As far as I know I'm the first one to ever dress like that in country comedy."

The parade of new talent to the Ryman stage continued, including two women. One was Margie Bowes, of Roxboro, North Carolina, who made her first appearance on the Opry as a contestant in the Pet Milk–Grand Ole Opry talent contest. She won. And stayed.

So did one of the other contestants—Melba Montgomery, out of Iron City, Tennessee. Roy Acuff was so impressed with her he invited her to join the Smoky Mountain Boys troupe.

That year also saw young Roy Drusky arrive from Atlanta, Georgia, to join the Opry cast. And there was a notable guest performer during the year, one Franklin Delano Reeves, of Sparta, North Carolina. He was in the Air Force at the time, but he had a hit record on the charts for Capitol titled "Love, Love, Love."

"I was at my home on a furlough," he said, "and on my way back to California I stopped off in Nashville. Jack McFadden, who was Buck Owens's manager, got me on the Opry that night.

"Backstage, Minnie Pearl told me, 'Boy, you sure have lots of charisma!' And I thought, 'What does she mean by that?' Because, God knows, I didn't know what charisma meant."

He was to learn.

iii On September 12, 1958—it was a Friday—Rod Brasfield died of a heart attack. He was only forty-eight years old.

The newspaper obituary said: "Brasfield, who had become a light-hearted part of Saturday night to families all over America as a star of the Grand Ole Opry, was stricken at 6:45 P.M. at his Dickerson Road trailer. He was DOA at St. Thomas Hospital."

A house trailer may not have seemed a fitting home for a star of the Opry, but he lived modestly.

WSM program manager Ott Devine told reporters: "There will be no happy faces at the Ryman tonight. Rod never had a serious moment in his life before his audiences. But in private life he had his troubles."

"Troubles" was a euphemism for his drinking, which served only to complicate his heart condition.

He was a private person, disliking interviews about anything but his onstage character. Thus, when a reporter did manage to corner him the answers always came out in jokes.

Rod loved to tell the story about alighting from a plane one day in Jackson, Mississippi, and being nabbed by FBI agents who mistook him for someone else. He told newsmen then: "I really feel sorry for that other bird. If the FBI wants him and he looks like me, why, Lordy, he's in double trouble!"

That was vintage Brasfield. Never taking himself seriously in the public eye.

Late in 1956 he got an opportunity that comes to few comedians. Film director Elia Kazan hired him to play a straight role in *A Face in the Crowd*, from a story by Budd Schulberg. It was an important film. Rod was Andy Griffith's right-hand man in a plot about a country musician who becomes a national figure and a menace. Critics praised Brasfield's performance.

He shrugged it off. "I was just Andy's flunky," he said.

Flunky was something Rod Brasfield had never been.

❧[iv]❧ As the fifties came to a close, the Grand Ole Opry continued to expand its roster at the same time a survey by *Radio Mirror* magazine showed that the Opry was the nation's most popular music program.

Once more the sure road to Opry status seemed to be the hit record. Billy Grammer, one of thirteen children of an Illinois coal miner, was added to the cast on the strength of a million-seller record, "Gotta Travel On." West Virginia–born, deep-voiced Harold "Hawkshaw" Hawkins (he reminded some of Ernest Tubb) joined the WSM show, his recording of "Sunny Side of the Mountain" already regarded as a country classic.

"Family" continued to be an Opry consideration, too. Tompall and the Glasers (Jim and Chuck), out of Spalding, Nebraska, came to the Ryman with their unique family harmony.

And Skeeter Davis, a.k.a. Mary Frances Penick, of Dry Ridge, Kentucky, joined the Opry as a single after an auto accident took the life of her partner in the Davis Sisters act, Betty Jack Davis. Skeeter quit show business after that, but was persuaded to make a comeback by Chet Atkins and Ernest Tubb. She toured with E.T. and it was through his intercession that she came to the Opry. There quickly followed two monster record hits: "Last Date" and "End of the World."

There was a noted departure from the Grand Ole Opry in 1959, as well.

Dee Kilpatrick, after less than three years at the helm, resigned as Opry manager. Why? There was some contention that Kilpatrick had crossed swords with several of the established stars. Be that as it may, Kilpatrick felt he had been undercut in the WSM executive offices, principally by Irving Waugh. Waugh, for his part, never denied he held Kilpatrick in disfavor.

The new Opry manager came from the radio station's staff this time: Ottis Devine, who had been the WSM program manager. He knew the Grand Ole Opry well, and he knew its people.

v She was a $65-a-week secretary from California. She had never been on a stage before. She had never sung in front of an audience before. She had never seen Nashville before. But there she was, standing in the wings of the Ryman Auditorium, waiting to be introduced for her debut on the Grand Ole Opry.

It was an October evening in 1959.

Her name was Jan Howard.

In one of those crazy flukes of show business, she had cut a demonstration record in a little studio in Pico Rivera, California, with Wynn Stewart's four-piece band. That record, "The One You Slip Around With," was a hit, suddenly blessed with top-ten status.

"I was terrified that night," she recalled. "Ray Price introduced me on the Prince Albert portion of the show [on the NBC network], and his exact words were, 'Tear 'em a new one, hon!' And I don't remember another thing that happened. That's how frightened I was."

The debut ended, she went back to California to her secretarial job and her husband, a struggling young songwriter named Harlan Howard. There was still no thought she was going to have a career in show business; she thought she was too shy for that.

But circumstances conspired against her. In June 1960 the Howards moved to Nashville, Harlan believing it was necessary to further his burgeoning career. Jan, because of the demo records she had cut of her husband's songs and because of her one hit with Wynn Stewart, was offered a recording contract. She also began to appear with some regularity as a guest on the Grand Ole Opry.

Her patron there was stage manager Vito Pellettieri. "I learned to dearly love that man," she said. "He'd say, 'Gimme two songs,' and I was so scared, because he was so brusque, I'd just say the first two songs that came into my mind. And he'd say, 'Those aren't your songs. You need to plug your own records.' So I'd say, 'Yes, sir,' and I'd sing whatever he told me to."

vi If there hadn't been a rebellion of sorts among Grand Ole Opry performers in 1959, Vito Pellettieri wouldn't have been around anymore when Jan Howard returned in 1960.

Mr. Vito was known as the contrariest man at the Opry. It made no difference who the Opry manager might have been, when the show went on the air Pellettieri 'ran it. His relationships with the artists were unique. And he was not shy about using four-letter expletives to get his point across.

"The rougher he talked to you," one Opry star said, "the better he liked you."

It was not uncommon for him to telephone a front-rank star and say to him: "Hello, you no-good hillbilly. What kind of garbage are you going to dish up this week?" No one was immune from the vitriol.

The rough talk, however, could not mask the affection which had built up between Mr. Vito and the performers. In mid-1959, when it was announced he faced mandatory retirement from both of his positions at WSM (music librarian and Opry stage manager) a shock wave swept through the Ryman.

Immediately, the Grand Ole Opry performers—every one of them—signed a petition demanding that Pellettieri be allowed to continue at the Opry. WSM officials relented; Vito stayed with the radio show, but was retired as music librarian.

That November, during the annual disc jockey convention hosted by WSM, Opry performers staged a surprise program in Vito's honor. Roy Acuff made a lengthy, off-the-cuff speech. "He is one of the men," said the King of Country Music, "who made the Opry what it is today."

There was a standing ovation. A five-minute ovation.

Vito, his eyes brimming with tears, said quietly: "This is the most impressive moment of my life."

❦〖 vii 〗❦ In the audience that night was a young pop singing star, an idol of teenage fans. His record of "A Rose and a Baby Ruth" had been a smash hit. He had toured with Buddy Holly.

"I was a 'teen balladeer,' " George Hamilton IV admitted, "and it really wasn't what I wanted to do.

"I sat there in the Ryman that night, and this may sound corny, and I had a musically religious experience. You hear of some people being born again spiritually; musically I was born again. Because I sat there and Ernest Tubb was on the stage . . . and I started to cry."

He turned to his manager, who sat beside him. "I told him I wanted to move to Nashville, I wanted to be a country singer. It may have seemed strange for a guy who was established in the pop field. But my manager called Jim Denny and asked Denny whether he'd try to book me. And I moved to Nashville with my wife, and my MG, and my Siamese cat, and my little baby boy, Payton.

"The first person who called me was Webb Pierce. He invited us to church, believe it or not. Chet Atkins signed me to RCA in 1960, and Ott Devine asked me to join the Grand Ole Opry.

"It was the greatest thrill in my life."

I fall to pieces
Each time I see you again,
I fall to pieces
How can I be just your friend?*

—Patsy Cline hit, 1961

For a lot of the members of the Grand Ole Opry the decade of the sixties began in an auspicious manner that had nothing to do with their music. At number 422 on Nashville's Broadway a garishly decorated bar called Tootsie's Orchid Lounge opened for business on March 29. Its back door led to the alley adjacent to the stage door of the Ryman Auditorium, giving the Opry performers a most convenient watering hole.

Very quickly it became the "in" place for Nashville's country music community. Fans soon learned they could see their favorite Opry stars close-up by visiting Tootsie's. Young performers went there to meet stars and agents and bookers. Song pluggers found it an ideal place to hawk their products.

Tootsie's was assured a place in the colorful lore of the Grand Ole Opry.

Across the alley, at the Opry itself, manager Ott Devine began the decade by adding to the roster a whole new crop of young performers. One was a girl singer.

Patsy Cline was born Virginia Patterson Hensley in the small town of Winchester, Virginia, positioned at the head of the fabled Shenandoah Valley. The year was 1932, the worst of the Great Depression. And in the show business vernacular of later years, she "paid her dues."

From the beginning she wanted to be an entertainer. She made her first public appearance at the age of four, winning a tap-dancing contest. Those were the days of the child movie star Shirley Temple, and there were dreams in poor families all across the land that, given the opportunity, their little girl could be another Shirley.

With Virginia, however, the emphasis soon switched from dancing to singing. Whenever and wherever she could sing she did—in churches, in clubs, in honky-tonks, on street corners. It was necessary for her, because of family financial needs, to quit school as a teenager and go to work as a clerk in Gaunt's Drug Store in Winchester. But the singing continued.

"Mother would pick me up at the drug store after work," she once told a reporter, "and would take me wherever I could get a job. We'd usually get home about three in the morning and a few hours later I was up again getting ready to go to work in the drug store. And you know something—I loved every minute of it."

That enthusiasm, accompanied by a total lack of shyness, enabled her to contact every name act that came through Winchester, always seeking an opportunity to perform. In 1948 Wally Fowler's Oak Ridge Quartet came to town; they were regular performers on Roy Acuff's "Dinner Bell" radio show on WSM. Patsy sought an audition with Fowler, got it, and Fowler suggested to Mrs. Hensley that her daughter go to Nashville. He'd get her an audition with Acuff, he said.

They went. Patsy was not yet sixteen.

"When I first came to Nashville in 1948," she recalled, "I drove in with my mother, sisters, and a few friends of the family. We shared expenses. I didn't have enough money to rent a hotel room, so the night before we were to audition, we stopped outside town at a picnic site and I spent the night sleeping on a concrete bench."

Acuff heard her, as Fowler had promised, was impressed, and offered her a job on his program. But the salary was minimal and Patsy had no money to fall back on. So the decision was made to return to Winchester and the drugstore. The reception she had received in Nashville encouraged her, however, and she kept singing, appearing as a regular vocalist with a local Virginia group known as Bill Peer and the Melody Playboys.

In 1953, at the age of twenty-one, she married Gerald Cline. Her professional name was established: Patsy Cline. As before, she sought out every opportunity to perform, and she had appearances on the "Louisiana Hayride," the "Old Dominion Barn Dance," the "Ozark Jubilee," and Jimmy Dean's television show in Washington, D.C.

The country music community began to notice her. Ernest Tubb, it is said, interceded with William McCall, president of Four Star Records, to get her a recording contract in 1955. Four Star had a distribution deal with Decca, and Decca producer Owen Bradley was approached to help with the new singer. Bradley told country music reporter Jack Hurst that the only thing he knew about Patsy Cline then was that she had a reputation of being "a little hard to get along with."

That wasn't true, he learned. The problem with Patsy, Bradley found soon enough, was that her voice was "too good."

"Patsy had such a beautifully silky voice," he said, "and . . . it was hard to get country radio stations to play her records. So we did things that, if you listen to her old records now, make you say, 'What in the world did you do that for?' We did it to try to rough those records up a little, so that maybe they'd be considered more country."

Her first record, released on the Coral label, was "A Church, a Courtroom, Then Goodbye," backed with "Honky Tonk Merry-Go-Round."

The big break came in January 1957, when she was accepted as a contestant on Arthur Godfrey's important "Talent Scouts" network television show. There she met Janette Davis, who was a regular singer on the Godfrey TV shows; Janette worked with Patsy to find the right material for her network debut. Patsy wanted to sing "A Poor Man's Roses," but Janette recommended that she do "Walkin' After Midnight," a song by Alan Block and Don Hecht; Patsy had cut a demo record of it. The song had been written for pop singer Kay Starr, but she didn't like it. In truth, neither did Patsy. But she decided to accept the advice of Janette Davis.

"Walkin' After Midnight" brought the studio audience to its collective feet. Patsy won the talent competition. And Decca (not Four Star) released the song immediately. It was a million-seller, going to number three on the *Billboard* country music charts.

Not everything was going well, however. Patsy's marriage to Gerald Cline collapsed and she divorced him. In September 1957 she married Charlie Dick, a Korean War veteran from Winchester.

After "Walkin' After Midnight," she recorded "A Poor Man's Roses," "Stop the World," and "Come On In." But there wasn't much magic in them. Owen Bradley said that one of the problems was that Four Star insisted that she sing songs published by that company, severely limiting her choice of material.

It didn't seem to matter much, though, because she went into semi-retirement in 1958 and 1959 following the birth of her daughter, Julia.

In 1960 several things happened that brought her back. Her husband, Charlie, realizing that she needed to perform, prodded her into accepting a spot on the roster of the Grand Ole Opry. And her contract with Four Star ran out. Decca, and Bradley, immediately signed her, and the first record released, the Hank Cochran–Harlan Howard tune "I Fall to Pieces," became her initial number-one on the charts.

Patsy's outgoing, hard-shelled personality was quickly evident at the Grand Ole Opry. She became a force there.

Jan Howard remembered an incident: "I was in the ladies' room at the Ryman, changing clothes, when the door opened and it was Patsy. And she stood there, and I will never forget it, because I admired her so much. She had on a cowgirl outfit—fringes and boots and everything—and she put her hands on her hips and she said: 'Well, you're a conceited little sonofabitch!'

"I said, 'What?!'

"She said, 'Well, you just saunter in here and you do your song and you change clothes and you leave. You don't say hello, kiss my ——, or nothin' else.' Those were her words.

"Well, then my Irish and Indian temper got up. And I said, 'Now, just a damned minute! Where I'm from, if a stranger moves to town it's the responsibility of the people who live there to welcome them and make them feel at home. There ain't a damned soul welcomed me to Nashville.'

"And then I said, 'I was a fan of yours, but I take it all back!'

"Well, she started laughing—and, you know, her laugh just boomed out—and she said, 'You're all right, honey. We're gonna be good friends. Anybody that would talk back to the Cline is okay.' "

On the male side of things, a smiling, open-faced Irishman named Hank Locklin came out of McLellan, Florida, to join the Opry roster in 1960. He had been born into a family of doctors, but Hank wanted to be an entertainer.

Beginning as a disc jockey, he soon graduated to performing, with an almost typical early result. His first job was singing in a Florida roadhouse for two dollars a night. But his expenses were five dollars a night; the simple arithmetic of that found him quickly broke.

Rather than quit, he packed up his guitar and some songs he had written and challenged Nashville. One of those songs, "Send Me the Pillow You Dream On," was a 1958 hit on RCA Victor, crossing over to the pop charts. And in 1960 another of his own songs, "Please Help Me, I'm Falling," was a million-seller for RCA.

Once more a great song had opened the doors to the Grand Ole Opry.

Another Floridian—Bobby Lord, of Sanford, Florida—also came aboard in 1960. He had made up his mind that he was going to pursue a medical career and entered the University of Tampa with that goal ahead of him. But a chance appearance on a local television show made him change directions; at nineteen he was committed to show business.

Like Locklin, Lord was a songwriter; "Hawkeye" and "Life Can Have Meaning" were early successes that led directly to the Ryman.

Yet another 1960 newcomer was Billy Walker, a native of Ralls, Texas, and a veteran entertainer before he joined the Opry roster. At fifteen he had won a talent contest that led to a radio show on KICA in Clovis, New Mexico. He joined a touring band, played on the "Big D Jamboree" in Dallas, and moved from there to the "Louisiana Hayride" and the "Ozark Jubilee."

"Actually, I first appeared on the Opry in 1954," Walker said, "when I had a big song about a telephone conversation, called 'Thank You for Calling.' I was in Nashville to record and they put me on the Opry as a guest. I was working the 'Louisiana Hayride,' and was from Texas, and didn't really have any thought about moving to Nashville.

A *wide-eyed, young Skeeter Davis performs at an Opry birthday celebration shortly after becoming a member in 1960.*

(1960) WSM PHOTO/LES LEVERETT

V*ito Pellettieri, the Opry's beloved stage manager, reviews the evening's lineup with Hank Snow.*

(1955) OPRYLAND USA ARCHIVES/JEANNE GORDON COLLECTION

A*rchie Campbell chats with Tennessee Ernie Ford before the Opry's 44th Birthday Celebration.*

(1969) WSM PHOTO/LES LEVERETT

Patsy Cline, whose heart songs made her the most popular female vocalist on the Opry, makes a glamorous appearance on stage. She is backed up by Harold Weakley on drums, Randy Hughes on guitar, and Lightning Chance on bass.

(C. 1961) WSM PHOTO/LES LEVERETT

During a May 1958 visit to Nashville as WSM's Mr. DJ, USA, future Opry member Bill Anderson shares a laugh with, from the left, Hawkshaw Hawkins, Jean Shepard, Stonewall Jackson, and Marty Robbins.

(1958) OPRYLAND USA ARCHIVES/JEANNE GORDON COLLECTION

"But in 1959 Randy Hughes, who was pretty well associated with the Opry and had Ferlin Husky and a couple of other acts, began to talk to me about coming to the Opry. By that time I had been on the 'Ozark Jubilee' with Red Foley and had left there to move back to Fort Worth. And when Hughes mentioned the Opry to me, I said, 'Well, usually you come to the Opry when you get a number-one record, and I don't have anything going at this particular time.' And he said, 'I don't think that will be the case.' So he got me booked in on 'The Prince Albert Show' as a guest. Ott Devine had taken over the Opry and he began talking to me about it and I said, 'Yeah, I'd love to be a member.'

"That was in November. I started working it regular the first of January, 1960."

And in that year Grand Ole Opry artists were dominating the record charts. Jimmy C. Newman had a major hit with "A Lovely Work of Art"; Cowboy Copas had a number-one single with "Alabam"; Faron Young scored with "Face to the Wall" and "Your Old Used to Be"; Marty Robbins had "Big Iron"; Hank Snow had "Miller's Cave"; there were Locklin's "Please Help Me, I'm Falling," and Ferlin Husky's "On the Wings of a Dove"; and Jim Reeves followed his classic "He'll Have to Go" with "Am I Losing You?"

Be it noted that there was also a solid hit in 1960 titled "Tips of My Fingers," by a soft-voiced young singer from Columbia, South Carolina, named James William Anderson III. He would become the only new act added to the Grand Ole Opry roster in 1961.

"I think what probably led to me getting on the Opry," Bill recalled, "was a show I did in Panama City, Florida, in late spring of '61. Opry manager Ott Devine was down in Panama City on a fishing trip and I was booked at the auditorium there as part of a package show. Ott came over to see the show. At the time I had the record 'Po' Folks' out and it was getting pretty hot across the country. I did it on that show in Panama City and got about two or three encores— just really stopped the show with it.

"Ott came backstage and seemed to be quite impressed. I had been a guest on the Opry a few times—the first time when I had my first record for Decca in '58, 'That's What It's Like to Be Lonesome'—but I hadn't really been on that much. Ott said when he got back to Nashville he was going to call me. So I was sitting home watching the All-Star baseball game on TV and about one o'clock in the afternoon my phone rang and I thought, 'Golly, I can't believe somebody is calling me and interrupting the ball game.' But it was Ott Devine and he said, 'How would you like to be a member of the Grand Ole Opry?' Needless to say, I forgot the ball game.

"I was totally in awe of the Opry. It was just so hard for me to believe that I was there with all those people I had listened to and idolized all down through the years. And it took me a long time to be comfortable. Because, if anything, I was a super fan. It was very, very hard for me to relax. And not just with the stars, but with the outstanding sidemen and musicians. It was very difficult for me to go up to them and ask them to play with me on the Opry. That was the days before I had a band.

"To me, the Grand Ole Opry had always been the pinnacle. I mean, it's like a kid growing up who wants to be a baseball player—in my era he wanted to play in Yankee Stadium, because that was the tops. Or if a guy wanted to be in the movies, he wanted to be in Hollywood. And for somebody who wanted to be in country music, the pinnacle, the top, the ultimate, was the Grand Ole Opry. And even though its role has changed somewhat in the modern concept of country music, to me it's still the pinnacle."

⋅⋅◖ iii ◗⋅⋅ Whisperin' Bill Anderson had reached that pinnacle on July 12, 1961, when he signed his Grand Ole Opry contract. Two days later, a near tragedy struck the Opry family.

Patsy Cline was seriously injured in an automobile accident just at the time her first really big hit, "I Fall to Pieces," was going to number one on the charts.

At times it seems that the stories of the Opry take on the aspect of a soap-opera script, and this was one of them. That accident would cement a unique relationship. One of the newest hopefuls in Nashville in July 1961 was an ambitious young singer named Loretta Lynn.

"I was on the Ernest Tubb Record Shop radio show that they do every Saturday night," Loretta wrote in her autobiography, *Coal Miner's Daughter*, "and I said, 'Patsy has the Number One Record, 'I Fall to Pieces,' and she's in the hospital.' Patsy heard it and asked her husband, Charlie Dick, to bring me to the hospital. She was all bandaged up. We talked a good while and became close friends right away. . . .

"The main reason we became good friends was, we were both struggling. Patsy had gotten cut out of a lot of money on a couple of her hit songs, and now she was in the hospital all banged up. We both felt we wouldn't try to hurt each other."

Cline was in the hospital for thirty-five days, and after leaving the hospital she was confined to a wheelchair for months. But she struggled back.

Grand Ole Opry announcer Grant Turner remembered her return to the Ryman: "They brought her down to the Opry and wheeled her out on the stage. She didn't sing, but just greeted the crowd. She still had scars on her forehead. You can't imagine the feeling in the place. Everybody in the audience and all of us onstage were so proud to see her."

Some weeks later, the youngster from Sevierville, Tennessee, Dolly Parton, was standing in the wings of the Ryman: "Patsy was just back to work after all that surgery from the car accident, and she came out on crutches and sang. I was still a kid, but that was one of the big thrills of my life because she was the biggest female singer ever."

Patsy also went back to the recording studio on crutches, to work again with producer Owen Bradley. He remembered that it took several weeks to finish the vocal on Willie Nelson's new song, "Crazy," because some of the notes were too high for her to hit with broken ribs.

"Crazy" was a major hit. Other hits followed: "She's Got You," "Leavin' on Your Mind," "Imagine That," "So Wrong," "When I Get Through with You," and even the Bob Wills country standard "Faded Love."

Music trade publications named her the top female vocalist in country music, ending more than a decade of dominance by another Grand Ole Opry star, Kitty Wells.

❧[iv]❧ On November 3, 1961, the Country Music Association announced the beginning of its Country Music Hall of Fame. The first performers honored were Jimmie Rodgers, "The Singing Brakeman"; Roy Acuff's partner, songwriter and publisher Fred Rose; and the tragic figure of the Grand Ole Opry, Hank Williams.

The Hall of Fame gave country music in general, and the Opry specifically, a place to assure the permanence of their stars. There was to be built on 16th Avenue South—Nashville's "Music Row"—a modernistic barnlike structure to house the Hall of Fame, to be a shrine for the very best in country music.

Over the years it has surprised no one that the Opry has provided the lion's share of the Hall of Famers (of the forty-five acts so honored through 1986, twenty-eight were of the Grand Ole Opry).

In 1962 Roy Acuff became the first living member of the Hall of Fame.

Electors couldn't agree on a majority choice in 1963—the only year that has happened—but in 1964 another Opry performer, cowboy Tex Ritter, went into the Hall of Fame.

It was Ernest Tubb in 1965, saying: "I don't deserve it, but I'm sure glad somebody thought of it."

In 1966 four new Hall of Famers were elected, all with roots in the Grand Ole Opry: singer Eddy Arnold, Opry manager James R. Denny, Opry "originator" George D. Hay, and the self-proclaimed world's greatest banjo player, Uncle Dave Macon.

Red Foley and Jim Reeves were honored in 1967, along with agent J. L. (Joe) Frank, who brought Acuff and Pee Wee King to the Opry. They were followed by the Carter Family (it was Mother Maybell Carter who played the Opry) and Bill Monroe in 1970; Chet Atkins and Patsy Cline in 1973; Opry musician Owen Bradley and Pee Wee King in 1974; and in 1975, belatedly most thought, comedienne Minnie Pearl.

There was a brief hiatus of Opry selections for the Country Music Hall of Fame until 1978, when Grandpa Jones was chosen. Then there was Hank Snow in 1979, Johnny Cash in 1980, veteran Opry announcer Grant Turner in 1981, and short-timer Lefty Frizzell and long-timer Marty Robbins in 1982.

Little Jimmy Dickens was honored in 1983, Lester Flatt and Earl Scruggs in 1985, and comedian Whitey Ford in 1986.

The Country Music Hall of Fame was never intended to be so overwhelmed by one radio show like the Grand Ole Opry. It speaks to the continuing strength of the Opry roster that the Hall of Fame *has* been so dominated. There is nothing to indicate that influence of the Opry on Hall of Fame electors will soon diminish.

We used to go out walkin' hand-in-hand,
You told me all the big things you had planned;
It wasn't long till all your dreams came true,
*Success put me in second place with you.**

—Loretta Lynn's first national hit

The story has been told in personal detail in the best-selling autobiography *Coal Miner's Daughter*, and in graphic detail in the hit motion picture of the same title. And yet there are nuances to the tale, and such basic human emotions to it that one never tires of hearing it.

It's the story of Loretta Webb Lynn.

She grew up in the grinding poverty of Butcher Hollow, a remote village in the coal-mining hills of eastern Kentucky. She was named for the glamorous movie star Loretta Young, and her mother literally papered the walls of the modest Webb cabin with magazine pictures of Miss Young, bringing a small measure of beauty to little Loretta's mean surroundings.

Her schooling was in a mountain grade school and she says she went through the eighth grade twice because she liked school so much she didn't want to quit, as most of the youngsters did. Loretta was only thirteen when she met a burly little man named Mooney Lynn (the nickname came from the fact he used to sell moonshine whiskey off the back of a mule) at a school social. He bought her

*"Success" by Johnny Mullins; copyright 1961 Sure-Fire Music Co., Inc.

homemade pie that night, they started "goin' together," and within a month they were married. Loretta was a few weeks shy of her fourteenth birthday.

Lynn was working for the Consolidated Coal Company at that time, but the job petered out. With Junior, Loretta's brother, Mooney hitchhiked to Washington state and found employment on a farm near the town of Custer. As soon as he could he sent money to his child bride, and she rode 3,000 miles on a train to her new home—frightened and pregnant.

"Custer was a lot different from back in Kentucky," she recalled. "It was a wide place in the road, but my goodness, there was electricity, there was farms, there was paved roads ever'where. We had three little rooms and an outhouse, no runnin' water."

The family grew and Mooney Lynn (Loretta always calls him "Doolittle," or the diminutive, "Doo") went from farm work to logging to service-station mechanic. On her eighteenth birthday he gave his wife a cheap guitar and told her, "You're as good as a lot of those women out there makin' records, and I think maybe this is what we ought to try to do."

Those weren't idle words. He persuaded a local band playing at the Custer Grange hall to give Loretta a chance on their radio show, and when they did, they liked what they heard. She became the band's vocalist on Saturday nights. For five dollars a night.

Encouraged by that, Mooney continued to push her. He entered her in a talent contest in a Tacoma saloon, for which Buck Owens was the host. Loretta won it, and Owens booked her on his local television show, at that time the only country music TV show in the Northwest. It was on that show that she was seen and heard by British Columbia businessman Norman Burleigh, who owned the small Zero Records label on the West Coast. Burleigh contacted the Lynns, and sent them to Los Angeles to record one of her songs, "I'm a Honky Tonk Girl": "I've lost everything in this world / And now I'm a honky tonk girl."

Since Zero Records didn't have enough money to promote the record, Mooney decided that he and Loretta would do it on their own. He secured a list of U.S. radio stations and mailed a 45-rpm record to every station on the list. And then they took off in their battered 1955 Ford and started a journey across the country, so that disc jockeys could meet this new singer, Loretta Lynn.

"We hit every station that was country," Loretta said. "Zero Records gave us money to buy gas—but not food—and we went all the way across the country, eatin' bologna and cheese and crackers and sleepin' in the car."

California disc jockey Hugh Cherry remembered their visit: "I was working as a late-night jock on KFOX in Long Beach. One evening—it was two in the morning—the buzzer rang downstairs and a voice said, 'Hello, I'm Loretta Lynn, and a disc jockey in Seattle, Washington, said I should come to Los Angeles and see Hugh Cherry. I've got a record for you.' So I let her in and she comes up very talkative and animated.

" 'I understand that if somebody wants to get a hillbilly record to break in California that you're the man to see. Well, I got one right here, "Honky Tonk Girl." It's mine!'

"I put it on the turntable and the record was really good. It was on a small obscure label, called Zero. Loretta told me that she and Mooney were distributing it themselves, personally taking it to every radio station along the way to Nashville.

"She said that she was going to Nashville to get the record played there and to be on the Grand Ole Opry. I said to her, 'But, honey, don't you know that it sometimes takes three to four years to get on the Opry?' And Loretta replied, 'I can't wait that long.' "

The road did lead to Nashville and to the offices of the Wilburn Brothers, Teddy and Doyle, an act she had met when they had toured in Washington state. Through the intercession of the Wilburns, Loretta was booked as a guest on the Grand Ole Opry.

The date was Saturday, October 15, 1960.

Loretta reminisced: "Ernest Tubb was the one who introduced me. I was on the Pet Milk part of the show. And I bought this dress to wear—it was real thin and had big puffed sleeves. It was kinda like a party dress. Lester Wilburn's wife cut my hair and got me ready for my first time on the Grand Ole Opry. I remember going out on the stage and I remember tapping my foot. I was so scared I don't remember anything else."

Of course, she sang "I'm a Honky Tonk Girl." Leslie Wilburn played bass behind her; Lester Wilburn was on rhythm guitar.

Was the audience receptive?

"Oh, yeah!" She laughed. "They figured if you was good enough to be on the Grand Ole Opry, you must be okay."

The strange odyssey continued, as Loretta and Mooney made the return trip to Custer, Washington, over a different route, stopping at every radio station to talk to disc jockeys and plug the Zero record.

"That record hit the top ten when there wasn't a soul could buy it." She laughed. "Record stores was callin' radio stations sayin', 'Get that thing off the air. People are drivin' us crazy.' "

When the Lynns returned to Nashville in mid-1961, they had sold everything they owned in Washington state, had packed the four kids in the car, and had come to stay.

It was then that Loretta Lynn met Patsy Cline.

···𝄞 ii 𝄢··· Nothing at the Grand Ole Opry really ever stayed the same. Indeed, there was a continuing subtle shift away from "hillbilly" and honky-tonk sounds in some of the new choices for the Opry roster in 1962. A shift to what was being called the "Nashville Sound." It was, in the simplest terms, more of a pop sound, smoother and sweeter. Chet Atkins, though, said: "Technically, there is no such thing as the Nashville Sound. It's the musicians. Southern people have a relaxed way of life, a relaxed way of playing."

Whatever the definition of "Nashville Sound," Sonny James, born James Loden in Hackleburg, Alabama, was recognized as a leading proponent of it. His beginning was in the traditional country vein, performing with a family group that featured the hillbilly fiddle and five-string banjo. Sonny was only five years old when he debuted with his mother, father, and sister at a business convention at the Muscle Shoals Hotel in Florence, Alabama.

From that point on it was a learning process, one he took seriously. He progressed year by year, honing his skills. There was an eighteen-month stint in the Korean War and when he returned he was ready to challenge for his place on the music charts. He was signed by Capitol Records (Capitol A&R man Ken Nelson gave him his stage name), and in Sonny James, Nelson and Capitol scored with a sensational crossover hit—one prominent on both country and popular charts—a teenage ballad called "Young Love." It soared to the top of the charts and sold more than a million records.

He followed that with "First Date, First Kiss," and the Grand Ole Opry beckoned in October of 1962. Throughout the sixties and seventies he was to have one country chart-topper after another—an astounding string of eighteen consecutive number-one records. Among them were "You're the Only World I Know," "True Love's a Blessing," "Only the Lonely," "Running Bear," "It's Just a Matter of Time," and "Empty Arms."

Also in 1962 the Opry added Leroy Van Dyke, another Nashville Sound devotee. Once more a great song catapulted an artist to the stage of the Ryman: Van Dyke had the number-one "Walk On By" in 1961, a Grammy Award winner as the Record of the Year.

Van Dyke, who came from Spring Fork, Missouri, was no hillbilly. He was a product of a distinguished family. One brother was an electrical engineer, another an obstetrician, a sister was a nurse, another a schoolteacher. And Leroy was a graduate of the University of Missouri with degrees in animal husbandry and journalism.

The image of the country singer was changing.

Somewhat more "country" was the act of Carl and Pearl Butler. They weren't strangers to the Opry stage, but in 1962 their duet of "Don't Let Me Cross Over" was a smash hit and they became roster members of the Grand Ole Opry.

Carl was a veteran solo performer and songwriter. Born and raised in Knoxville, that hotbed of country music activity, he had worked, and learned his trade, on WROL and WNOX in Knoxville, and WPTF in Raleigh, North Carolina.

It was in 1948 that he first played the Opry, an association that continued right into the sixties. He was a prolific songwriter: "If Teardrops Were Pennies," "My Tears Don't Show," "Crying Alone," "Grief in My Heart," "Loving Arms," "A White Rose," "I Like to Pretend," "So Close," "Hold Back the Dawn," "Guilty Conscience," "Country Mile." A collaboration with Earl Scruggs produced "Building on Sand" and "Crying My Heart Out over You."

Pearl Dee Jones was a native Nashvillian who married the young Carl Butler when he was just beginning his career. She had a fine natural voice, but for a good many years was content to remain in the background, singing with Carl only at family get-togethers. But then they decided to record the "Don't Let Me Cross Over" duet for Columbia Records, Carl's label.

By 1963 they were voted the top duo in country music, and on record and from the stage of the Opry they turned out a string of duet hits: "Forbidden Street," "I'm Hanging Up the Phone," "Just Thought I'd Let You Know," "We'll Destroy Each Other," "Little Mac," "Little Pedro," "Call 29," "Same Old Me," and "Too Late to Try Again," a number-one record in 1964.

Two other lesser developments of 1962 should be noted here. A young songwriter named Willie Nelson made his debut on the charts with a song called "Touch Me." And a drummer who had been playing in Atlanta, Georgia, joined Ernest Tubb's Texas Troubadours. His name was Jack Greene. "The first year I was with Tubb," he said, "we worked three hundred and five days on the road."

··◁[iii]▷·· Loretta Lynn, meanwhile, had settled in with the Opry, although she was not a roster member. There were seventeen consecutive weeks when she was a guest on the Grand Ole Opry. And not without trouble.

"It seems there were a lot of girl singers who were trying to get to the top at the same time," Loretta would write later. "When I came along they got jealous and started complaining at the Opry because I got invited back so much. Then they started telephoning me and saying I ought to go back to the West Coast.

"One girl asked me who I was sleeping with to get on the Opry so fast. It hurt so much that I cried day and night. My husband said, 'If you don't quit this crying, I'm gonna take you back to the West Coast and forget it.' And he would have."

(Jan Howard had had a similar experience: "I'll tell you what—it wasn't all beautiful when I moved here. I got some threatening phone calls; a few things like that. They said, 'The Grand Ole Opry doesn't need you. Who do you think you are, having one record and appearing on the Opry?' I mean, I cried many a night.")

Just as Patsy Cline had quieted the jealousies by embracing Jan Howard, she also came to the defense of Loretta Lynn.

Loretta recalled: "I guess the other girls didn't know about me and Patsy being friends. They called a party at one of their homes to discuss how to stop me from being on the Opry; and they invited Patsy! There were about six of them. . . . I'm not saying who they were, but they know it themselves. The only thing I will say is that Kitty Wells wasn't one of them. . . .

"Anyway, inviting Patsy was their mistake. She called me up and told me what the deal was and said we both should go to that meeting. I said I didn't have anything to wear, and besides the meeting was about me. She said going was the best thing to do. She told me to get my hair done, and she came over to my house with a new outfit she had bought for me and she made me go.

"When we got to the house, there were all these Cadillacs belonging to the top women singers in the country. We went in there, and they didn't say a word. That ended their plan. Patsy put the stamp of approval on me and I never had any problems with them again. . . . But I made a point of it when new girls came along to give 'em all a chance, because I wouldn't treat anybody the way they treated me. If you're good, you're gonna make it."

(There was an interesting aside to all of this in 1974, when Australian pop singer Olivia Newton-John, who had recorded several country-style hits, was named Female Vocalist of the Year at the Country Music Association awards show. The hue and cry over the award was bitter. Loretta made a point of going to a Newton-John concert, coming onto the stage with a bouquet of flowers, and publicly embracing the young singer.)

On September 24, 1962, Loretta was called to Ott Devine's office and given a contract as a Grand Ole Opry roster member. "I jumped about three feet off the floor," Loretta said, laughing, "and WSM photographer Les Leverett made a picture of it.

"I guess my fondest memory of the Opry is seeing my picture up on the wall backstage at the Ryman, with the light in back of it. When I saw that I thought, 'Boy, I'm big!' I really hadn't even started, but I was there on the Opry wall."

❦[iv]❦ And then it was December 1962—
The scene was Carnegie Hall in New York City, packed to capacity. Fire marshals had closed the doors, leaving several thousand bluegrass fans outside on the streets.

Lester Flatt and Earl Scruggs and the Foggy Mountain Boys came onstage at Carnegie Hall to screams of delight from the standing-room-only audience. Bluegrass was the hottest sound around. In September of '61, Flatt and Scruggs appeared live on the NBC News television magazine, "Frank McGee: Here and Now," and Earl tried to explain in the simplest terms what his banjo technique was all about.

McGee asked: "Earl, how about a close-up view of the Scruggs-style picking?"

As the camera zoomed in tight on the banjo, Earl answered: "Sure, Frank. The fifth string is plucked by the thumb—and these two fingers"—he wiggled his index and middle fingers—"take care of the rest of the strings. The picks are for sharpness and brightness. These two extra pegs mounted here enable me to change the pitch while I'm playing." And then he demonstrated by going into "Shucking the Corn."

Rudimentary? Certainly. But it introduced millions of viewers to the magic of bluegrass music, to the driving intensity of traditionalist music played on non-electric stringed instruments. It was basic stuff.

The originator of it all, Bill Monroe, also found there was a new demand for his talents. He and the Blue Grass Boys appeared before an enthusiastic audience at the University of Chicago in February 1963. In the same month he had a successful New York City concert and in July he was featured at the famous Newport Jazz Festival.

Bluegrass had become the most popular export of the Grand Ole Opry.

Sweet dreams of you, ev'ry night I go through,
Why can't I forget you and start my life anew,
Instead of having sweet dreams about you. *

—Patsy Cline hit, 1963

Patsy Cline was in the recording studio in February 1963, putting together the songs for a new album. She cut "I'll Sail My Ship Alone," "Crazy Arms," "Always," "Blue Moon of Kentucky" (the Bill Monroe song with which Elvis Presley got started), "Someday You'll Want Me to Want You," Don Gibson's haunting "Sweet Dreams," and "Faded Love," a Johnnie and Bob Wills tune dating back more than a decade.

Of the last song, Patsy's husband, Charlie Dick, remembered: "She and I had been driving back to Nashville late at night and Jackie DeShannon came on the radio singing 'Faded Love.' I thought Patsy was asleep in the backseat, but she popped up, scaring the devil out of me.

" 'Everybody's modulating these days,' she said. 'I wonder why Jackie modulated down?'

"I said, 'Probably the song is not in her key and it would be hard to do without modulating.'

" 'No, it wouldn't,' Patsy replied. 'I can do it.'

"I said, 'Oh, you can, huh?' and she said, 'Yep, I sure as hell can!'

"At that session Patsy took 'Faded Love' and made the high notes even higher and sang it all the way through without the least bit of modulation. 'I told you I could do it,' she boasted. I was fairly amazed and a little impressed, though by then I should have known that Patsy could do anything she set her mind to. She was really something—years ahead of her time, musically."

In spite of her self-confidence, however, Patsy sought the reassurance of her friends. She invited Dottie West and Jan Howard to the studio for a preview of the album, and then, on Thursday evening, February 28, 1963, she telephoned Loretta and Mooney Lynn.

"It was late at night," her husband said, "but Patsy asked them to come over to the house. She thought highly of Loretta and Mooney and she wanted to make sure they approved. Loretta sang authentic country and I think Patsy wanted to be reassured she wasn't getting too far away from country with her string arrangements."

Loretta's recollections of that evening were vivid:

"Me and Doo sat and listened. She was all excited and so proud. 'I want y'all to tell me if I'm getting a little too far from country.' I said, 'No, Patsy, it's beautiful.' What else could I say? That's what it was. It was *fantastic*.

"I remember that while we listened to the tapes, Patsy embroidered a tablecloth. She did that to relax. Her little boy, Randy, was on a rocking horse, rocking very hard. I was worried that he'd fall off and get hurt, but Patsy said not to worry. That night we made plans to go shopping when she returned from doing a benefit show in Kansas City for some disc jockey. . . .

"Just before I left her house about midnight, she said she had something for me. Then she gave me a great big box filled with clothes for me to take home. One thing in that box was a little red sexy shorty nightgown. She told me, 'This is the sexiest thing I've ever had. Red is the color men like.' . . .

"I remember that before we said good-bye, we'd usually hug each other, but that night I was carrying that huge box. Patsy said, 'Aren't you going to hug me?' I put down the box and hugged her. Then . . . she said, 'Little gal, no matter what people say or do, no matter what happens, you and me are gonna stick together.'"

When Patsy Cline left Nashville the next day she headed for a concert date at the Birmingham, Alabama, municipal auditorium. On the bill with her would be Jerry Lee Lewis, Charlie Rich, Lester Flatt and Earl Scruggs, and Tex Ritter.

ii It was Saturday, March 2, 1963.

Birmingham News reporter Rebel Steiner, Jr., wrote of the happenings at the municipal auditorium:

"The first show was sold out. The second performance was standing-room-only. Still, more than 500 fans were outside wanting tickets.

"Many of those stood in line along Eighth Avenue North . . . to see and hear country music's most popular woman singer.

"For two shows the promoter was paying Patsy Cline $1,000 cash, a hefty fee then. The crowd grew, and the promoter wanted all the performers to do a third show. But he wouldn't give them more money.

" 'Well, I'll do it if everyone else does,' Miss Cline replied.

"So she swaggered on stage and sang her traditional first number, 'Come On In (Sit Right Down and Make Yourself at Home).'

"After the song and applause, the set . . . went a little like this:

"Turning to her band, she said, 'Oh, dogies, never heard such a swingin' beat in all my life.' And, then, turning back to the audience: 'Howdy, everybody! You havin' a good time? Well, let your hair down and let's see what you look like. We're havin' a ball. Here's one that's a kinda true-life story.'

"Then she . . . looked at her guitarist to begin 'Crazy,' a song written by Willie Nelson that was high on the charts. 'Leave it right in the same gear as that, hoss, and we'll see what damage we can do to it.' "

··◦[iii]◦·· It was Sunday, March 3, 1963.

The concert in Kansas City was to be a benefit for the widow of country music disc jockey Cactus Jack McCall. Playing the benefit with Patsy were Roy Acuff (without his band), Billy Walker, Cowboy Copas, Wilma Lee and Stoney Cooper, and Hawkshaw Hawkins.

When the concert was concluded, the Coopers drove to their next engagement, Walker left on a commercial flight, and Acuff turned down the offer of a free plane ride back to Nashville. He chose to go back by car. Patsy, Copas, and Hawkins boarded the private plane of Randy Hughes, Copas's son-in-law.

They never made it back to Nashville.

As a matter of fact, the wreckage of the private plane wasn't found until dawn of March 6, in a remote area known as Fatty Bottom, some twenty minutes' flying time from Dyersburg, Tennessee. Debris was spread over a sixty-yard-wide area in a heavily wooded tract between a rural highway and a ranger tower, approximately five miles west of the Tennessee River. It was clear that no one had witnessed the crash. Searchers said that the bright yellow plane apparently had struck a large tree before hitting the ground. At the crash site, Patsy's cigarette lighter, hairbrush, and mascara wand were found.

Soon the whole world knew. Radio commentator Paul Harvey reported the tragedy in his clipped, distinctive style. This is the script, exactly as he typed it:

Three familiar voices are suddenly silent today.
And over an ugly hole on a Tennessee hillside, the heavens softly weep. No more mournful ballad was ever sung on the Grand Ole Opry than the one which was hammered out on the nation's newsprinters this morning.
The Nashville country music stars . . .
Hawkshaw Hawkins and Cowboy Copas and Patsy Cline . . . and her manager . . .

In 1961, Opry stars set off for New York's Carnegie Hall for a benefit for the Musicians' Aid Society. From left bottom: Grandpa Jones, Patsy Cline, and Bill Monroe; from left top: Minnie Pearl, Jim Reeves, and Faron Young.

(1961) SPECIAL COLLECTIONS, VANDERBILT UNIVERSITY

"I jumped three feet off the floor!" said Loretta Lynn about the day Ott Devine called her into his office to sign with the Opry.

(1962) WSM PHOTO/LES LEVERETT

*Loretta Lynn appeared with
the Wilburn Brothers on their
syndicated television show shot
at WSM. From the left, Shorty
Lavender, Don Helms, Harold
Morrison, Leslie Wilburn,
Doyle Wilburn, Lester
Wilburn, Loretta Lynn, and
Teddy Wilburn.*

(1962) WSM PHOTO/LES LEVERETT

They'd flown in a one-lung Comanche to Kansas City . . . for a benefit performance.

For the benefit of the widow of a friend . . . who'd been killed in a car wreck.

And they were returning to home base—Nashville, Tennessee. They'd refueled at Dyersburg.

Some severe thunderstorms had been raking that area along the Tennessee River. At least one commercial airliner had detoured.

Precisely what happened thereafter will be subject to conjecture forever.

And what terror there was toward the end we'll never know.

But there was no pain.

When they found the plane this morning its engine had entered the earth straight down.

Somebody will write a cow country classic about this night ride to nowhere. Because hill folks are a sentimental lot.

But the highest compliment their eulogies are likely to include . . . is that the somber citizens who converged this day on that ugly scar in the woodland where pieces of four bodies lay . . .

That there are real tears in their whispered words . . .

And that they refer to each of the suddenly deceased by his or her first name . . .

For none of them ever thought of Randy and the Cowboy, Hawkshaw and Patsy any other way . . . than as homefolks, kinfolks, friends.

There were residual tragedies to the terrible plane crash. On March 7, Jack Anglin, of the veteran Grand Ole Opry duo Johnny and Jack, was hurrying to memorial services for Patsy Cline. His car crashed, and he was killed instantly.

And on the Opry roster was singing star Jean Shepard, the wife of Hawkshaw Hawkins. They had been married four years earlier and had one son, Don Robin, named for their close friends Don Gibson and Marty Robbins. At the time of the plane crash, Jean was pregnant with their second child.

When another son was born a month later he was named for his father—Harold Franklin Hawkins II.

⟨[iv]⟩ It was Saturday, March 9, 1963.

Time for another performance at the Grand Ole Opry.

Announcer T. Tommy Cutrer said, "Ladies and gentlemen . . . Ott Devine, manager of the Grand Ole Opry."

A sober-faced Devine came to the microphone, nervously clutching a piece of paper.

"All of their friends standing with me tonight on the stage of the Ryman Auditorium know that it is impossible to put into words our thoughts, our feelings, our love for Patsy, Hawk, Cope, Jack, and Randy. And so we ask that you in our audience please stand and join us for a moment of silent prayer in tribute to them."

Only a quiet sob or two broke the stillness enveloping the old Ryman.

Then, Ott Devine again:

"Thank you. Patsy Cline, Cowboy Copas, Hawkshaw Hawkins, Jack Anglin, and Randy Hughes never walked on this stage without a smile. They would want us to keep smiling, and to recall the happier occasions. I feel that I can speak for all of them when I say . . . Let's continue in the tradition of the Grand Ole Opry."

The Jordanaires came forward to the microphone and sang "How Great Thou Art."

There was a slight pause when the sacred number was finished and then, suddenly, Roy Acuff and the Smoky Mountain Boys struck up a fast fiddle tune. As he played Acuff looked over at Minnie Pearl, standing in the wings, crying softly. Their eyes met and she nodded almost imperceptibly to him.

The fiddle tune ended, Acuff leaned into the microphone and said, "Now let's make welcome . . . Cou-sin . . . Min-nie . . . Pearl!"

She took a deep breath, swallowed hard, forced a smile to her face, and made her tripping, dancing entrance.

"How-dee!" Minnie Pearl bellowed.

"How-dee!" the audience roared in response.

"I'm just so proud to be here!"

Unhappily, the tragedies weren't ended.

Less than three weeks later—on March 29, 1963—Texas Ruby Owens, who, with her husband, fiddler Curly Fox, was a popular act at the Opry in the late thirties and the forties, died in a fire that destroyed their trailer home in Nashville.

It seemed a pall hung over the Grand Ole Opry family.

All the chapel bells were ringing
In the little valley town,
And the song that they were singing
*Was for baby Jimmy Brown.**

—The Browns hit,
circa 1959

On September 27, 1963, the National Life and Accident Insurance Company purchased the Ryman Auditorium from what was known as the Ryman Auditorium Corporation, a general welfare corporation. In other words, National Life took the old building off the hands of the city of Nashville for something in the neighborhood of $200,000. It was a necessary move to give the Grand Ole Opry exclusive use of the building and to enable National Life to do maintenance repairs, which the municipal owner hadn't been doing.

The price was modest, considering that the building sat on a piece of land smack in the middle of downtown Nashville. But it was old, even with repairs it was a firetrap, and any reasonable person could conclude the Grand Ole Opry wasn't going to be able to stay there forever.

Nevertheless, it was a historic building, and because the Opry was there, it had been dubbed "The Mother Church of Country Music." National Life turned it over to its wholly owned subsidiary, WSM, Inc., and the building was renamed the Grand Ole Opry House.

They might as well not have bothered. It would always be called "The old Ryman."

Inside, several new acts were delighting the fans in 1963. One was a family trio out of Sparkman, Arkansas—the Browns; the other was a young lady from Birmingham, Alabama, who used the stage name Marion Worth (a.k.a. Mary Ann Ward).

The Browns—Jim Ed, Maxine, and Bonnie—had that unique, tight harmony which seems to accrue to sibling singers. Their beginning was not unlike the start of many performers who had come to the Opry. "It's the same old story you've heard a thousand times," Jim Ed said. "We listened to the Grand Ole Opry every Saturday on a battery-operated radio." Sister Maxine would order all the songbooks advertised on the program and they would sit and sing along with the Opry acts.

In 1954 Jim Ed and Maxine wrote a humorous ditty called "Looking Back to See," and it was offered to RCA Victor, King Records, and most of the major labels. It was also turned down by all of them. Finally they signed with the obscure Fabor label in Shreveport, Louisiana, and recorded their song; Jim Reeves played rhythm guitar and Floyd Cramer was at the piano during that session. "Looking Back to See" was a major hit.

By 1955 sister Bonnie had joined the act and the trio was something very special. They became cast members of Red Foley's "Ozark Jubilee," and a year later RCA Victor made up for its earlier error by signing the Browns.

Then, in 1959, they recorded what seemed to be an unlikely piece of material by a French composer, *Les Trois Cloches.* English lyrics had been written for "The Three Bells" (also known as "The Jimmy Brown Song") a decade earlier, and the Browns added their distinctive harmony to the poignant life-to-death tale. It was a million-seller. A gold-record effort.

The Browns were in demand on all the network TV variety shows, and in 1963, after having made numerous guest appearances, they became roster members of the Grand Ole Opry. Jim Ed and Maxine moved to Nashville; Bonnie never did. It was Maxine who persuaded RCA's Chet Atkins to record her brother as a single. In 1965 he made his record debut as a soloist with "I Heard from a Memory."

Eventually the sisters retired from show business to raise families, but Jim Ed stayed to become a fixture at the Opry.

Marion Worth came out of Alabama after having won a talent contest as one-half of a sister duet, and having had her own radio show on WVOK in Birmingham. She was regarded as a "singer's singer" at the Grand Ole Opry, capable of going from sultry love ballads to belting barn-dance tunes.

As a songwriter, she turned out "That's My Kind of Love," "I Lived a Lifetime in a Day," "Are You Willing, Willie?," "A Woman Needs Love," and "Mama Says." As a recording artist, Marion Worth had national hits with "Shake Me, I Rattle (Squeeze Me, I Cry)" and "Crazy Arms."

·◁[ii]▷· Nashville in the sixties was an ever more powerful magnet for talent. It had made its peace with rock 'n' roll, as many rock acts recorded there. It had become "Music City, USA." Then, too, loyal country fans had returned to the music they knew best, once more packing the Ryman. Thus, Music

City was centered around the Grand Ole Opry and along what has become known as Music Row, a semi-decaying residential area of 16th and 17th Avenues South that was home for record companies, and recording studios, and music publishers, and talent agents, and songwriters, and television producers, and press agents, and every stripe of entrepreneur who operates on the fringes of the volatile music business.

Music City was a small town, really, its inhabitants being basically small-town people. They hailed from places that most others hadn't heard of: from Byhalia and Bell Buckle, Strawberry Plains and Sale City, Emory Gap and Eastabuchie, Dewy Rose and D'Lo, Soddy and Sessums. And they got off the Trailways and Greyhound buses, carrying their instruments and their dreams, to gravitate immediately to Music Row. And to spend some time in Tootsie's Orchid Lounge and hoist a few brews, and to try to get backstage at the Grand Ole Opry where someone might listen to them, or look over one of their songs.

Music Row itself was an enigma. It was a place where millions could be made. It was a place, too, where dreams were destroyed. It was a place for the most honorable of men, where a handshake was better than a signed contract. A place, too, for the most dishonorable of men, who would sell mica as precious jewels.

It was a city growing beyond itself, in a sense. And it needed more than million-seller records and millionaire singers in rhinestone-studded costumes. It needed someone from outside the country music establishment to tell it: "Hey, this country music boom is *legitimate*."

Perhaps that came in 1963, when the American Society of Composers, Authors and Publishers (ASCAP) opened a Nashville office. ASCAP represented the prestige of the music business; it offered now an imprimatur it had previously denied to country music writers. There had been a time when ASCAP had refused to license "hillbilly songs," on the basis that they really weren't music. And that was one of the reasons for the success of its music licensing rival, Broadcast Music, Inc. (BMI). From its beginning, BMI had embraced country music songwriters, giving them a place to go to protect their songs when ASCAP had slammed the door.

But now ASCAP had recognized Nashville, however belatedly, and that was important. To country music and to Music City, USA.

❧[iii]❧ Nineteen sixty-four began with the Grand Ole Opry on the front pages of the Nashville newspapers. For a different kind of performance.

It seems that a priest, Father Jack Miller, arrived in Nashville with a story he wanted to tell to some people he long admired—several of the Grand Ole Opry stars. He "had got off the beaten path," he confessed, having violated some of his priestly vows, and he wanted to make a fresh start. But he was penniless. He needed help from his Opry "friends."

Jim Reeves, approached first, agreed to finance a brief stay by Father Miller in a downtown hotel. And he gave him several free tickets to the Grand Ole Opry, because the man had said he had three ambitions in life: He wanted to be a priest—which he already was, although it wasn't going too well; he wanted to see the Grand Ole Opry; and he wanted to visit the Soviet Union.

At 12:30 A.M. one night, Father Miller showed up at Hank Snow's Nashville home with the same tale. Snow let him in and they discussed the priest's problems. After the visitor had left, Hank missed a pair of his favorite hand-tooled boots. Also a watch. He went to the police.

Reeves also came forward then, telling the police that when he was sent the hotel bill he learned that the priest had run up charges for tips, room service, and long-distance phone calls more than double the room rent. Another Opry star, Stoney Cooper, volunteered the information that he had contributed twenty-five dollars in cash to Father Miller's "rehabilitation."

But the bogus priest was long gone from Nashville.

A somewhat bemused Nashville detective, Leo Ladd, told reporters: "From the way he operated, the suspect may have 'touched' several other stars for funds, but there's no way of knowing unless they contact us." No one else complained.

Did the police have any idea where the con man had gone?

"Well, he's realized two of his lifelong ambitions," Detective Ladd said lightly. "He's been a 'priest,' and seen the Grand Ole Opry. Maybe he's headed for Russia."

It wasn't too many days later that Ladd learned the con man's destination had been Memphis, where he was involved in the same "Father Jack Miller" scam. He was tripped up by two Roman Catholic motel clerks, who were suspicious of his unpriestly demeanor.

Returned to Nashville, the man admitted the errors of his ways. Police identified him as Ralph Edward DeLaval, thirty-three, of Toronto, Canada, and charged him with grand larceny.

Reeves still had to pay the inflated hotel bill. And Stoney Cooper never saw his charitable twenty-five dollars again.

But Hank Snow got his boots back.

···❧ iv ❧··· On the stage of the Ryman it was business as usual, with Ott Devine continuing to add new acts.

On March 7 it was Ernie Ashworth of Huntsville, Alabama, who was put on the roster. Ashworth was "hot"—"Most Promising Male Artist" in surveys by both *Cash Box* and *Billboard* magazines. And again, there was that big song.

"Talk Back Trembling Lips," only his third release on Hickory Records, had sailed to the top of the country charts and stayed on the charts for thirty-six consecutive weeks. That was "open sesame" for the Opry.

Several weeks later (March 28, to be exact) a pretty young housewife and mother from Ohio was backstage at the Ryman as the guest of Bill Anderson. Connie Smith was awed by it all.

"I remember," she said, "when I was five years old saying, 'Someday I'm gonna sing on the Grand Ole Opry.' My daddy's favorite was Ernest Tubb; my Momma's favorite was Eddy Arnold. I had a crush on Justin Tubb when I was a teenager and I loved the Louvin Brothers—those were my favorites. And I just always loved the Grand Ole Opry.

"Then, when I was married and had a little boy about four months old, I wound up getting a chance to sing at a park near Columbus, Ohio. Bill Anderson was on the show that day and I got to meet him."

That was in 1963. Some six months later she and her husband went to see Bill Anderson at a concert in Canton, Ohio, and the Opry star invited them out to dinner. The talk was all about country music.

Bill said, "You really like it, don't you?"

She agreed that she wanted to do nothing but sing.

"Well, why don't you come to Nashville?" Anderson said.

"Just like that?"

"Sure," Bill answered. "I'm scheduled to host the Ernest Tubb Record Shop show on March twenty-eighth. If you'll come to Nashville, I'll let you sing."

On that date, then, she was in Nashville and backstage at the Opry. "I remember sitting on the Coke cooler watching Bill Phillips's little boy while Bill was onstage. And then I went down to the 'Midnight Jamboree' at the record shop and sang 'Walk Out Backwards,' and was scared to death."

It was back to her home in Warner, Ohio, after that exciting evening, and in May, Bill Anderson asked her to return to Nashville to cut some demonstration records of some of his songs. A few days later, Anderson called her from on the road—he was in Minneapolis—to tell her that Chet Atkins, who had heard the demos, wanted to sign her to an RCA Victor contract.

That head-swimming development came in June. By July she had cut her first record for RCA—a Bill Anderson song titled "Once a Day."

It wasn't noted by anyone in particular, but in that same June (on the first of the month, to be precise) the bosomy, ambitious teenager from Sevierville, Tennessee, made her permanent move to Nashville. Dolly Parton came to Music City on the day after her graduation from high school.

On July 8 Dottie West, an attractive redhead who was the oldest of ten children of a farm family from nearby McMinnville, signed the papers that made her a roster member of the Grand Ole Opry.

There was almost a direct career line from McMinnville to Nashville. Almost, but not quite. Music was a big part of her growing-up years. She was taught to play the guitar by her father, Hollis March, who "could play anything with strings on it." She also sang in the local Southern Baptist church.

Dottie wanted to be more than just a country singer; she wanted to understand music. Not just country music, but *all* music. In the early fifties she enrolled as a music major at Tennessee Technological University in Cookeville. In her first week there she met an engineering student named Bill West, who could play excellent steel guitar. They teamed their talents at numerous campus events, they married, and when they both graduated they moved to Cleveland, where Bill got a job with an electronics company.

The music continued, however, as they supplemented their income by appearing as a country music team. One of their gigs was as regulars on the television show "Landmark Jubilee" in Cleveland. In 1959, after Dottie got a recording contract with Starday Records, they moved to Nashville, where they became a part of a community of young artists seeking the gold of stardom: Willie Nelson, Hank Cochran, Roger Miller, et al.

"It was through guitar-pulling sessions that I really became a writer," Dottie told an interviewer. "When I first went to Nashville, Patsy Cline was my best friend. I had idolized her singing before that, and we became good friends. . . . She never wrote songs, but she really got me going to what we called guitar pullings at the time. We'd sit with one guitar in the room and we'd pass the guitar around and everybody would sing the song they had written that week and try to knock each other out. So it really kept you on your toes and you wrote a lot of songs that way."

Dottie West's first song growing out of the guitar-pulling experience was "Is This Me?," written in 1961. Jim Reeves recorded it and had a hit with it. After that, matters progressed reasonably fast. She signed with RCA Victor Records, got a songwriter contract with Tree Publishing, and hit it big on her own with "Here Comes My Baby (Back Again)" in 1964.

That was also the year that she did her first duet, pairing with Jim Reeves on Justin Tubb's "Love Is No Excuse." By July, when she joined the Opry roster, that record had soared into the top ten on the charts.

Reeves was, without question, the biggest star on the Grand Ole Opry at that time. After joining the Opry in 1955, he had had hit after hit: "Four Walls," "A Touch of Velvet," "Guilty," "Blue Canadian Rockies," "Tahiti," "Heartbreak in Silhouette," "Golden Memories and Silver Tears," "I Could Cry," "I'll Follow You," "Where Does a Broken Heart Go?" In 1960 RCA released his "He'll Have to Go"; it sold more than three million copies.

Trade publications named him the number-one male artist in country music. Reeves and his wife, Mary, became a virtual miniconglomerate: publishing, broadcasting, major concert tours.

He also had a vast popularity base overseas—in England, Germany, Norway, and strangely, South Africa. He was practically a national idol in South Africa; he was mobbed by crowds in that country, playing to tens of thousands on his tours there. To solidify his base there, he recorded a number of records in Afrikaans, learning the lyrics phonetically.

It was in South Africa that Reeves made his first and only motion picture—*Kimberly Jim*, advertised as a "robust, action adventure, starring Jim Reeves as a guitar-strumming gambler from Dixie seeking his fortune in the South African diamond rush." The film further endeared the Texan to South Africans, because the songs in it were written by South African composers: "Born to Be Lucky," "A Stranger's Just a Friend," "Dolly with the Dimpled Knees," "I Grew Up," and "Diamonds in the Dust."

At the height of his popularity he was on the road so much that his time at home in Madison, Tennessee, was limited to fewer than ninety days a year. It made sense, then, that he should fly a great deal, and become a pilot himself.

On Friday, July 31, 1964, Jim and his manager-pianist, Dean Manuel, had flown to Batesville, Arkansas, on business in a small rented Beechcraft Debonair. They were returning to Nashville; Reeves planned to appear on the Grand Ole Opry the following evening.

A summer storm was whipping the Nashville area. Air traffic controllers at Berry Field received a call from Reeves. Ten miles out, he said, in the vicinity of Brentwood, flying into heavy rain. Within seconds the plane's blip disappeared from the radar screen.

It was forty-eight hours later (Sunday, August 2) that the wreckage of the Beechcraft was found in a tangled patch of woods on "Old Baldy," a hill near Brentwood. Ironically, it was discovered only fifteen hundred feet from where the search had originally begun late on Friday. The plane had come to rest behind a white fence, only one hundred yards from a residence. A man there had told police that he had heard the plane's engine cut out during the thunderstorm. It wasn't found immediately, apparently, because the impact of the crash had broken the plane into many small pieces which were effectively hidden by dense under-brush.

Many of Jim's friends had participated in the search, including Chet Atkins, Ernest Tubb, and Eddy Arnold. It fell to Arnold to identify the bodies.

In Carthage, Texas, Jim's grave was marked by a lifesize statue on a fourteen-ton granite base. On it is engraved:

> If I, a lowly singer, dry one tear or soothe
> one humble heart in pain, then my homely verse
> to God is dear, and not one stanza has been
> sung in vain.

〔 vi 〕 Twice in just sixteen months the Grand Ole Opry had been hit with the gravest of tragedies. Its leading female and male singers had been lost. Those were severe blows, but the Opry continued. In keeping with the growing popularity of bluegrass music, the show added two more such acts in 1963: Jim and Jesse McReynolds of Coeburn, Virginia, and the Osborne Brothers, Sonny and Bobby, from Hyden, Kentucky, in the mountainous coal-mining region of the southeastern portion of the state.

Also added to the Opry roster, on November 28, was a smooth-shaven song-writer-singer from Abbott, Texas, who eschewed cowboy outfits, appearing on the Ryman stage in polyester suits, white shirts, and fashionably narrow ties. Willie Nelson's talents as a songwriter were already apparent at that time. But as a performer . . . well—he really hadn't scored in any important way.

He had come to Nashville at the start of the sixties, after having spent seven years as a disc jockey on stations in Texas, Oregon, and California. He wanted to be a performer and he needed to test the waters in the country music capital. He met Hank Cochran at Tootsie's Orchid Lounge and Cochran helped Willie get a writing contract at Pamper Music, partly owned by Opry star Ray Price. Price also took him on as a bass guitarist in his band.

But it was Nelson's songs that got him noticed. Patsy Cline recorded "Crazy," radio personality Ralph Emery had an interesting recording of "Hello Fool," and Faron Young had a smash hit with Willie's "Hello Walls." In 1961 he wrote a song, "Funny How Time Slips Away," that was to become a country classic. Patsy Cline did it first; Ray Price would later see it become perhaps his best recording.

Liberty Records signed him in 1962, and he had two top-ten single releases: "Touch Me" and a duet with Shirley Collie, "Willingly." Then came November 1964, and his induction as a Grand Ole Opry regular. In the same year, RCA Victor gave him a recording contract.

But something wasn't right. "I always thought I could sing pretty good," he told an interviewer years later, "and I guess it kinda bothered me that nobody else thought so. I guess I was into a lot of negative thinking back then. I did a lot of bad things, got in fights with people . . . all that stuff. My head was just pointed the wrong way, you know."

Willie's Opry tenure was limited. In 1972, seeking a new start, a different direction, he would leave Nashville and return to Texas.

Connie Smith, the housewife from Ohio, was finding Nashville something drastically different. That July 1964 recording—her first—of "Once a Day" immediately soared to the number-one position on the trade charts. Connie was an overnight sensation.

In November she sang on the Grand Ole Opry for the first time, but it wasn't really a planned event. "Actually, at disc jockey convention time, I came backstage at the Opry," she recalled. "Loretta Lynn was on that night and she asked me whether I was going to be on and I said, 'No.' And she said, 'How come? You got the number-one song and you're not on the Grand Ole Opry?' She had the song 'Happy Birthday, Merry Christmas, Happy New Year,' and she had me go out and sing harmony with her on that song. And then she talked about me having the number-one record."

There was to be a lot more to the Connie Smith story.

···❧ vii ❧··· Away from the stage there were other developments that would eventually have an impact on the Grand Ole Opry.

For one thing, WSM president Jack DeWitt hired a young executive of the parent National Life and Accident Insurance Company as his administrative assistant. E. W. "Bud" Wendell was a native of Akron, Ohio, and he had graduated magna cum laude from the College of Wooster with a degree in economics. After joining the National Life sales corps, he immediately became aware of the influence of the Opry.

"My father sold insurance for National Life," Wendell said, "and I can remember listening to WSM as a small youngster. When I became a salesman, my territory was basically southern Ohio, northern Kentucky, West Virginia—I worked some down in the coal-mining area of Logan and around in there—and those folks were all staunch listeners to and supporters of the Grand Ole Opry.

"And the salesmen had a little booklet that National Life put out that had pictures of the Opry artists in it—a little free giveaway door-opener, we called it. And I'd go up and knock on the door and I'd say, 'Hi, I'm Bud Wendell with the National Life and Accident Insurance Company of Nashville. That's the company that owns the Grand Ole Opry; the Opry's our broadcasting service. But we also have another service of financial security and I'd like to leave this little booklet with you. May I step in?'

"It was a great door-opener. And a lot of people had insurance with National Life because it was the company associated with the Opry and the Opry always stood for the right principles, and they felt that the insurance company must be good because it was part of the Opry."

Early in 1963 Wendell had moved to Nashville. By 1964 he was Jack DeWitt's administrative assistant.

"At that time," Wendell remembered, "DeWitt gave me several specific assignments relating to the Opry. Then the Opry was still a radio program, as opposed to what it has evolved to as a separate division of the company. We were just beginning to sense the resurgence, I would say, after the Elvis rock-'n'-roll impact. We could see that attendance was beginning to come back and there were some growth pain–type problems that DeWitt asked me to get involved with."

In that same year, staff announcer Hal Durham became involved with the Opry. "It was in August or September that I was assigned to the Opry," he said. "Ralph Emery was working the Opry and he wanted to leave. Another announcer, T. Tommy Cutrer, left to go into station ownership. So Dave Overton, who was the program director, assigned himself and me to the Opry; Grant Turner was there, of course." Durham smiled. "I was assigned because I was the junior announcer and the other announcers didn't want to do it because it meant working every weekend, you know.

"But I was glad to do it. As a matter of fact, even though I was not heavily involved in country music, the reason I came to WSM was the Grand Ole Opry. I thought the Opry made this radio station different [from] any other station in the country."

··❦[viii]❦·· That difference also put WSM Radio on display in a public fishbowl.

On Sunday morning, December 6, 1964, Nashvillians awoke to find spread across the top of their newspapers an eight-column banner headline in bold type usually associated with war or public disaster: "**OPRY DROPS 12 TOP STARS.**"

"Twelve top country and western music stars," the story read, "will not appear on the Grand Ole Opry in 1965, and have been prohibited from using the Opry name in their outside billings, it was learned yesterday.

"Another entertainer, long-time favorite Minnie Pearl, has been given a leave of absence from the show for the coming year, but will continue to use the Opry billing in her present contracts, a WSM spokesman said."

Dismissed from the Opry roster were George Morgan, Don Gibson, Billy Grammer, Johnny Wright, Kitty Wells, the Jordanaires (background singers on Elvis Presley's records and concert dates), Faron Young, Ferlin Husky, Chet Atkins, Justin Tubb, Stonewall Jackson, and Ray Price. Opry officials, after using the policy only minimally before, had insisted on strict adherence to a rule that said Opry performers had to appear on twenty-six shows in a year to be retained on the roster.

WSM public relations director Bill Williams tried to put the best face on it, insisting, "Nobody is mad at anybody. It's just that periodically we have to take stock. It's just a routine thing."

Irving Waugh, somewhat removed from the Opry in his capacity as general manager of the WSM television station, nevertheless thought the announcement was ill advised. He viewed the action as an "antagonism" of the country music community by WSM president Jack DeWitt.

Looking back on it, the "Purge of '64" might have been a monumental public relations goof. Within a day of the release of the original story, Opry manager Ott Devine had to remove Chet Atkins's name from the list of the original twelve. His name should not have been included, Devine said, because "Chet has not been officially connected with the Opry for many years." That admission suggested to some that the entire incident reflected adversely on the quality of Opry management.

Money is what really generated the hassle. Faron Young remembered: "When they insisted on the twenty-six-week thing, I put a pen to it and figured it out. I was gonna lose $180,000 a year to work the Opry twenty-six weeks out of the year."

Percentages paid by the artists to the WSM Artists' Service Bureau (make that read "booking agency") also were in contention. Johnny Wright, Kitty Wells's husband, explained: "They booked some of our dates, and then some of the dates were booked by our personal managers and booking agents. They were charging us fifteen percent on the dates they booked, and then if they didn't book a date you still had to pay them five percent of the dates that you booked yourself.

"Some of the artists stopped paying the five percent, a lot of them. But Kitty and I paid it right up to the very last, and I told Ott Devine: "Ott, I don't think it's fair for us to pay that and some of them not paying it. Unless you get everybody to pay it, then I'm not gonna pay it.'

"They didn't fire anyone. We just quit because we didn't wanna pay the five percent."

Quit or fired? It didn't make any difference; the public perception was that their favorites had been summarily dismissed. If anything good came out of the incident, it was a realization in the city—in some quarters, for the first time—that the Grand Ole Opry was really important to Nashville.

On Tuesday, December 8, the *Nashville Tennessean* ran an editorial under the heading: "Opry Has Duty of Protection." It said: "The Opry has been—and continues to be—the nucleus of Nashville's $40 million music industry. There is hardly a successful music enterprise in the city that does not owe its origin and its longevity to the Opry.

"Thus, it seems the Opry has a responsibility to compel observance of reasonable restrictions for its own protection and for the protection of the rest of the [music] industry in Nashville. . . . Most of the thousands of people who line up at the Opry House every Friday and Saturday night have traveled long distances to see in person the stars they have come to love by radio. It must be a disappointment for these fans to arrive at the Opry on this one big night for them and find that their favorite stars have found a more profitable audience in some other state.

"Opry Manager Ott Devine says the 11 released stars will be missed. And they will be. But there is a feeling that such a loss would be more keenly felt if the stars had not already been missed too often at the Opry."

With that, the *Tennessean* put the onus squarely on the artists, perhaps unfairly. But a lesson was learned, expressed best in a bit of old country philosophy: "Don't try to fix what ain't broke."

Who did you say it was, Brother?
Who was it fell by the way? . . .
I heard the crash on the highway,
But I didn't hear nobody pray.*

—Roy Acuff hit, circa 1942

The pall that had descended on the Grand Ole Opry with the deaths of stars Patsy Cline, Cowboy Copas, Hawkshaw Hawkins, and Jim Reeves was not easily dispelled. Indeed, the day-after-day, night-after-night touring of country music acts was an open invitation to disaster.

In May 1942 Roy Acuff had recorded a somber song, with overtones of country gospel, titled "The Wreck on the Highway." He had heard the song during his early days at the Opry, believed it to be in the public domain, recorded and released it. It was an immediate hit.

Acuff's mail brought a letter from a North Carolina weaver, one Dorsey Dixon, who was also a singer and guitarist who had done some recording. Dixon claimed authorship of "The Wreck on the Highway," which he also referred to as "I Didn't Hear Nobody Pray." Letters of that type were not unusual; any number of stars heard from people who claimed to have written their hit songs. But when Acuff investigated he was convinced that Dixon was telling the truth.

Acuff-Rose Publications made a deal with the North Carolinian: He was to receive all of the royalties on the song accruing to that date—a sum of approximately $1,300—and his name would be listed as the songwriter in perpetuity. (It must also be noted that in signing the agreement Dorsey Dixon gave up any rights to *future* royalties on the song.)

In any event, the sad lyrics of "The Wreck on the Highway" became reality in 1965.

On June 20, Ira Louvin, the older of the Louvin Brothers act, was killed in an automobile accident. The surviving brother, Charlie, was devastated. He didn't know whether he could continue, or whether he even wanted to. But the Grand Ole Opry family rallied around him and he was eventually able to go back to the Ryman stage—as a single.

Less than three weeks after Louvin's tragedy, Roy Acuff and the Smoky Mountain Boys were on the road, as they always seemed to be. The date was Saturday, July 10, and they were on their way to an engagement in Terrell, North Carolina, about three hundred miles from Nashville. It was raining when they left, in two cars, at 7:30 A.M.

By 10:30 they were about seven miles west of Sparta, Tennessee, moving along the two-lane State Highway 26 in increasingly heavy rain. Acuff, driving a cream-colored Chrysler Imperial, was in the lead; Shot Jackson sat in the front seat, singer June Stearns was sprawled out on the backseat, trying to sleep. Trailing in a blue Pontiac station wagon were sidemen Onie Wheeler, the driver; Oswald Kirby, Jimmie Riddle, and Jimmy Fox. There were seat belts in both cars. Unused.

The Chrysler came up on a slower-moving car and Acuff decided to pass. But when he pulled out he found there wasn't just one car in front of him, but two! And another car was approaching him over a small rise. He applied the brakes to ease back into his own lane and his car skidded out of control on the wet highway. It happened very fast.

Acuff, anticipating a head-on collision, steered toward a ditch on the left-hand side of the road. Not fast enough. A '63 Ford, driven by Edward Blish of Smithville, a laborer with the Army Corps of Engineers, smashed into the Chrysler, unable to avoid it.

"Roy's had a wreck!" Onie Wheeler shouted to the others in his car. All had been dozing. When Wheeler pulled off on the berm, Jimmie Riddle was the first out of the station wagon and the first to reach Acuff's crumpled car.

"Help Shot," Roy said weakly.

It was obvious that Shot Jackson was seriously injured. Oswald remembered: "The whole side of Roy's car was caved in. The metal was sticking midway into the car, and the glass was broken out on that side. The doors wouldn't open. So then we tried to open the doors on the left side. They were also jammed. We knocked out the glass. I honestly don't know what we used to get into them from that side. I guess we must have used our fists, because Jimmy Fox cut his hand badly trying to get out the glass.

"Time and time again Shot grabbed me and tried to pull me down to him as he was looking up at me and screaming, 'Oswald.' But we couldn't do anything except try to comfort him as he sat there in blood, screaming. The most terrible thing that can happen to a man is to look in a person's eyes like that and not be able to do anything. We just couldn't get into the car."

Even after a wrecker, and ambulances, arrived from Sparta, it took fifteen minutes to free the trapped passengers.

Jackson's condition was critical. He sustained a skull fracture when he was thrown forward into the windshield; he suffered a broken jaw, eighteen broken ribs, a punctured lung, and a contused kidney.

Acuff was listed as "seriously" injured. He had two pelvic fractures, a broken collarbone, and broken ribs.

June Stearns, tossed forward from her sleeping position, had a broken ankle.

The unfortunate driver of the other car, Edward Blish, had a broken jaw and smashed teeth.

On Saturday, August 28, leaning on a cane, Acuff was back at the Ryman. "Let's forget about the accident," he said. "I'm not an invalid."

He was introduced, to standing applause. The cane was left backstage and he limped on carrying a ukulele and went into a spirited version of "Tennessee Central No. 9." Shot Jackson was there, too, although he did not perform.

The sum of it all was that Acuff canceled all personal appearances for the rest of the year, except for a USO tour of South Vietnam, the Philippines, Okinawa, Japan, and Korea from December 6, 1965, through January 3, 1966.

Shot Jackson didn't make that trip. In the following year he was to have several operations to restore his fitness, but his full recuperation took a long time.

June Stearns, considering herself lucky to have escaped with only a broken ankle, decided to forgo future touring. She never appeared with the Smoky Mountain Boys again.

In one of the many interviews Acuff had to give after the accident, he had said, "You know that song which talks about the 'Wreck on the Highway'—the one that says nobody was prayin'? Well, that song is wrong, 'cause there was somebody prayin'—it was me."

ii Admittedly, Woodward Maurice Ritter had come to the downside of a colorful career when he moved to Nashville in 1965 to accept an offer from WSM Radio to join the cast of the Grand Ole Opry and to host an all-night talk show. But as Tex Ritter, he had been one of the movies' most important singing cowboys, and the invitation to come to Nashville came on the impetus of yet another record hit, "I Dreamed of a Hillbilly Heaven."

Born the youngest of six children in 1905 at Murvaul, Texas, he was somewhat spoiled as a child. But he had ambition, even if it was not directed toward becoming a Texas farmer. After graduating from high school in Beaumont at the top of his class, he entered the University of Texas, taking pre-law courses. The twig was bent there, but not toward law. At the university he met J. Frank Dobie, renowned authority on southwestern history; John A. Lomax, well-known collector of American folk music; and Oscar J. Fox, composer of cowboy songs and director of the university glee club. All three were to influence the young man's future. Ritter joined the glee club, throwing himself into its activities with such enthusiasm that his studies were neglected.

In 1928 the Shubert Company presented the operetta *Maryland, My Maryland* at the Hancock Opera House in Austin, and Ritter never missed a performance. When the show left town, he was with it as a singer in the male chorus. The road led to New York City.

It was there that he was first called "Tex." Pickings were lean at first, but he eventually landed a spot in the men's chorus of the Hammerstein-Romberg musical *The New Moon*, both on Broadway and in the road company. Then, in December 1930, he opened in a Theater Guild production on Broadway, *Green Grow the Lilacs*, playing a cowboy (Cord Elam) and understudying the star, Franchot Tone. During the course of the play-with-music he sang "Git Along Little Dogies," "The Old Chisholm Trail," "Goodbye Old Paint," and "Bury Me Not on the Lone Prairie." The play was a hit, but not once did Tone miss a performance; Tex never got an opportunity to play the lead role of Curly McClain. (Years later, when Rodgers and Hammerstein were turning that play into the musical *Oklahoma!*, Ritter auditioned privately for Oscar Hammerstein II. Unsuccessfully.)

There were two more Broadway shows, *The Round-Up* and *Mother Lode*. And a lot of radio: "The Lone Star Rangers," "Maverick Jim," the "WHN Barn Dance," "Cowboy Tom's Roundup," the "ENO Crime Club," "Gang Busters," and his own local show, "Tex Ritter's Campfire."

In that period he began to record for the veteran A&R man Art Satherley, and his first release in 1933 was "Rye Whiskey," backed with "Goodbye Old Paint." But Satherley seemed to lose interest in him and Tex signed with Decca Records.

In 1936 came what seemed to be the inevitable summons to Hollywood. Two years earlier Gene Autry had burst onto the movie scene and had become a major box-office draw for Republic Pictures as the first of the singing cowboys. Producer Edward F. Finney, associated with Grand National Pictures, wanted to duplicate that success. He selected Ritter after hearing him on "Cowboy Tom's Roundup" on New York's WINS. A deal was quickly struck, and by late November 1936 Tex's first starring picture was released: *Song of the Gringo*. In it was the hit song "Rye Whiskey."

In less than two years there followed eleven more Grand National "oaters," starring Tex Ritter and his horse, White Flash. From there he moved to Monogram Pictures, where he made twenty more B features. Then to Columbia, where he was teamed with Bill Elliot; next came Universal, and shared billing with Johnny Mack Brown; and finally PRC Pictures, with Dave O'Brien. In all, he made sixty features through 1945, too many of them, in his view, in costarring circumstances.

What good came out of that was his marriage to actress Dorothy Fay Southworth, who had been his leading lady in several of the Monogram films, and his contract with the new Capitol Records organization. He hit big with Capitol: "Jingle, Jangle, Jingle" and "There's a New Moon over My Shoulder" were major hits. In 1952 the Russian-born composer Dimitri Tiomkin came to Tex with a song that was going to be the theme of a motion picture titled *High Noon*, starring Gary Cooper and Grace Kelly. Ritter wasn't asked to be in the film; he was simply to sing the title song for the soundtrack. It was a unique hit, both as a movie song and as a record for Tex. It won an Oscar for Tiomkin, and Tex sang "High Noon" during the 1953 Academy Awards ceremonies, the first to be televised nationally.

But Ritter's career stalled after that. His television efforts on the West Coast never seemed really to work out, and the music publishing company he launched with his old friend Johnny Bond—Vidor Publications, Inc.—didn't generate the profits they had anticipated.

More and more, Tex was turning his attention to Nashville. He became active in the Country Music Association, serving two terms as president, in 1963 and 1964. In the latter year he was elected to the Country Music Hall of Fame, honored as an "untiring pioneer and champion of the country and western music industry."

It was on June 12, 1965, that he was inducted as a member of the Grand Old Opry family. He would become its elder statesman. A hardworking citizen of both Nashville and the state.

⋅⋅⋅⟨ iii ⟩⋅⋅⋅ The other Opry personnel additions in 1965 were on the more youthful side.

Bobby Bare, a thirty-year-old native of Ironton, Ohio, drew the Opry nod on the basis of his hit recording of Mel Tillis's anthem of the country boy's discontent with the industrialized North—"Detroit City." And while he didn't stay very long at the Ryman, it was perhaps because he was always searching for something different.

Writer Michael Bane would say of him: "Pigeonholing the Bare is like searching the green hills south of Nashville for traces of the woolly mammoth; don't be surprised if you come home empty-handed."

Norma Jean's elevation to the Opry roster was more in the nature of a graduation. She had come out of Wellston, Oklahoma, in 1960 to be the "girl singer" with the Porter Wagoner troupe and to appear as a regular on his widely syndicated weekly television show. That, of course, got her on the Ryman stage. Her experience and her hit records kept her there.

When she was only thirteen, she had her own three-time-a-week radio show on KLPR in Oklahoma City. By the time she was twenty she got an invitation to join the "Ozark Jubilee" in Springfield, Missouri. It was there that she dropped her last name—Beasler—and became simply Norma Jean. And when Wagoner spotted her in 1960, she moved to Nashville.

By 1963 she had a contract with RCA Victor and a major hit, "Let's Go All the Way." In the following year she hit again with "Go Cat Go" and in 1965 found the charts with "I Wouldn't Buy a Used Car from Him." The Grand Ole Opry roster assignment followed.

The Browns (from the left, Maxine, Bonnie, and Jim Ed) became roster members of the Grand Ole Opry in 1963. Their recording of "The Jimmy Brown Song" was a million-seller in 1959–60.

(1963) COUNTRY MUSIC FOUNDATION LIBRARY AND MEDIA CENTER

Grant Turner (on the right) interviews Jim Reeves about WSM's Mr. DJ contest on October 7, 1963.

(1963) WSM PHOTO/BEV LECROY

Left to right, Haze Jones looks on as Ott Devine hires a clean-shaven, obviously happy Willie Nelson for the Opry roster.

(1964) WSM PHOTO/LES LEVERETT

Johnny Cash, the Man in Black, plays a mean guitar while Roy Acuff struts his stuff. From the left are Luther Perkins, Marshall Grant, W. S. Holland (on drums), Johnny Cash, Lightning Chance, Willie Ackerman, Roy Acuff, Tom Hanserd, and T. Tommy Cutrer.

(1963) WSM PHOTO/LES LEVERETT

One of Hollywood's most popular cowboy actors, Tex Ritter moved to Nashville in 1965 to join the cast of the Opry and to host an all-night talk show on WSM. Pictured backstage at the Ryman are (from the left) Hank Locklin, Jan Howard, Tex Ritter, and June Carter.

(1965) WSM PHOTO/LES LEVERETT

Another girl singer of note, Connie Smith, also received roster status at the Opry in 1965, after numerous guest appearances following her phenomenal "Once a Day" debut hit a year earlier. Even though she was no longer a stranger at the Ryman, her first performance as a regular was an emotional experience.

"I joined the same night as Bob Luman," she said. "And I had totally no control over my voice at all. I was scared to death; it just meant too much to me. I had heard about people's knees knocking, and I thought it was a fake. But mine actually did while I was out there singing; I was that shook. And when I came off the stage I busted out crying. It was just my dreams come true.

"It's hard for me, if I stop and think about it, to realize that week after week I got to be out there and be onstage with Roy Acuff. It's hard for me to believe that I can actually be around people like Roy and Bill Monroe and Hank Snow and Bashful Brother Oswald and Jimmy Dickens—it's like me being able to walk in history."

Connie's fellow inductee that night, Bob Luman, was a performer who was as close to being a rock 'n' roller as anyone given roster status. Certainly, the native of Tyler, Texas, was a rockabilly. His launching pad had been the "Louisiana Hayride," where he had appeared at age seventeen after winning a talent contest. That sent him to Hollywood to appear in a movie, *Carnival Rock*.

And in 1960 he scored with a million-seller recording "Let's Think About Living," still considered a rockabilly classic. But the military draft intervened and after two years in the service he had to start over again.

He did that by signing a contract with Hickory Records, from which came a steady stream of hits: "The File," "Go Home Boy," "Interstate Forty," and "You Can't Take the Boy from the Country." And as one rockabilly was joining the Grand Ole Opry, another was departing.

Johnny Cash had come to the Ryman in the mid-fifties, had been there with regularity for about two years, and then had gone on to superstardom—to Hollywood, to the major concert halls across the nation, to a steady string of number-one hits. But he had never severed his ties with the Opry; he'd appear as a special guest as often as he was in Nashville.

Yet the pressures of his stardom had become too much for him. Amphetamines and alcohol were his crutches. And he started missing concert dates. He canceled nine out of every ten recording sessions booked by his producer.

In his autobiography, *Man in Black*, Cash candidly wrote of a 1965 evening at the Ryman:

"One Saturday night, in Nashville for an appearance on the Grand Ole Opry, I arrived at the Ryman Auditorium [after] having taken pills regularly for weeks. My voice was gone as were a few more pounds of body weight. I was down to about 165. . . .

"The band kicked off a song, and I tried to take the microphone off the stand. In my nervous frenzy, I couldn't get it off. Such a minor complication in my mental state was enough to make me explode in a fit of anger. I took the mike stand, threw it down, then dragged it along the edge of the stage, popping fifty or sixty footlights. The broken glass shattered all over the stage and into the audience.

"The song ended abruptly, and I walked offstage and came face to face with the Grand Ole Opry manager [Ott Devine]. He kindly and quietly informed me, 'We can't use you on the Opry any more, John.'

"I couldn't answer. I had sobered again in the time it took to blink.

"I walked out of the back door of the Grand Ole Opry House, got in my car, and started driving. After a few blocks, I headed south through the residential areas to avoid police cars out on the highway. I was crying now, and I couldn't see well enough to drive.

"It began to rain, and as I reached to turn on the windshield wipers, the car swerved and crashed into a tree beside the street.

"I woke up in the emergency room at the hospital with a broken nose and a broken jaw. The car was totaled out."

As it turned out, Cash's departure from the Opry did not end his career. Nor did it end his battles with the demons seeming to possess him. There followed a divorce from his first wife, an eventual marriage to June Carter, a religious conversion, a "kicking" of the drug habit, and a step up to the lofty position of "superstar."

Johnny Cash was always a complex man. In a sense, a *driven* man. But that drive made him a superb songwriter, a recording star, a movie star, a television star, a best-selling author.

And while he never again was a member of the Grand Ole Opry, he made his peace with the Opry. In 1969, when the ABC television network signed him to host a weekly country music variety show, he insisted it should originate from the stage of the old Ryman Auditorium. The tradition of the Opry, he reasoned, *had* to be a part of his show.

Then, too, when the Opry was moved to its new home at the Opryland amusement park in the spring of 1974, it was Cash who was chosen to be the host of the first network TV special originating from the new building. The title of the show was "Country Comes Home."

Johnny Cash came home, as well, that night.

There goes my reason for living,
There goes the one of my dreams,
There goes my only possession,
There goes my ev'rything.*

—Jack Greene hit, 1966

The last half of the sixties decade was nothing but change. Change so drastic that the doomsayers were predicting a demise of the Grand Ole Opry. As before, they were wrong.

On the stage of the Opry the new faces were Ray Pillow, and Jack Greene, and Stu Phillips, and Del Reeves, and Charlie Walker, and Jeannie Seely, and the Four Guys, and Jeanne Pruett, and Tom T. Hall, and Dolly Parton.

And behind the scenes there was a complete changing of the guard, with decisions being made that would lead to an era of unprecedented growth that even the most enthusiastic Opry supporter could not have imagined.

But with it all, the stories were still about people. About their dreams, their foibles, their triumphs.

*"There Goes My Everything" by Dallas Frazier; copyright 1965, 1966 Acuff-Rose/Opryland Music, Inc.; Husky Music, Inc.

❧ ii ❧ Since 1962, Jack Greene had been "learning the ropes" with Ernest Tubb's Texas Troubadours. Learning too of E.T.'s determination to help everyone he could in the country music business.

Tubb had permitted Jack to sing "The Last Letter" as a solo effort on the 1964 album *Ernest Tubb Presents*. It was a modest success, good enough to earn Greene a recording contract with Decca. On his second session there he recorded Dallas Frazier's "There Goes My Everything."

"On Christmas Day of '66," Jack recalls, "that record was number one across the board—*Record World*, *Cash Box*, and *Billboard*. Ernest said, 'Well, you better start making some plans.' So we decided to continue to work together through 1967 . . . and make the break then. But we worked Shelley's Club [now Gilley's] in Houston and it was a madhouse. I was sitting back there playing the drums and they were hollering, 'Let the drummer sing!' They loved Ernest down there, but they were embarrassing him. I had already done my show, you know, 'cause Ernest would let Cal [Smith] and [me] do our numbers, and then he'd come on. But all they wanted to hear was 'There Goes My Everything' again.

"We went on to the 'South Louisiana Hayride' in Ponchatoula the next night and after that show Ernest said, 'Well, son, I think it's time for you to go.' "

The venerable E.T. had brought another sideman to stardom.

❧ iii ❧ There are as many different stories about coming to the Opry as there are Opry performers.

Ray Pillow, singer-guitarist-songwriter out of Lynchburg, Virginia, came to the Opry as a "loser." In the early sixties he was in Nashville to compete in the National Pet Milk Talent Contest. He didn't win it. But there's something about ambition that enables a performer to shrug off the dark moments.

He honed his skills, going the usual tough route of small clubs and radio stations, a coffee-and-cakes existence. Until 1964, when his manager, Joe Taylor, after shopping Pillow's demo tapes around to major record labels, finally got him signed with Capitol. The opportunity was all he needed; his "Left Out," "Take Your Hands off My Heart," and "Thank You Ma'am," all made their way to the charts.

Capitol Records showed its pleasure by releasing his first album, *Presenting Ray Pillow*, in December 1965. And in 1966 two top-ten hit duets with Capitol's female star, Jean Shepard—"I'll Take the Dog" and "Mr. Do-It-Yourself"—caused the Opry to reach out and make Ray Pillow a roster member. By year's end, both *Billboard* and *Cash Box* were calling him "Most Promising Male Artist of 1966."

Pillow was to have a lot of company the following year because Grand Ole Opry manager Ott Devine seemed determined to give a "new face" look to the roster.

On June 1, 1967, established Canadian star Stu Phillips, who was gaining a reputation in the States under the direction of RCA Victor producer Chet Atkins, joined the Opry. Likewise a Nashville pop country harmony group, the Four

Guys. And veteran Charlie Walker, who had come from Texas a decade earlier to make his Opry debut, found himself a roster member on August 17 on the strength of back-to-back record hits, "Pick Me Up on Your Way Down" and "Don't Squeeze My Charmin."

And then there was Del Reeves, who had appeared as a guest on the Opry in 1958 while still in the U.S. Air Force. Reeves had had some modest success in the West, playing the Las Vegas–Tahoe–Reno circuit with the "Judy Lynn Show." But it was stardom in Nashville he sought.

"In 1963, we had a song my wife had written, 'The Only Girl I Can't Forget,' on Reprise Records, and it got to number twelve on the charts. And Jesse James and forty thieves could not have even stole that record, much less buy it! But the disc jockeys were playing it. So I called Hank Cochran—I had known Hank in California, because we were on different television shows together—and he said, 'Hey, get your butt back here [to Nashville] right now. They're talkin' about your record.'

"Well, I loaded up the car and I said, 'Hey, honey, me an' you an' them two girls is goin' to Nashville.' Lo and behold, we come here. Dean Manuel, who got killed with Jim Reeves, got me my house I lived in on Saunders Avenue, next to Kitty Wells, and he done everything for me, really. We were great friends. But not until '65 did I find 'Girl on the Billboard,' and that started the whole thing.

"At that time if you wanted to be on the Opry you had to do twenty-six Saturday nights per year. When 'Girl on the Billboard' made number one, and 'Belles of Southern Bell' made number one, they called me to join the Opry. And my manager, Hubert Long, rest his soul, says, 'It's an impossibility. You can't join the Opry now.' That almost broke my heart. I told Hubert: 'But I worked all my life, from a little boy in Sparta, North Carolina, to be a member of the Grand Ole Opry! And you tell 'em I can't join!' He said, 'Don't worry, they're gonna call you back.'

"And in 1967 I finally joined the Opry, during the DJ convention week. Porter Wagoner introduced me. And my mother and daddy, who at that time were seventy-eight and eighty-one, were in the audience to see one of their seven sons—there were four girls too—make the Opry.

"I don't even think I got out 'Doodle-do-do-do-do,' which has been a trademark with me, before I started cryin'. Porter came up and put his arms around me. And when he done that I laid my head on his shoulder, and the band kept playin', an' Porter started gettin' tears in his eyes, an' it was just one big cryin' mess. I think I finally did begin to compose myself.

"An' then Porter, being the showman he is, said, 'Ladies an' gentlemen, his mother and father is in the audience.' An' they stood up, an' when they did I just fell apart. I mean, there ain't no way I'm gonna be able to sing. An' Porter's got tears runnin' down his face, an' I'm cryin'—literally boo-hooin'. So Porter just stood there with his arms around me. An' I'm tryin' to think 'Where am I at in the song?' I finally went to the last verse an' got through the last verse an' the chorus. An' that was it. The whole place stood up at the old Ryman."

A reflective sigh. "Those were the days," Reeves said quietly. "Lord, it seems like such a short time ago."

⁘❴ iv ❵⁘ "My mother says I was four years old when I found 650 on the radio," Jeannie Seely remembered. "We had one of those big consoles—remember those old Philco consoles?—and she said, 'You were barely tall enough to turn the knob, and you couldn't really see the numbers, but when you hit 650, then that's where it stayed.' "

WSM Radio was, and is, at 650 on the dial.

"I was born in Titusville, in northwestern Pennsylvania," Seely said. "People that know their history know that's where oil was first discovered, and not a damned thing has happened there since then. But our farm—oh, a huge farm, thirty-eight acres—bordered the Pennsylvania State Game Preserve land, so we were way out in the country.

"I'd be the best little girl you ever saw all week long, and I'd do all my chores, if they'd promise to take me to Hillbilly Park in Franklin. And there was always the Opry. Back then we didn't have radio stations playing country music all the time. We were lucky to find some little, local fifteen-minute show on Saturday morning—which, by the way, I started doing when I was eleven—and the Opry was one of the things I looked forward to.

"On the weekends my parents would go to different people's houses to play cards. And I used to cry if we were gonna go to somebody's house where I couldn't listen to the Opry. So Mother started a thing where she fixed up a big bowl of popcorn, and got some soda pop, and Daddy would make sure the battery was charged up on the old Ford, and they'd let us sit out in the car and listen to the Grand Ole Opry. Really and truly, it's just been there all my life for me."

Thus, everything she did was pointed to being on the Opry—from her debut at eleven on a radio station in Meadville, Pennsylvania, to the grind of small clubs, auditoriums, and country music parks, to a stint as the hostess on an Armed Forces Radio Network disc jockey show, to secretarial jobs with Liberty and Imperial Records in Hollywood in the early sixties. And to her own recording contract with Monument Records.

"I had recorded Hank Cochran's 'Don't Touch Me' on March 12 of 1966," Jeannie recalled, "and it was my first hit record and won the Grammy award and everything. Anyway, in June it was pretty close to number one and they asked me to make a guest appearance on the Opry. I don't believe I've ever been through such a mixture of emotions: 'Oh, I can't go out there, but I can't wait to get out there.'

"Later, then, they finally asked me to join. I was working with Hal Smith of Pamper Music and Hal sat me down and said: 'You know it's a heavy commitment. Don't be one of those who join and then don't show up when the *new* wears off.' Well, for me, the Opry could never get old.

"So it was September 16, 1967, when I joined. My parents came down from

Pennsylvania for the show. About halfway through 'Don't Touch Me' the realization hit me [of] what this really meant. I was twenty-six, and from four years old I wanted that moment. I started crying. Then I encored and that was even worse. Strictly emotional."

Emotion plays such a powerful role in any performer's career. At times it's pure emotion that motivates a turning point toward stardom. Barbara Mandrell's story is a good example.

She had been a professional performer since the age of nine, playing accordion, banjo, saxophone, and steel guitar in the Mandrell Family act, with mother Mary and father Irby, and later her sisters, Louise and Irlene. At eleven she was being featured with the legendary Joe Maphis in Las Vegas lounges.

At eighteen and a half she was ready to quit from show business, having married a young Navy pilot, Ken Dudney.

"I was going to retire," she reminisces, "and be a serviceman's wife, after the Mandrell Family band made a trip to Vietnam to entertain the troops.

"When we got back, Daddy wound up his business in California, and I went to Washington state to be with Ken, who was in Navy pilot training there. Daddy took a job with the Mosrite musical instrument company as a 'troubleshooter,' you might say. He had to work all over the country, so the family moved to Nashville because it was centrally located—Daddy, my mother, and Louise and Irlene.

"Then, when Ken was assigned to overseas duty in 1967, he brought me to Nashville to be with my family while he was gone. I had never been to Nashville before, and I really had not known a lot about the Grand Ole Opry. We didn't hear it in California, although I had worked with a lot of people who were on the Opry. But being in Nashville, you wanted to see the Opry.

"Daddy took me to the old Ryman and we sat in the balcony and watched the show. And while I was watching I got the idea, 'Hey, I can do that.' I turned to Daddy and said: 'I want to do that. I can't just sit out front here. I want to be up there.' And I guess I pointed to the stage. 'And I want you to manage me.'

"Well, Daddy never hesitated. He said yes. And I remember that he told me, 'I'll bet my last cent on you making it.' " Barbara laughed heartily. "As it turned out he almost had to do that."

Barbara Mandrell wasn't the only future female superstar to find a starting point at the Grand Ole Opry that year. Another was the young lady from Sevierville, Tennessee—Dolly Parton.

Unlike Mandrell, of course, Dolly was thoroughly indoctrinated in the mystique of the Opry. She had haunted the Ryman for several years, she had had that teenage experience of singing on the "Friday Night Frolics," and she felt a kinship with the people on that stage.

"I saw Johnny Cash for the first time on the Opry," she remembered. "It was when he first came there; when he had 'Ring of Fire' and 'I Walk the Line.' That was also my first encounter with what sex appeal was. I was in the audience—I must have been maybe ten or eleven—and I saw Johnny Cash and, I'll tell you, it was a feeling like I had never had before. I found out years later that what he had was called charisma."

Dolly brought her own brand of charisma (and sex appeal, to be direct) to the Ryman in 1967 as a member of the Porter Wagoner show. She had replaced Norma Jean as the Wagoner "girl singer," Norma Jean having decided to quit to get married.

"My first time on the *real* Opry was with Porter," Dolly said, "and we sang a duet, 'Last Thing on My Mind.' That was our biggie then. And I'll never forget when I walked out on that stage. It was one of the biggest thrills of my whole life—even to this day."

She paused, searching for a comparative circumstance. "I guess, outside of my marriage, that was *the* biggest event."

⋅∘[v]∘⋅ The changing of the guard behind the scenes at the Opry began in August 1967 when WSM president Jack DeWitt called Irving Waugh, the television station general manager, into his office and startled him by announcing that he, DeWitt, was going to take an early retirement, starting in March 1968. And he suggested that Waugh, as heir apparent to the WSM presidency, might want to do some thinking about what would be his new job.

When Waugh did come to power, one of his first acts was to put E. W. "Bud" Wendell in charge of the Grand Ole Opry. He wanted his own man there, and Ott Devine was placed on the WSM retirement rolls.

"I wasn't bright enough to know what to do with an administrative assistant," Waugh said lightly, referring to Wendell's role under DeWitt. "But I thought Bud showed more administrative ability than any of us had, and the Opry certainly needed someone down there. It needed a businessman, it needed someone to start courting the music industry and try to get us back into the swim. The music industry in Nashville thought the Grand Ole Opry was a real backwater. And that was reason enough to send Bud down there. He told me afterward he thought I was exiling him to Siberia."

"I started at the Opry in April of '68," Wendell recalled. "I can pinpoint that because it was during the period when we were having the civil rights marches in downtown Nashville."

The Reverend Dr. Martin Luther King had been assassinated in Memphis on Thursday, April 4, and authorities in cities across the nation feared a massive black backlash. By Saturday a 7:00 P.M. curfew was imposed in Nashville. Immediately affected was the Grand Ole Opry. The live performance was canceled for the first time in its history and a taped version was played on the air.

But Saturday morning, hundreds of would-be Opry-goers were lined up outside the Ryman Auditorium waiting to get tickets, as they had every Saturday morning for years. It was beyond belief to most of them that there would be no performance of the Grand Ole Opry that evening.

Roy Acuff's biographer Elizabeth Schlappi picks up the story: "About this same time, 10 A.M. [Saturday], the Music City Playhouse was having its grand opening around the corner from the Opry House. Its premier attraction was a 39-minute film showing some of the Opry performers, with interviews of others. Roy and many celebrities were in the audience.

"At the conclusion of the film the lights went on and the audience of celebrities and tourists prepared to leave. Just then Roy Acuff stood up in the middle of the theater and said:

" 'Friends, can I have your attention for a minute? There's something I'd like to say. We all know there's a curfew on in Nashville. It starts at seven o'clock and there's not going to be an Opry tonight. It seems a shame that so many people have come in from out of town and won't be able to see it. Let's see if we can find a place and give them a show!' "

Acuff owned a storefront building on nearby Broadway, just around the corner from the Ryman; he used the first floor to exhibit his collection of old musical instruments. On the floor above it was a square-dance hall called Mr. Ed's, run by one Eddie Cummings. It was there, with Cummings's approval, that the emergency performance of the Grand Ole Opry was given.

The word spread to the milling crowd outside and by 2:00 P.M. the place was jammed. It was a tense moment. There was a major civil rights march uptown, and the air was filled with the screams of police car sirens. Some other buildings on Broadway were closed by uniformed officers carrying rifles.

But in the square-dance hall there was laughter and applause as the makeshift Opry was carried on by Roy Acuff and the Smoky Mountain Boys, Harold Weakley, Sam and Kirk McGee, and a few other Opry performers who dropped in.

As though underscoring the change of the hierarchy at the Opry, on Wednesday, May 8, came the news that George Dewey Hay had died at his home in Virginia Beach, Virginia. The following Saturday night, Opry announcer Grant Turner, a protégé of Hay, paid him tribute:

"He called himself The Solemn Old Judge. If he was solemn, it was only in the face of those who sought to change or corrupt the purity of the barn-dance ballads he sought to preserve. We, the performers and friends of the Grand Ole Opry, salute the memory of one whose influence is felt on the stage of the Opry tonight—The Solemn Old Judge, George D. Hay."

It was almost as if the words could be heard again, ghostlike now, with which Hay closed every performance of the Grand Ole Opry. A colorful bit of nonsense that had become his trademark:

That's all for now, friends . . .
Because the tall pines pine
And the pawpaws pause
And the bumble bees bumble all around,
The grasshoppers hop
And the eavesdroppers drop
While, gently, the ole cow slips away . . .
George D. Hay saying, So long for now!

❧[vi]❧ Bud Wendell's recollections of his first weeks as the new chief of the Grand Ole Opry:

"We didn't do a lot, nobody does, in tampering with the format of the show. But we had a lot of opportunities insofar as trying to increase attendance, or improving our tourism situation.

"The Opry had been for so long just a radio show. It received very little management attention. It was something that was broadcast every Saturday night, but we didn't have any ticketing situation. We wanted to get more into a typical theater situation; we wanted to set up a system whereby people could order tickets ahead of time, and buy reserve-seat tickets. For specific seats.

"And we felt an opportunity there for a tour business. Up to that point, I guess, the Opry had not been perceived as a potential base for a huge tourism industry. That entailed setting up a large support staff.

"We were sensing some desire on the part of television people to do more with country music. We hadn't been getting any national exposure on TV up to that time. So we made ourselves available, you might say. The CMA awards was one early show—"

Wendell was speaking of the Second Annual Country Music Association Awards, scheduled for October 1968. The CMA, unable to find a network home for its awards ceremonies in 1967, turned to Irving Waugh and Jack Stapp, then president of Tree Publishing, for help. What happened next simply added to the lore of the Grand Ole Opry.

Waugh and Stapp went to New York City to canvass their substantial contacts in the advertising industry, seeking a sponsor for the CMA awards show. Their search ended at the J. Walter Thompson agency, which was responsible for "Kraft Music Hall," seen Wednesday nights on NBC television.

Thompson agreed to include the country music awards within the "Kraft Music Hall" format. That was accomplished by canceling one of its planned programs at the Texas State Fair. But Roy Rogers and Dale Evans had already been signed to contracts to host the state fair show; the only way to honor those contracts was to make Roy and Dale the hosts of the awards show. That was done.

(Gary Smith and Dwight Hemion, the producers of "Kraft Music Hall," became the executive producers of the awards show; the author, having just left NBC News after twenty years as a producer of news specials, came aboard as the line producer.)

From the very beginning of the planning neither the Thompson agency nor the NBC network wanted to chance a "live" show with "hillbilly" artists they didn't know. Thus, the CMA awards ceremonies would be videotaped on Friday, October 18, for airing on Wednesday, October 30. A glitch developed; the October 30 airing was suddenly canceled. The announced reason was that it was preempted by a broadcast by President Lyndon Johnson. The truth was something else again.

Bill Greeley, writing in *Variety*, the show business bible, revealed: "Although it was billed as a political preemption, NBC-TV's cancellation last week of 'Kraft Music Hall's' presentation of 'The Second Annual Country Music Assn. Awards' was in reality due to circumstances arising out of the network's current troubles with the Federal Communications Commission regarding questionable program practices on quiz and award shows.

"Since receiving severe written reprimands from FCC regarding the telecast of the Golden Globe Awards, doled out by the Hollywood Foreign Press Assn., and the daytime quiz shows, 'Hollywood Squares' and 'PDQ,' NBC top brass has called for up-tight security measures and thorough investigations of any shows susceptible to similar reprimand.

"At the 11th hour (airdate last Wednesday, Oct. 30, that is), it was discovered that NBC programming standards & practices folk had neglected to make the required investigation on the annual c&w music awards. Although the c&w awards have the reputation of being above reproach, the awards special, pretaped at ceremonies in Nashville, was yanked at the last minute. The hour was filled with a Presidential pitch lasting 25 minutes; an old print of a half-hour summer replacement musical show, 'The Lively Ones,' apparently exhumed hastily from deep in the vaults; and what must have been the first five-minute 'musical interlude' in network broadcasting since Walter Damrosch had a coughing spell back in 1931."

NBC finally got its house in order; the CMA awards show—"from the home of the world-renowned Grand Ole Opry in Nashville, Tennessee"—was finally aired on Wednesday, November 20. Even with all of those problems, the telecast was a ratings success. It won in its time period over the CBS powerhouse rural duo of "The Beverly Hillbillies" and "Green Acres," and doubled the rating of the November 13 "Kraft Music Hall," "Comedy in the Year 2001," starring Steve Allen, Shelley Berman, Bill Dana, and Julie Harris.

(From that day forward, right through 1985, the CMA awards shows were sponsored by Kraft and always originated from the stage of the Grand Ole Opry.)

Staging the awards ceremonies for TV in the Ryman Auditorium, however, imposed some monumental changes, however temporary, on the old house. The stage was nearly doubled in size, accomplished by removing eight or nine rows of church-pew seats and thrusting forward a whole new stage on top of the old one.

Kathy Sawyer, writing in the *Nashville Tennessean* after the event, captured the essence of what had happened: "The Grand Ole Opry House played Eliza to NBC's Henry Higgins. . . . The old hall obediently sucked in her waist, put on her shoes and did not speak unless spoken to, while sober faced aliens hustled on and around her stage removing—for an evening—her accent. . . .

"The backdrops advertising work pants and pipe tobacco were masked by more sublime solid blue; the orchestra played behind white gauze hangings; and there were sprinklings of white lights everywhere, like a starlet's mirror."

In the awards ceremonies themselves, Glen Campbell, who had flown into Nashville in a Learjet from a movie location in Colorado where he was filming *True Grit* with John Wayne, was named Entertainer of the Year and Male Vocalist of the Year. Tammy Wynette, not yet on the Opry roster but soon to be, was voted Female Vocalist of the Year.

For the Grand Ole Opry perhaps the biggest plus was the selection of the duo of Porter Wagoner and Dolly Parton as Vocal Group of the Year.

There was a bittersweet nostalgic moment, too. Red Foley, who had been such an integral part of the growth of the Opry, had died just a month earlier while on tour in Fort Wayne, Indiana. Only a year before he had been named to the Country Music Hall of Fame.

On the awards show, then, tribute was paid to Foley when his son-in-law, Pat Boone, appeared to reprise the last song Red Foley had ever sung, "Peace in the Valley."

⋅⋅❋ vii ❧⋅⋅ Almost lost in the lavish coverage of the televised awards show was the announcement by Irving Waugh, WSM president, that the Opry's days at the Ryman Auditorium were numbered.

Strangely—and perhaps it seems strange only in hindsight—the Waugh announcement was lumped together with another music industry story in the Saturday morning, October 19, issue of the *Nashville Tennessean*. The headline on the story read: "STARDAY BUYS KING RECORDS."

Within the article was the big news for the Grand Ole Opry family: "The initiation of plans for the relocation of the Opry, possibly as the center of a multimillion dollar hotel and amusement complex, was announced at a breakfast at Municipal Auditorium sponsored by WSM."

What was announced was that WSM's parent company, National Life and Accident Insurance Company, was investigating the possibilities. There was no site at that moment, and not even a clear goal for the project. That would be determined when Economic Research Associates of Los Angeles, which aided in the development of Disneyland and Sea World in San Diego, would come to Nashville to study the economic feasibility of the project and a possible location for it.

"Our feeling is that the Grand Ole Opry needs a new, modern facility," Irving Waugh told those at the breakfast. "And we would like a facility that would be very active. . . .

"It is estimated the center, which would be called Opryland, USA, would require between one hundred fifty and two hundred acres of land. The location would not be in the Music Row area."

An entirely new day was dawning for the Grand Ole Opry.

Joshua, Joshua,
Why, you're just what I been a-lookin' for!
Joshua, Joshua,
*We ain't gonna be lonesome anymore.**

—Dolly Parton's first #1 Record

At the Grand Ole Opry in 1970 manager Bud Wendell was being cautious about adding new acts, although he did see a need to add two.

One was a newly constituted group, Lester Flatt and the Nashville Grass, formed after Flatt and Earl Scruggs split in 1969. The two bluegrass giants had come to a parting of the ways over a matter of "concept." Scruggs, the father of three teenage boys who had become musicians in the soft-rock genre, wanted to be more modern with the sound of the Flatt and Scruggs band. Flatt objected vehemently. In the end, they were left with no choice but to end their association.

Flatt formed the new Nashville Grass, still a traditionalist band, to be accepted immediately at the Opry. Scruggs fronted a new group, featuring his sons, called the Earl Scruggs Revue. In no way was it an act tailored to the Opry; country music purists complained that Scruggs had subverted his great natural talents. Ultimately, the sons would branch out on their own, making names for themselves

*"Joshua" by Dolly Parton; copyright 1970 Owepar Publishing Company.

as sidemen, writers, and record producers. And Scruggs, beset with ill health, never returned to the greatness he had known as a member of Bill Monroe's Blue Grass Boys and in his partnership with Flatt.

Opry manager Wendell was also impressed in 1970 with a young songwriter from Olive Hill, Kentucky—one Tom T. Hall. He had made a guest debut in '69.

"I think it was Ernest Tubb," Tom recalled, "who went to Bud Wendell and said, 'You know, there's a young guy out there singing odd kinda songs. He's really good. His name is Tom T. Hall and you oughta get him as a guest on the Opry.'

"So, the first night on the Opry, Roy Acuff introduced me as 'Tom P. Hay'! I guess he was thinking of George D." He chuckled. "But I didn't mind. I went out, took a bow, and sang 'A Week in a County Jail.' "

Hall was to become the first new Opry roster act of the seventies.

"I was amazed at the informality of it all," he said. "Wendell called me back to his office and said, 'Well, Tom, do you want to be a member of the Opry?'

"And I said, 'Yes, sir. That would be a great honor.'

"And he said, 'Well, you'll have some insurance in case you get killed out there on the road, you know.' "

A grin started. "I never really understood what I had to do to collect."

And Tom P. Hay laughed.

⋅◦ℑ ii ℘◦⋅ Bud Wendell admitted that he began his job at the Grand Ole Opry as a fan.

"I never got over being a fan," he said. "Artists intrigue me. I can remember lots of nights, exciting nights, at the Ryman. Frequently, I would be reluctant to put a particular artist on the program only because I liked to hold back a few surprises for the people in the audience. And I think one of the fondest memories I have was the night I didn't announce that Loretta Lynn was on the program. She and Ernest Tubb had a thing going on 'Sweet Thing,' a duet that was doing very well. Ernest went out and started doing 'Sweet Thing,' but without Loretta, and then she just casually walked out and joined him. It just tore the house down.

"I remember one time when Dinah Shore came in as a guest on the Opry. And she arrived with her accompanist, who had a fistful of music in his hand. After I had passed some pleasantries with Dinah, the accompanist said, 'Who do I see about passing around my music?' And I said, 'Me, I guess. I'm probably the only one here who knows it's music. The rest of them don't read music.' And I laughed about it and he got uptight about that. Dinah knew what was going on. She just kind of left him by the side of the stage and went out and did her thing with the staff band. And it was great.

"There was another night when Loretta Lynn was onstage. And the way the

Ryman stage was, I guess it was only thirty-six inches higher than the floor of the auditorium. Well, some rabid fan started running from the back of the downstairs main floor and just leaped right up on stage. And stood there while she finished her song. He didn't touch her, he didn't cause a problem. He just wanted to stand beside her, you know.

"I guess some of the finest memories I have of the Ryman deal with Marty Robbins. And the eleven-thirty show. That would always turn out to be a Marty Robbins crowd. The way that he could hold that audience spellbound was astonishing.

"One night he was down there, and there was a rather large woman in the balcony who had worked her way down to the front row. And as he started into one of his better-known love songs, she started to take her clothes off. And Marty stopped playing and started just looking at her, as he would do, you know. And started carrying on a conversation with the lady—on the air! As I recall it, he somehow calmed her down to where she stopped taking her clothes off."

≪iii≫ The Marty Robbins 11:30 show—a legend within the legend of the Grand Ole Opry—began because of what became Marty's second career: auto racing.

Opry announcer Hal Durham explained: "When I first started announcing, Marty would occasionally work the first show. And then he would go to the racetrack here in Nashville and race. And he would come back and do that last show. He wanted to do the last show because it enabled him to race and still work the Opry.

"I think he was more at ease working that last show. He didn't have the constrictions of time; somebody else waiting in the wings to go on. So when more and more people began expecting him on the last show, he gave up working the first show altogether.

"And, as the eleven-thirty segment became more and more 'his show,' so to speak, he began to take liberties with the time. Instead of running over five minutes, he'd run over fifteen minutes. Some of the other people grumbled a little bit about it, particularly if they were down at the Tubb Record Shop show waiting to go on. But we saw that the people at the Ryman enjoyed it very much and we never had any intention of squelching it. The eleven-thirty show with Marty was something very special at the Grand Ole Opry."

Robbins didn't undertake his racing career without some concern about the fans of his music. He told an interviewer: "I didn't know if my fans would accept my racing, but I decided to give it a try. I started playing around with micro-midgets in '59 and '60. Then, in 1963, I started to really learn how to drive by dirt-track racing in a modified stock car I called 'Devil Woman.' In '65, I graduated to late-model modifieds on the half-mile asphalt track at the Nashville Speedway, but kind of had a setback along the way."

That "setback" was a massive heart attack late in 1969 while he was touring in Ohio. Later he would say that he "felt like a hot dog ready to pop open." He was hospitalized in Cleveland, then transferred to St. Thomas Hospital in Nashville. His life expectancy was put at three to six months.

There was a new operative technique, but dangerous because it was so new, that would enable the doctors to do a triple arterial bypass. The main arteries into his heart, he was told, were blocked with cholesterol. He prayed on the decision overnight and then gave his permission to operate.

Tens of thousands of "get-well" cards poured into the hospital from the fans. It seemed to be in perfect character for the tough little man from Arizona that he pulled through. And with a joke on his lips. Nashville newspaper columnist Red O'Donnell wrote: "Marty instructed—cajoled would be a better word—his nurse to phone me and to come out to St. Thomas, bring a photographer and 'make a picture of the most carved up chest in Nashville.' "

It seemed strange to many that Robbins, a man who didn't drink or smoke and who kept himself slim, would suffer such a serious heart attack. But he did have his excesses. "I used to eat a dozen eggs for breakfast," he told a writer, "just to show people I could do it. I'd drink a quart of milk. I wouldn't eat a dozen every day. Usually, I'd have the cook bring me four eggs to see if she was a good cook. Then, if she was, I'd get eight more."

The bypass operation was performed on January 27, 1970. On Saturday, March 28, the curtain opened for the final half-hour of that evening's Grand Ole Opry. It was 11:30.

Reporter Jerry Thompson was there: "The sound from the jam-packed crowd was deafening. They couldn't hear the words to the song the familiar figure behind the Opry mike was crooning, but there was no mistake—Marty Robbins was back where he belonged. . . .

"Midway through the show Robbins sat at the piano and told the audience: 'I had so many things I was going to say tonight. I want to thank all my friends for their concern and I want to thank God for letting me be here. Now, I can't think of anything to say, so I guess I'll have to sing for you.'

"And sing he did until 12:27 A.M. when the curtain closed amidst repeated shouts of 'More, more, more.'

"Throughout his performance, a woman in the third row remained in a condition best described as just short of hysteria. She would clap her hands to her cheeks, rise out of her seat and, in a shrill, trembling voice, shout phrases such as: 'Lordy, Lordy!' 'Oh, mercy, Marty!' Or 'Lordy, I can't hardly stand it!' "

Marty Robbins had once more extended the Opry a half-hour past its assigned off time. Performers waiting at the Ernest Tubb Record Shop to begin the "Midnight Jamboree" must have smiled; the Grand Ole Opry was once more back to what might have been described as normalcy.

Gradually, Robbins resumed his full singing career. Within a year he would announce that he was returning to auto racing.

*E*rnest Tubb introduces longtime friend and former Texas Troubadour, Jack Greene, on the night of his Opry induction.

(1967) WSM PHOTO/MARVIN CARTWRIGHT

E. W. "Bud" Wendell was named Opry Manager in 1968. Here, he chats with Dottie West backstage at the Ryman.

(C. 1968) WSM PHOTO/LES LEVERETT

Dolly Parton became Porter Wagoner's "girl singer" in 1967. Their duets made country music history and launched Dolly to superstardom.

(C. 1968) *COUNTRY MUSIC FOUNDATION LIBRARY AND MEDIA CENTER*

Barbara Mandrell joined the Opry roster in July of 1972. Here, she performs on that special night with her father, Irby (far right), and Jerry Reid (center).

(1972) WSM PHOTO/LES LEVERETT

Tom T. Hall uses his smooth and easy style to weave another musical tale.

(1982) WSM PHOTO/LES LEVERETT

Marty Robbins, shown here in 1959 with his micro-midget racer, eventually gave up the first show on the Opry so that he could be at the track. His late show at 11:30 became an event for his adoring fans.

(1959) *RONNIE ROBBINS COLLECTION*

The exhilirating *Tennessee Waltz* at Opryland USA.

(MID–1970s) *BILL LAFEVOR*

Opryland's breathtaking *Wabash Cannonball.*

(MID–1970s) *BILL LAFEVOR*

Opryland's musical salute to the nation, "I Hear America Singing."

(MID–1970s) *BILL LAFEVOR*

··**{ iv }**·· Roy Acuff was introduced as "a senior statesman of country music" to a small crowd standing in the field on a plot of land along the multilaned Briley Parkway, hard by the Cumberland River.

He was to officiate at the ground-breaking ceremonies for the Opryland amusement park, whose construction was indicative of National Life's determination to go ahead with plans for moving the Grand Ole Opry and, at the same time, to become an even bigger factor in the economic growth of Nashville.

The date was Tuesday, June 30, 1970.

Acuff said, "This is a beautiful day in my life." Then he blew on the steamboat whistle Judge Hay had given him, the one used by Hay during his long tenure at the Opry. And he used The Solemn Old Judge's favorite phrase, "Let 'er go, boys!"

With that, Beecher Kirby—Bashful Brother Oswald—broke the ground with a plow pulled by two mules, signaling a new beginning for a radio show that once was known as the "WSM Barn Dance."

··**{ v }**·· At that same time, Acuff's old friend Tex Ritter was engaged in something Roy could understand: a statewide political race for United States senator.

His decision had been made early in January. In hindsight, it was a rather strange one. An avowed conservative, Tex didn't have the support of the Tennessee Republican party organization. That went to millionaire William Brock, a four-term U.S. congressman. And thus Ritter faced a tough, uphill primary campaign before he could hope to face incumbent Senator Albert Gore in the general election.

Ritter worked hard. And his country music friends rallied to his cause; most of the Nashville stars participated in a plan to each donate a day's time to appear with Tex on platforms across the state. But the "big money"—the promised financial support from Tennessee's conservative businessmen—somehow never materialized.

California friend Johnny Bond, Tex's partner in the music publishing business, recalled an appearance at a university "where only a handful of students sat in an otherwise huge auditorium." Ritter went ahead with his planned speech, extolling the virtues of his hard-line conservative program.

In his biography of Ritter, Bond would write: "Following the speech, Tex took on an open question session and I thought he was going to lose his temper.

" 'It's easy for you to stand there and talk like that when you've already got it made,' said one militant [student]. 'What about us? What's in it all for us? You're a movie star and a television star, but we've got to scrape it all together.'

" 'May I tell you somethin'?' said Tex. 'You think I've got it made. That's what a lot of folks think. But I'll tell you this: If I lose this election—and lose it I could—I'll be singing "The Boll Weevil" the rest of my life to try and pay for the campaign.' "

As it turned out, that was the exact truth.

In the August Republican primary, William Brock crushed Ritter's bid, garnering more than seventy-five percent of the vote.

Once more country music stardom on the Grand Ole Opry couldn't translate to victory in the political arena.

∘[vi]∘ There seemed to be a quickening of the pace at the Grand Ole Opry—and in all of country music—as the seventies sped along.

The annual Opry Birthday Celebration, begun in 1951 to recognize disc jockeys who played country music, had grown so large in twenty years that it had become unwieldy. What had happened was that hard-core country music fans had been registering in ever-increasing numbers and had finally overwhelmed it. WSM's solution, in concert with the Country Music Association, was to establish a separate celebration for the fans. Dubbed "Fan Fair," it was inaugurated in the spring of 1971—a roaring success right from the beginning.

Another new development, this one in February '72, was "Grand Ole Gospel Time," which recognized the long, close association between country music and gospel music. It was the brainchild of the Reverend Jimmie Snow, son of the Opry's Hank Snow. "Grand Ole Gospel Time" was installed as a late-night show following the "Friday Night Opry."

And in the spring of 1972, Opryland amusement park opened its gates as an American music theme park. There was country music, of course, but all pop music was included: Dixieland, Broadway, Big Band, and a patriotic music show. There was also a wide variety of amusement park rides, including a steam train, dubbed "The Wabash Cannonball," which circled the tree-lined park. Attracting some 1,400,000 customers in its first season, Opryland far exceeded the first-year attendance forecasts.

Talent matters were fast-paced, too. In February 1971 Opry star Loretta Lynn made her debut as a duet partner with Conway Twitty, a former rock 'n' roller from Friars Point, Mississippi, and their first record release, "After the Fire Is Gone," was a major hit. There would be other hits, and in 1972 Loretta was named the Country Music Association's Entertainer of the Year, and she and Conway would be honored as the CMA's Vocal Duo of the Year, an award they were to win for four consecutive years.

In 1971, also, Jan Howard would become an Opry roster member. But Jan Howard had been a member of the Grand Ole Opry since 1959, right? Wrong.

"I was a guest for years," she said, laughing. "I started guesting there when Ott Devine was manager and then Bill Anderson and I started working together in '65, and so I was part of the Bill Anderson show on the Opry. In the meantime, Bud Wendell became manager and I saw him at a party one Thursday night.

"He said, 'Well, I'll see you at the Opry tomorrow night.'

"And I said, 'No, I'm not going to be there.'

"He said, 'What do you mean, you're not going to be there?'

"I said, 'I'm not a regular member and I just happen to not be booked.'

"And he said, 'Well, you *are* going to be there!' And the next night—it was a Friday in March—I was made a regular member."

Much the same thing happened to Connie Smith. She had been in the limbo of being a "regular guest" until Wendell discovered it and added her to the roster in '71.

He also noted the guest appearance on the Ryman stage that summer of a young singer-songwriter from Texas, Larry Gatlin.

"I was on the Opry the first time with Dottie West," Gatlin said. "Steve and Rudy and I, and our sister, LaDonna, sang at the old Ryman on a Saturday afternoon matinee with Dottie. It was the first summer I moved to Nashville. We went out and bought these wool suits and it was like 194 degrees in that sucker! But it was a great thrill. We sang 'Here Comes My Baby Back Again' with Dottie. That was before we had any records of our own."

In 1972 two more young performers were added to the roster. One was David Houston, of Bossier City, Louisiana, a direct descendant of Sam Houston and Robert E. Lee, and a godson of Gene Austin, the pop singer who had gained fame with his recording of "My Blue Heaven." Houston had debuted professionally at the age of twelve on the "Louisiana Hayride," had toured with Johnny Cash and Elvis Presley in their early days, and in 1966 had a smash hit record, "Almost Persuaded," which was number-one everything that year.

The other '72 newcomer was Barbara Mandrell.

"It was in July," she remembered, "when Bud Wendell asked me to join the Grand Ole Opry. I was very honored. And I was introduced on the Roy Acuff segment. At the time, while I was acquainted with Mr. Acuff, I can't say we were friends. By coming to the Opry we became dear friends and now he's so special to me.

"You know what I recall most about the old Ryman? It's dressing and getting made up and all in the toilet, which was the women's dressing room. That was really close, and warm and friendly, sharing that crowded space with Loretta Lynn and Connie Smith and Dolly Parton and Jeannie Seely—"

···⟨ vii ⟩··· When the Opryland amusement park opened there was a shift in executive responsibilities. Bud Wendell was named to the new post of general manager of Opryland *and* the Grand Ole Opry, and he asked announcer Hal Durham, a native of McMinnville, Tennessee, and a high school classmate of Dottie West, to take over as the Opry manager.

He knew that it wouldn't be too many months before the Opry would leave the Ryman Auditorium to be housed in a new multimillion-dollar Opry House under construction next to Opryland. And when it did, the job would no longer be a reasonably comfortable position of simply managing a long-running radio show. He'd be in a new fishbowl, with all of the attendant pressures.

WSM president Irving Waugh and Bud Wendell were involved in a series of tortured meetings with the board of directors of National Life concerning how much money was being spent on the lavish new Opry House.

"There was never any row about building the new house," Waugh reminisced. "Everybody agreed that was necessary, but we had problems getting appropriations for the studios behind the Opry House. It took a lot of selling to get that going. At one big meeting with the National Life people, I remember Bill Weaver [National Life chairman of the board] jumping up and saying loudly, 'I'll say this to you!' And he stuck his finger down in front of my face. 'You better sell a helluva lot of popcorn!' "

Wendell recalled: "When we built the new Opry House we agonized over how many seats to put in the building. We were coming from a 3,000-seat house; actually, there weren't 3,000 salable seats in the Ryman. And here we were building a new house with 4,400 seats. Could we fill them? We weren't really sure.

"So in the early concepts of the Opry House we talked about ways to hide the balcony, because we just felt that the balcony probably wouldn't get used other than in the summertime. We talked with the architects about a 'light shield' to hide it. And there was talk about a mechanical ceiling—they had one in the Sydney, Australia, opera house—whereby the ceiling could come down and totally hide the balcony, while not affecting the acoustics. We looked into three or four of those sorts of things, just because we thought the house might be overbuilt. But we wanted the additional capacity as much for other shows as we did for the Opry.

"There was a *lot* of agonizing! I remember at one meeting with Dan Brooks, the CEO at National Life, and Bill Weaver, and Irving Waugh, and myself, Brooks said: 'I've got to see some numbers. You're going to have to put some numbers together that will, in fact, give me an idea of the income and expense levels, so that we can justify the investment.'

"I recall telling Irving after the meeting that I didn't have the foggiest idea how to approach numbers on the new building. Based on what we were doing at the Ryman we were talking apples and oranges. But I put together some numbers that did reflect, in fact, that it would be, as they termed it, 'a thin but acceptable' investment. Some of the figures were accurate, some of them weren't accurate. As I recall, the investment for the building was somewhere around twelve million, without any television equipment. That equipment was another two or two and a half million dollars. It was a big gamble simply because we had no television business. We were rolling the dice. . . .

"I remember going out, when we first got the equipment, to a seat-cover shop and asking them if they'd be interested in designing some covers for the cameras and the switchers and assorted gear, because I didn't think we were going to use the TV equipment that much." Wendell laughed. "But before we ever got them ordered, business started coming in."

There was a great deal about the planning of the Opryland complex that was speculative. *All of it*, actually.

"In the very early plot plans that were taken to zoning," Wendell said, "we felt that we should have a little motel—a hundred-fifty-room motel—to take care of a few folks who might be coming in."

Nobody fully appreciated what kind of bear they had by the tail once the full potential of the Grand Ole Opry was unleashed.

Our d-i-v-o-r-c-e becomes final today,
Me and little J-o-e will be going away;
I love you both and this will be pure h-e-double-l
  for me,
Oh, I wish that we could stop this d-i-v-o-r-c-e.*

—Early Tammy Wynette hit

He was a fertilizer salesman. A good one, setting all kinds of sales records for a Yazoo City, Mississippi, agricultural chemical company, while regaling his customers with a seemingly unending supply of stories about the friends he grew up with in rural Amite County.

A story of a coon hunt, for example, in which one John Eubanks gets caught up in a tall sweetgum tree with a "souped-up wildcat," while his friends on the ground, unaware that what he's tangling with is *not* a raccoon, keep shouting: "Knock him out, Jo-o-h-h-h-h-hn!" Or stories of the notorious Marcel Ledbetter, including one in which he is denied a cool drink at a tavern, getting his revenge by attacking the tavern screen door with a chain saw, reducing it to a twisted pile of wire and splinters. Complete with unique vocal sound effects.

After eighteen years of employment by the Mississippi Chemical Corporation, and nearly that long in storytelling, his friends finally convinced him that his stories had show business potential. "Ever since I met my manager, Tandy Rice of Nashville, in 1971," Jerry said, "my life's been boilin' like a great big Alka-Seltzer." His first storytelling album for MCA, *Jerry Clower from Yazoo City, Mississippi, Talkin'*, was an unqualified hit.

At the Grand Ole Opry, where there had not been a new "straight comic" signed in years, manager Hal Durham saw Clower's potential. He was added to the Opry roster in November 1973.

Jerry remembered it emotionally: "It's undescribable, because, you see, I had prayed as a little boy that at the end of a crop year we'd clear enough money for us to go see the Grand Ole Opry. And we never did make it. Now, here I was on it! *Grand Ole Opry star Jerry Clower!* Woooo!"

·∘⟦ ii ⟧∘· Once more at the Opry there was an oversight corrected in 1973.
Jeanne Pruett had come out of Alabama to become a force in Nashville, first as a songwriter with Marty Robbins Enterprises and then as a singer. Robbins had used his considerable influence to get her a recording contract with RCA.

"I can remember the first time that Ott Devine called me and invited me to come on the Opry," she said. "I think probably Chet Atkins twisted his arm. Anyway, Ott called me and it just surprised me so much. I knew that if I didn't say yes that first time there might not be a second time. So immediately I said yes and then started scurrying around looking for a suitable attire. That goes back to '64 or '65, around in there."

Jeanne became what she characterized as "the only semiregular who was not a cast member."

She went on: "Actually, as it turned out, I had been a member of the Opry for almost a year before I could get inducted. Dolly Parton wanted so badly to introduce me as the new member of the Opry, but her schedule and mine conflicted and we just couldn't seem to find a time to arrange the introduction. Anyway, I finally 'joined' on July 21, 1973. And Dolly did introduce me."

That moment came just as Jeanne's hot record "Satin Sheets" reached number one on the charts. It was one of the top five records of the entire year, attaining that lofty position with the likes of Charlie Rich's "Behind Closed Doors," Olivia Newton-John's "Let Me Be There," Merle Haggard's "If We Make It Through December," and Kris Kristofferson's "Why Me?" A vintage year for country hits.

"I was the last singing artist to join the Grand Ole Opry while it was still at the Ryman Auditorium," Pruett pointed out. "Jerry Clower joined after I did.

"You know, it was always a thrill for me at the Ryman when they said, 'Here's Jeanne Pruett!' For some reason that stage takes precedence over everything else. It might be the mystique of the years and years and years of talent that stood on that stage. It's kind of almost hallowed ground, so to speak, when you think back to Hank Williams, George Morgan, Patsy Cline, Marty Robbins—people no longer with us.

"But even more than that, it represented a way of life in my mind. I have total recall of Saturday nights when my whole family gathered around a little battery-operated radio on the farm in Alabama where I was raised and listened to the Grand Ole Opry. I was one of ten children and we all sang, and we all played music, and we all learned to *love* country music from hearing the Opry."

Also in 1973, the Opry took on one of the most mercurial couples in country music history—Tammy Wynette and George Jones. George, actually, had been on the roster before and now was returning. Both were at the height of their popularity, not only as an outstanding duet act, but individually as well. And that's the way they came on the Opry roster.

Tammy, a former hairdresser born in Red Bay, Alabama, was hot. She had been named the Country Music Association's Female Vocalist of the Year for three successive years—1968, 1969, and 1970. She was one of the leading record-sellers in the business in 1973. And she had a finely tuned feeling for the heritage of the Grand Ole Opry.

"Daddy used to play 'Wabash Cannonball' on the harp [harmonica] when I was growing up," she said. "That and 'The Great Speckled Bird' were the first two songs I ever remember singing."

She had been a guest at the Opry many times, the first time when she was just beginning to be recognized as a record artist in 1966.

"Roy Acuff introduced me the first time I was on the Opry," Tammy recalled, "and I sang 'A Good Girl's Gonna Go Bad.' I had out that record and 'Apartment #9' at the time. Then he introduced me again when I had 'D-I-V-O-R-C-E,' and [my daughter] Georgette crawled out on the Ryman stage and pulled on my dress and waited till I finished. I had to carry her off.

"I love Roy Acuff. God, he paved the way for so many of us. In those days when they didn't make hardly anything he was out there working and setting it up so that we all could make something later."

She paused, then laughed. "Oswald told me a story one time about how the Smoky Mountain Boys used to put rubber bands around their blue jeans at the knees, and walk out into the audience where they worked and sell those songbooks. Instead of trying to put the money in their pockets, they'd drop the coins down the bib of their overalls and it would go all the way down the legs of their pants. Then they'd stand in a No. 3 washtub, and pull the elastic bands off their pants, and let all the money drop out into the tub."

George Jones was already regarded as a country music "legend" when he rejoined the Opry—a singer's singer. He had started as a teenager in the late forties with his own show on KTXJ in Jasper, Texas, and then graduated to a half-hour show with the act of Eddie and Pearl in Beaumont, for room and board and $17.50 a week. There followed the usual period of existing in honky-tonks, and in 1953 he cut his first record, "There Ain't No Money in This Deal."

Later, Jones told an interviewer: "I didn't get into this business even thinking about money, what I would do, and where I would go. I just wanted my guitar in my hands and to keep on going. I just wanted to sing."

And sing he did. In 1962 and 1963 he was voted the number-one male vocalist by *Billboard* and *Cash Box* magazines. He established a style like no other. Unique. (Even with all his personal problems—broken marriages, too much booze, missed bookings—Jones persisted. In 1980 and 1981 the CMA voted him Male Vocalist of the Year.)

Tammy and George divorced in 1975, their tempestuous marriage later to be detailed in Tammy's soap-operaish autobiography, *Stand by Your Man*. In it the violent coupling, highlighted by George's drinking and irresponsibility, was given full exposure. The book would become the subject of a 1981 CBS television movie of the same title.

An honest evaluation of the film is that CBS didn't do either Tammy or George any favors.

⸨ iii ⸩ "A man who plays the five-string banjo has got it made," Dave Akeman used to say. "It never interferes with any of the pleasures in his life."

He recorded a song once, titled "Goin' to the Grand Ole Opry to Make Myself a Name." And that's exactly what he did. He was a superb banjo player, fine enough to have been a member of Bill Monroe's Blue Grass Boys. But what he was, first and foremost, was a naturally gifted funnyman. A rube comic, with a sad-sack delivery, raised-eyebrow expressions, and a Chaplinesque stance. He elicited sympathy. Love.

Country music fans *loved* Dave Akeman, even though most of them didn't really know his name. They knew him as "Stringbean," the character he was on the Opry stage. He had come out of Anneville, Kentucky, a tall, skinny young man, and he exaggerated that appearance with a costume that featured a long, long shirt, tucked into pants that were belted somewhere around the knees. It was a sight not easily forgotten.

His best friend, Grandpa Jones, recalled: "He said he got some of that costume from Slim Miller up at the 'Renfro Valley Barn Dance.' He thought Slim was the funniest man he ever seen."

When the rural version of the "Laugh-In" comedy show began on CBS television in 1969—it was called "Hee Haw"—Stringbean was one of the first comics selected for the cast. And it opened up a whole new career for Akeman. He didn't much care about that, though; the extra money was nice, but paramount to him were the simple pleasures of life with which the five-string banjo didn't interfere.

That meant hunting and fishing. And *not* driving a car. He never did drive a car.

Back in the forties, an article about Stringbean concentrated on that fact: "Talk about women drivers—Mrs. Estelle Stanfill Akeman, of the Maury County Stanfills, ought to get some kind of medal for cross-country performance.

"She's the 'driving woman' of the one-and-only Stringbean of Grand Ole Opry fame in every state of the 48 covered by the American Flag and all provinces of Canada. Seems that Estelle's the only one in the family who knows how to pilot that Cadillac. . . . Dave likes to hunt and fish and play the banjo, but he never has hankered to learn to drive an automobile. . . .

"Estelle must be about the best woman driver hereabouts. Certainly the best to get back last week from a 15,000-mile tour of Kansas, Nebraska, Iowa, Missouri, Texas, etc. Stringbean took part in the Minnie Pearl Show that toured the fair circuit to a fare-thee-well.

"To finish up the journey, Estelle pushed the Cadillac from Dallas to Nashville (750 miles by road) during the interval from 2:30 A.M. to 6:30 P.M."

Another Opry star with whom Akeman shared the "Hee Haw" experience was Archie Campbell: "String was the greatest guy in the world. I never heard him say one mean thing about another human being. He was really fine. And he was a wealthy man, you know, and the word got out that he wore overalls and he carried lots of money in them. And he did. He was warned about it different times. I know Bill Carlisle went up to him one time and said, 'Somebody's gonna knock you on the head.' "

It was the second weekend of November 1973 and Opry announcer Grant Turner was leaving the Ryman Auditorium at the end of the broadcast. "I'll never forget that night," he said. "I saw Grandpa Jones and Ramona [Grandpa's wife] talking with Stringbean and his wife. They were having so much fun; they were planning to go fishing. I was going to stop and say something to them, but they were busy talking. That was just a short time before Stringbean and his wife . . ." The sentence trailed off.

When the Akemans reached their rural home they were surprised by burglars who had obviously heard the stories of Stringbean carrying large sums of money. It may have been that the Opry star resisted them. The terrible sum was that Dave and Estelle were gunned down—shot in cold blood.

Eventually two murderers were caught, tried, convicted, and sent to jail.

It simply added to the legacy of tragedy visited upon the Grand Ole Opry family.

···❊ iv ❊··· "Hank Williams got kicked off the Opry for drinkin' too much old wine," Skeeter Davis said. "Me? I got kicked off for singing about the new wine."

It was just two weeks before Christmas 1973, when Skeeter was going to the Ryman for yet another performance. She witnessed the arrest of a paddy wagon full of what were known as "Jesus freaks" in those days—young people protesting on the Nashville streets about what the world had become.

Those were troubled times: corruption in government uncovered in the Watergate investigations, a new war in the Middle East, U.S. military forces on "precautionary alert," environmental concerns. It seemed to some, even though the Vietnamese adventures had been ended in January 1973, that there was a need for new moral values. And they defied the establishment by demonstrating in the streets. Nashville police met that defiance with arrests.

It enraged Skeeter Davis and she expressed that rage on the Opry that night—talking about it, singing about it, weeping about it. In total, she used the Opry microphones to editorialize about it. She was dismissed from the Opry.

Later, a newspaper account of it encapsulated the event: "Her support of the 'Jesus loves you' street people made headlines, made enemies, made for a quick review of the unwritten rules [against editorial comments on the Opry]. She was stunned when told she was no longer a member.

"She was invited back 18 months later, after she had taken to playing for people 'in places that I had to look up on the globe.' "

Perhaps it proved one thing: Opry family members did not exist in a vacuum.

Through the years we've been together,
Singin' songs of life and love;
It was at the Grand Ole Opry
Where we shared this common bond. *

—TV special song, 1974

It was Tuesday, January 2, 1974.

Grand Ole Opry star Tex Ritter was getting ready to leave his Nashville home for a trip to Philadelphia, where he would be playing a three-day engagement at the Bijou Café dinner theater.

Several days earlier, *Philadelphia Evening Bulletin* columnist Ed Weiner had written: "Tex Ritter at the Bijou Café? What with the Bijou's usual pop and jazz fare, it's a bit of an incongruous change-of-pace booking . . . enough to make one sit up and take notice. . . . And whether this is high camp at its best, or an honest attempt to showcase a true musical legend will probably reside in the ears of the beholder."

Johnny Bond, author of the biography *The Tex Ritter Story*, told what happened on that early January day:

"Over his morning coffee, while visiting with Dorothy [his wife] and son Tommy he scoffed at the morning sports pages announcing the defeats of his favorites, [the University of Texas] by Nebraska and USC by Ohio State.

*"Will the Circle Be Unbroken?" by A. P. Carter; copyright 1935 Peer International Corporation. New lyrics by Chet Hagan by special permission of the copyright holder.

" 'Danged Woody Hayes!' Tex scowled, throwing the newspapers on the floor. . . .

"After breakfast, he called several of his band boys and asked them to meet him at certain places in Nashville [for the trip to Philadelphia].

" 'What about Jack Watkins? Is he going to be able to go with us?'

" 'Jack's in jail,' was the report.

" 'In jail!'

" 'Yeah. An old non-support charge.'

" 'Well, I'll be damned,' said Tex, beating his pipe on the table. 'I'll have to go down there and bail him out. . . .'

"Tex Ritter hung up the phone, sat by it for a silent moment, arose and kissed his wife goodbye. . . . Then he and his son drove away on the icy streets for downtown Nashville."

Reporter Jerry Bailey, writing in the *Nashville Tennessean*, picked up the story:

"Sheriff Fate Thomas said Ritter visited the jail to see if he could pay bail for the release of a member of his band, Lamar (Jack) Watkins, 35, of Springfield, Tenn., who had been charged Tuesday with being a fugitive for non-support.

"Jail Lt. Johnny Brewer said Ritter came to the jail about 5:30 P.M. and was sitting in a chair in his office when he 'just all of a sudden went limp in the chair. . . . He had been acting in just the best of spirits. He was kidding around and cutting up and having a good time. He told us it was the first time he had been to the jail and he was amazed at how it was run.'

"One of Ritter's two sons, Thomas Ritter, a law student at Vanderbilt University, was with him at the time. . . . He said his father suddenly 'grabbed at his chest' and slumped down.

"Sheriff Thomas said Watkins was being processed for release when Ritter had the attack."

Tex died instantly, the victim of a heart attack.

There was a memorial service in Nashville and the body was flown to Nederland, Texas, for the funeral.

Johnny Bond again: "All during the night of January 4 and all day January 5, Tex lay at the funeral home, where thousands upon thousands came to pay their last respects.

"Early in the afternoon of the fifth, in my hotel room, I turned on the television and watched the taped Porter Wagoner show. Guest star Tex Ritter sang 'Fall Away.'

" 'He would have wanted it shown,' I thought."

Radio and television personality Ralph Emery worked with Tex on his all-night radio shows on WSM: "I used to kid Tex a lot about movies, about how he could shoot fifty times without reloading.

"So on the very last show [taped at WSM studios just two weeks before his passing] it seems that I said, 'Well, Tex, this is where you ride off into the sunset, isn't it?'

" 'Yeah,' said Tex. 'I'll get on my horse, ride off down the trail about thirty yards or so, turn around, wave my hat and say "*Adiós, amigos*."

"As it turned out, just a couple of weeks or so after his passing, we aired the taped show, and Tex Ritter was able to voice his own farewell: '*Adiós, amigos!*'"

›❪ ii ❫‹ At the Opryland site along Briley Parkway in the spring of 1974, work was being completed on the construction of the *new* Grand Ole Opry House, begun November 12, 1971.

It was so different from the old Ryman as to defy comparison. And yet the auditorium was designed in such a manner that its cushioned pewlike seats (it still meant to be "The Mother Church of Country Music") were as close to the performers as possible, from one side of the theater to the other, in an effort to maintain the intimacy of the Ryman. There were no pillars anywhere to obstruct any views. And the balcony was there in all its glory; early tentative plans to find a way to "hide" it had long since been abandoned.

The auditorium was air-conditioned, and jammed with the ultimate in modern electronics, acoustics, lighting, and audiovisual equipment. While it was the new home of a radio show, the auditorium, boasting 4,400 seats, was a giant television studio. "The world's largest broadcasting studio," Grand Ole Opry press releases trumpeted.

The total width of the "workable stage"—that portion of it seen by the audiences—is 80 feet, with a depth of 63 feet. That can be extended forward, however, to 75 feet by means of a 12-foot hydraulically operated thrust stage. And in the maple flooring of the stage had been inserted a large oak disc cut from the stage of the Ryman, which brought the ghosts of the old house with it. Visiting singer Jimmy Dean would say: "Cutting that piece of the old Ryman stage out and putting it in the stage of the new Opry House was a stroke of damned genius."

Backstage there was ample space in the wings so that the clutter of bodies known as the Ryman was no longer a necessity. And there were thirteen dressing rooms—large ones. No one had to dress and get made up in the toilets any longer. Only one dressing room was permanently assigned: *Number One* went to Roy Acuff. "It beats changing clothes in the back of a car," he quipped.

He quickly hung a small plaque on the door. It read:

> Ain't nothin' gonna come up today
> that me and the Lord can't handle.

❪ iii ❫ But before the Grand Ole Opry could move to its new home there had to be a farewell to the old.

A schedule was set up. Saturday, March 9, 1974, would mark the last Saturday-night show at the Ryman. Then, because tradition dictated that the new house ought to open on a Saturday, the final broadcast of the Grand Ole Opry from Captain Tom Ryman's gospel tabernacle was set for Friday, March 15. (As it turned out, the *very last* broadcast from the Ryman on WSM was the "Grand Ole Gospel

Time" program; this was a fitting conclusion, somehow, that would have pleased the ghost of evangelist Sam Jones.)

It was no surprise that the Friday Opry was a tearful one.

Minnie Pearl remembered: "The night we left, the last night we played at the Ryman, I was crying. I was so sentimental about the old building. I never felt that way about the War Memorial, and that's where I started on the Opry. But we had thirty years or more at the Ryman and it had so much ambiance. The church pews, the haze of hair spray in that ladies' room, Henry leaving me out of the car in the alley and me running up those cement steps to the stage door, the people out front—"

"That last night was a very sacred moment," Jan Howard said. "But I'm glad we left. Listen, when you see people pass out in front of you because of the heat, and you're performing on a stage that's a hundred ten degrees, and there's no air—yes, I'm glad we moved. But it still was a reverent moment that night, almost like being in church. You knew it was history and you were a part of it.

"I've heard some other artists say, 'Well, the new house is not the Opry.' But, to me, the Opry is the people, not the brick and stone."

Jeanne Pruett said her most moving moment at the Grand Ole Opry was that last night at the Ryman: "Marty Robbins and I did the last show [the 11:30 segment]. I can remember when that curtain came down—well, we were going from what we knew and loved and held dear, to the unknown. And I just wondered to myself if it was the end of the Opry, or was it the beginning?"

Roy Acuff had the final word. With complete candor he told the audience: "Certainly there are memories of this old house that will go with us forever. Not all of them are good. Not all of them. Many of them are, but some of them are *punishment*.

"Punishment in the way that we ask you to come to visit with us and then we sit you out in this audience here and in the hot summer we sell you a fan for a dollar. You do your own air-conditioning. And some of you, we sell you a cushion to sit on because the seats are not just the most comfortable they can be. But out in Opryland, when you come to see us, we'll furnish the air conditioner. We'll furnish the cushion seats.

"You just don't know how much we do appreciate you people. It's *you* who have made the Grand Ole Opry so successful. Will you not forget us when we move into our new building? You'll love us for being out there and we'll love you for coming to see us. Thank you. God bless you all—good night."

Inevitably, there was a bit of controversy involved in the geographical change. Tom T. Hall elected not to continue on the Opry roster in the new house. A page-one newspaper story said he had quit because Grand Ole Opry executives had denied him permission to use his own band, which included horns.

"It's true that when the Opry left the old Ryman I didn't go with it," Tom explained. "But I'm a romantic, you know. I didn't care about the new Opry House at first—it just didn't set right with me. Just out of a romantic notion.

"So the newspapers called my agent, Bob Neal, to find out what it was all about. They got Sonny Neal, Bob's son, on the phone. And he says: 'Well, I'll tell you, by God, they won't let Tom use his horns on the Opry.' That got me in all kinds of trouble. There was a lot of press about it.

"Of course, I didn't have a damned orchestra. I had a hillbilly band, like everybody else. But I had made a record, 'The Year that Clayton Delaney Died,' with a trumpet on it; I used a Jimmie Rodgers kind of arrangement on that song. So, Sonny took my 'cause' in hand.

"But I finally got back on the Opry a few years later—I think it was 1980—the same way I got on there in the beginning. I was at the Opry House doing something else; doing my TV show. And I met Ernest Tubb in the parking lot and he said, 'You get back here on the Opry. You belong over here.'

"And I said, 'Yes, sir.'

"You know, what could you say to Ernest Tubb? I went back on the Opry again."

···✠ iv ✠··· Saturday night, March 16, 1974. It was 6:30 P.M., Central Time. The new Grand Ole Opry House was packed to the very last row of the balcony. There were hundreds of specially invited guests in the audience, most of the men in somber business suits and ties, the women in fashionable cocktail dresses. One suspected that a lot of them had never been to a Grand Ole Opry broadcast before. But this was a special occasion, one deemed worthy of Nashville's and Tennessee's business, political, and cultural leaders.

In the auditorium, too, was a corps of sober-faced young men, tiny identity buttons in their lapels. Secret Service men. For the President of the United States was coming to help inaugurate the *new* Opry.

President Richard M. Nixon was a beleaguered leader on that night, caught up in a peculiar kind of madness that historians will forever refer to as Watergate. The value of his being there on the Opry stage could not have been lost on a consummate politician like Mr. Nixon. He knew, of course, that the new building was a tribute to the Opry's very substantial appeal to grass-roots America—a grass-roots America whose support he needed in his time of trial.

Nevertheless, President Nixon had demonstrated his support of the country music community over the years. There seems no doubt that he would have attended the ceremonies in Nashville under any circumstances. And it was a proud moment for the Opry family. The President was going to be there!

It all began with the familiar sounds of the Fruit Jar Drinkers, those veteran musicians who had been at the Opry since the earliest days. And with the voice of Grant Turner, who had been an Opry announcer for thirty years.

Formal proceedings began with Opry star Billy Grammer giving the invocation, and WSM president Irving Waugh pointing out that in 1976 the United States of America would celebrate its bicentennial. "By then," he said, "for more than one-fourth of the nation's years there will have been a Grand Ole Opry."

*T*ammy Wynette and George
Jones, one of the best-known
duos in Opry history, onstage
at the Ryman on May 17, 1969.
(1969) *WSM PHOTO/MARVIN
CARTWRIGHT*

*S*tringbean (Dave Akeman) adopts one of his
characteristic Chaplinesque poses. His
murder in 1973 devastated Opry fans and stars.

(*LATE 1940s*) *GRAND OLE OPRY ARCHIVES*

President Nixon plays the piano as the audience sings "God Bless America" at the Grand Opening of the Grand Ole Opry House in 1974.

(1974) WSM PHOTO/LES LEVERETT

President Richard M. Nixon addresses the crowd at the Grand Opening of the "new" Opry House in 1974.

(1974) WSM PHOTO/LES LEVERETT

Roy Acuff tries to teach a befuddled Richard Nixon how to yo-yo—without much success—at the Grand Opening of the Grand Ole Opry House in 1974.

(1974) WSM PHOTO/LES LEVERETT

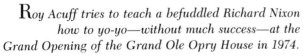

··❧[v]❧·· Much earlier, when construction had just begun on the new Opry House, Roy Acuff had said: "I've made my request that if I'm still here when the Opry House opens, they let me be the first one to go on the stage. I just want to open the curtain and sing two songs. Then they can have it."

But when that day came, Acuff had trouble getting into the Opry House. He arrived with his arms loaded with clothes and instruments he would need for that night, and was stopped by Secret Service men. He tried to explain who he was, but one young man had his doubts. Finally a senior agent came on the scene: "He's telling you the truth. I've seen him on television."

The speeches were ended and the show was about to start; a democratic decision had been made. The Opry acts would appear in more or less alphabetical order, thus assuring Acuff his opening spot.

The house lights dimmed, the curtain rose, and there was a huge white scrim. Projecting on it was the picture of George Dewey Hay from the 1940 movie *Grand Ole Opry*.

"First we're gonna hear from Roy Acuff and his Smoky Mountain Boys," the movie voice of The Solemn Old Judge intoned. "Smoke it up, Roy!"

And there was Acuff. A young Acuff. Of thirty-four years earlier. A dark-haired Acuff of serious demeanor. Bashful Brother Oswald's wailing dobro gave him his cue. And *that* Roy Acuff began to sing. In the powerful voice that used to knock small radio stations off the air:

> *From the great Atlantic Ocean to the wide Pacific*
> *shore,*
> *From the queen of flowing mountains to the*
> *south bells by the shore,*
> *She's mighty tall and handsome and known quite*
> *well by all;*
> *She's the combination on the Wabash*
> *Cannonball.*

Then the scrim began to rise slowly. And through it the audience could see the 1974 Roy Acuff and his Smoky Mountain Boys, making a perfect musical segue from the film to the live performance on the new Opry stage.

The effect was electric. There was a standing ovation, prolonged through most of the song. And there were some tears. But not from Acuff; he was in his element. This was his moment.

Stage lights came on full and behind him came the other roster acts of the Grand Ole Opry. Nearly sixty in number. All singing.

"This is nonrehearsed," Roy shouted joyfully. "Believe me, this is the first time we've been on this stage together."

Acuff made a few introductory remarks, led the assembled cast in the country standard "You Are My Sunshine," brought on Ralph Sloan and the Tennessee

Travelers clog-dancing group, and then introduced the next Opry star in the long alphabetical list, Whisperin' Bill Anderson.

[vi] The Presidential party arrived in the Opry House at a few minutes past seven. Mr. Nixon was accompanied by his wife, Governor Winfield Dunn, and Tennessee's United States senators, William Brock and Howard Baker. They were escorted to seats in the balcony.

Someone shouted, "Ladies and gentlemen, the President of the United States!" Everyone rose, glancing at the balcony and applauding.

And the show continued. Comedian Jerry Clower told his story about Marcel Ledbetter demolishing the roadside beer joint with his chain saw. Jack Greene came on with his duet partner, Jeannie Seely, who elicited wolf-whistles from the audience with her bare-midriff pantsuit as she sang "Don't Touch Me."

President Nixon watched the show for about half an hour before Roy Acuff appeared on the stage again. (It's part of the lore of this evening that several of the politicians present wanted to introduce the President. Mr. Nixon had other ideas. "Roy will do it," he said.)

At the appointed time, Acuff came to the microphone again: "Tonight we're honored by the very first President to visit with us at the Grand Ole Opry—and you can know that we boys and girls, we're just delighted that this has happened while *we* are here at the Grand Ole Opry. I just couldn't say the words that would *really* let you people know how delighted I am that I can be here and take the microphone and ask the President and Mrs. Nixon, with their troupe, if they would mind honoring us and coming down and be on the stage here this evening. We would be delighted to have you."

That was vintage Acuff. Totally sincere. His words tinged with the accent of the hills of east Tennessee. Unpretentious. And there was no doubt that Acuff understood that the President was to have the center spotlight; the "troupe" he mentioned included a governor and two U.S. senators. They were never introduced to the audience.

While Acuff was speaking, the Nixon party came to the wings of the stage, accompanied by National Life board chairman Bill Weaver and Mrs. Dorothy Ritter, Tex's widow. Just before the final introduction, Weaver gave Mr. Nixon a yellow yo-yo. "Mr. President," he said, "if you want to bring the house down, pull this out of your pocket when you get onstage."

"Hail to the Chief" was played by the Opry band: a hillbilly version—the anthem had never sounded like that before. And its playing never seemed more appropriate. The Grand Ole Opry cast, crowded together on center stage, applauded wildly; so did the appreciative audience.

There was a presentation of a handmade dulcimer to Mrs. Nixon by Dorothy Ritter, and then Acuff suggested that everyone sing "Happy Birthday" to the First Lady, adding a further suggestion that the President play the piano.

"Well, in this very professional company," Mr. Nixon said, "I'm a little embarrassed to try and play that thing there." A nod toward the old upright piano. "I haven't even learned to play with this thing."

Out of his jacket pocket came the yellow yo-yo, which promptly fell to the end of its string. Acuff was completely surprised. But Bill Weaver had been right: The audience roared its approval.

The surprises weren't ended, however. Mr. Nixon went to the piano and played "Happy Birthday" and everyone joined in on the singing. And then he added an encore of "My Wild Irish Rose" for his wife, Pat Ryan Nixon.

It seemed almost an intrusion on the happy informality when it came time to dedicate the plaque memorializing the opening of the new Opry House. When the unveiling was completed, Acuff once more approached the microphone.

"Must be time for a commercial," the President quipped.

In an aside to Opry announcer Grant Turner, one not heard on the microphone, Roy whispered: "He's got me stunned."

Stunned, too, must have been the members of the White House press corps who had made the trip to Nashville. They had never seen *that* Richard Nixon before.

Acuff began his formal introduction of the guest: "Ladies and gentlemen, about a year ago I was invited to the White House, along with many others, to entertain the [Vietnam] prisoners of war. After I sung my song, Mr. Bob Hope, who was the master of ceremonies, asked me back to the stage and I remarked that it was the highlight of my career. But you know, I never *dreamed* that a night like this would ever come to Roy Acuff. So I'd like to say to the world that is listening in, from our new home here in Opryland, USA: Ladies and gentlemen, the President of the United States, Richard Nixon."

Smiling, Mr. Nixon said: "Somebody was telling me that there is only one thing stronger than country moonshine, and that is country music. I saw a couple of fellows outside that were combining the two and, believe me, it was plenty strong."

The audience laughed loudly.

The President praised the character of the Opry's music: "First, country music is American. It started here, it is ours. . . . It is as native as anything American we can find. It comes from the heart of America, out here in Middle America. Country music talks about family. It talks about religion, the faith in God that is so important to our country and particularly to our family life. And we all know that country music radiates a love of this nation—patriotism. Country music, therefore, has those combinations that are essential to America's character, at a time when America needs character."

The import of that last phrase was not lost on political observers.

Mr. Nixon seemed reluctant to leave. Once again he pulled out the yo-yo and made an inept attempt to operate it. Those listening on WSM Radio, and on a live 200-station network, and on the 1,135 stations of the Armed Forces Radio Network, must have been wondering what was going on.

Acuff: "Turn your hand over and let it go. Now, jerk it back!" The President's yo-yo didn't respond. "You don't need to be in a hurry to get back up there [to Washington]—we need you down here for a while."

Nixon, chuckling: "I'll stay here and try to learn how to use the yo-yo, and you go and be President, Roy."

Acuff, in full laughter: "This is such a wonderful program. We'll never see another one like it in our state. Never have before."

It wasn't finished. Roy led the assembled Opry cast in singing "Stay All Night, Stay a Little Longer."

Acuff again: "Mr. President, do you belong to the musicians' union? You'll get some talk on this if you don't. Come on over here, I want you to play the piano again."

Mr. Nixon replied that he was an honorary member of the musicians' union in New York City. He returned to the piano and accompanied the Opry folk as they sang "God Bless America."After that, the Nixons left the stage.

But the Grand Ole Opry broadcast had to go on. Singer Jan Howard was the next up: "I've had some tough acts to follow in my career, but this is unreal. I wouldn't wish a spot like this on a dry cleaner."

Backstage, Roy presented the President with a special gift: a replica of George D. Hay's steamboat whistle, the side engraved with the names of the entire Opry cast. The Presidential party left the Opry House shortly after eight o'clock.

And the inaugural broadcast in the new house went on. Minnie Pearl didn't make it to the microphone until 9:30 P.M. "I've been waitin' to go on for so long," she joked, "my dress has gone out of style."

In one sense, that March night at the Grand Ole Opry could not recapture for President Nixon the public image he had once had. One hundred forty-five days later (the date was August 8), the realities of Watergate caught up with him; he announced his resignation, the first President in the history of the nation to leave office so.

··⟨ vii ⟩·· Once the Opry House was opened, it became necessary to prove the merits of the auditorium as the television studio it was meant to be. A major television special was mounted for NBC, utilizing the newly instituted Opryland Productions facilities. Joseph Cates, a veteran producer of variety shows, was brought in to head it up.

Johnny Cash was signed as the host, but the show featured the strength of the Opry roster: Acuff, Monroe, Tubb, Lynn, Hall, Pearl, Anderson, Greene and Seely, Mandrell, Parton and Wagoner. And others.

The special opened with a wide helicopter shot of the new house and Cash's words: "Hello . . . and welcome to an emotional experience—the first nationwide television special from the new home of the Grand Ole Opry. It is, in truth, a reaffirmation that country music *is* the music of Americans . . . not only the performers on this stage, but the tens of thousands of Americans who have witnessed the Opry over nearly fifty years. For country music—this is home!"

An opening ensemble number, a special piece of material based on A. P. Carter's old tune, "Will the Circle Be Unbroken?," set the tone:

Home, it's said, is where the heart is
No matter where we may roam;
Well, our hearts are at the Opry,
Country music has come home.

So, the circle won't be broken,
By and by, friends, by and by;
Our real strength is country music,
It won't die, friends, it won't die.

"Country Comes Home" (for that was the title of the telecast) marked the last television appearance of the duet of Porter Wagoner and Dolly Parton. By the time the show aired on April 26 they had gone their separate ways.

Candy kisses, wrapped in paper,
Mean more to you than any of mine;
Candy kisses, wrapped in paper,
*You'd rather have them any old time.**

—George Morgan hit

Moviemaker Robert Altman celebrated his fiftieth birthday in 1975 while working on his newest film, *Nashville.* Some called it a "hatchet job" on the country music business. Others loved it, and the movie was very well received at the box office when it was released in June. One writer said *Nashville* "sought a symbol in the hopes and failures and betrayals of the country music industry." It was a popular game in Nashville to try to match up the characters in Altman's movie with real people.

In one sense, Altman's film forced a new look at country music. And in country music in general, and at the Grand Ole Opry specifically, 1975 brought a realization of a *new reality.* The Opry, while amazingly successful as an economic entity, no longer "made" stars. That was a simple, cold fact.

There was a new generation of country music stars developed without the imprimatur of Opry rostership. Kris Kristofferson was a star. And Charlie Rich. And Tanya Tucker. And Charlie Pride. And Donna Fargo. And Jerry Reed. And Merle Haggard. And Anne Murray. And Crystal Gayle. And Freddy Fender. And

*"Candy Kisses" by George Morgan; copyright 1948 Hill and Range Songs, Inc.

Mickey Gilley. And Glen Campbell. And Waylon Jennings. And T. G. Sheppard. And Willie Nelson—*after* he had left Nashville. And others.

They all maintained an appreciation of what the Grand Ole Opry was. Most of them accepted guest appearances at the Opry, but becoming a member of the roster was no longer that important to them.

The ready availability of national television was partly responsible for that. Easier travel on jet planes and in luxurious air-conditioned buses was partly responsible for that. The siren songs of West Coast agents and managers were partly responsible for that. Times had changed.

Indeed, so had the Grand Ole Opry.

T. G. Sheppard gave a candid evaluation: "I played the Opry only once. I guess we could play it more, but we just don't, because we're what they call the 'new breed.' And a lot of the 'new breed' doesn't play the Opry."

What were his emotions?

"Well, it was very strange," T.G. said quietly. "I don't know—I think every performer experiences that whenever you go to the Opry for the first time. You know, you're standing in the middle of history. I guess it's pretty much like if you're a politician and you get to walk into the Oval Office and sit behind the President's desk for two or three seconds. You know that you're sitting where all the greats have sat.

"My appearance on the Opry was a real humbling experience for me, no matter what my music form may be. I sang 'Last Cheater's Waltz'—a very country song. And 'Devil in a Bottle,' another very country song. The reaction was good. The audiences at the Opry are very enthusiastic people. Most of them come from all walks of life, from all across America, to witness whoever is on that night."

A thoughtful pause. "It's strange to me that in a time when everybody's complaining about business being off, the Opry still packs them in every weekend and nobody knows who's going to be there. There's no box-office draw! The music form itself, I guess, is the draw."

T. G. Sheppard had discovered the truth, the "secret" of the Grand Ole Opry—there in the open for anyone who would seek it.

··◖ ii ◗·· One who could play it good and play it right and do it justice returned to the Grand Ole Opry roster on February 8, 1975, after an absence of eighteen years.

Little Jimmy Dickens was back.

Hank Snow introduced him: "Jimmy is one of the greatest showmen of all time. It's like replacing the most important spoke in a wheel to have him back on the Opry. We need more Jimmy Dickenses."

Jimmy sang "The Family Reunion."

"I thought that it was appropriate," he told a reporter that night. "It's hard to put in words and say how you feel about being back in the family. It's been so long."

There weren't many roster changes in the latter half of the seventies. It was more of a reordering, a keeping of the house in fine tune. Don Gibson also returned to the roster in 1975. And George Hamilton IV, who had built himself a solid fan base in Europe, came back on the roster in 1976. Larry Gatlin and the Gatlin Brothers were added in 1979.

But basically, the principal work of the Grand Ole Opry management of those years was to build on the base it already had. New promotional activities were needed to keep the big new house filled; to keep what had become a big business running smoothly; and to look to corporate expansion. In 1975 National Life executives announced plans for the construction of the Opryland Hotel. Not the originally conceived 150-room motel, but a major hotel and convention and exhibit center.

❧[iii]❧ Marty Robbins remained one of the key stars of the Opry in the mid-seventies. But one who was bringing some gray hairs to Opry officials and to his loyal fans who continued to pack the 11:30 show at the new Opry House.

For Marty's auto-racing enthusiasms had graduated to the highly professional, high-speed, big-league NASCAR Grand National circuit, competing against the likes of champions Richard Petty and Bobby Allison. His concerned fans and his worried family counseled against it, but Marty persisted.

Things went well for a time; he had several NASCAR commendations as a promising rookie driver. Then, on October 4, 1974, on the second lap of the National 500 at the Charlotte Motor Speedway, Robbins hit the front straightaway wall head-on trying to avoid a ten-car pileup in front of him. On February 16, 1975, Robbins recorded three laps when he was involved in a multicar crash in the Daytona 500. On May 4, 1975, he had finished sixty-two laps when he crashed again, in the Winston 500 at Talladega, Alabama.

Three races. Three successive wrecks. But none of them his fault.

Indeed, his quick reflexes in the race at Charlotte certainly saved lives. When he saw cars ahead of him spinning and crashing he deliberately turned his #42 Dodge into the wall—at a speed in excess of 150 miles per hour—to avoid smashing into other drivers. Richard Childress, one of the drivers in the melee, told reporters: "There's no doubt in my mind I wouldn't be here talking to you right now if Marty Robbins hadn't risked his life."

Characteristically, Marty made light of all that and continued to race.

❧[iv]❧ Since 1948, when he had been added to the Grand Ole Opry roster as the replacement for Eddy Arnold, George Morgan had been a major force. And a backstage legend. As already suggested, Morgan was an inveterate practical joker.

It seemed to some that George never took anything seriously. That was a critical misjudgment of him. He may have seen the foibles of life as something unmitigatedly funny. But he was deadly serious about one thing: his music.

Morgan's early life had not been easy. He had been born on a small family farm at Waverly, Tennessee. His father, Jack, augmented the meager farming income by cutting cross-tie timbers for the railroad. One day he was walking along a stretch of railroad track when one of his boot laces caught in a switch. Try as he might, he could not free himself. A train approached.

At the last moment he threw himself backward to avoid being struck by the train, breaking his leg. But his leg was still across the switch and the train severed it.

Later George told the story to Dixie Deen of *Music City News*: "That put an end to his farming and cutting cross-ties. And when I was about two years old, after my brother Bill was born, my daddy had to move to Ohio to get work. . . . He got a job hauling coal with a horse and wagon."

Within a year, Jack Morgan moved his family to Barberton, Ohio. "He got a job with the Sieberling Rubber Company," George said, "and he got a wooden leg around that time. I can remember times during the Depression that he would come home, take off that wooden leg, and the blood would be seeping out of that old stump stocking. These are not pleasant things [to talk about], but it is pleasant in my mind to know how much Dad loved us to go through all that. I mean, he would work around the clock sometimes just to feed us.

"Every Saturday night, Mom and Dad, both being from Tennessee, would tune into the Grand Ole Opry. . . . I grew up listening to country music and my love for it was instilled because to my folks it was something from 'down home.' "

When George graduated from high school in Ohio, he had a variety of jobs: in restaurants, a rubber plant, surveying. But he also bought a guitar and, by 1947, "we got a little band together and started working for peanuts, and sometimes not even for that."

A new radio station opened in Wooster, Ohio, and Morgan and his band auditioned and were hired. "There was no money in it. Our little country band opened up the station every morning for a couple of months, then the other guys in the band couldn't see any future in it and they all quit. I stayed on with my guitar."

It was during that period that he wrote "Candy Kisses." "I was on the way to the station one morning," he recalled, "and I was thinking about a girl and it occurred to me that my kisses meant less to her than the candy kisses my mother used to bring home had meant to me when I was a kid."

"Candy Kisses" opened all the doors: to a "real" job at WWVA, Wheeling, West Virginia; to a Columbia Records recording contract; and to WSM and the Grand Ole Opry.

That song was a monster hit. In 1948–1949 there were four top-ten releases of "Candy Kisses"—his own, Cowboy Copas's, Eddie Kirk's, and Red Foley's. In '49 he also charted with "Crybaby Heart," "Please Don't Let Me Love You," "Rainbow in My Heart," and "Room Full of Roses." A substantial career was started and other hits followed: "Almost," "I'm in Love Again," "You're the Only

Good Thing," "Slipping Around," "You Loved Me Just Enough to Hurt Me," "A Picture That's New." A lot of hits.

In 1956 he left the Grand Ole Opry to star in his own show on WLAC-TV in Nashville, but by 1959 he was back at the Ryman. To stay.

Today, no one can speak of George Morgan without mentioning the practical jokes. "He was a kind of a danger," Tom T. Hall said, chuckling. "Everybody kept an eye out for him. He'd be standing there talking to you, and he'd be patting you on the back and untuning your guitar at the same time. He did that to me. I was introduced and walked out on stage and said, 'Thank you very much,' and hit my guitar and it was just like a screen door! Man, there was nothin' there!"

Music publisher Bill Denny, Jim Denny's son, remembered the Morgan pranks: "You know, life on the road for a country music entertainer is not all applause—sometimes it gets pretty boring. You've got to go from one town to the next and pretty soon all the towns get to look a whole lot alike, and the inside of a Holiday Inn is pretty much the same in every town. So the people on the road would find ways to amuse themselves.

"George Morgan's show expanded a bit and he finally bought a second limo— this was the days before the big buses. To amuse themselves they would drive down the road side by side, and open the windows, and throw eggs at each other as they went on down the road."

Chocolate-coated cherries, too, another story has it.

Backstage at the Opry, though, the major George Morgan innovation was the "Ugly List."

Jeanne Pruett explained: "George would post his Ugly List every Friday night at the Opry. And before the show was over it was the gathering place for all of the backstage people. We'd all gang around the bulletin board to see who was on George's Ugly List. He had a list from [number] fifty to number one. And I used to stay after him all the time because I wanted to be on his list so bad; it was a place of honor because George only put people on there that he really cared about.

"And I can remember one Friday night when I came in there he had a little notation down at the bottom: 'Jeanne Pruett has been begging me for three years to get on the Ugly List just so she could see her name here. I can't really in good conscience put her on the list, but I am going to mention her name.'"

Vic Willis was often a confederate in Morgan's practical jokes and he had vivid memories of the Ugly List.

"Hal Durham made it every time." Willis laughed. "And there was this little drummer with Stu Phillips—Paul Russell, a good little drummer, a good entertainer. And Paul did everything a person could do to make himself look good. He wore stylish clothes, had his hair styled, and was always neat. But when he came on the Opry, George walked right up to him and said, 'Hello, my name is George Morgan. You're the ugliest SOB I ever saw! How would you like to be in the Ugly Hall of Fame?'

"So George put him one-two-three with a bullet. And he kept putting him on the list."

Daughter Lorrie Morgan remembered that Russell was sometimes "number one through nine, with a bullet. I mean, he was tops. He was Dad's Number-One Ugly."

Just before the Grand Ole Opry moved to its new home, George proudly introduced his daughter—full name: Loretta Lynn Morgan—for her Opry singing debut.

"I was thirteen years old," Lorrie recalled, "and it was down at the Ryman Auditorium. I was a little skeptical about doing it. I was real nervous and I really wasn't sure I wanted to sing. But I could sing and Dad asked me if I wanted to try to go on the stage. We got to the Opry House and I went and rehearsed the song 'Paper Roses' with the guitar player. And I was shaking. And Dad told me—he used to call me Fussy—'Now, Fussy, before I bring you on I'm gonna look at you over in the wings. And if you wanna come on you shake your head yes, and if you don't, no.'

"Well, I got a new dress and everything, but I still wasn't sure I was going on. So he went out there and he started talking about something and he looked over at me and I shook my head yes. And he introduced me. Before I went on I had asked my guitar player, 'What do I do if I get an encore?' 'Well, you won't,' he said, 'but if you do, you come back in and sing the chorus again.' So I went out and I sang and I got a standing ovation.

"And from then on I said, 'Okay, this is it!'

"I appeared with Dad sometime on the road and when they started having Opry guests out in Opryland park, I was on those shows quite a few times with him."

In May 1975 George Morgan suffered a heart attack while installing a television antenna on the roof of his Nashville home. He recovered sufficiently enough to return to the Opry in June, where his friends celebrated his fifty-first birthday on the stage. But then he learned that he needed open heart surgery and entered Baptist Hospital in Nashville in early July.

There were complications. He died on July 7.

Vic Willis again: "After George died we kept putting up the Ugly List every week, in his memory, you know. And we kept putting Paul Russell's name on it every week, the way George used to.

"But I got worried about it; I thought maybe we were overdoing it. I went to Paul and said, 'Paul, do you want me to stop all this stuff?' And he said, 'Why?' And I said, 'Well, it might have gone too far.' He said, 'Naw! Vic, till George started the Ugly List stuff nobody paid any attention to me. And now I got a lot of friends down here.'"

⌁⟦ V ⟧⌁ On Saturday night, April 2, 1977, eighty-seven-year-old Vito Mario Pellettieri worked the Grand Ole Opry as its stage manager. But he was ill; his duties had become largely "honorary," the old gruffness lost in age.

It was to be his last night at the Opry.

Not too many days later he suffered a stroke. He died on April 14.

It was difficult to assess his value for anyone who had not been associated with the Opry. But he was missed. And he was never replaced.

Eight years after his death, as the Grand Ole Opry approached its sixtieth anniversary, one of the veterans of the Opry roster bemoaned the lack of a tough stage manager: "I miss Vito. You know, we don't have a marshal anymore. What we have out there is a piece of paper in a box, with a list of the acts and when they're supposed to go on. But we don't have anybody encouraging us, goading us, giving us advice on how to do better. Nobody to jack us up."

The second half of the seventies took a terrible toll on the Opry family: George Morgan and Vito Pellettieri, and Skeeter Willis of the Willis Brothers, and Sam McGee, and Bob Luman (only forty years old at his death), and Lester Flatt, and Mother Maybelle Carter, and Lefty Frizzell, and Hattie Louise "Tootsie" Bess, the flamboyant owner of the old hangout across the alley from the Ryman, Tootsie's Orchid Lounge.

And, of course, the young man from Memphis who had found the Grand Ole Opry such a bitter disappointment: Elvis Presley.

⁂[vi]⁂ But if there was any proof needed as the eighties approached that the Opry still had power and influence, it came when the executives of the Public Broadcasting System approached their counterparts at the Grand Ole Opry with a startling proposal. They wanted to do what had never been done before: put an entire evening of the Grand Ole Opry on television!

PBS, faced with ever-increasing cuts in appropriations from the federal government, needed to expand the base of its subscribers. It needed to reach people, for contributions, it had never been able to reach before: grass-roots America, as it were. PBS could best do that, it was thought, with the Grand Ole Opry.

Thus, on Saturday, March 4, 1978, the Opry was fully on TV, carried coast to coast, just as it happened, on the PBS network. The only real concession to television came when PBS "covered" the radio commercials with backstage interviews and features.

Pledges to contribute to PBS poured in on the telephone lines. It was so successful that it was repeated again in March 1979, 1980, and 1981.

*Here she comes, look at her roll,
There she goes, eatin' that coal;
Watch her fly, huggin' the rail,
Let her by, by, by—the Fireball Mail.**

—Country music standard, circa 1943

ith the coming of the 1980s, and the Grand Ole Opry firmly established in its lavish home, there was a new image inherent in country music. It was fashionable now in the broad sweep of the nation; it was no longer an embarrassment to be recognized as a country music fan.

There were some unique things happening in country music. In January 1980 ancient comedian George Burns reached the country charts with his nostalgic recording of "I Wish I Was Eighteen Again." And no less than three major motion pictures—all successes at the box office—advanced the cause of country music.

One was *Urban Cowboy*, starring John Travolta, a good portion of it filmed at Mickey Gilley's giant country music honky-tonk in Pasadena, Texas. It started a western-clothing fad in the cities; but perhaps more important, it passed on a message to urban dwellers that it was really okay to like country music.

Another important film was *9 to 5*, with a story line about sexual harassment of women office workers. It marked the highly successful motion picture debut of Grand Ole Opry star Dolly Parton, who also wrote the movie's theme song and whose record of it would go to number one on the popularity charts.

*"Fireball Mail" by Floyd Jenkins (a.k.a. Fred Rose); copyright 1943 Milene/Opryland Music, Inc.

And then there was *Coal Miner's Daughter*, a film adaptation of Loretta Lynn's best-selling autobiography. Filmed in Tennessee and Kentucky, it starred Sissy Spacek as Loretta (eventually winning Spacek the Best Actress Oscar of the Academy of Motion Picture Arts and Sciences), Tommy Lee Jones as Loretta's husband, Mooney Lynn, and Beverly D'Angelo as Opry star Patsy Cline.

Coal Miner's Daughter had its world premiere in Nashville on March 4, 1980; it was the occasion for much pride demonstrated within the Grand Ole Opry family.

The successes of those two women—Lynn and Parton—both nurtured by the Opry, serves to mirror what had happened to country music over the years. Not only has it become acceptable, but it has also shed its poverty roots, leading to life-styles of which a young Roy Acuff or a young Minnie Pearl could not even have dreamed.

···❴ ii ❵··· It's almost impossible to equate the Loretta Webb born into the grinding poverty of the coal-mining settlement of Butcher Holler, Kentucky, with the Loretta Lynn of today. For the two entities are light-years apart.

"When I first came to Nashville," Loretta said, "people called us 'hillbilly singers' and hardly gave country music any respect. We lived in old cars and dirty hotels, and we ate when we could. Now country music is big business. Why, they've even got a country music station in New York City. So I've seen country music go uptown, and I'm proud I was there when it happened."

Uptown, indeed!

Today Loretta owns a 3,500-acre ranch in Tennessee, which includes the entire small town of Hurricane Mills; a seaside home in Mazatlán, Mexico; and a hunting lodge in British Columbia. And the old cars are gone too. When she goes on the road now it's in a long, luxurious traveling home, a custom-fitted bus featuring bathrooms and bedrooms and TV and stereo tape decks.

Loretta calls all of that her "glamorous" life, as if it were separate from her, because she never forgets her humble beginnings. She doesn't want to forget; it's an inextricable part of her.

Which is not unlike Dolly Parton, who has come her own light-years away from a mountain cabin in the hills of east Tennessee to wealth and superstardom. And with all the trappings: luxury apartments in New York City and southern California, first-class travel accommodations, glamorous clothes and jewelry.

But the hill country is always in her. She's now the developer and owner of a theme amusement park near Pigeon Forge in east Tennessee, Dollywood. And country music fans have made it a success.

More glib than Loretta, perhaps more sophisticated, Dolly nevertheless remembers her beginnings. "I learned about the facts of life in the barn," she told an interviewer. "We had uncles and cousins that were maybe two or three years older than us that knew a lot of stuff. As soon as we got a chance, we'd try it."

She's adept at poking fun at herself: "I patterned my look after Cinderella,

Mother Goose, and the local hooker." Of her ample bosom, she says: "No silicone injections. There ain't that much plastic in the world. When somebody says that a doctor claims he did it, I always say that plastic surgeons are all alike, they're always making mountains out of molehills."

Dolly is not awed by her successes in Hollywood. "This town doesn't own me," she said. "If you know who you are and you know what you can do, you can't be sucked in. I'm a happier person than most out here. I can make my own rules. If it gets to the point where I feel burdened or troubled or used in any way, Hollywood can kiss my ———.''

In the fall of 1987, Dolly was selected by ABC television to headline a new musical variety show, a category that had all but disappeared from network schedules. It was a recognition of Parton's universal appeal.

It should not be imagined, however, that Lynn and Parton are the only ones of wealth in country music today. The fashionable suburbs of Nashville are crammed with big homes owned by Grand Ole Opry artists, or former Opry stars. Luxury touring buses are commonplace. And more than a few who have come up through the roster of the Grand Old Opry are certifiable millionaires.

Yet there have been signs all through the eighties that George D. Hay's frequently voiced admonition—"Keep it close to the ground"—had not been forgotten. The more earthy country music, the more traditional sounds, were returning.

··❦〖 iii 〗❦·· His name was Lecil Travis Martin and he was born on September 1, 1931, in Sterratt, Texas, in a little frame house hard by the railroad tracks. And now there he was on June 19, 1980—some forty-nine years later—dressed as a hobo, calling himself "Boxcar Willie," and making his *debut* at the Grand Ole Opry.

It had been a long road, indeed, from Sterratt to Nashville, to the realization of his greatest dream.

There was no bitterness that it had taken him so long. And no apologies for what he was: 99 $^{44}/_{100}$ percent pure country. There was nothing but joy in his recollections of that night.

"I had played the Wembley Festival in England," Boxcar said, "and Wesley Rose saw me there. And he said, 'Would you like to be on the Opry?' I said, 'Man, I've been trying to get on there forty years.' He said, 'You come to see me when you get to Nashville. I want Acuff to meet you.' Of course, Mr. Acuff had never seen me work, you know.

"I almost beat Wesley back to Nashville. And he set up a ten-minute interview with Mr. Acuff down at his office. Roy came in and that ten-minute session lasted over three hours. He and I just set there and talked. And he asked me questions about my life, my family, my desires, my dreams, and when he got through he stood up and he said, 'I'd be proud to put you on the Grand Ole Opry.' And I just—I couldn't believe it, you know.

Hal Durham, General Manager of the Grand Ole Opry, welcomes the "hobo singer," Boxcar Willie, to the cast in 1981.

(1981) WSM PHOTO/LES LEVERETT

George Morgan (center), who joined the Opry in 1948, quickly made a name for himself as the preeminent practical joker backstage. Here he is with Bobby Osborne (left) at the Grand Ole Opry Birthday Celebration.

(1968) WSM PHOTO/LES LEVERETT

Backstage at the Ryman Auditorium, Dolly Parton reminisces with other country music women about the old days of the Opry for a taping of her ABC television show. From the left, Del Wood, Jan Howard, Skeeter Davis, Minnie Pearl, Dolly Parton, Jeanne Pruett, Norma Jean, and Jean Shepard.

(1988) DONNIE BEAUCHAMP

"That first night then—well, I've had similar feelings when I looked at my children when they were born. It's a hard feeling to describe. How do you describe when you look down and see your wife laying there, and she's got a little boy and a little girl on each arm? And they're both healthy and she's all right. How do you describe that feeling?

"But then comes the nail-biting. And the stomach butterflies. I've never been so nervous in my life."

He paused, searching for the words. "I kept getting up out of the dressing room and going backstage, and standing looking out at that stage, and my mouth was just like cotton. I mean cotton-cotton! And Jimmy Riddle was standing right beside me—bless his heart. He said, 'Are you nervous?' And I said, 'I'm scared to death.' He said, 'I always chew gum when I'm nervous.' He handed me a stick of chewing gum. I don't think I could have gone out on the stage, my mouth was so dry, but that chewing gum loosened it all up.

"And Mr. Acuff started introducing me, and I thought, 'I can live up to that introduction.' This man had never seen me play, you know. If his introduction had lasted fifteen more seconds, I think I'd have fainted. But he introduced me and, as I live and breathe, it's only . . . what? . . . thirty feet from the wings to the center stage? No, it's two miles!" A laugh. "If it's a foot, it's two miles. And the more I walked the farther it got. The microphone kept getting smaller and smaller.

"And I finally got to center stage. I didn't say nothing; I couldn't. I started my rhythm on the guitar and I 'blew' the train whistle. The train medley lasts two minutes and forty-eight seconds, right? No, it don't. It lasts two hours and four weeks!"

Boxcar's train medley, a tribute to the preoccupation there has always been in country music with the lore of the steam engine, encompassed "Fireball Mail," "Train of Love," "Walking Cane," "Wreck of the Old 97," "Orange Blossom Special," "Wabash Cannonball," and "Night Train to Memphis." It brought the audience to its feet.

"When I got through," he went on, "I didn't want to immediately run off the stage, I wanted to linger just a little bit, you know. The applause was thunderous. And I looked out and I swear to God I saw my mama! Standing there, smiling. I mean, I didn't see her, but in my mind I knew she was there. And the people were standing up and they were applauding. I started crying. I couldn't help it.

"Acuff brought me back to the microphone and I *knew* I couldn't say a word. He made me stand there and he put his arm around me, and they were still applauding. When they got quiet, Roy said, 'They wanna hear you do another one.'

"I'm not smart enough to describe how I felt; I don't have the education. I don't know that many adjectives. It was unbelievable. A dream, you know. I promised Mama—I guess I was probably ten—that someday I would be on the Opry. And it took forty years to keep that promise. It's seven hundred miles from the Opry House to my home and it took me forty years to get those seven hundred miles. A centipede could have made it faster."

But where had he been for those forty years?

"I can't remember when I didn't sing," he said. "I did my first radio broadcast when I was about ten years old, and my dad played fiddle. I just grew up singin' and playin'."

But reaching his goal of the Grand Ole Opry was an odyssey: Some Texas honky-tonks at thirteen; a brief stint on the "Big D Jamboree"; a tour of duty in the Air Force (he became a pilot); a disillusioning experience on the "Cowtown Hoedown" in Fort Worth, where "everybody wanted to sing rock 'n' roll"; a second tour of duty in the Air Force; two years on a daily live country music television show in Lincoln, Nebraska; and then a job in Idaho as a country music disc jockey, calling himself Marty Martin.

"KGEM in Boise, one of the Intermountain Network stations," he explained. "I was there almost ten years. In 1964 Ernie Ashworth submitted my name for what used to be a thing called 'Mr. DJ, USA.' The Grand Ole Opry would bring in a disc jockey each week. He would do the Friday-night show with Grant Turner and they would present him on the Ryman stage Saturday night, for a bow, you know. Kinda wine and dine him. And in turn, hell, we pushed the Grand Ole Opry.

"It was a big thing, because I went back to Boise and I was a big thing: 'Hey, Marty Martin wins Mr. DJ, USA! This ole boy must be pretty good. We'd better buy some spots on his program.' "

But even being a successful disc jockey had its limitations. In 1970, having married an Idaho girl, he moved back to Texas, continuing the odyssey: work as a refrigeration mechanic; flying with the Air National Guard; a year in Spain as an instructor for the Spanish air force; an auto repair business in Texas; and back to being a disc jockey again.

Then, in 1975, Marty and his wife were watching the Country Music Association awards telecast from Nashville in their Fort Worth home. Entertainer of the Year honors went to pop singer John Denver, who accepted via satellite from Australia, where he was on tour. The Texas viewer was disgruntled. Turning off the TV set, he said to his wife: "Honey, I'm going to win a major country music award within five years."

And he went into his bedroom and slid a box from under the bed. In it were a beat-up hat, overalls, and a ragged coat—the costume of Boxcar Willie.

"I had the idea for many years before that, even had the costume under the bed," he said. "But it took that moment in the CMA awards for me to decide to put all the other work aside and decide that I was not going to disc jockey anymore, not going to be a mechanic, not going to fly airplanes, but to devote a hundred fifty percent of my time to being Boxcar Willie!"

He struggled, but plugged away every waking moment promoting the character of Boxcar Willie. Nashville record producers weren't interested in a hobo singer. But in 1977, during the period of the annual Grand Ole Opry Birthday Celebration, Boxcar Willie made an appearance at George Jones's Possum Holler nightclub.

"The reception was just out of this world," Boxcar recalled. "And that's where Drew Taylor, a booking agent from England, first saw me. He was looking for an unknown, and I was about as unknown as anybody, but he thought I'd be good for the British audience. So we made a deal and I went over there in 1978."

What had been planned as a seventeen-day tour turned into thirty-four days. As a matter of fact, he made three thirty-day tours of England that year. In '79, now as popular as any country act in Britain, he was a smash hit at the Wembley Festival. And the next year he was back at Wembley: "When I just walked out on the stage that time I got a standing ovation."

Enter Wesley Rose, the long, warm interview with Roy Acuff, and the June 1980 debut at the Grand Ole Opry. On February 21, 1981, he was added to the Opry roster.

And the major award he had promised his wife?

In the spring of 1981 he was named the Most Promising Male Vocalist on the nationally televised *Music City News* awards show.

At age fifty.

§[iv]§ January 1981 brought some disquieting news. Marty Robbins suffered his second heart attack.

It was diagnosed as a mild attack, not requiring additional surgery, but doctors ordered him to cancel his February schedule of personal appearances, and to give up any idea that he would ever drive a race car again.

In March his career was resumed and the big bus that carried the self-deprecating sign on the front "No One You Ever Heard Of" was on the road once more.

§[v]§ "I made sure to stand on the circle from the stage of the old Ryman," John Conlee said of his first appearance on the Grand Old Opry. "That circle had been so important to me because so many big stars had stood on that wooden flooring."

Conlee was thirty-four years old when he came to the Opry roster in February 1981, and he admitted that he was somewhat different from earlier performers on the radio show. He was a child of the television era, "so the Opry was not a ritual of every Saturday night tuning in, but my dad was an Opry fan. There was a time when the Opry was more important to a career than it is now. All of the record-seller acts of an earlier day were a part of the Opry. Unfortunately, that wasn't true anymore."

There was no doubt, however, that John was a *country* singer. There was a rich, powerful voice; some compared it to Merle Haggard's. But he could belt out a song, clearly enunciating every word, and in that sense he was not unlike a young Acuff. He was John Conlee first, though, and not an approximation of any other singer. His own man.

For one thing, he was a licensed funeral director in his native Kentucky. "Usually, when you say 'funeral director' or 'undertaker,'" he said, "you associate those words with death. But the funeral is not for the dead person—it's for the family left behind. And as long as you look at it that way, it's very self-satisfying work because you're dealing with people when they're at their worst. In many respects, once you've helped a family through a situation, you're thought of as someone just below their minister. They kind of hold you in reverence. And there's a lot of satisfaction in that; thinking that, maybe, you're helping people through a tough time. I still keep my licenses up and I always will."

Yet there was another side to young Conlee. Every Saturday morning when he was a youngster, his mother would take him and his sister from Versailles, Kentucky, to Lexington for guitar lessons.

"That was a shopping day for Mom," John explained. "She'd go out and hit all the stores in downtown Lexington, which means we ate up half a day every Saturday. Well, after the guitar lesson—which was only thirty minutes—I had time to kill. So I started hanging out at the local radio station across the street. That's where I fell in love with radio, and wore my family out with it because I'd take old news copy home with me out of the trash basket and all week long, instead of practicing guitar probably as much as I should have, I'd be up in my room—pretending to be an announcer."

As an adult, the pretending ended. After six years as a funeral director, he decided to take a gamble with radio "at a little ole station in Fort Knox. And I certainly don't regret the move."

He moved on to stations in Elizabethtown, Kentucky, then in his hometown of Versailles, and eventually to Nashville. Being a disc jockey in Music City was a definite plus for him: "It was a means of making contact with people on Music Row, more than I could if I was clerking in a hotel. I had a reason to meet them and they had a reason to know me."

He was known first as a songwriter. Joe Stampley cut Conlee's "Backside of Thirty" in the mid-seventies without a great deal of success. Success would come when Conlee started to record on his own for ABC Records in the latter part of '76.

" 'Backside of Thirty' was my first release," Conlee recalled. "It didn't make it at all—just three or four markets. Next was 'Let Your Love Fall Back on Me.' The third one was a thing called 'The In Crowd.' Not the old rock-'n'-roll song, but a totally different song that Tommy Cash also released after I did. It didn't work for either one of us." Conlee laughed.

"Then 'Rose Colored Glasses' took off."

An understatement: "Rose Colored Glasses," which John cowrote with George Baber, was a smash hit—fully two and a half years after it had been recorded!

There hadn't been a lot of singing artists added to the Grand Ole Opry roster since the move to the new house in Opryland. But in 1981 Opry manager Hal Durham reached out for John Conlee.

·◦⟦ vi ⟧◦· That same year, wrecking balls and bulldozers began to raze the old headquarters building of the National Life and Accident Insurance Company in downtown Nashville. Disappearing forever would be the original studios of WSM Radio and, of course, the original "homes" of the Grand Ole Opry.

And on November 3, 1981, WSM Television (WSM-TV, Channel 4) became the property of the big Gillett Broadcasting Company. Executive Bud Wendell explained: "We sold it on the basis that we felt we had developed a good deal of expertise in production of television programming. We did an awful lot of live television, both on our station and as the Opryland Productions unit grew. We thought that there was going to be a future in programming on cable television; we thought there was a desire out there on people's part for more country music programming.

"Obviously, the networks had got out of variety show programming, the syndicated country music shows had somewhat dried up, but we staunchly believed that if we put out a good product there was an audience out there and we were the logical people to get into that area. We had great optimism about the future of cable television.

"So we sold the television station to get the seed money, the capital, to build The Nashville Network."

It was not to be the last such corporate development.

Show me where I start,
Find a horse and cart,
I'm just a country boy,
*Country boy at heart.**

—Ricky Skaggs hit

It's a pleasure to take part in this salute to the King of Country Music, Roy Acuff," the President of the United States said from the White House. "Roy, a product of the hills of east Tennessee, is the epitome of the American dream."

It was the evening of March 1, 1982, and the Grand Ole Opry's most enduring star was being honored in a two-hour special telecast on the NBC network.

The program was in the planning stages for months, long enough to have been the impetus for a "roast" of Acuff planned by the Buddies of Nashville in the preceding September, when some of the out-of-town stars were in the city for TV tapings. A crowd of some 700 paid $100 each for the charity event at the Hyatt Regency Hotel.

Everyone tried valiantly to really "roast" Acuff, but they all had trouble with it. Minnie Pearl set the tone: "Roast Roy Acuff? It's very hard for me to roast someone who's the dearest friend I have in the world. He's one of the finest men

*"Country Boy" by Tony Colton, Ray Smith, and Albert Lee; copyright 1977 Island Music Ltd., London, England; USA rights, Ackee Music, Inc.

who ever lived. Instead of a roast, I'd say a toast—a toast to the King of Country Music!"

But a lot tried lighthearted jokes. Vice-President George Bush: "You know the East Tennessee Wilderness Act? That was the act Roy was caught committing in east Tennessee."

Tennessee's Democratic U.S. senator, Jim Sasser, poked fun at Acuff's 1948 gubernatorial campaign: "Roy was quoted in the press as saying he didn't really understand the issues. And that's when the Republicans decided he was the man to run."

Tennessee's Republican U.S. senator, Howard Baker, whose father was Acuff's campaign manager: "The first time Roy was in Huntsville he asked my dad, 'How's the campaign going? How're we doing?' My father said, 'Roy, they're telling lies on us and they're proving part of it.' "

Nashville mayor Richard Fulton: "Roy, when you introduced me to sing on the Grand Ole Opry, I decided you were about the dumbest man I'd ever seen."

(Fulton announced that Hawkins Street in the Music Row area would be renamed Roy Acuff Place. "It's only one block long, and it dead-ends," the mayor said, laughing. "We thought Roy Acuff *Place* was better than street or drive since it didn't go anywhere.")

Cowboy star Gene Autry: "Roy Acuff has been on radio so long that when Marconi invented it and turned it on, the first damned thing he heard was Roy singing 'Wabash Cannonball.' "

Chet Atkins: "There was the time Roy was signing autographs at Opryland, and a country boy said, 'I bet you wish you had a dollar for every one of those you signed.' And Roy said, 'I have.' "

But most didn't even try to roast the venerable Acuff. When it came down to the last speaker of the night, bearded Charlie Daniels, his cowboy hat pulled low over his eyes, summed it up: "I idolized him. He's everything good to me in country music. I admire him with all my heart."

There were two particular cases in which performers who had been booked had to pull out at the last minute. Dottie West got laryngitis and was so guilt-stricken about having to cancel that she insisted her doctor hand-deliver an affidavit of her affliction to the producers. And Johnny Cash was rendered *hors de combat* by a kick in the ribs from a full-grown ostrich at his small game preserve near Hendersonville. The ostrich was a male named Waldo who recently lost his mate. The newspapers had fun with that one.

But on the show itself more than thirty stars cavorted with Acuff: He sang "That Silver-Haired Daddy of Mine" with Tom T. Hall and Chet Atkins in a mini-salute to the visiting Gene Autry, played a fiddle duet with Charlie Daniels on "Fireball Mail"; warbled with Crystal Gayle on a song he had introduced for his partner, Fred Rose, "Blue Eyes Crying in the Rain"; traded quips with Dolly Parton about making movies in Hollywood; sang "I Saw the Light" with Hall of Fame comrades Grandpa Jones, Minnie Pearl, Chet Atkins, Pee Wee King, Merle Travis, Kitty Wells, and Ernest Tubb; reprised a song from the last record he had released, "I Wonder If God Likes Country Music?," a duet with Bill Anderson; and worked with his Smoky Mountain Boys on "The Great Speckled Bird," "Wabash Cannonball," and "Down Yonder."

President Ronald Reagan's words set the tone for it all: "Roy Acuff has been the troubadour of the American people—out there on the highway at the wheel of a truck, in the mill, the factory, and on the farm. His songs have told their stories—of their disappointments, of their triumphs, of their loves, of their faith. And each year more than eight hundred thousand of them come from all corners of the nation to see Roy Acuff at the Grand Ole Opry."

At the very end, Tom T. Hall, "The Storyteller," introduced his latest composition:

> *You're the king of country music Smoky*
> > *Mountain boy,*
> *You climbed that hill with happiness and pain;*
> *You're the king of country music Smoky*
> > *Mountain boy.*
> *You sung your way into the Hall of Fame.*

Tom couldn't resist a closing editorial:

> *The movies tried to make you change your style,*
> *Some made fun of your music and your ways;*
> *Lookin' back, it makes us want to smile,*
> *'Cause the whole damned country's country*
> > *today.**

ii In May 1982 the Grand Ole Opry took a hard right turn along the road to the "traditional" country music Roy Acuff represented. It signed to the roster a twenty-eight-year-old bluegrass musician and singer who had been raised along Brushy Creek at Cordell, Kentucky.

His name was Ricky Skaggs.

"That was a childhood dream of mine," Skaggs said. "Because I used to go to sleep on my grandfather's lap listening to the Grand Ole Opry in his Ford pickup truck out by the barn. We'd pull away from the house where all the electric lines were and we'd pull down to the barn, and he would turn his radio on—an old tube radio that he had in his pickup—and, of course, Nashville always came and went, you know, the frequency and the signal would just come and go up in those Kentucky mountains.

"But, you know, when it would come back in, you'd hear Earl Scruggs playing the banjo—it was the greatest sound in the world. And I used to listen to that.

*"The King of Country Music" by Tom T. Hall; copyright 1981 Hallnote Music Company, Inc.

I'd been playing since I was five years old, when I played with Bill Monroe up in Martha, Kentucky, in a little high school.

"When I was seven my dad had moved us down to Nashville to try to further my career, to try to get me on the Opry. They wouldn't let me on it because I was too young. But Flatt and Scruggs heard me backstage one night at the old Ryman and said, 'Well, come down an' do an audition for the television show.' That was the Martha White show. I did and I was good enough to play on their TV show."

The precocious and highly talented young man could not be stopped. At the age of fifteen he joined the important bluegrass group the Stanley Brothers, hired by Ralph Stanley after the untimely death of his brother, Carter. It was with that act that he first stepped on the Ryman stage, appearing on the Roy Acuff segment of the Opry show when he was seventeen years old. But it was a tough life: exhausting travel, long hours of work, short pay. He quit the Stanley Brothers and moved to Washington, D.C.

There he was recruited by the Country Gentlemen, an innovative group that was heading up what was called the "newgrass movement." It was traditional bluegrass married to young musical talent of the seventies. It was what he had been looking for; it was the stimulation he needed to progress. After that he played with J. D. Crowe and the New South until he formed his own group, Boone Creek. By age twenty-five he was known by insiders as a musician's musician.

Emmylou Harris asked Skaggs to join her Hot Band in late 1977. One of his first assignments with her was working on the famed Dolly Parton/Linda Ronstadt/ Emmylou Harris trio album. Under her guidance he became a seasoned commercial performer. The public started to become aware of him; for the North Carolina label Sugar Hill he released a solo LP, and he was no longer a background musician.

In the spring of 1981 he was asked to debut at the Grand Ole Opry.

"I had just left Emmylou's Hot Band," he recalled, "and I had a couple of singles out, one of them being 'I'll Take the Blame,' and it was really doing well in Nashville. It had gone to number one in Houston. Also the *Sweet Temptation* album was getting a lot of airplay.

"Hal Durham asked me to be a guest on the Opry and, boy, I was very into doing that, you know.

"I had just started to put my own band together and it wasn't ready yet, but I had the Whites—Sharon and Cheryl came out and sang background with me on 'I'll Take the Blame.' Emmylou Harris was in town and she came out with me on the second song, 'Could You Love Me One More Time.' It was a very touching time, a very beautiful experience. I also did 'Sweet Temptation,' and the fans really responded. It was a very moving time for me. I felt welcomed."

Welcomed he was. By May 1982 came the invitation to join the Opry roster.

"I was on the Ernest Tubb part of the Opry that night," Ricky said, "and Ernest read a couple of telegrams. Bill Monroe sent a telegram in, saying he was very happy that I was being a part of the Grand Ole Opry family. It was just a . . . well, you know, the Opry was the only place in the world that made me nervous.

"And I don't ever—ever!—want to get to the point where I can't come and play the Opry, where I feel like I'm too good to play the Opry. Mr. Acuff said that I would do that. He said, 'You'll get so big you'll do just like all the rest of them.' And I said, 'You don't know me. You just watch me and see. I'm not made that way. I didn't join the Opry for that.'"

···𝄢 iii 𝄢··· On June 19, 1982, the Opry added another young act with traditional roots: Riders in the Sky.

With a keen appreciation of the western side of what once was known as country-and-western music, the trio of Ranger Doug Green, Woody Paul, and Too Slim (his real handle is Fred LaBour) not only brought the songs of Gene Autry, Roy Rogers, Tex Ritter, and the Sons of the Pioneers back to the Grand Ole Opry, but also added their own brand of broad humor to the Opry proceedings.

One thing is certain about the Riders in the Sky: They do not take themselves seriously. Their music, yes. Their own personas, no. They have fun on the stage. The audience benefits from that.

Ranger Doug, the emcee of the group, is the Douglas B. Green who wrote the 1976 book *Country Roots: The Origins of Country Music* while he was on the staff of the Library and Media Center of the Country Music Foundation. Gerry Wood, writing in *Billboard*, said: "With respect and reverence for the roots, Green paints an historically accurate portrait of what has happened and will happen in country music. A valuable enlightening chronology."

In light of that, then, it seemed that Green was the logical man to ask for an opinion on what makes the Grand Ole Opry so special.

"It beats me." Doug chuckled. "It just comes so loaded with tradition and emotion and feeling for anybody who cares the least little bit about country music. The first time we were on it was just a magical experience. We guested on the Opry twenty-five times and then they made us members in June of '82, and it's still a magical experience. It's still really wonderful. I'm not as scared as I used to be, but you just feel like you're part of this continuous line of tradition."

Woody Paul added: "I remember when we joined we had been playing a lot on the road. We played in Texas at noon and they chartered a plane and flew us to Fort Worth to get a plane to come be here our first night as members of the Opry. When we walked in at seven o'clock, Hal Durham said, 'Welcome home.' He was sincere about it and suddenly we were just part of this great family."

"You know, the old-timers say it was a lot more intimate in the old days," Green interjected. "I hear that so much that I have to believe it's true."

Paul thought it might have to do with the environment: "I think at the Ryman it was a warmer audience to perform for. I think it's more difficult to establish that feel here in the new house."

Ranger Doug nodded agreement. "When we did this part in the *Sweet Dreams* movie, re-creating the life of Patsy Cline, we were on the Ryman stage as the Opry backup singers—that was the Riders in the Sky's part of the movie—and to be back on that stage we realized how the people are right on top of you. The stage is so compressed there."

··◦[iv]◦·· There was not much fun, though, in the disquieting news of July 1982, which revealed that the stable foundation of the Grand Ole Opry—the National Life and Accident Insurance Company—had been acquired by a major Houston-based insurance firm, American General Corporation.

In the sort of corporate takeover that had become so fashionable in financial circles, American General was the owner of the assets of the NLT Corporation, the holding-company entity of National Life. Included in those assets, of course, was the profitable insurance company. But to the Grand Ole Opry family it also meant that the Opry itself, the Opryland amusement park, the Opryland Hotel, radio station WSM, the new Music Country Radio Network (a joint venture of WSM and Associated Press), Grand Ole Opry Tours, and the soon-to-be-completed Nashville Network cable television facility were now part and parcel of a company without a Nashville orientation.

What did all of that mean to the future of the Grand Ole Opry? New rumors, many of them foreboding, surfaced almost daily.

Bud Wendell remembered: "American General . . . [is] primarily and totally in the business of selling insurance, and so here was an entertainment complex that didn't fit the rest of their structure. They made the announcement that they would sell it. It was that simple!"

Now the rumors and the fiscal shuffling reached a fever pitch. "First of all," Wendell said, "Walter Robinson, who was the CEO of the old NLT, attempted to put together a local group to acquire us, but that didn't work out. And the American General people had hired First Boston investment bankers to oversee the sale of the Opryland complex. They brought twenty or thirty prospective buyers through." Wendell laughed. "I devoted a year of my life to tours of the properties."

Wendell and his associates weren't the only ones concerned about what might happen. Tennessee governor Lamar Alexander was also upset.

"When word got out that the Texans who bought NLT would sell the Opry, I was worried," he said, "and so were a lot of other Tennesseans. I interrupted a family vacation and flew to Houston to talk to a board meeting of American General. . . . All the way to Houston I was thinking, 'Just what can I say to these Texas business people—most of whom have probably never been to the Opry—to explain what the Opry means to Tennesseans?'

"By the time I arrived I knew just what to say. 'Think of it this way,' I told the American General board of directors. 'For us, selling the Opry would be like Texas selling the Alamo. All I can ask, on behalf of millions of people, is that you be mighty careful with it when you let somebody else have it.' "

v But life at the Opry went on. And death.

On July 2 DeFord Bailey died in Nashville at the age of eighty-two. Nashville newspapers carried page-one obituaries of the black harmonica player who had had such a vital role in the earliest years of the Grand Ole Opry.

Bailey had been admitted to Baptist Hospital on June 7, gasping for breath. Doctors said the musician's kidneys and heart were failing, and that his lungs were congested. They offered little hope for his recovery.

He was released from the hospital on June 29 and taken to the home of a daughter, Dezoral (Dee) Thomas. On Friday of that week he died in Mrs. Thomas's arms, as another daughter, Christine Bailey Craig, stood by his side.

Mrs. Thomas told reporters: "He was such a beautiful little man. I'd say, 'Hey, old man, how you doin'?' He was always dressed in a three-piece suit and a hat to match, and always had those shined shoes. I'd say, 'You could just die right now and we could put you right into the casket,' and we'd just laugh.

"I sure hate to see him go. The legend is finally gone."

Only a few months earlier, in April, DeFord made his last appearance on the Opry stage, working a reunion show of old-timers. He played "Pan American Blues," his signature; "Fox Chase"; and "It Ain't Gonna Rain No Mo'."

No one got a bigger ovation than did DeFord Bailey.

His death revived the controversy about the failure of the country music community to elect him to the Country Music Hall of Fame.

John Egerton, who wrote the 1979 bicentennial history of the city, *Nashville: The Faces of Two Centuries*, said: "It would be a tragic miscarriage if the industry failed to honor Bailey. This man was not a Johnny One-Note, and people in country music ought to be embarrassed for their gallery of heroes to remain all white. They owe too much to black musicians and black music."

David Morton, a Dallas housing planner who became a friend of DeFord's while seeking his doctorate at Vanderbilt University, said: "Not only does he belong in the Hall of Fame because of his firsts, but because he was a fixture, a mainstay, of the Opry from its beginning until its thrust changed in the early 1940s. Aside from Uncle Dave Macon, Mr. Bailey was the most popular artist on the Opry during that time."

The "firsts" Morton spoke of involved the fact that Bailey was the first performer to play on the WSM radio show after George D. Hay had dubbed it "The Grand Ole Opry" in 1928. Further, he was involved in the first recording session in Nashville history, when RCA field technicians came to town in October 1926 and recorded not only Bailey, but also the Binkley Brothers' Clodhoppers and Paul Warmack and the Gully Jumpers.

A year after his death, there was a twin celebration in Nashville in memory of DeFord Bailey. For one, a monument was unveiled at his gravesite in Nashville's Greenwood Cemetery, as Bill Monroe and Herman Crook played the music DeFord loved.

For another, there was a reception at the Country Music Foundation to receive the donation of some of Bailey's personal effects: the megaphone he used in performance, a short film of him in later years, a couple of hats, a business card from his shoeshine stand, a walking cane that folded into a chair, and a series of photos taken by Nashville photographer Dennis Wile.

But as of this writing, DeFord Bailey's name still has not been added to the Country Music Hall of Fame.

···**{ vi }**··· On October 11, 1982, Eddy Arnold announced from the stage of the Grand Ole Opry, during the Country Music Association awards show, that the newest member of the Country Music Hall of Fame was Marty Robbins.

Delighted, his face beaming, Marty came up from the audience. He was proud and at the same time humble.

"I never had any idea this would happen," he said, "because I feel there are other people that deserve it before I should get in. But I think possibly it might not happen again, so I'm gonna take it tonight!"

Less than two months after his induction into the Hall of Fame, Robbins suffered a third heart attack. Doctors performed a second bypass operation. It consumed eight and a half hours, but this time the damage was too severe. Although the hospital staff members reported that he fought valiantly to sustain life, he died on December 8.

His funeral was like none seen before in Nashville. Thousands of floral tributes filled every corner of the church. One was a checkered racing flag, made of black and white carnations, from Bobby Allison. Another was a huge white carnation map of Texas, with gold letters across it spelling out "El Paso." It was from Willie Nelson.

Marty's had been a full life. But had it been a totally satisfying one for him? Earlier, in a wide-ranging interview with music columnist Jack Hurst, he had mused about what he might have been in another time.

"If I could have been born a hundred years ago," Marty said, "when you had open range and could ride wherever you wanted to, I would have made a good drifter. Just traveling over the country, seeing it and working only when I had to . . . Yeah, I think about that sometimes."

The early eighties had been devastating years for the Grand Ole Opry family, taking Marty Robbins, and DeFord Bailey, and clog dancer Ralph Sloan, and Guy Willis, and Doyle Wilburn.

Sadly, the time for tears was not ended.

Where the tumbleweeds are growin'
I know it's there that I am goin' to stay;
I've been a Texan since my birth,
No place like it on this earth,
*I gotta go, I got Texas in my soul.**

—Ernest Tubb hit, 1947

Although 1983 began without a buyer for the Grand Ole Opry and the Opryland complex, plans for the beginning of The Nashville Network (TNN) had to move ahead. Too many millions were at risk to allow for any doubts.

On Monday, March 7, the country music cable television network kicked off with a five-hour live show, originating not only from Nashville, but also from New York City, Denver, Chicago, Los Angeles, and Austin, Texas.

David Hall, general manager of TNN, summed it up: "To my knowledge, the TNN launch was the most elaborate entertainment production since the Bicentennial—seven years ago. The talent assembled, the locations used, and the personnel required, outdo anything I can think of short of coverage of the Olympics or a national election."

Cable networking was a monumental gamble for the Opryland people. Even as the debut show was being aired, workers were rushing completion of a $5.8 million headquarters and studio building for TNN next to the Grand Ole Opry

*"Texas in My Soul" by Ernest Tubb and Zeb Turner; copyright 1947 Noma Music, Inc.

House. And the whole thing, the entire gamble, was begun with the belief that country music's universal appeal would make TNN a success.

As it turned out, that belief was correct, adding to the attractiveness of the Opryland complex for a potential new owner.

·◦⟨ ii ⟩◦· Friday, July 1, 1983, was a key date. Maybe the most important date in the saga of the Grand Ole Opry since Saturday, November 28, 1925, when WSM program director George D. Hay began what he called the "WSM Barn Dance."

American General Corporation of Houston announced there was a buyer for the Opryland complex: Gaylord Broadcasting Company of Dallas, Texas, a subsidiary of the Oklahoma Publishing Company of Oklahoma City.

Bud Wendell recalled: "Quite a few of the interested lookers were only interested in part of it—some only wanted the hotel, some only wanted the [amusement] park, some only wanted the park and Opry—the bits and pieces. But it works best when it's all held together. Now I had known the Gaylords because they came in [to Nashville] about twice a year when 'Hee Haw' was in production, and early on they said they would be interested in pursuing the acquisition if it could be worked out."

"The Gaylords" meant Edward L. Gaylord and his wife, Thelma, of one of America's largest privately owned newspaper and broadcasting enterprises. Among their holdings were the "Hee Haw" syndicated television series and Gaylord Productions, formed in 1979 to produce programs for television, including cable, and theaters.

Inevitably, there was much talk about how much money was spent to acquire the lock, stock, and barrel of the Opryland complex. The sale price was never announced. Newspapers, however, speculated that $250 million to $300 million had been expended for the multiple properties. No one ever came forward to dispute that speculation.

Later, in a TV appearance, Mr. Gaylord quipped that he had spoken of the purchase price to his wife over breakfast one morning. "The figure left her speechless," he said, "and that made it worth every penny of it."

◦⟨ iii ⟩◦ In 1984 the Opry added two new acts to the roster. One was Lorrie Morgan, daughter of the late George Morgan, the same Lorrie Morgan who made her singing debut on the stage of the Grand Ole Opry at the age of thirteen. The other was a family act solidly steeped in traditionalist sounds: the Whites.

The Whites were what one newspaper headlined "Just Plain Downhome Folks"—the father, Buck White, and his daughters, Sharon and Cheryl.

H. S. White ("I named myself Buck when I was about ten because I liked the old cowboy movie star Buck Jones") began his musical career as a western swing and country pianist in the forties, moonlighting from his construction business in Wichita Falls, Texas. He played as a sideman with the likes of Lefty Frizzell, Webb Pierce, Hank Snow, Ernest Tubb, and others "who would pick me up as an extra to play dances in northern Texas and southern Oklahoma when they'd come through."

But there wasn't any serious thought then that music would be his life. It was all just "fun" at the beginning: a Wichita Falls TV show with a couple of friends, some schoolhouse bookings nearby. In 1962 it began to turn around. Buck and his wife, Pat, decided to move to Greenwood, Arkansas, because it seemed a perfect place to raise their young daughters. Rural, quiet, traditionally American.

It was in Greenwood that Buck and Pat began a group they called the Down Home Folks, first with some friends and, then, as daughters Sharon and Cheryl grew into teenagers, it became more of a family act. "We played old country stuff," Buck said. "Bob Wills stuff, gospel stuff, some Bill Monroe stuff, and some Sons of the Pioneer stuff. When the girls got into high school they decided they wanted to sing professionally. That was okay with me. In 1971, after the idea had already been kicked around for several years, they said, 'Let's move up to Nashville.' So we did."

They started to record on small labels, turning out several bluegrass albums, and performing more and more on the road, building a solid reputation. In 1975 their touring took them to a concert in Washington, D.C., where they played on the same bill with Emmylou Harris. Sharon and Cheryl would eventually sing backup to Emmylou on one of her most successful albums, *Blue Kentucky Girl*.

In their association with Harris they renewed acquaintance with one of Emmylou's sidemen, Ricky Skaggs, who was about to burst out to stardom on his own. They had met him first years earlier when he was a teenager with Ralph Stanley's bluegrass band. The "Ricky Skaggs connection" was to be very important to them.

Sharon married Ricky in 1981. By the time the Whites joined the Opry, Sharon was pregnant with their first child. On March 8, 1984, Molly Kate Skaggs was born.

Three weeks later, Molly Kate, content in her mother's arms, was introduced to the public from the stage of the Grand Ole Opry.

Again—family.

iv Ernest Tubb, the Texas Troubadour, had not appeared on the Opry since August 14, 1982. Even his touring had ended. A long bout with emphysema had made him too ill to continue and he became something of a recluse because he refused to be seen in public with the oxygen tank he needed with him at all times.

E.T. was a proud man. He wanted no outpourings of public sympathy.

On Thursday, September 6, 1984, his long struggle ended at Nashville's Baptist Hospital. He was seventy years old.

Tubb's Grand Ole Opry compatriots were devastated. So was the entire country music community.

Willie Nelson said: "Ernest Tubb was one of my heroes. The first songs that I learned were out of Ernest Tubb songbooks. Before I was ever known he had asked me to come up and play on his Record Shop show. He was really a special person."

Waylon Jennings put it succinctly: "It's like the passing of the beginning."

The day after Tubb's death, songwriter Hank Cochran offered a eulogy at a showcase performance:

> *I believe there's a heaven, tho' I've never been.*
> *But I sure would have liked to been there*
> *   yesterday*
> *When Ernest Tubb walked in.*

More than a thousand friends jammed into the Two Rivers Baptist Church, just across the parkway from the Grand Ole Opry House, for his funeral services. B. J. Thomas sang Tubb's "Tomorrow Never Comes." And throughout the service recordings of his hits were played: "If We Never Meet Again This Side of Heaven," "I Love You Because," "Precious Memories," "I Will Miss You When You Go," "Stand by Me."

And finally, "I'm Walking the Floor over You."

Jack Greene reminisced: "He was a great man for taking enough time for a songwriter that was trying to get a song cut; he'd listen to all their songs and he'd write 'em a letter back. And he'd take time for the disc jockey that wanted an interview, and he'd take time for the fan that wanted an autograph. He'd take time for the promoter; he'd always mention the promoter's name on stage. He knew all those promoters all over the country and he wanted everybody to make a dollar. I've seen him take all the money from a gate and put it back in the guy's pocket. He'd say, 'You didn't make a dime on this, so I don't want any money.' He'd really do that.

"I'm still learning something about him every day. Like Hank Snow—I didn't know before that he paid Hank's way up here from Texas and got him on the Opry. Of course, the same thing happened to Ernest. He told me that [agent] Joe Frank paid his salary out of his own pocket when the Opry said, 'We don't want him.' So Ernest returned that favor to other people.

"It never ceases to come up that Ernest helped somebody else in this business."

··◦[v]◦·· Thus, Ernest Tubb's absence was deeply felt when the Grand Ole Opry reached its sixtieth anniversary in 1985. But there's no doubt he would have approved heartily of the mid-eighties trend on the venerable radio show— the return to traditional country music sounds.

More than a few at the Opry recalled Tubb's words: "Country music is good. It is humble and simple and honest and relaxed. There are those who cross over the bridge and mix their music"—and he spoke with rare disdain then—"but I personally have no desire to do this."

In its first sixty years the Opry had survived through the shifts in its home base, through the phenomenon of the urbanized sound of "uptown country," and through the traumatic period when it seemed it was about to be eclipsed by rock 'n' roll. And now it was bigger than ever, a portion of it being televised on The Nashville Network every Saturday night, quickly becoming the highest-rated program on TNN, and it was returning to its earthy, country roots.

One such demonstration of that was the signing of Johnny Russell, late of Sunflower County, Mississippi, to an Opry contract in August 1985—the sixtieth act on the anniversary-year Grand Ole Opry roster.

Although he was born in Mississippi, he became a Californian as an early teenager when his family moved. He grew up in an entertainment atmosphere, acting at a young age, appearing in clubs and on TV. And also writing songs.

One of his first to be recorded was "In a Mansion Stands My Love," put into a Jim Reeves recording session by producer Chet Atkins. It was a B-side song, but happily, the A side of the RCA Reeves release was "He'll Have to Go," the number-one country hit of 1959. Thus, Russell was in the enviable position of drawing royalties from a million-seller, even though it wasn't his song doing the selling.

Later, in 1963, his "Act Naturally" became a legitimate best-seller when Buck Owens recorded it. Johnny also became a recording artist himself, turning out hits with "Mr. and Mrs. Untrue," "Rain Falling on Me," "Rednecks, White Socks and Blue Ribbon Beer," "The Baptism of Jesse Taylor," "Hello I Love You," "Ain't No Way to Make a Bad Love Grow," and "Song of the South."

In John Bright Russell, the Grand Ole Opry added a veteran entertainer, one in the traditional country vein.

❧[vi]❧ The date was Thursday, November 14, 1985. Millions watched as the CBS television network aired a two-hour, prime-time salute to the Grand Ole Opry on its sixtieth birthday.

Backstage, an auburn-haired, doe-eyed young woman waited nervously. She had come a long road from her native Oklahoma, and as she waited, she remembered a summer day when she was only five. She had gone to the Cheyenne Frontier Days in Wyoming with her family.

"I was in the lobby of our hotel," she recalled, "and my brother Pake came up and told me somebody had just given him some money for singing a song. I said, 'I can do that.' So I got him to sing 'Jesus Loves Me' with me right there in the lobby. Somebody came up and gave me a nickel. That just amazed me."

Reba McEntire had made her debut.

Roy Acuff adjusts the microphone for DeFord Bailey while he performs the classic "Pan American Blues" in one of his last Opry appearances.

(1975) WSM PHOTO/LES LEVERETT/ROY ACUFF COLLECTION

Ricky Skaggs and Sharon White pose backstage at the Opry House with daughter Molly Kate.

(1987) DAVID SCARLETT

Representing two generations of bluegrass musicians, Bill Monroe and Ricky Skaggs chat backstage at the Opry on April 7, 1984.

(1984) LES LEVERETT COLLECTION

Aspiring "Honky Tonk Angel" Patty Loveless responds to a warm reception by the Opry audience.

(1988) *DONNIE BEAUCHAMP*

Ricky Van Shelton, left, and host Keith Bilbrey discuss Shelton's rapidly developing career on the Nashville Network program, "Grand Ole Opry Live Backstage."

(1987) *LES LEVERETT COLLECTION*

From the left, Rosie White, Buck White, Sharon White, and Reba McEntire swap road stories between Grand Ole Opry shows.

(1987) *DONNIE BEAUCHAMP*

Randy Travis, who joined the Opry family in 1986, is one of country music's superstars. His stage appeal reminds many admirers of an earlier Opry legend, Hank Williams.

(1988) *DONNIE BEAUCHAMP*

There is no such thing as an overnight success, and Reba didn't have one. But she was at ease with performing, not awed by audiences and applause. She had understood those things since her earliest days, because every year the McEntire family would jam into an old green Ford for a summer on the rodeo circuit. Traveling day and night, the four McEntire kids would sleep across the backseat, floorboards, and rear dash, whiling away long hours on the road by singing.

The young girl understood too what it was to be a star, if only secondhand. Her grandfather and father were rodeo champions. When she married, husband Charlie Battles was also a rodeo champion. A measure of stardom came for her in January 1983, when she had her first number-one country record, "I Can't Even Get the Blues," followed immediately by another number-one hit, "You're the First Time I've Thought About Leaving."

By October 1984 she was the Country Music Association's Female Vocalist of the Year. And again in 1985.

"People used to say that my mama could have been a successful singer if she had any breaks," she mused, "but she was teaching school and raising a family. My mama always used to say to me, 'Reba, I'm living my life through you.' "

Onstage, announcer Grant Turner was introducing the newest member of the Grand Ole Opry—Reba McEntire.

She was sober-faced as she walked into the spotlight, planting her feet firmly on the circle of wood cut from the stage of the old Ryman Auditorium. When she spoke, her words were soft, sincere.

"You know, it's real funny that I've been waiting on this for twenty-five years," she said, "and it's an honor and a thrill for me. And you know, this little piece of wood has probably heard more sad songs than I'll be able to sing all the rest of my life. But if you'll let me, I'd like to do one more song just for it."

She looked down at the relic of the storied Ryman.

"It has a lot to do with sadness, and country music, and what country music is all about. It's a song about a man and a woman who just can't seem to talk to each other anymore. And you know, the worst thing about it is, is that there's kids involved."

She began to sing, the hurt pouring out of her conjuring up visions of Patsy Cline and Kitty Wells and Jean Shepard and Dottie West and Dolly Parton and Loretta Lynn—all of the great women singers who had been on that stage before her.

"Somebody should leave," she sang, *"but which one should it be?*

"You need the kids, but they need me."

The audience was deathly quiet; there was no movement there.

"Somebody should leave, but we hate to give in;

"We keep hoping somehow we might need each other again."*

The last note of the music faded away. There was a momentary complete

---

*"Somebody Should Leave" by Harlan Howard and Chick Rains; copyright 1984 Tree Publishing (BMI), Cross Keys Music and Choskee Bottom Music (ASCAP).

silence. Suddenly the applause came, louder and louder. The crowd rose to its feet—a standing ovation for the sixty-first roster member of the Grand Ole Opry as its sixty-first year began.

A hand fluttered to her mouth. And tears flowed.

Reba McEntire had come home.

··⸨ vii ⸩·· An observer couldn't help but note that a new generation of young country music superstars was being put into place at the Opry.

Opry manager Hal Durham commented: "The Opry will always be the cornerstone of country music. And we will continue to tie what we have today to the beginnings—that very strong, basic, traditional country music that was here at the start."

The eighties had seen Ricky Skaggs added to the Opry roster. And Reba McEntire. And Oklahoma-born honky-tonker Mel McDaniel in February '86. And, then, in November of that year, Durham invited one Randy Travis, whose plaintive, gutsy style recalls the strong appeal of a Hank Williams, to become a member of the Grand Ole Opry family.

There are those who believe Travis might eventually become greater than all who have gone before him at the Grand Ole Opry.

His story reads like fiction or a screenplay—pulp fiction and a B screenplay. Born Randy Traywick in Marshville, North Carolina—population just over 2,000, thirty miles or so removed from Charlotte—in 1959, he picked up his first guitar at the age of eight, his interest in the instrument generated by what he heard on old 78-rpm records of Williams, Lefty Frizzell, Ernest Tubb, Gene Autry, and Tex Ritter. By the time he was fourteen, he and an older brother were singing in local beer joints and school halls. There was not, however, any great dream of being a professional entertainer; there was a great deal more motivation to sow wild oats.

At sixteen he left home. "I didn't like school," he explained. "I couldn't stand it, to tell you the truth. I started runnin' away from home, drinkin' an' gettin' into trouble. After about the seventh grade, I just almost wouldn't go to school at all."

The police and Randy Traywick were well acquainted. Jail seemed to be in his immediate future. At that point there entered his life a woman named Lib Hatcher, who had "discovered" Randy in a talent contest at a Charlotte club she owned. Hatcher convinced the authorities to release the young man in her custody, promising to keep him out of trouble.

So strong was her belief in his ultimate greatness that she sold her North Carolina club in 1981 to stake a move to Nashville. Lib gave him a new name, Randy Ray, and when that didn't seem quite right she dubbed him Randy Travis.

In Nashville, Hatcher got a job as manager of the Nashville Palace nightclub, very near the Opry House. Randy became the Palace's short-order cook, frequently called away from his kitchen chores to sing on the club's stage. During the day, Travis's personal manager—for that was what Hatcher became, although she had no previous experience as one—haunted the record companies on Music Row, Randy's demonstration tapes in hand. They all turned her down.

Finally, in 1985 Hatcher persuaded Warner Bros. artist and repertoire chief Martha Sharp to come to the Nashville Palace to see and hear Randy Travis. It was a lightning-strike evening. Sharp signed Travis to a Warner contract and put him in the hands of veteran producer Kyle Lehning.

Randy's first solo effort, "On the Other Hand," was a modest success. But his next release, "1982," shot him to the top of the country charts. "On the Other Hand" was quickly rereleased and also went to the top of the charts. His first album, *Storms of Life*, released in June '86, became the first debut album by a solo country artist to sell more than a million units in less than a year.

In the spring of '86, the West Coast–based Academy of Country Music gave Randy Travis its Most Promising New Male Vocalist award. In the fall of the same year, the Country Music Association gave him its similar Horizon Award, followed almost immediately by the invitation to join the Grand Ole Opry roster.

Ricky Skaggs, in introducing Travis to the Opry audience, spoke of the George Jones hit, "Who's Gonna Fill Their Shoes?," which wonders lyrically who is going to fill the shoes of the Acuffs and the Williamses.

Skaggs said simply: "This is the man who's gonna fill their shoes—Randy Travis!"

··◦❴ viii ❵◦·· Traditional musical values had indeed returned to the Grand Ole Opry, not alone in the signing of Travis to the Opry roster. He was to be followed by others in the traditionalist mode.

And yet, as new members were welcomed into the Opry family, elders passed away. Veteran comedian Archie Campbell, originally of Opry fame and later a staple player on the long-running TV show "Hee Haw," died of a heart attack on August 29, 1987, at Tennessee Memorial Research Center. He was seventy-two.

On a happier note, on August 22, the Opry management corrected what may have been an oversight for many years: they put Virginia-born traditionalist Roy Clark on the roster.

Roy Linwood Clark was born into a family with a musical heritage (April 15, 1933), and the first instrument he played was made for him by his father, Hester; a cigar box with a ukulele neck on it and four strings rigged to enable young Roy to play in a school band at Meherrin Elementary. When he was fourteen Roy got an honest-to-gosh guitar at Christmas—a Silverton model from the Sears catalogue.

"When I came downstairs Christmas mornin'," Roy said, "and saw the guitar, I grabbed it, went back upstairs, and never turned it loose. My fingers got sore and bled. I got cold water, dipped 'em in it 'til the pain went away, and went right back at it. I didn't want to go to school or anything. I just wanted to sit there and hear that sound."

It was with his father's bluegrass band that he started playing professionally; he got $7.50 for his first gig. And right from the beginning, Roy began to exploit the availability of a new medium called television. In 1947–48 the teenager appeared on "The Hayloft Conservatory of Country Music" on Dumont's channel 5 in Washington, D.C., and then on the "Ozark Jubilee" and Connie B. Gay's pioneering "Town and Country Time."

His musical versatility—he played guitar, banjo, fiddle, and five other instruments, including trumpet—got him network TV guest shots on Arthur Godfrey's "Talent Scouts" and Ed Sullivan's famed "Talk of the Town." With his warm, comedic personality he was in constant demand, appearing on television with Dean Martin, Mitzi Gaynor, Dinah Shore, Merv Griffin, Mike Douglas, Johnny Cash, the Osmond Family, the Muppets, and others, as well as hosting his own TV specials.

Clark racked up an imposing list of "firsts"—the first country music artist to be guest host on Johnny Carson's "Tonight Show"; the first country music artist to begin major TV guest appearances abroad, i.e., "The Tom Jones Show" from London; the first country music artist to headline a major hotel showroom along the Las Vegas strip; and, of course, the first country performer to host a major TV show, "Hee Haw," for more than twenty years.

It can be argued that Roy Clark has appeared on television more than any other country artist.

He was also named Entertainer of the Year in 1972 and 1973 by the Academy of Country Music, and Entertainer of the Year in 1973 by the Country Music Association.

With all of that success and adulation, his induction into the Grand Ole Opry family left him genuinely teary-eyed.

Perhaps what has kept Roy Clark on top for so many years in a highly competitive business is his native modesty. "I never compare myself to anything or anyone," he once told an interviewer. "And if anybody else does, all I can definitely say is one thing: 'I'm the best Roy Clark I know of.' "

When the Opry moved into 1988, general manager Hal Durham saw additional opportunities to add two more talented young traditionalists to the show's roster: Ricky Van Shelton of Grit, Virginia, on June 10, and Patty Loveless of Pikeville, Kentucky, on June 11.

Van Shelton was introduced to the Opry audience by the venerable Roy Acuff.

"I hope I can carry on," Ricky told Acuff, "with what you and the rest of the Opry [members] have done over the years, 'cause you and everybody else that belongs to the Opry—you are country music."

Ricky's rise to Opry status had been swift, really based on the smashing success of his initial CBS-Columbia album, *Wild-Eyed Dream*, which produced five chart hits. In addition to the title song, there were "Crime of Passion," "Don't We All Have the Right," and two consecutive number-one singles, "Somebody Lied" and "Life Turned Her That Way."

He was quickly named Top New Male Vocalist by both the Academy of Country Music and *Billboard* magazine. On the Monday before his Friday induction into Opry membership, he was voted the Star of Tomorrow by the readers of *Music*

City News. In October of 1988 he won the prestigious Horizon Award given by the Country Music Association, just a few weeks after the release of only his second album.

Patty Loveless, it might be said, came from a Grand Ole Opry background. A cousin of Opry superstar and Country Music Hall of Famer Loretta Lynn, Patty remembers sitting on the kitchen table at age three or four listening to the Opry broadcast while her mother mopped the floor. By age five she was singing along with the Opry performers.

She was only twelve when she began singing with her brother, Roger, who was to become her manager. Two years later they visited Nashville where Opry stars the Wilburn Brothers—who years earlier had hired Loretta Lynn as their "girl singer"—signed the Kentucky youngster as a staff songwriter.

During the next few years she spent her winters in Kentucky finishing high school and her summers in Nashville honing her talents. In 1986 MCA released her first album, from which came the chart songs "Wicked Ways," "I Did," "After All," and "Lonely Days, Lonely Nights."

Early in 1988 her second album, *If My Heart Had Windows*, was released and the title song became her first Top 10 hit.

It was a family affair as Patty Loveless joined the Opry. Her mother and five of her seven brothers and sisters stood proudly in the wings as Opry veteran Porter Wagoner introduced her to the listeners.

"My family," Patty said, "has always had the dream, and I have always had the dream" to be a member of the Opry. "And now they've accepted me and the music that I do and have made me a part of the Opry family."

The days of June 10 and 11 were happy ones for Van Shelton and Loveless, but there was a pall of sadness among the old-timers backstage. For the Nashville newspapers of Saturday, June 11, reported the death the night before of eighty-nine-year-old Herman Crook at the Park View Hospital.

Crook, a "hillbilly" harmonica player, had been the last surviving member of the original 1926 Grand Ole Opry cast. That final link to the colorful past had been severed and a new generation of country music traditionalists was in place.

❧[ix]❧ It's a country music radio show.
In 1989 it's in its sixty-fourth year.

By conservative estimate, some 24 million have sat in its audiences, with nearly a million more being added to that total each year.

The additional millions who have heard it on 50,000-watt, clear-channel WSM Radio out of Nashville, Tennessee, or have seen portions of it on television, are as uncountable as the grains of sand on a beach.

It's a genuine phenomenon. An American treasure.

And yet, with all of the great songwriters who have been associated with the Grand Ole Opry over the years, there has been only one song capturing the essence of it all. Paradoxically, it was written in 1979 by two men—Mel McDaniel and Bob Morrison—who had no close ties with the Opry at that time. McDaniel could not have guessed that he'd be asked to join the Opry seven years later.

Indeed, the artist who recorded the song and made it a hit, Conway Twitty, was likewise somewhat removed from the Opry during his illustrious career. He had been a guest at the Opry, true, but had not "lived" with it week by week as had so many other performers.

It may be, of course, that full appreciation of the Opry requires a kind of detachment, a step or two backward when viewing it. As songwriters McDaniel and Morrison must have had when they created "The Grandest Lady of Them All":

> *She's never in the spotlight,*
> *But everybody knows that she's the star;*
> *And once she shines upon you,*
> *She'll make you truly proud of where you are;*
> *She'll wipe away the pain of all the dues you had*
> *   to pay;*
> *When the curtain to her world starts to unfold,*
> *With mother-tender hands, she will applaud and*
> *   feed the hunger in your soul.*
>
> *And she's known as the Grand Ole Opry,*
> *Where the legends come to call*
> *On the queen of country music,*
> *On the grandest lady of them all.*
>
> *She's sung of desperados,*
> *The lonesome whistle of a midnight train;*
> *The coal mines of Kentucky*
> *And how it feels to be out in the rain;*
> *She's sung of Texas cowboys, of hoboes and*
> *   heroes*
> *But most of all, she's sung about the common*
> *   people just like me and you.*
>
> *And she's known as the Grand Ole Opry,*
> *Where the legends come to call*
> *On the queen of country music,*
> *On the grandest lady of them all.**

*"The Grandest Lady of Them All" by Mel McDaniel and Bob Morrison; copyright 1976 Music City Music, Inc.

Index